Commercial Driver's License Exam

by Cory Adams

A Wiley Brand

Commercial Driver's License Exam For Dummies®

Published by: **John Wiley & Sons, Inc.**, 111 River Street, Hoboken, NJ 07030-5774, www.wiley.com

Contents at a Glance

Table of Contents

Introduction

While I may be a bit biased, I truly believe this book might be the most important thing any prospective driver could read. Within these pages, I guide you through the process of becoming a professional driver, from getting into a truck for the first time, to performing inspections, to driving buses, to backing a trailer, to getting good fuel mileage, and everything in between. I will help you understand the material you need to know in order to pass the Commercial Driver's License (CDL) written exams and prepare you for the behind-the-wheel tests as well.

About This Book

I have seen too many new drivers who were given a CDL but weren't taught concepts to be good drivers. Maybe the instructors desired to instill some safe driving concepts but were hindered by time restraints, or maybe they didn't know how to bridge the gap between their experience and the student's experience. The result is the same — an ill-prepared professional driver.

Unfortunately, I was not given a thousand pages in which to write this book (although would you have looked at a thousand-page testing guide with fear in your eyes?). And you and I are not in a truck together, so you are not able to ask me questions. Nevertheless, the goal of this book is to help you gain a greater understanding of driving a commercial motor vehicle — more than what you would obtain through a website or study guide or a question-and-answer book. I want this book to help you leapfrog other drivers with the same amount of experience.

Commercial Driver's License Exam For Dummies is conveniently divided into the areas that you will need to focus on. If you need guidance on how to use this book, refer to the "Where to Go from Here," section later in the introduction.

>> In Part 1, "Getting Started on the CDL Journey," I give you a picture of the broad field of driving commercial motor vehicles, encourage you with a look at the testing that takes place when getting your Commercial Driver's License, and a glimpse of what a career can look like when you get your CDL. I really don't do justice with what can happen in your life once you have a CDL as there are so many different positions in the transportation industry.

>> In Part 2, "Reviewing General Knowledge," I begin where you generally need to start and that is with the general knowledge of driving, and the responsibilities that professional drivers have when they are not driving. Please ignore anyone who says, "I am just a truck (or bus) driver." To be a good professional driver, you must be more than a steering wheel holder.

>> In Part 3, "Exploring Air Brakes," I get somewhat in-depth talking about air brakes. It might seem excessive but not for the student who really wants to understand their commercial vehicle.

>> In Part 4, "Combing Though Combination Vehicles," I share the extra knowledge needed to safely drive a vehicle that has a trailer — to ensure your safety and thus the safety of those around you. I dedicate an entire chapter to helping you understand the concept of backing a trailer. I really hope you practice what I shared in that chapter. After you obtain your CDL, it can be really valuable.

>> In Part 5, "Examining Other Endorsements," I share the physics of driving a vehicle with a tank. I encourage you to go ahead and add endorsements (additional certifications to haul a specific type of cargo) to your CDL as a resume enhancer. Endorsements will take a little more work, but you can do it. You were smart enough to buy this book!

>> In Part 6, "Passing the Tests," I share how to inspect your commercial vehicle. This is one of the most important aspects of driving. You will notice that I mention something about inspecting your vehicle throughout the book. But in this part, I focus on passing the pre-trip inspection test as well as road tests.

>> In Part 7, "The Part of Tens," I give you warnings of how to fail a test, but more positively, I share ways to pass your tests. Be sure to use both the backing successfully and the efficient driving chapters for your new CDL or for your personal vehicle driving.

Some of the chapters have practice questions. The chapters that don't reflect content where there will be no written exams. (Exams are referred to as "written" but are most likely to be electronic multiple choice.) The questions that I created are somewhat like the exam questions you will encounter — tricky at times and poorly worded. Exam questions seem to have been designed to trick you instead of seeing what you know. I've tried to follow that format.

Foolish Assumptions

I am writing this book presumably to someone who has little knowledge of commercial motor vehicles. But if you have some knowledge, I assume you lack some knowledge to pass the CDL tests. (After all, you bought this book — or perhaps it was a gift.) I try to bridge any gap between my knowledge and experience with the lack of experience I assume you have. I assume you have some enthusiasm to learn more about commercial motor vehicles and to obtain your CDL. I hope I can feed your enthusiasm and be a good coach while cheering you on!

Note: Throughout this book, I will use terms like exam and test interchangeably, so treat them as the same thing. The same goes for some vehicle terms. For example, a truck might be a semi-tractor, but a semi-tractor will always refer to a truck that is designed to pull a semi-trailer — the traditional tractor-trailer combination. A bus will *always* be referred to as a bus, and a vehicle can be any of the equipment you can operate with your CDL.

Icons Used in This Book

Throughout this book, icons in the margins highlight certain types of valuable information that call out for your attention. Here are the icons you'll encounter and a brief description of each.

TIP

The Tip icon marks tips and shortcuts that you can use to make passing tests easier.

REMEMBER

Remember icons mark information that's a little more likely to be on a test or is simply for doing your job correctly. If you are about to take a CDL test, skimming these icons might help refresh your memory for answering test questions correctly.

I occasionally will insert a bit of personal insight or hopefully helpful story, but I won't bore you with a bunch of success or failure stories — definitely not all my failures!

There isn't a lot of information in this book that is technical so it's fine to ignore. When you see a paragraph with this icon, skipping it won't hamper your success with passing the CDL test.

The Warning icon tells you to watch out! It marks important information that may save you headaches, or an accident, or a chat with an officer.

Beyond the Book

In addition to the abundance of information and guidance related to passing your CDL exams that I provide in this book, there is even more information online at Dummies.com. Check out this book's online Cheat Sheet to help you prepare for driving at your new job and know what to bring with you. Just go to www.dummies.com and search for "Commercial Driver's License Exam For Dummies Cheat Sheet."

Where to Go from Here

This book doesn't have to be read in order from the first chapter to the last. If you have some familiarity with commercial motor vehicles and the transportation industry, you may want to jump ahead to the general knowledge chapters in Part 2. You can skip some of the endorsements chapters in Part 5 if your goal is to start driving with the basic professional license. It's up to you. If you are scared of backing a combination vehicle (semi-tractor trailer for one example), go to Chapter 11 on backing a combination vehicle and maybe it won't be quite so scary anymore.

If commercial vehicles are a completely foreign concept to you, I suggest you read the first three chapters before moving on to the chapters in Part 2. If you don't have an idea what you want to do next, just keep reading. But feel free to skip chapters that may not be applicable to you, such as hauling hazardous materials, until you are more comfortable with the information in other parts of the book.

If you're looking for a quick return on your investment of purchasing this book, read Chapter 23, "Ten Tips for Safe, Efficient Driving." If you truly adopt these practices in your driving, you will see a substantial increase in your fuel economy and encounter fewer close calls with mediocre motorists, bold cyclists, and absent-minded pedestrians. (I am a cyclist and a pedestrian so hopefully that qualifies me to make that observation of a segment of our self-transporting communities.)

1
Getting Started on the CDL Journey

Meet the people who have become commercial driver's license holders and find out how you can be one of them.

Begin your test preparation by exploring what the exams entail and use tips, tricks, and strategies to pass them.

Discover the many driving careers available to CDL holders. Consider what career path to take and understand how you can increase your opportunities with your CDL.

Chapter **1**

Taking a Big-Picture Look at Commercial Driving

When I was a kid, I thought that all truck drivers, like my dad, were big and strong. My friends' fathers, who were also truck drivers, were big guys — at least for the most part. One of the fathers, who didn't have these attributes, had an accident when a steer tire blew on the truck, and he ran off the road. I asked my dad why he had the accident. My dad replied, "because he wasn't stout enough to hold the truck on the road." This reenforced my belief that all truck drivers were big and/or strong — and men.

At that time, it did take a lot of strength, nerve, and sometimes recklessness to drive big trucks in the 1960s and '70s. Trucks didn't have power steering, and roads were generally narrower. A truck might have had 30-plus gears, and the tarps for covering loads were heavier. Truck drivers didn't have cell phones to call for road service when their trucks broke down. Dispatchers and brokers were commonly known to threaten drivers with docked pay, lost opportunities, and other such illegal tactics. But as you probably know, the world is different now, and the transportation industry has drastically changed.

What has changed? To start, the demographics of commercial drivers include all ethnicities and genders who are no longer constrained by physical strength or stature requirements. Trucks have power steering. Computers can shift transmissions, so the driver doesn't have to do it manually. Not only are lighter tarps used for covering loads, but some *shippers* (the business facility from where cargo is picked up) also have devices that help drape a tarp over the cargo. A truck driver can use a cell phone to call for road service or take a picture of that broken *thing-amajig* (a component of your vehicle that you don't know the name of) and send that photo to a service person to identify. And drivers have more power behind them than in the past with whistleblower protection. Today, the lanes of city roads are wider, and the number of lanes on interstate highways have increased. Big money lawsuit verdicts have changed the way much of the industry acts and thinks.

In this chapter, I describe commercial driving and informally introduce you to various government agencies that mandate regulations for the transportation industry. I also give you a glimpse of what commercial motor vehicles (CMVs) there are as well as a preview of the Commercial Driver's License (CDL) testing.

Recognizing the Need for Drivers

In the past, the commercial driver pool was made up of baby boomers (born between 1945 and 1964), and many came from the agricultural community. Coming from an agricultural demographic, these drivers had a lot of applicable skills. They knew how to take care of, drive, and operate heavy equipment.

Over time, the baby boomers provided a sufficient supply of truck drivers in the United States. Now, many of those baby boomer drivers are retiring or not working full-time, and the number of people coming from farms has been greatly reduced. Families are generally smaller than in the past, and there has been a societal push towards college education and white-collar jobs. Even still, the need for transportation and the movement of goods has continued to grow.

For a large portion of current CDL holders, driving was not their first profession. There are drivers with doctorate degrees. There are former government agents and law enforcement officers who made the switch to driving. Retail store clerks, school teachers, Elvis impersonators and other singers, ministers, and hospital administrators have all changed careers to start driving a truck.

However, you don't necessarily have to change to a different career or company. Your current employer may have jobs that require material to be moved from one location to another, so applicants need to have a CDL to operate a vehicle. In this case, driving isn't the main focus of the company, but in order to have the required materials and tools at the jobsite, vehicles requiring CDL drivers are used.

AUTHOR SAYS

Buses also require a CDL to operate them. I have driven buses for many school field trips, athletic events, and music events for my kids' school. I thoroughly enjoyed it (although kids in junior high school were a little challenging). I would get free admission to most of the events, and when we stopped at a restaurant for a meal, guess who got their meal free?

Knowing the Public's Perception

"They're *just* a truck driver." Some people have an idea that driving a truck or bus is an easy job. It isn't an easy job if you do it well! Unfortunately, there are some people who think commercial drivers are less intelligent or can't make it in another career. I'm here to tell you that this perception couldn't be further from the truth. (See my reference to drivers with doctorate degrees in the previous section.) Don't let these sorts of misperceptions keep you from pursuing a career as a professional driver. Good companies know the value of a driver and will treat you accordingly.

Hollywood movies often portray truck and bus drivers as the hero or the villain who drives recklessly in order to save someone in distress or themselves, respectively. But within the real-life industry, everyday people drive commercial vehicles — people who are parents, married or single, young adults, middle-aged, or seasoned. Sometimes a couple will drive in the same truck!

UNDERSTANDING HOW DRIVERS THINK

There is an old saying that a wise man learns from his mistakes, but the wisest of men learn from the mistakes of others. If you don't know this already, you are setting yourself up to repeat the same mistakes as a commercial driver.

Driving is a career where you must always be in the process of learning and relearning in order to succeed, maybe not in a traditional academic way but through driving experience. Sometimes a new driver who needs your guidance will force you into new thoughts and theories.

A typical truck driver doesn't just gather knowledge by reading but will greatly benefit from putting learned skills into practice because the human brain stores up information to use when the opportunity arises. When the weather conditions change, or a life-threatening event unfolds before your eyes, you don't have the time to read a book about the situation. You must be able to react. Much like a professional athlete, a professional driver must train and prepare for "real-game" scenarios.

Experience is a great teacher, and in many areas, it's the only way to practice the skills needed to become a professional driver. Remember to watch other drivers to learn from their experiences.

Although there may be mixed perceptions about who commercial drivers are, no one else's perception is more important than your own. You should realize that driving a CMV is a highly responsible job. A driver makes many decisions like a surgeon performing surgery, and planning is important for both jobs. While surgeons have some assistance from a surgical team (including nurses and anesthesiologists), commercial drivers may only have help on limited occasions. Hazards come from many directions and only the driver is there to spot those hazards.

Taking a Look at the CDL Governing Bodies

It is time to examine some of the acronyms that get tossed around like everyone knows what or who they are. There are many government agencies that are involved in the transportation industry. Although there are more regulating agencies than can be discussed in this book, this section highlights the most important governing bodies that you should remember.

Thinking about federal regulations

The federal government's main contribution to regulating transportation — at least for vehicles, drivers, and the safe operation thereof — is the Federal Motor Carriers Safety Administration (FMCSA). The FMCSA is responsible for most of the commercial driving regulations in the US, which helps to ensure the safety of CMVs and the people who drive those vehicles.

Regulating the industry

All the compilation of federal regulations is called the Federal Motor Carriers Safety Regulations (FMCSR). It states requirements (regulations) of integrity for the major components of vehicles. Components that have defects as listed in the FMCSR are defined as *out-of-service*, meaning that the vehicle is not allowed to be driven until the defect is repaired. Within these regulations are the rules that the transportation industry must abide by. These regulations cover driver qualifications, medical examiners, the commercial vehicles, required paperwork, and the list goes on.

Training the industry

Once upon a time, all the states did everything on their own testing, taxing, and licensing; and it was a nightmare for the transportation industry. When there was a regulation or law, especially that would be an inconvenience for the driver, someone would ultimately find a way around it. Many drivers would have more than one driver's license. When too many tickets were issued on one license, another license would be obtained from another state.

Licenses were easy to get in some locations — at least at certain times. In 1992, the CDL became the law, consisting of federal guidelines for potential drivers to study and pass. The FMCSA provided a CDL study guide, and in 2005 gave it to each state to publish and brand on their own. Each state (known collectively in this book as State Departments of Transportation) basically had their own spin on the testing.

Becoming effective in 2022, the FMCSA set up the requirements and mandated new training for commercial drivers as well as the instructors who provide the training. This training, called *Entry-Level Driver Training* (ELDT), prepares individuals for the tests needed to obtain licensing for different classifications of vehicles. (See Chapter 2 for more information on the ELDT.)

Any entity, or provider, desiring to offer training to potential CDL drivers or to drivers looking to add to their license must certify that they meet the requirements — qualified instructors, sufficient equipment, proper curriculum, and classroom space — as stated in the FMSCA regulations. Potential drivers can look online for the FMCSA registry of these providers at `https://tpr.fmcsa.dot.gov/` to find an authorized training facility. Individuals can register as ELDT providers but may only offer training for their employees.

Figuring out state regulations

As you're driving your commercial motor vehicle down the interstate, you'll see a sign that says, "All trucks must weigh." While the FMCSA created most of the regulations, it's the states that do the majority of enforcement (along with help from county and local law enforcement). There are weigh stations scattered across the country where they not only ensure that your vehicle weighs within legal limits, but inspectors occasionally check drivers and their vehicles for safety and regulatory compliance. Inspectors might have you pull your vehicle around behind their building for an inspection. Weigh stations are generally found on major highways, but officers can set up portable scales that can be used away from the weigh stations but in a safe location. Officers can conduct business at these temporary locations just like the permanent weigh stations.

While the federal government will make regulations, it can't always make states agree to enforce or adopt those regulations. You may encounter different regulations or weight and size limits as you travel state to state because some states had their own laws prior to the federal government's laws. So state laws and regulations can be *grandfathered in* or take precedent over the federal law.

In spite of licensing regulations coming from the federal government, State DOTs administer the licensing of drivers. State DOTs follow the federal regulations but might also add some additional restrictions, like who would be allowed to be a school bus driver.

STATE TAXES ON FUEL

States collect money by taxing the fuel that commercial motor vehicles must buy. Generally, these fees go to the road and bridge funds within the states. However, if you are operating a CMV in multiple states you might think, "I want to buy fuel in a state where the tax is lower," or "I will buy fuel where the retail price is lower." However, the tax portion of the fuel price is irrelevant because as a commercial driver you have to keep track of the miles you drive in each state and then pay a tax for each mile you drive within each state. Periodically, these miles are reported and rectified between the states. So when you're trying to get the best deal on fuel purchases, remember to subtract the fuel tax per gallon when you compare prices. Electronic GPS devices that transmit information back to your office, usually keep track of the miles you drive in each state to make tracking easier for you.

Discovering an Array of Commercial Vehicles

Eighteen wheelers are what many people think of when commercial vehicles are discussed, especially when they are thinking about which vehicles require a CDL to drive. City municipalities commonly have commercial vehicles that include garbage trucks, snowplows, and dump trucks. Some trucks have a vacuum apparatus for working with sewers. Utility companies need drivers with CDLs for their trucks that service customers and pull trailers.

And of course, there are many types of buses: school buses, activity buses, tour buses, prison buses, daycare buses, city buses, airport shuttle buses, and so on.

Plumbing and electrical contractors need CDL drivers for their trucks and heavier trailers. Construction companies need CDL drivers because they might be hauling heavy equipment, like cranes, well-drilling vehicles, and other specialty machinery. Others in the building industry need to drive dump trucks and concrete mixer trucks, not to mention all the equipment that needs hauled from site to site like bulldozers.

Mobile medical units are often semi-trailers pulled by a semi-tractor. Football teams and marching bands have their own trailers that need pulled by semi-tractors. Musicians, race car drivers, and others in motor sports need people with CDL's to move their equipment from one event to the next. (See Chapter 3 for more information on the types of careers that require a CDL.)

And, in case you are wondering, the Weinermobile does not require a CDL. While I am not sure why, I know the smiles it creates don't have weight ratings.

Knowing More Than How to Drive

I hope to never hear you say, "I'm just a truck driver." (Note that "bus" can be substituted for "truck" here.) Truck drivers are always more than truck drivers. The earliest transportation engineers did not consider themselves to be just camel operators; they were traders and business people!

Earlier drivers had to perform much of their own repairs and maintenance (some still do). Today, many driving jobs involve loading and unloading the cargo. I see beverage haulers physically stocking store shelves with their sodas and energy drinks. The same goes for drivers from bread and snack chips companies. Some drivers are filling static tanks at a fuel station or unloading them like septic tank truck drivers who — by the way — have some of the nicest looking trucks on the road.

Bus drivers are often assisting passengers, loading and unloading luggage, and occasionally being tour guides.

TECHNICAL STUFF

When a load is picked up at a shipper (legal term and "person" contracting the transportation), by a driver (also known as *an agent for a carrier*), the carrier has taken responsibility for the load. The load belongs to the carrier, meaning that if something happens to the cargo, the carrier pays the shipper for it instead of the *consignee* (transportation name for the receiver of the cargo). The driver again is more than just a driver, they are security.

REMEMBER

In this book, for the sake of brevity and your reading satisfaction, I will often use the generic term, "driver" or "truck driver" when talking about any kind of commercial driver. So feel free to substitute "bus" or "crane" for truck!

Exploring the CDL Exams

There are four categories of exams for acquiring a CDL, not just one — sorry. The good news is that the written test(s) will be on a different day. Testing is how a state certifies that you know what you are doing and have the skills to do it. Now, if only every driver exhibited the same skills in their daily driving . . .

Here's a brief summary on the type of exams you'll need to take to obtain a CDL:

>> **Written.** It is called a "written" exam, but you will more likely have a bunch of multiple-choice questions at a computer terminal. Which written exam you will take depends on what type of vehicle you want to drive and the type of work you desire. This exam consists, at a minimum, of a general knowledge test. Examples of additional written tests would be an air brake test and a combination vehicle test. These exams would be required for driving a tractor-trailer combination (also known as eighteen wheelers). Passing these written exams grants you a Commercial Learner's Permit (CLP); see Chapter 2.

>> **Pre-trip inspection.** Inspecting your commercial motor vehicle is critical. Yes, I know most people don't inspect their personal vehicles the same as what is required for commercial motor vehicles. But then again, your personal vehicle probably doesn't endure the same type of intense day-in, day-out use — nor is it as large, meaning the capability of doing greater damage if something goes wrong.

The test is harder than real life because you must *talk* about the vehicle in front of a license examiner. However, I'll give you lots of help with inspecting your vehicle, which is scattered throughout the book. (See Chapters 17 and 18 for more information on passing the pre-trip inspection test.)

>> **Behind-the-wheel — skills.** There will be a course that was designed to test drivers on a few maneuvers. Most states have you drive forward and stop with the front end of the vehicle in a box. They have you back up straight for a set distance. They'll have you perform a maneuver that is much like pulling away from a curb from in between two other vehicles. Then, there's a reverse maneuver that puts you right back in the same spot, stopping with the back end of your vehicle in a box.

License examiners give you a couple of times to Get Out and Look at your vehicle (known as GOAL) and a couple of strategic pull-ups or adjustments. (See Chapter 19 for more information on passing the behind-the-wheel test.)

» **Behind-the-wheel — road.** When the inspection is complete, and you've aced the skills course, or at least passed, you'll move on to the final test, which is the road test. The road test will vary, especially between the different types of vehicles. Your license examiner will likely have you drive along roads to test specific tasks, like someone driving a bus will have to drive across some railroad tracks. When there isn't a required scenario in the neighborhood of the licensing facility, your license examiner will simulate that scenario. For example, when there isn't a railroad track, or a hill to park on, or passengers to pick up, or a real breakdown in progress nearby, you can still expect to know what to do and explain these situations.

Becoming the Nation's Superhero

Our society only functions as it does thanks to people who have and use a CDL. Imagine the chaos if every person who had a CDL stopped driving a commercial motor vehicle. No superhero would be able to save the country from the mayhem that would ensue.

Whatever stereotypes you might have had in your head of bus and truck drivers, you can now throw them out. You can throw out many excuses you've been using to not go ahead and procure a CDL. I'll admit that driving a bus or a truck is not for everyone. To be a good driver, it takes a person who is smart, conscientious, communicative, determined — while giving attention to details — and is willing to learn. Okay, maybe I am overselling the profession, but since you have this book in hand you have at least a little bit of interest. Don't make excuses and continue your path into the world of driving commercial vehicles by obtaining a CDL.

IN THIS CHAPTER

» **Understanding when a CDL is required**

» **Figuring out the classifications and endorsements**

» **Making sense of the skills needed**

» **Taking the Entry-Level Driver Training**

» **Getting ready to take the required tests**

Chapter **2**

Embracing the CDL Exam Preparation

Students looking to obtain a Commercial Driver's License (CDL) have many reasons for doing so. Their employers need people with a CDL to operate their equipment. Often a business finds out the hard way by receiving a citation for operating equipment without the proper license classification or finding out that they haul enough hazardous material (when they just thought it was cleaning supplies) that a CDL is required. Layoffs and businesses downsizing are motivators for a drastic job change. People also experience burnout with their previous job and need a new challenge in life, or they desire a career where they can make a positive contribution to society. Yes, moving cargo really does contribute to society because CDL drivers safely deliver food and supplies around the country.

Look at preparation for the CDL exam as an intense exercise in making the process less stressful. Understanding why the government insists that people have a CDL for various transportation vocations will help give you the correct mindset for this task.

I don't intend for you to pass all your Commercial Driver's License (CDL) tests and then toss this book aside because it has useful information you might want to explore for adding to your vehicle certification. In this chapter, I assist you with making some informed decisions on getting a CDL and help remove roadblocks that some people place in their own path by sharing with you some important strategies in passing the CDL tests.

WEIGHT ACRONYMS

Equipment ratings are determined by manufacturers to inform users what can be safely hauled on their vehicle. Tires, axles, and the whole vehicle are given these ratings. The following ratings are also used by the government to determine if a driver is operating safely or not, meaning if they are properly licensed and if they are on a road or passing over a bridge that is built to handle that much weight.

- **GVWR** (Gross Vehicle Weight Rating) is the maximum weight that a manufacturer says a vehicle can safely weigh with all its cargo. This is assuming that the vehicle is equipped with the appropriate y rated tires (this is always presumed).

- **GCWR** (Gross Combination Weight Rating) is the manufacturer's rating of the vehicle's capability when combined with a trailer or with a towing unit.

- **GVW** (Gross Vehicle Weight) is not a rating but simply an acronym referring to the gross weight of a vehicle including cargo and passengers. It is usually used for the purpose of limiting weights passing over roads and bridges, and determining licenses of both drivers and equipment.

- **GCW** (Gross Combination Weight) adds to the GVW by including any attached trailer.

Knowing When You Need a CDL

Determining when a CDL is required can be confusing after reading federal or state regulations. Basically, you need a CDL to drive a commercial motor vehicle (CMV). A CMV is defined as a vehicle that is used on highways for interstate commerce (cargo shipments that begin in one state and end in another), and for most intrastate commerce (cargo shipments that begin and end in the same state), that has a gross vehicle weight rating (GVWR), or a gross combination weight rating (GCWR), or a gross combination weight (GCW) of 10,001 pounds or more, whichever of these weights is greater.

REMEMBER

Let me put the definition above in everyday speak, using four criteria. If a vehicle driven on the road can *weigh 10,001 pounds or more loaded, for any type of commerce*, it is probably a commercial motor vehicle. If a vehicle is designed for *more than eight passengers* including the driver and is used for compensation, it is a commercial motor vehicle. If a vehicle can *hold 16 passengers* including the driver, regardless of compensation, it is a commercial motor vehicle. (Small buses are often used by nonprofit organizations and thus their drivers don't always require a CDL.) Finally, if a vehicle is *transporting hazardous materials in quantities that require placards*, it is a commercial motor vehicle.

Acquiring the Necessary Credentials

There are times when it makes sense to build incrementally, over time. However, when it comes to obtaining your CDL, I encourage you to consider the classes and the endorsements to expand your job possibilities. If the opportunity exists to "go big" (obtain a Class A instead of a B, for example) you may save yourself time later. And, you could already have that resume enhancer in hand.

Classifying CDLs

Now that you know how a commercial motor vehicle is defined, you will probably want to know what type of vehicles require a CDL.

REMEMBER

There are different classifications that are required to drive various CMVs, which are defined as:

>> **Class A** is needed for combination vehicles (a towing vehicle and a trailer) that together weigh over 26,001 pounds, as long as the trailer weighs over 10,000 pounds.

>> **Class B** is required for a large bus or *straight vehicle* weighing over or rated for over 26,001 pounds or more. These CMVs can pull a trailer, but it must be under a 10,000 pound haul.

>> **Class C** is required for vehicles designed to carry 16 or more passengers (driver included) or when hazardous materials are hauled in quantities that require an HM placard.

No matter what CDL classifications you choose to obtain, you will need to pass a general knowledge test. In the chapters on general knowledge, you will read what every driver (commercial driver or not) should know but doesn't. Driving safely in all kinds of road situations needs to be the top priority of every driver of any vehicle.

Endorsing your CDL

You may want to have a slightly more enticing resume and decide to obtain endorsements to add to your CDL. *Endorsements* are additional certifications that allow you to drive specific types of CMVs or specific cargo.

For example, driving a bus requires adding a *passenger endorsement*. To add this endorsement to a CDL, you will need to drive a bus of the proper size, or larger, for your driving test. If you are planning to drive for a bus company, they will provide a bus for you to use. States (specifically, State Departments of Transportation) have their own rules and regulations surrounding school buses. Again, they will help you navigate the requirements and a school bus to use for your test. However, if you simply want to drive for a nonprofit organization that has a vehicle that can transport 16 passengers or more, you will need to have Entry-Level Driver Training (ELDT), which will be discussed in a later section.

Any load that has containers of liquid or gas that are larger than 119 gallons *and* cumulatively has more than 1,000 gallons capacity — such as a tanker truck — requires a *tanker endorsement*. With a tanker endorsement, you can have loads of liquid (or gas) containers while pulling a box trailer or driving a box truck. You only need to pass a written test to obtain a tanker endorsement; there is no behind-the-wheel tests for it.

Adding the doubles/triples endorsement might enhance your resume. You can choose to pull two or three trailers or not. Most states only allow doubles but since the CDL program is a federal program, triples are still part of the endorsement, even it they are not allowed in your state.

Restricting your CDL

Restrictions generally sound negative. However, if you didn't acquire any endorsements when you obtained your CDL and you're now applying for your dream driving job but it requires you to also be qualified for air brakes and combination vehicles for an occasional local task, you won't qualify for the job.

In this case, *not* having the proper classification or specific endorsement is considered a restriction. *Restrictions* are identified on CDLs to tell people that you haven't officially proven that you are qualified for a skill. A restriction might be more of a physical one, like I have a restriction that says I must wear corrective eyewear when I drive. Common restrictions include automatic transmission only and no air brakes.

TIP

I encourage you to expand your CMV knowledge to include learning to shift a manual transmission (see Chapter 4) and to use air brakes (see Part 3). Having these skill sets and not having the restrictions on your license will make you a more desirable job candidate, even if the job doesn't require these qualifications.

Taking CDL tests in your traditional semi-tractor trailer vehicle will help eliminate restrictions on your license.

Understanding the Skills and Responsibilities

A fellow driver wrote an article in a newsletter about the hardest easy job in the world — being a truck driver. His take was some people look at driving a commercial vehicle (being a truck or bus driver) as an easy job, but they don't know what's involved in doing a *good* job.

Inspecting for safety and performance

At the beginning of your driving day, whenever you stop for personal reasons or for a delivery or pickup, and at the end of your driving day, you need to inspect your vehicle. Some of the inspections are minor and don't take too long, but you should do them anyway. Inspecting your vehicle is the most critical part of driving that the other motorists don't get to see.

WARNING

You inspect your vehicle for your safety and for the safety of others. You want your vehicle to keep performing to the best of its ability because it is the tool that helps you make money. To neglect your inspection, especially in this age of litigations, is to play Russian roulette. Don't take that chance! Be a responsible citizen by keeping your vehicle well-maintained through inspections, which is also helping to protect others.

Driving safely under any conditions

When I was a kid, I made ramps to jump with my bike, and I would do wheelies. I did my share of not-so-safe things on my bike, but not now when I drive a commercial vehicle. I have to examine the cost of a single mistake that was due to my negligence. I take pride in getting the load delivered safely. (For more information about safety requirements, see Chapter 4.)

REMEMBER

Hazards are everywhere. The weather can be unpredictable, bad drivers will make themselves a problem, animals will run out in front of you, or your cargo can become a challenge to keep secure. Always drive with safety in mind!

Caring for your cargo

As a CMV operator, you have more responsibility than just holding onto a steering wheel. You're responsible for the cargo to be safely secured behind you, regardless of being able to see the cargo in your mirrors. Although Federal Motor Carriers Safety Administration (FMCSA) regulations require CMV drivers to do inspections on their cargo periodically, a good driver knows why — it's for safety! (See the section that follows for more on the FMCSA.)

Bus drivers have the advantage of being able to check on their (human) cargo continuously. (Some drivers might differ with me on the word "advantage," especially after a two-hour trip with the words, "The wheels on the bus go round and round" on a repeating loop at 85 decibels.) Every bus driver's objective is the same: to make sure their passengers are delivered safely to their destination(s).

Fulfilling the Entry-Level Driver Training (ELDT) Requirements

The FMCSA, the agency with the US Department of Transportation that oversees CDL testing standards, determined that in order to obtain a CDL prospective license holders must complete Entry-Level Driver Training (ELDT) for two classifications and two endorsements, which are:

>> Class A

>> Class B

>> Passenger endorsement

>> Hazardous materials (hazmat) endorsement

The FMCSA set up minimum testing requirements whereby a person must be trained; therefore, training facilities must certify that they meet the criteria for providing CDL training. The requirements include having classroom facilities, qualified instructors, and proper equipment and curriculum. The curriculum is to include theory (classroom for the most part) and behind-the-wheel training.

REMEMBER

In order for you to obtain a CDL, you will need to receive ELDT from a school, company, or some other entity like a nonprofit organization that is on the FMCSA ELDT registry (https://tpr. fmcsa.dot.gov/). You don't necessarily have to pay for the training. A company that hires you might conduct their own training, but it may require you to stay employed at the company for a set period of time — possibly a good thing!

The first step to getting your ELDT is to pass a written test for a Commercial Learners' Permit (CLP). Most schools and companies that conduct their own training will give you training prior to you taking the test to receive your learner's permit. There are a few training facilities that require you to get a learner's permit prior to taking their classes. While this doesn't make sense to me, it's legal.

Identifying Each Part of the CDL Exam

This section provides a brief description of each section of the CDL exam. You will need to prepare for your written test and your behind-the-wheel tests (including inspections) separately. Normally, there will be at least three weeks between the day you pass your written test (to obtain your CLP) and the day you have your inspection test and behind-the-wheel skills and road tests. (The absolute minimum waiting time, by regulation, is 14 days.)

Use this information here to compartmentalize your test-taking skills. Once you have completed the written test, you will work for a few weeks on the driving skills.

Get some rest! After you have completed all your studying, used flash cards, had friends or family members quiz you, get a good night's sleep the night before each of the tests. Concentration and alertness take energy, so you won't be able to focus if you're not completely rested.

Taking the written test

The first written exam will be for *general knowledge*. (Even though your test will likely be electronic of some sort, it is called a written test.) You must pass it before going on to another test. The information on general knowledge is contained in Part 2 of this book.

You will likely take an air brakes test next, if you want to drive commercial motor vehicles with air brakes. While not all CMVs have air brakes, many do, including larger buses. You can find information on air brakes in Part 3.

The exam for *combination vehicles* might be your next test. This test is required for semi-tractor trailer combinations. If you plan to drive a smaller vehicle while pulling trailers weighing over 10,000 pounds with cargo, you will need to take this written test. Combination vehicles are covered in Part 5.

Here are some tips for taking the written exams:

>> **Take your time.** Don't rush through the tests. Take your time. License examiners will give you plenty of time to pass each test.

>> **Read each question carefully.** By carefully I mean read questions more than once. Catch any words that turn a positive statement into a negative one. State exams are often tricky. Sometimes questions in a test just don't make sense — maybe that is a hint to which choice is correct? Don't just choose the first correct answer. The best answer might be — "all of the above"!

>> **Pass up a question.** You should be able to pass or skip on a question. Do so if you are not confident of an answer. There might be another question that gives you the answer to the question you skipped. The states' exams that I am familiar with use multiple-choice questions, which will increase your chances of passing. You need to get 80 percent of the answers correct. Once you've achieved 80 percent, many tests will stop and won't give you any more questions.

So if you go through all the questions but haven't answered 80 percent yet, you will get the questions that you passed on. This time around you might be more confident of the answer.

After you pass the written test portion of the CDL exam, you can breathe in a breath of fresh air and relax for a little bit. Then, it is time to get back to studying. You will still have to complete a pre-trip inspection test, a behind-the-wheel skills test, and a behind-the-wheel road test. I intend to help you in Part 6 that covers the testing material, but let me give you some encouragement first.

Planning for the pre-inspection test

When it comes to inspecting your vehicle, it's as simple as it sounds — you are to look at a vehicle component, identify it (many places will let you point to it instead), be able to say why you inspect it and how you inspect it. Seriously, you can be like the speaker who seems to just be talking to you instead of reading a script. Learn the components and what they do and how to inspect them and know what can happen when you don't inspect them.

One day when I was listening to a student practicing their inspection presentation, they were really struggling. I wasn't looking at them because I needed to tilt my ear to them to hear. When I finally looked at the student, the student was looking at the ground beside the vehicle attempting to remember what they wanted to say next! Your objective shouldn't be to memorize and then recite a script of information during the pre-inspection test. You should talk during the pre-inspection in a natural progression.

Present your inspection the same way that you would read a novel — from left to right, top to bottom. You wouldn't skip words or paragraphs and then go back to what you missed, would you? If you are under the hood, start at the top left and look for clues to jog your memory. For instance, you see a container with a liquid in it, and you recall that it is coolant. Then you see the lines on its tank that are labeled "minimum" and "maximum." The lines are clues that the coolant needs to be at the proper level.

With the modernized test that is most widely used, the license examiner is not to *assess points* (State DOTs use either a maximum or minimum of points for test assessments) for you forgetting the name of the *whatchamacallit*. If you point to or touch an item, that will take the place of naming it. You need to remember why you would inspect it and most importantly what to inspect it for.

Here are some tips you will want to use for the pre-inspection exam:

>> **Utilize your allowed sheet.** There is an official inspection cheat sheet that you are allowed to use. Your instructors or even the license examiner might give it to you prior to the test. You are not allowed to add any notes on it, but it does have some components on it that can be helpful. But I doubt you will need the cheat sheet because you know that you have the outline in front of you.

>> **Know what you shouldn't see with the components.** Some key things to remember are that liquids and air should not leak. Also, everything should be properly mounted and secured. I can't name a single component that should be cracked bent or broken. Rubber lines should not be rubbing on other components but should be being held still.

With just this bit of information, you have a good foundation for learning the pre-trip inspection. Make yourself a video of the vehicle that you will be testing with and then you can practice at home conducting your inspection.

>> **Listen to the license examiner.** When you have your CDL, you will want to have a systematic process for inspecting your vehicle. However, in the pre-inspection test, a license examiner will tell you which area of the vehicle they want inspected. Don't expect the test to be in the order that is logical. So, in each area of the vehicle, remember to inspect everything and in the same order.

Most places have adopted an abbreviated process for testing, but you can *inspect* more than the license examiner wants to hear. In this case, the examiner can't count your added information as wrong. Some examiners may not like that you're inspecting everything, but they will get over it. They should quickly figure out that you know what you are doing. A DOT officer would be proud of your complete inspection.

Driving behind-the-wheel tests

The pre-inspection test and the two behind-the-wheel tests (skills and the road) should take place on the same day. I will say again to always start the night before the test day with a good night's rest. Chapter 19 has more information on passing the skills and road tests, but the following are some guidelines to consider.

Skills test

One of the most important things to do on the skills test is to listen to your license examiner. If you don't hear or understand what you're being asked to do, politely ask them to repeat what they said, or you can say what you believed they've said, asking for confirmation. Block everything out of your mind, except for the tests you are going to complete. Take your time and don't rush.

Road test

You will have spent several days at a school or other training facility in preparation for the road test day. Go slow on the turns. Stop behind stop signs and stop lines. Stay in the right lane unless told otherwise. Again, listen to your license examiner and ask questions when you need to. Pretend you are with the person who has been coaching you for the past several days. Get comfortable but stay focused at the same time. Remember what size vehicle you are driving.

REMEMBER

There are some differences in CDL regulations from state to state, so listen to your ELDT instructor for those subtle differences. Don't focus on how you can fail but focus on listening to the license examiner.

Chapter **3**

Making a Career with Your CDL

aving a Commercial Driver's License (CDL) isn't just about the added flexibility that you can provide to employers, it also confirms that you have the required training as a professional driver. CDL holders have received training and passed tests that demonstrate they have the knowledge and skills to be a safe driver. (I know, I know it doesn't guarantee that a candidate *is* a safe driver, but they have the skills to be a safe driver.)

In this chapter I discuss possible career options you can have with a CDL, which job to choose, how to spend your off time, and moral choices. This chapter will help you make some informed decisions on whether a commercial driving career is right for you.

You don't have to choose a career path while your exploring your driving options. You can go to a driving school, pass your tests, and then see what opportunities are out there. In the past, some transportation companies hired experienced drivers only but that has changed. Job qualifications have gone from requiring two years of driving experience to hiring a person before they even have a CDL and then proceed in training them.

Introducing Different Types of CMVs

As in most industries, terms are somewhat foreign to people outside of the industry. The words can be interchangeable with other terms or be very specific. To assist with terminology, Figure 3-1 shows several examples of commercial motor vehicles (CMVs) that correspond to terms in the list below.

>> A: Semi-tractor with a flatbed.

>> B: Semi-tractor, tractor, or truck.

>> C: Tanker as a *straight truck*. A straight truck is not a semi-tractor and does not hook to a trailer like a semi-tractor because it doesn't have a *fifth wheel* (the locking mechanism to attach a trailer).

>> D: Concrete mixer.

>> E: Truck with snowplow and salt spreader or just "snowplow."

>> F: Garbage or refuse truck.

>> G: Dump truck.

>> H: Semi-tractor with van trailer.

>> I: Panel truck or box truck or delivery truck.

>> J: School bus.

>> K: City bus.

>> L: Crane truck.

>> M: Tour bus.

FIGURE 3-1:
Examples
of CMVs.

© norsob/Adobe Stock Photos; © Md Tarikul Islam/Adobe Stock Photos; © RR Design/Adobe Stock Photos;
© jazz jackrabbit/Adobe Stock Photos; © Rajkumar/Adobe Stock Photos; © Mazharul/Adobe Stock Photos;
© munja02/Adobe Stock Photos; © Mechanik/Adobe Stock Photos; © Yuri Schmidt/Adobe Stock Photos;
© ABDA/Adobe Stock Photos; © Yuri Schmidt/Adobe Stock Photos; © Mmm/Adobe Stock Photos;
© KBL Sungkid/Adobe Stock Photos

Choosing a Career That Uses Your CDL

In localities where there's a lot of commerce, there will likely be several choices for driving jobs. Some opportunities might not be advertised, so you might have to go and apply in person for the jobs that interest you. Talk to the recruiters or hiring managers and see what they have to say about their driving positions.

Every company has someone in charge of hiring drivers. Larger companies have recruiters whose main job is to hire new drivers. Some driving schools will accept job posts from companies that need drivers. To find driving career opportunities on your own, search the social media and websites of transportation companies as well as companies that use professional drivers. Read driver reviews of companies but discern what is true and what is not.

AUTHOR
SAYS

Be wise, some companies will promise the world, and act like their place is free from the problems that other driving jobs would have. Choose a company that accepts the reality of transportation work and is honest with you.

Going over-the-road

Over-the-road (OTR) driving is driving far enough from home so that you must stay in the sleeper berth of your semi-tractor or truck on a regular basis. A *sleeper berth* is an area in the cab of a semi-tractor that is designed for sleeping. (Believe it or not, there are regulations on what can considered a sleeper berth, but I digress.) Some of these jobs can take you all over the country while others might keep you within a certain area of the country. Some jobs will have you driving the same familiar route over and over, while other jobs present you with the adventure of going to another new place every week.

A few OTR jobs will use a truck called a *day cab*. This is a semi-tractor that does not have a sleeper berth. When you are away from home and it is time for rest, your employer will put you up in a hotel.

All OTR jobs are not always semi-tractor trailer driving jobs. There are *straight trucks* that are utilized in a similar manner. Some straight trucks have a sleeper berth, while others don't. These straight trucks typically have a different niche in the transportation field. Often, there will be an order for parts or supplies that must be delivered expediently. This type of work is usually referred to as *hot-shot hauling* or *expedited freight*. Because the delivery must happen quickly, the transportation cost goes up. So, a straight truck can deliver a smaller amount for a lower fee than the transportation cost of a semi-tractor trailer delivery.

Driving locally

Perhaps you love to drive but you also love seeing your family and friends, or maybe you just like your own bed. You may be surprised to know that there are more local driving jobs that require a CDL than there are OTR driving jobs. This section provides a look at career options using your CDL to drive locally.

Delivering the last mile

There is a segment of the transportation industry where delivery of cargo is often referred to as *final mile delivery*. When something is delivered the "last mile," it infers that it was delivered most of the way to its final destination by a larger truck, probably to a hub or distribution center, where the cargo gets redistributed to smaller vehicles that deliver it to the final destination — the *last mile*.

This type of transportation is necessary because the delivery destination is in a residential area or to a facility that does not have the space for a big truck. If the streets and intersections are not practical (sometimes not legal) for a long semi-tractor trailer to navigate, the delivery must be made by a smaller vehicle.

Delivering the last mile not only serves a specific transportation need for businesses and their customers, but it also allows their drivers to go back home every night.

TIP

You might ask if you need a CDL for the last mile delivery? That would depend on the vehicle. There are a variety of vehicles that make the last mile of delivery, including cargo vans, straight trucks, and *short-pup trailers* (trailers that are commonly pulled as doubles [two trailers at a time] but can be used singularly). However, if you have a CDL that covers all these commercial motor vehicles (CMVs), you will be more valuable and marketable to companies. The CDL might give you the edge over another job candidate.

Working for city/state government

In our society, citizens like to have certain services provided in exchange for some of their tax dollars. Many of these services require drivers with CDLs, which are outlined below.

>> **Hauling waste: garbage trucks.** Other choices for staying local can include work for municipalities, agencies, or private contractors hauling waste material. Garbage haulers are generally large enough to require a CDL. Garbage or waste haulers are in more demand than in past decades as rubbish used to be burned. Many items can be recycled — including cardboard, paper, plastics, and glass — but need to be collected and hauled to the appropriate facility to process back into useful materials.

Even organics like leaves and landscaped waste are recycled and need trucks to pick up and distribute material to appropriate facilities, such as farms and energy plants. I guess waste haulers (another name for garbage haulers) can consider themselves as hauling raw materials for production.

>> **Pushing snow: snowplows.** You get a job operating a snowplow. Most state and local governments will turn their CDL-required dump trucks into snowplows. Some governments will even equip garbage trucks with snowplows.

TIP

Most states do not have enough people on the payroll to operate snowplows 24 hours a day, so they might hire some part-time drivers to operate the plows.

>> **Transporting passengers: buses.** Another career option for you is driving a bus. You can find city buses in many locations as well as bus services in many rural areas. Your local school district might have a fleet of buses, or the district may have contracted a bus company to provide transportation for its students. (I have seen at least one area of the country where "School Bus" signs were stuck to various personal vehicles, so you might be out of luck if that is happening in your area.)

Taking the tour bus: I'm with the band

If you want to try something driving part-time, some tour bus companies have need for drivers. You must concentrate on your driving while transporting sightseers, but you might get in a little sightseeing time on your own at stops (after you have performed all appropriate inspections and bus maintenance like fueling, of course).

Athletic teams and bands will often use coach buses to travel to their competition sites. You can take advantage of this opportunity to inform the coach or conductor what they should change for the next time (not while you are driving though, as passengers are not to be holding conversations with you, or you with them). There might be the possibility that you would need a combination vehicle license if you are also pulling a trailer. It might depend on how much the tubas weigh. Many high school marching bands will go to several competitions in the fall. So if you have a child in the marching band and have a CDL, you will at least have "free" transportation to the event.

Moving concrete

Drivers are needed to transport concrete with large concrete mixers for making a road, a parking lot, or a driveway. Then aggregate (such as sand and gravel) and asphalt need to be hauled to the job site. Depending on where you live, you might not have much work during the wintertime — unless . . . you had a lot of snow (see the snowplow reference in the previous section).

Distributing food and beverages

Have you heard kids ask where their food comes from? Well, it comes from trucks that haul it to grocery stores, restaurants, caterers, hospitals, schools, convenience stores, prisons, and the list goes on. But where does this food come from? Well, it comes from distribution centers and warehouses who received the food from the processing plants that make pasta, vegetable oil, ice cream, snack chips, bread, and so on. It also comes from canneries that process beans, tomatoes, corn, and baby food. How does the food get to these places? Truckloads of raw products are delivered to these places. It is amazing how many trucks are utilized, and most of the trucks are local, meaning drivers get to drive to the delivery locations, make deliveries, and go back home in a day.

Delivering food and beverages generally means a considerable amount of physical activity. Oh, have I not mentioned the beverage trucks? Not only are there options to deliver sodas, juices, and adult beverages, but you also have trucks delivering water — in heavy cases of 16.9-ounce bottles or in 5-gallon containers. The physical activity, if you can lift and move the product ergonomically correct, will help to keep you in shape.

Avoiding Driver Turnover

Don't let anyone fool you, driving OTR is difficult. You must have the discipline to drive when it is time to drive, take your breaks when the regulations demand, and utilize the break time to accomplish goals like showering and eating. If these are the only goals that you accomplish (or fail in), you will likely become a turnover statistic. I don't believe that you will fail at these tasks because this section helps to identify ways that you can avoid becoming a statistic.

Setting goals

As a driver, it's easy to get yourself into a predicament. Mindlessly wasting your off-duty time is one way and proceeding without a plan is another. For me, it was easy to do what I needed to do during my on-duty (work) time. However, during my breaks, I had to have a plan or else I would rob myself of sleep. Setting goals for driving, both small and big, generally benefit safe driving and your mental health.

There was a period when I was driving that, to a slight degree, I was bored. A thought came to me that I could start to track what kind of fuel mileage I could get. I added to my habits of employing slow efficient starts, choosing efficient driving speeds, and timing traffic lights by reducing my engine's idling time (time the engine ran with the truck going nowhere). I didn't always apply all the tricks that contribute to good fuel mileage, but the driver managers at the dispatched office noticed how high my fuel mileage was and would occasionally ask how I did it. After I got into the office, incentives were given to drivers, I shared with drivers my tactics and the fleet's fuel mileage increased dramatically.

There were other times, during breaks, that I simply read a book. What could have been idle time for me to do *nothing* was used for a productive activity. Similarly, you should avoid activities that can negatively affect your driving. For example, a driver who gets involved in time-consuming activities — like online gaming — for hours may find themselves needing sleep when it's time to start driving!

Have a goal and create a schedule for yourself — an itinerary for the day — for on duty *and* off duty. Discipline yourself to do the things on the work list but also include something that you can look forward to. It might be a hobby where you are crafting an item or practicing playing a guitar (isn't that on your bucket list?). Just remember to allot a specific length of time for your hobby so that you get your rest for the next driving day.

Working to stay healthy

You have received your CDL and your new company has given you additional training. You are getting the miles or hours of driving that you desired (OTR jobs generally get paid by the mile, while local jobs, by the hour). However, if you don't take of yourself properly, you're likely on the road to poor health. This section explains the federal government's physical requirements for drivers and gives practical tips for keeping in shape while in a fairly sedentary job. I have included tips for safe work habits as most OTR jobs don't give you enough physical activity for good health and when you occasionally have to do some strenuous work, your body is not ready for it.

Passing a physical

Generally speaking, drivers need to pass Department of Transportation (DOT) physicals every two years. If you don't do well on the physical or have certain medical conditions, you will have to have a physical examination every year. If the DOT medical examiner has a greater concern about your health, you will likely need to return more frequently. Drivers who have good exams return for another examination every two years. Certain health conditions automatically require more frequent visits. Look at these positively, like an accountability session.

Don't get mad at the DOT medical examiner when they ask for more information, possibly from one of your doctors. Many doctors may not be aware of what medications a CDL holder can (or can't) take, but a DOT examiner is certified to know. When they ask for more information from your doctor, they are verifying and documenting what is safe for you to take when you're out on the road. They cannot give a medical certificate saying a driver passed their exam just because they like or feel sorry for them. They must eliminate a reasonable level of potential driver failure. Otherwise, their own licenses and livelihoods could be on the line, not to mention the reasonable potential for catastrophe (an accident involving a driver) that is on their hands.

DOT examiners must conduct thorough examinations to ensure and document that drivers are meeting the health standards that the DOT has established. Drivers and their companies receive a certificate or card (which can be a digital version) that certify successful examinations and document it to cover a specific period of time. Each state's licensing department receives this certification to include on your driving record.

The DOT examiner should refer you to your physician when something is detected that keeps you from complying with the driving regulations. They should also educate you when applicable. As a group, DOT medical examiners promote wellness and programs that help drivers keep or regain the ability to safely operate commercial vehicles.

Be thankful when they identify a potential or existing medical problem. They are performing a critical service for you and for your employer.

Exercising

When you finish your driving day, you might feel drained and don't have the energy or desire to go run, walk, or ride a bike — especially if it's raining or too cold outside. I understand that. But, in order to sustain your driving career, you really need to exercise or as a fellow driver once said, "just do something!" Choose an exercise that you enjoy. Many drivers have fold-up bikes in their truck and use them! It makes a lot of sense to start the day off with exercise (that gets rid of the "end of the day" excuses).

TIP

If you don't have an exercise regime, here's what I suggest you do to get started. Engage your muscles one group or several groups at a time by flexing them. Then move your muscles and body parts with the same movements that you use in weight-bearing exercises and with stretches (see the next section for suggestions) and even yoga positions. Just concentrate on engaging all your body parts (not necessarily at the same time) for 10 minutes. Use a heart monitor to keep from escalating your heart rate too high. Do these exercises four to six days a week, possibly before you start with your driving day. You will feel like you are more ready to take on the day and may experience other positive results as well. (As always, consult a physician prior to starting any exercise regimen.)

WARNING

If you fail to exercise regularly, getting your heart pumping and muscles stretched, you will eventually become a driver turnover statistic, and not simply because you desired a different career.

Working smart

You battled through construction zones and stayed patient in stop-and-go traffic and even found an alternative route that helped you make your delivery on time. You exit out of your vehicle, walk to the back to open the rear doors, and begin to move boxes. If you don't proceed with caution, an injury can occur. Use the following tips in handling cargo or whenever you are switching to physical activity after sitting in the cab of a truck.

Before you begin:

>> **Stretch your back muscles.** Bend over at the waist and let the weight of your body increase the length of your back muscles. Don't force any movement or bounce.

>> **Flex your thighs and calves.** Immediately follow these movements with stretching.

>> **Stretch your shoulder and chest muscles.** Stretch upward, backward, sideways, but again, do not bounce or force any movement.

>> **Stretch your neck muscles.** Alternate stretching your head out from your body, like a turtle poking its head outside its shell, and then tuck your chin in towards your chest just below your neck.

Begin to move the box (or other cargo) with deliberate muscle effort, meaning you're not putting any strain on your joints. Here are some things to remember:

>> **Place your hands under the box.** Of course, you can use the handholds (like cut-outs on the sides of the box) if present.

>> **Bend your legs.** Lift a box from a lower level by keeping your back in a straight vertical position.

>> **Use a dolly if possible.** Strap the cargo to the dolly (to move heavy objects) for more support.

>> **Ask for help.** When you need to move heavy and/or awkward items, ask for assistance. "Driver assisted unloading" is not the same as the "driver does-it-all-alone unloading."

>> **Slide a box down to the boxes beneath for an appropriate lifting height.** If you must move a box that is above shoulder height, this will aid in controlling the box.

>> **See where you are walking.** Avoid or remove any trip hazards.

>> **Use gloves with good grip.** You don't want the box to slip out of your hands.

If you aren't convinced that keeping a check on your health and being proactive about it is important for driving a bus or any CMV, think about this: You are given a great deal of responsibility when you acquire a CDL. You might be hauling children or operating an 80,000-pound vehicle or driving a high-center-of-gravity concrete mixer. Whether you are protecting lives in your vehicle or protecting the lives of those around you, you are responsible for your cargo as a CDL holder. This takes work and effort that is generally outside of work time. And if that doesn't convince you, your health is worth more than just driving responsibly as it helps a driver perform some lesser spoken goals of being able to play with children or grandchildren or to climb some stairs while on a vacation.

Finding the right company

Your first step in searching for the right company is by reading this book. Seriously, you want to make an informed decision by knowing what to look for and what type of jobs are available. You will find that there are companies that take care of their customers by taking care of their employees. Conversely, there are companies that sacrifice their employees, thinking that this is the way to conduct business.

Many companies do not understand that taking good care of their customers and employees is part of a good business model. Customers will positively respond to a company that is taking care of them, and customers will also appreciate having friendly, happy drivers who deliver to their facilities. They will also appreciate clean and properly maintained vehicles. These are all fairly simple business practices but are not always followed.

TIP

Observe the drivers of a company that you are considering for your new driving job. Do they seem happy or at least content? Or are they ready for quitting time just one hour into the day?

AUTHOR SAYS

HAPPY EMPLOYEES

I used to occasionally haul loads with multiple delivery stops to hardware and other building supply type stores. I could almost always count on the employees at one chain to be discontented with me delivering special customer orders to them. Another chain where I delivered had employees who were simply content but not winning any prizes for enthusiasm though. However, when I delivered to small local operations, the employees (possibly owners) were happy to see me with the product that their customers had ordered and did everything in their power to make a successful delivery of their customers' orders.

Do you see the difference in the stops I had to make? I am not attempting to disrespect chain stores, but I am "dissing" the lack of proper philosophy that is needed to run a thriving business where employees are happy to work at each day, even if the work is hard! I believe that the problem or success starts at the top and works its way down. Each layer of employees must convey to the next level the same philosophy of which they have been entrusted.

The moral of the story is to look for the companies that take care of their in-house employees and their drivers — where driver turnover is less frequent.

Staying Compliant with Regulations

AUTHOR SAYS

I have made both bad and good decisions in life. Many decisions cannot be undone but many decisions can be left behind. Just remember that forgiveness brings freedom. Your decision to start a new career with a CDL will probably give you a new start in some ways. But always attempt to make things right with someone you have wronged or with someone who has wronged you. If you had felonies in your past, you may be able to get a driving job. If you had convictions that involved drugs and/or alcohol (assuming you didn't have a CDL), you can still obtain a CDL and get a driving job. With your new CDL, you change things.

You should start your driving career with a determination to stay compliant with transportation laws and regulations. You may find that you are not 100 percent successful with all the obscure points. But if you are honestly attempting to be compliant, you go on to a successful driving career. This section examines some very important requirements and regulations that you need to closely follow.

Drugs and alcohol

REMEMBER

Failing a drug or alcohol test adversely affects a person's driving career. Employers are required to have 50 percent of their drivers randomly tested each year for drugs and 10 percent of their drivers for alcohol. The odds are great that you will get sent for a drug screening every year or two. Screenings can only take place when a driver is on duty and presumably able to report to duty. This means that such a screening would not take place after you have an adult beverage with a Saturday night meal, and you don't report to work until Monday. Nor would the screening take place when you are off duty due to a surgical procedure that has you on painkillers that CDL holders are banned from using.

Whenever a driver fails such a drug test, the failed results are sent to the Federal Motor Carrier Safety Administration's (FMCSA) Drug and Alcohol Clearinghouse, which is a database of commercial drivers with the record of any failed drug and alcohol screenings. Once a driver is in this database, employers cannot hire them nor can licensing facilities grant them a license. In order for a driver to regain driving privileges a driver must complete a lengthy return-to-work process.

Once you have your CDL, protect it. Stay away from drugs and alcohol. But if you do drink any alcohol, you are forbidden to drive for 4 hours before reporting for duty. I would extend that, for everyone's sake, to 24 hours. That should make it obvious that no alcohol is to be consumed while you are on duty. Again, if you are going to drive, just don't consume alcoholic beverages.

CDL disqualifications

There are various ways that you can be disqualified from having a CDL or the Commercial Learner's Permit (CLP) in addition to failed drug and alcohol screenings. These *disqualifications* are anything from 60 days to a lifetime disqualification and might vary among states. But they mainly involve committing a crime while driving a CMV, receiving serious traffic violations, or committing violations at a railroad crossing. Depending on the type of offense, the frequency of events, the state that you are licensed in, or if you are driving a CMV at the time of the offense, there are various lengths of time for disqualifications. Here's a list of some disqualifications:

>> Leaving the scene of an accident, commercial vehicle or not — 12 months minimum disqualification.

>> Committing a felony with a CMV or not — 12 months minimum disqualification.

>> Being convicted of one of the above two offenses while carrying placarded hazardous materials — 3 years minimum disqualification.

>> Failure to stop when you should stop at a railroad crossing — 60 days disqualification up to a year disqualification.

   This failure can happen in several ways: failing to stop when the tracks aren't clear, failing to stop when you are required to, or failing to realize there isn't enough clearance under your vehicle to clear the tracks.

   Do your research to determine if your cargo dictates if you should stop at railroad tracks and be vigilant for all railroad crossing hazards and warnings.

>> Two serious traffic violations in a three-year period — 60-day disqualification, 120-day disqualification for three violations.

   Serious violations include excessive speeding, reckless driving, improper lane usage, cell phone usage, among others.

Stay focused on always driving legally and responsibly. This will take care of any potential problems that may result in losing your CDL. You won't have to remember what the above abbreviated list contains!

Certain health conditions

In spite of our good efforts, there are some health conditions that you and I have little or no control over. For some of the items in the following list, most drivers can be proactive and work with their doctors to avoid disqualification.

The following are some medical conditions that disqualify a driver with a CDL.

>> **Vision.** Vision seems obvious: you must have at least 20/40 vision in both eyes, with or without corrective lenses. You must be able to identify the colors of traffic signals and have at least 70 degrees of horizontal peripheral vision.

- **Epilepsy.** This category also includes other conditions that cause a sudden loss of consciousness. Drivers can be granted exemptions in some instances.

- **High blood pressure.** Any high blood pressure will result in some sort of restriction. If you have stage three hypertension (blood pressure readings of 180/120 mmHg or higher), you must get your blood pressure down to get medical certification.

- **Heart conditions.** Certain heart conditions can disqualify you, but not all conditions. It is important to work with a physician to improve your chances of qualifying.

- **Hearing loss.** You are allowed to wear a hearing device to pass a hearing test, but some levels of hearing loss without one can disqualify you.

It is possible to regain your medical certification if you lose it. Work with your doctor and the DOT medical examiner to see what can be done. It is not unheard of to reverse a medical status and regain the certification to drive.

TIP

For good transportation companies (those that have higher job satisfaction and retention rates among their employees), health disqualifications are one of the biggest contributors to turnover. Work with your doctors and other healthcare professionals to help you maintain a healthy lifestyle — physically and mentally.

2

Reviewing Relevant General Knowledge

IN THIS PART . . .

Find the information you need and gain superior practices to enable you to become one of the elite professionals on the road.

Learn how to drive safely in adverse driving conditions.

Glean the knowledge that a professional driver needs apart from safe driving skills.

Secure your cargo to keep the cargo intact, and the people around you safe.

IN THIS CHAPTER

» Checking out a vehicle for the first time

» Identifying the pedals, controls, and gauges

» Understanding how to operate your vehicle

» Determining braking distance, speed, and proper spacing

» Focusing your mind on driving

Chapter **4**

Driving Safely at Any Time

When you pass all your Commercial Driver's License (CDL) tests and have in hand your new license, you have become a professional driver of commercial motor vehicles. Commercial motor vehicles (CMVs) require greater knowledge and skill to operate than other vehicles. They are heavier than other vehicles and have a high center of gravity or may have hazardous or precious cargo in them (like hazardous materials or children).

When you understand the best practices contained in this chapter and pass your CDL exams, you will be among the safest drivers on the road. These tactics, in this chapter, if employed by every new driver, will reduce the number of accidents and even create a pleasant driving environment for all drivers. Remember, a CMV is not like a four-wheeler (CB lingo for passenger vehicles; see the sidebar, "CB Lingo" later in this chapter) and thus should not be driven like one.

In this chapter, I introduce you to the interior of the truck and to proper driving techniques, both physically and philosophically. I will explain the process of shifting a manual transmission. Study this chapter as it contains foundational guidelines for professional driving.

Making Adjustments to Drive the Vehicle

On the first day, after all your orientation and training with your new job, your boss says, "take the new truck we received and deliver the load to Acme Warehouse." While you might want to panic, don't! Follow these steps in this section to make the trip a safe delivery and more comfortable for you as well.

Adjusting the driver's seat and steering wheel

You must be able to reach the pedals with your feet and operate them properly (such as pressing the clutch pedal to the floor when you have a manual transmission). So the first step is to get in the driver's seat and adjust it.

EVOLUTION OF TRUCK SEATS

Truck seats, in my lifetime, have come a long way. Seats would have a cushion, period. Drivers had health issues that stemmed from poor seats. Springs were added to seats, and many adjustments were added to help fit the driver. Engineers started designing the seat to absorb the shock of the bumps and holes in roads. Today, air ride seats are common and have adjustments for "everything." Controls and adjustment knobs can be found on either side or both sides of the seat. Use these features and don't just have the seat sitting on the floor so you can look cool. You won't look cool when you are walking around in pain.

Place your hands on the left and right sides of the steering wheel while sitting back firmly in your seat. Find the controls to adjust the seat up/down or forward/back as needed; the seat might have knobs and switches on both sides and the front. You might need to reference the owner's manual or search the Internet for information on the vehicle's seat controls.

Next, adjust the steering wheel, if possible; some older model vehicles may have steering wheels that aren't adjustable. Steering wheels in over-the-road trucks generally can be adjusted up and down and forward and back. Move it to a comfortable position, but don't spend too much time as you will figure out what is most comfortable for you as you gain more driving time.

Positioning the mirrors

REMEMBER

Never start to drive without checking your mirrors first for proper adjustment. Some companies have a mirror check station, but most will not. You should know how to adjust the mirrors in any case. Start by adjusting the big mirrors on both sides of the vehicle so that you see a sliver of the side of your truck, bus, or trailer as shown in Figure 4-1. Notice the figure, the sliver of the trailer in top-left and the top-right mirrors; these are the *big mirrors.* The smaller mirrors on the bottom-left and bottom-right are *convex mirrors,* which show wider angles. You don't need to see all your vehicle or trailer as you know where it is and what it looks like. Everything around you will be changing, and that is what you must be able to see in relation to your vehicle. Adjust the mirror to show as straight as possible from top to bottom.

FIGURE 4-1:
Proper
mirror
positions.

LAW ENFORCEMENT OFFICERS

The main law enforcement officers that perform inspections of CMVs are state troopers. Even among state troopers, there are troopers who specialize in CMVs. An officer can randomly pull you over to the side of the road (in some states), or inspect your vehicle at a weigh station, or pull you over for a traffic infraction and then conduct an inspection. However, any officer can notify a specially trained officer when they have spotted an unsafe vehicle on the road. A Department of Transportation officer (a state trooper who has special training to inspect commercial motor vehicles) will gladly come. After all, who doesn't want to pull an unsafe vehicle off the road?

Next, adjust the smaller mirrors that are on each door. Don't adjust them to see the same objects that your big mirrors show — that would just be redundant. However, there should be a little overlapping. Adjust the left convex mirror to show 30 to 35 feet back from your mirror, revealing the "lane" to your left or where a little car might be. Adjust the right convex mirror to do the same except to see about 60 to 70 feet farther back.

Your vehicle might have one or two fender mirrors. These mirrors offer even broader views of what is behind you. Adjust the fender mirrors to see the rear of your vehicle or trailer and partially away from the vehicle. You will use these mirrors to verify that you are making turns correctly and guiding the rear of the vehicle in the correct path.

TIP

Prior to starting a trip, and each time you have an opportunity, clean your windows and mirrors. It is sort of like making your bed each morning, it gives you a good feeling and it looks good. Dirty mirrors can also tell an officer who is inspecting your vehicle or maybe observing your vehicle as it passes over the scales at a weigh station, that you are not taking care of small items, so the rest of your vehicle needs to be inspected.

Getting Familiar with the Pedals

TIP

"Feet, meet your pedals!" You don't want your feet getting caught up or fumbling around the pedals when you need to bring the vehicle to a stop, especially in an emergency situation. This is your opportunity to familiarize your feet with the pedal locations and relationship to each other.

Here's how you can get started:

1. **Place your right foot on the fuel pedal (also known as the accelerator), then on the brake pedal.**

2. **Repeat enough times that your feet are comfortable with instantly finding the pedals.**

Even if you don't like the way the vehicle manufacturer placed the pedals, don't make excuses and skip these steps. Build a memory of where the pedals are by *repeating the back-and-forth movement*, so you will press the pedal with confidence and accuracy when an emergency arises. If you have a manual transmission, do the same with the clutch pedal. Repetitively practicing where to place your left foot on the clutch pedal will build muscle memory (or is it simply your brain remembering?).

Finding the Controls and Gauges

You already know that it's bad when you don't know where the brake pedal is instantly. You should also know where the other dashboard controls are located when you need to utilize them. You will find all these controls when you perform a pre-trip inspection (see Chapter 17), but your mind will be focused on a different task at that time. Know where these controls are beforehand and how to operate them when needed. If you fail to do this, you may be guilty of being a distracted driver when you were simply looking for the wiper switch!

Identifying the dashboard controls and switches

Here is a list of important controls that you should familiarize yourself with:

>> Headlights

>> Defroster

>> Heater

>> Wiper switch

>> Turn signal

>> Cruise control

>> Horn(s)

>> Windshield washer fluid

>> Transmission selector or shift lever

>> Engine brake switch and setting

Here is a list of controls that are optional before the pre-trip inspection:

>> Traction control

>> Four-way flashers, also known as emergency flashers or just flashers

>> Hillside assist

>> Differential lock

>> Suspension height

>> Fifth wheel release

>> Power Take-Off (PTO) switch (the switch that powers other operations of some CMVs, like a dump truck)

There are many other controls that are specific to the type of vehicle you are driving. Ask the person familiarizing you on the vehicle what the unknown control buttons are for, or search in your owner's manual or on YouTube for an instructional video. I'm sure that someone has made a video about it.

Looking for the gauges

Looking at your gauges to ensure that your vehicle is operating properly is a characteristic of a professional driver. You had to find a few of these gauges while performing your pre-trip inspection. However, there are more gauges to observe than what you looked for during your inspection. If your truck doesn't have analog gauges all around the dashboard, you will likely have a screen that you must toggle through to find the various gauges. Practice scrolling through finding the gauges while you are just sitting so you won't be distracted doing so when driving.

Here is a list of gauges to find:

>> Amp meter or voltmeter: shows battery charge level

>> Coolant temperature: temperature of engine coolant

>> Air pressure in supply tank(s): air pressure to operate brakes

>> Oil pressure: oil pressure for proper engine lubrication

>> Fuel: amount of fuel in tanks

>> Diesel exhaust fluid: amount of DEF in the tank

>> Speedometer: speed of your vehicle

>> Tachometer: speed of your engine or RPM (rotations per minute)

>> Differential temperature(s): temperature of the drive axle(s)

>> Transmission temperature: temperature of the transmission

>> Turbo boost pressure: pressure the turbo is operating

>> Brake application pressure: amount of air pressure applied to brakes

>> Suspension pressure(s): amount of air pressure in air bags

>> Outside thermometer: temperature of the weather outside

More information on gauges can be found in Chapter 17 on inspecting your vehicle and in Chapters 8 and 9 on brakes. Like the switches, ask someone, check the owner's manual, or look for a video to get information on what other gauges control in your vehicle.

Inspecting Your Vehicle

To comply with federal regulations, you must inspect your vehicle for the following: before you start your day, after you get out of the vehicle including for required stops, and when you finish your day. You might be thinking of other reasons to inspect, like avoiding breaking down on the side of the road. But federal laws require that a driver must *know* that their vehicle is safe to drive. This section outlines when you should inspect your vehicle.

WARNING

Don't drive an unsafe vehicle! If I haven't told you yet, as a professional driver, you are the one who is responsible for whether an unsafe truck is taken out on the road or not. The buck indeed stops with you!

Pre-trip inspection

Inspect your vehicle and your load/cargo when you start your day. This is commonly referred to as the *pre-trip inspection*. There is a common saying that you should inspect everything and always inspect everything in the same order. See Chapter 17 for a complete run-down of a pre-trip inspection.

During the trip

After you begin your trip, inspect your vehicle and your cargo within the first 50 miles, then again every 3 hours or 150 miles, whichever comes first. This is commonly called the *enroute inspection* because you conduct it while you're still "in route" or have driving left to do during the day.

First, you will need to be aware of a few things you *should not do.*

>> **Don't inspect everything.** You're not making a pre-trip inspection.

>> **Don't touch anything hot.** This is self-explanatory.

>> **Don't check fluids.** Fluids expand with heat.

>> **Don't check the pressure of your tires.** The tires will be hot, and the pressure will be higher than the cold tire pressure, which is when you should check the tire pressure.

The following are inspections you can and *should do.*

>> **Thump the tires with a hammer or a tire thumper.** If the tire feels or sounds like the pressure is low, use a tire pressure gauge to confirm your suspicion. If your tire has lost pressure, you need to have the tire repaired or replaced.

>> **Check your wheels.** Hold your hand in front of the wheel to feel for excessive heat. If one of the wheels is hotter than the other wheels, a failure is in the process, like a bearing going bad. Also look for hub oil leaks.

>> **Inspect your trailer and dolly connections when appropriate.**

>> **Listen for air leaks and look for fluid leaks.** Look on the ground for leaks and around on the frame and tires.

>> **Inspect the securement of your cargo as much as is feasible.** For drivers of truck flatbeds, take your winch bar with you as you walk around your *rig* (truck), ensuring tie downs are still tight. All drivers should check that doors are closed and nothing from inside the cargo area is leaking out.

Post-trip inspection

When your day is over, inspect everything you inspected during the pre-trip inspection, except anything that is affected by heat or is hot. This inspection will take you a little longer to conduct than an en route inspection.

REMEMBER

If you hook to a trailer after your initial pre-trip inspection, perform a pre-trip inspection on the trailer. Every time you hook to a different trailer, inspect it. Also, every time you unhook from a trailer, perform a post-trip inspection on it.

Where to inspect

When you start or end your day, you should already have chosen a safe location to inspect your vehicle. But when it is time to conduct an enroute inspection, you must choose an area that has limited traffic and where you can keep safe. The shoulder of an interstate highway or ramp is not a safe place. It's also helpful to find a convenient location ahead of time, like a truck stop, rest area, weigh station, or maybe in an industrial area that has extra-wide streets.

Operating Your Vehicle Properly

You might not give much thought to making left and right turns while driving your personal vehicle, but when you are driving a large commercial motor vehicle (CMV), driving intentionally is imperative.

Making a turn safely in a commercial vehicle takes planning. If you haven't already switched to your alter-ego of professional driver from ordinary driver, it's time to make that switch now. If you make a turn with a big truck or bus the same way you drive a personal vehicle, you will soon be in trouble, big trouble.

Turning left or right

If you're making a left or right turn and have more than one lane designated for making that turn, always use the widest lane. This means you choose the lane with the largest radius or the outside turning lane as shown in Figure 4-2.

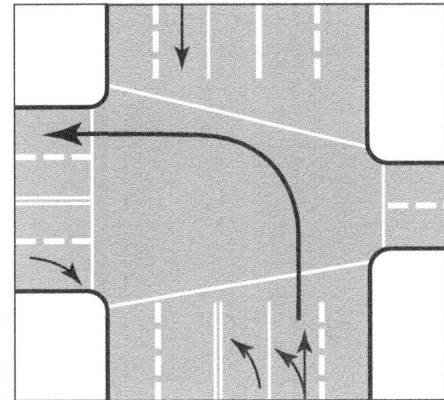

FIGURE 4-2: Use the widest turning lanes.

You must wait a little longer before turning the steering wheel, when making a turn in a longer vehicle. If you turn too soon, your last axle will be running over curbs, stop signs, traffic lights, or a pedestrian who is standing too close to the curb. The rear axle doesn't follow the steer tires perfectly, not even close sometimes. The term for the rear axle taking a different path than the steer tires is called *off-tracking*. Some reference to off-tracking is likely to be on your written test.

You must also take the turn slowly. The tighter the turn, the slower you should drive. There are too many things to account for and to do, for you to drive fast. There are steering wheels to turn, curbs to miss, mirrors to constantly monitor, other drivers to avoid, and people to watch for.

Slow down before you get to the turn, unless you want to test Newton's law of motion that goes something like this, "An object in motion tends to stay in motion." I saw a driver of a concrete mixer truck test this law. Besides taking out someone's privacy fence (it wasn't private after that), the concrete hardened in the mixer before the truck was placed back on its wheels.

Left turns

Wait until you get to the middle of the intersection before you start turning, maybe longer. At the same time, make sure you turn before you run into the far curb (diagonally to the left or straight in front of you if it is a "T" intersection), sidewalk, parked cars, and so on.

If you were to make a left turn from the inside lane, you may discover that you have to swing wider to miss the vehicles waiting their turn to go or to miss a median, and you won't be able to see all vehicles that would be on your right side creating a hazardous situation. So always remember to use the outside lane to make your left turns.

Right turns

Right turns are inherently tighter turns than left turns (unless you are driving in England, but this is a book about getting your license in America so . . .). Take the right turns very slow. "How slow," you ask? You may go slower than you need to, and that's okay.

TIP

If your right turn is going to take more lanes than the one you are turning from and turning onto (even if you stay as wide as your lane allows), you would be making an illegal turn, and your driving examiner may have an issue with you using the wrong lanes. This is known as *a jug handle turn*, which is shown in Figure 4-3.

You can use the opposite lane of the road you are turning onto, known as a *button hook turn* (see Figure 4-4), but you are not allowed to use the opposite lane of the road that you are turning from (jug handle). One of your objectives is to eliminate the possibility of someone driving between your vehicle and the curb (or whatever is to your right). If another motorist drives into that space, it will not go well for them. Since *you are* the professional driver, you will be held accountable for making space that other drivers can drive into.

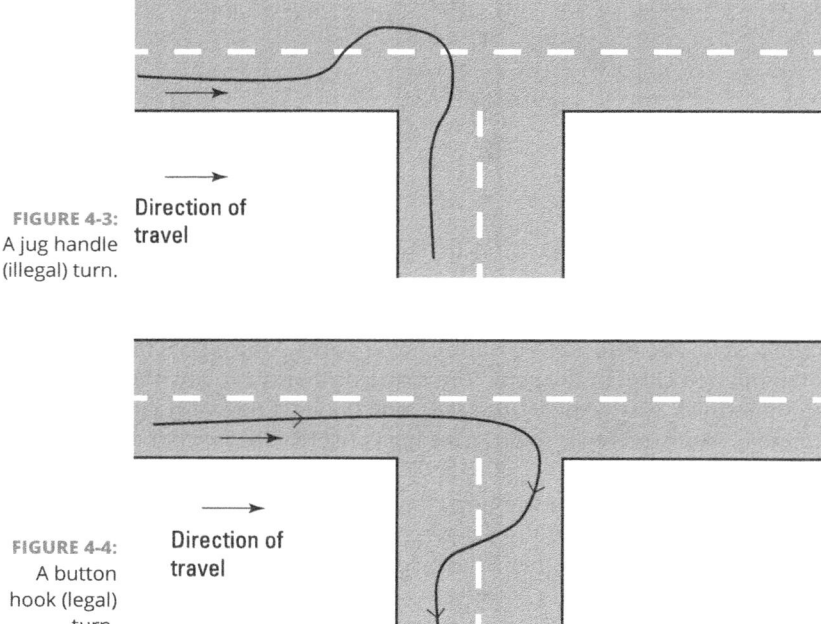

FIGURE 4-3: A jug handle (illegal) turn.

Direction of travel

FIGURE 4-4: A button hook (legal) turn.

Direction of travel

Here are the steps for making a right-hand turn:

1. **Turn on your right-hand turn signal and slow way down.**

2. **Steer into the proper lane (if there is a choice and as discussed above).**

3. **Wait until the other vehicles (that are in your way of making a safe turn) have cleared.**

4. **Drive forward enough in your current lane for your rear-most tire to miss any obstacle on the right when you make the turn.**

   The rear-most tire should stay completely on the road.

5. **Steer to the right.**

   Notice how your vehicle reacts to the turn and learn from it. But be aware that the next vehicle you drive may react a little differently. Be a student of the physics of turning.

6. **Watch your mirrors.**

   Pay attention to your right mirror more than your left for right turns (vice versa for left-hand turns). Use both the convex and hood mirrors if you have them.

7. **Avoid turning too soon into the right-most lane if you have a long vehicle.**

   Turning too soon will bring the rear tire into the curb. (This is especially true if you are pulling a trailer.) Remember, you can use the oncoming lane of the road you are turning onto.

8. **Turn completely into the right lane.**

Centering your vehicle

A little but important thought process for you to employ is to center your vehicle. Centering your vehicle in your lane forces you to check your mirrors often. (More on mirror usage later in this chapter.) Your view in the driver's seat provides part of the picture, while using your mirrors will provide the rest of the picture that you need. Your mirrors may even surprise you as to where your truck or bus is really positioned on the road, particularly when in narrow lanes.

Backing up

Backing up a commercial vehicle is a potentially dangerous maneuver and should be avoided when possible. However, you might need to back into a dock to deliver cargo. In this case, you must take some safety precautions.

Before you begin, you should start from the easiest path possible. Positioning your truck to move straight back is best option with a gentle curve as a second option. Avoid making an "S" curve path because in order to execute, causes increased blind spots and hazards.

As you back into a dock, constantly check both mirrors so that you can fine-tune the truck's position. Being in the correct position will enable you and the dock workers to enter and exit your truck or trailer safely. Having your truck straight in a dock space will keep other drivers from getting mad at you for getting too close to their truck. Another driver can potentially block your door with their vehicle if you get too close to their dock space. There's more on backing a combination vehicle in Chapter 11.

REMEMBER

There are two common acronyms in the trucking industry: one is *GOAL*, which means Get Out and Look, and the other is *WATER* or Walk Around the Entire Rig. Always use these steps to safely back up your vehicle.

TIP

Ask a helper, such as a dock worker or another truck driver, to provide a better vantage point for your path backward. You will need to ensure that your helper knows what *you* need to know as the driver and understands the agreed-upon hand signals — especially the one for stop!

Understanding the basics of shifting gears

To convert the energy of an engine to make your vehicle move, you need a transmission. A *transmission* transfers that energy ultimately to the drive wheels/tires. A transmission will have gears or other components that enable the vehicle to move faster.

Shifting gears using an automatic transmission or an automated manual transmission is easy. An *automatic* transmission in a CMV operates like most car transmissions as it makes all the decisions for the driver. (An *automated manual* transmission is a manual transmission that a computer is operating; the truck has a clutch and gears, but there is no clutch pedal for the driver to operate.) To move the vehicle forward, you place the *gear shift lever* (also known as a gear shift tower or gear selector) in "drive" or in "forward." To move backward, you place the gear shift level in reverse. (Just like in personal vehicles, these might be labeled "D" and "R.") This is probably just like your personal vehicle, so let's move on to the manual transmission.

TIP

Automatic and automated manual transmissions make up the vast majority of transmissions placed in trucks and buses today. However, in most, if not every state, you must test in a manual transmission vehicle to avoid being restricted from driving a vehicle with a manual transmission. While this is not about you becoming "a real trucker," I advise that you learn to drive on a manual transmission so that you won't be restricted in what you are licensed to drive.

The examiners have a specific shifting process that they usually have potential CDL holders to perform; it's referred to as double clutching (see the section "Double clutching" later in this chapter). While there are various manual transmissions, this section addresses the most the common option — the 10-speed transmission. When you gain experience with the 10 speed, you can learn how to shift a 13- or 18-speed transmission in just a minute or two because the most difficult parts of shifting gears are used for the 10 speed.

Knowing which gear to use

You won't always start driving your vehicle in the same gear. When your vehicle is heavy (has cargo), you might choose second gear. If your truck is empty (not carrying cargo), you might choose fourth gear. Your driving instructor will advise you as to what they want you to do during your classes.

A 10-speed transmission has ten forward gears and two reverse gears. Low gears are made for going a low speed. The low gears are also the gears that help you work up to the high gears so that you can go a higher speed. The high gear for reverse is a dangerous gear to use. I accidentally used it once and scared myself, and I am not afraid of much — though I do have a very healthy respect for many varmints, like skunks.

OPERATING THE CLUTCH PEDAL

As part of the gear shifting process, you must use a clutch pedal. Your clutch pedal is the pedal on the left as shown in Figure 4-5. Pushing the pedal with your left foot operates the clutch. If you use your left foot for the brake in your personal vehicle, — *stop!* Your left foot should forevermore be used only for the clutch pedal or nothing at all.

When you push in the clutch pedal, the first 1½ to 2 inches of movement is *free play,* meaning nothing is activated or disengaged in this distance. Pushing the clutch pedal all the way to the floor operates the clutch brake, not to be confused with the brake pedal. The clutch brake stops some internal components of the transmission from turning. You will only want to use the clutch brake when you are stopped and shifting into reverse or into your first forward gear. In between the free play and clutch brake is where you want to do most of your work with the clutch pedal.

FIGURE 4-5:
From left to right the clutch pedal, brake pedal, fuel pedal.

While the engine is turned off, practice operating the clutch pedal with your left foot by doing the following:

1. **Push the clutch pedal in halfway.**

2. **Release the clutch pedal all the way.**

3. **Push the clutch pedal in halfway again.**

4. **Release the clutch pedal twice as slow as the first release.** (This provides for a smoother engagement of the gears with the engine. Releasing it fast results in more jerking and jumping of the truck. It will help the components to last longer.)

From the first depression of the pedal to the final release should be close to 2 seconds.

WORKING THE GEAR SHIFTING PATTERN

As previously mentioned, this section focuses on using the most common shifting pattern for manual transmissions — an H pattern, shown in Figure 4-6. (Some trucks will have a label showing the shift pattern and a shifting sequence; an example is shown in Figure 4-7.) Note where the numbers are in the H-pattern; you will shift up and down in numerical order. In between the numbers is neutral. When the gear selector is in this area, it is not in a gear, thus neutral. Remember that you don't start driving in first gear (in most cases), and your instructor might have you starting in a higher gear than second gear. You can use first gear when you just want to slowly creep forward — which is called *granny low* — like during the behind-the-wheel test (see Chapter 19).

In a truck with a manual transmission, use the following steps to become familiar with how to shift gears with a gear shift lever:

1. **Sit in the truck and leave the engine off.**

2. **Ensure that the brakes are set (pull out the yellow knob).**

FIGURE 4-6:
Shift
pattern of
a 10-speed
transmission.

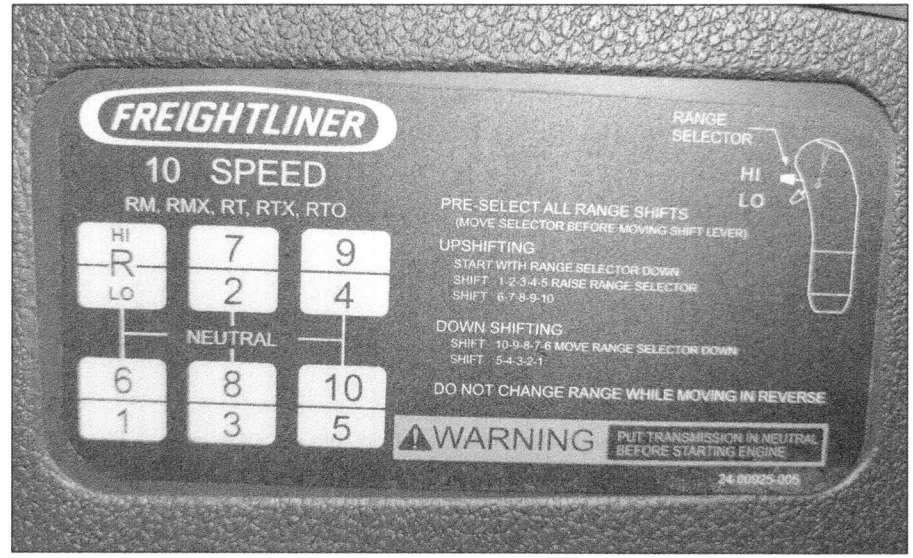

FIGURE 4-7:
A shifting
sequence
label.

3. **Wiggle the gear shift lever left and right.** You might have to pull or push the selector out of gear if the previous driver left it in gear.

4. **Pull the lever left towards you.** You may feel the spring giving a little resistance.

5. **Push the lever up to the "R" position to go into reverse.**

6. **Pull the lever down to the "1" to go into first gear.**

7. **Pull the level out of gear and release it.**

8. **Let the lever rest on the left edge of the wiggle position in Step 3.** It might rest to the left on its own, so you may need to gently push it into that position.

9. **Practice finding the gears by gently pushing them into one of the four gear slots (gears 2, 3, 4, or 5).** Since the engine is not running, the transmission may not be completely cooperative. One of the gears should cooperate and let you slide it in with a *two-step slide* (a little slide, then a little resistance and then a slide into the gear position).

10. **Repeat these steps until you are familiar with the shifting pattern.**

TIP

When you are driving with a manual transmission, I want you to select gears like holding a teacup with your pinkie sticking out or like you are gently shoving a little kitten out of the way. Don't grasp the gear shift like a hammer or baseball bat. Gently move the gear shift in and out of gears and back in again. This movement will help you to treat the transmission with care and not try to ram the gear shift into a gear. If you force the transmission into a gear, you will hear noises coming from the transmission and a different kind of noise coming from your instructor.

Using the splitter

There is a lever on the front side of the gear shift lever that can be moved up or down. It is commonly called the *splitter* or as the range selector as illustrated in the drawing in the previous shifting sequence photo. In the down position, you can select the lower gears — first through fifth gear — and low reverse. In the up position, you can select gears six through tenth. Please don't use the high reverse. You will start with the splitter in the down position. It's okay to move it up and down when the engine is off or even when it is on. In fact, go ahead and try it. You won't hurt anything. Just remember move it down when you are getting ready to drive.

Looking at the tachometer

While shifting gears, the main gauge to refer to on your dashboard is the tachometer. The *tachometer* shows the engine's rotations per minute (RPM). As your skills progress, you will learn to use the speedometer in combination with your tachometer to determine gears to be in. For now, just use the speedometer to keep your speed in check. Your vehicle will likely *idle* (the engine running without a foot pressing on the fuel pedal) at around 600 RPM. For the purpose of learning how to shift a transmission properly, I don't want you to make the engine go higher than 1500 RPM.

TIP

Revving an engine (increasing the RPMs) above 1500 RPM, makes it harder to manually shift gears.

Double clutching

In order to shift the transmissions in larger CMVs, you must employ the process of double clutching. *Double clutching* means that you are using the clutch (and clutch pedal) twice each time you shift a gear. Most license examiners will officially state that this is the only way to pass your driving test. Trying to single clutch will fail you in more ways than one as the gears will not sync properly most of the time.

Up-shifting gears

Here's an example for up-shifting to a desired gear:

1. **Depress the clutch pedal halfway.**

2. **Slide the gear shift level into your desired gear.** If it is grinding or vibrating, move your clutch pedal somewhat slowly to the floor. If you are keeping a little pressure on the lever, it should slide into position. If there is no grinding but it doesn't want to let you put it in gear, slowly let out on the clutch. As soon as the lever slides into the gear, push the clutch pedal back in.

3. **Check to make sure that it's safe to proceed and *slowly* lift up your foot on the clutch pedal.** When you feel the truck start to move (transmission takes hold), completely release the clutch pedal. Now you're moving!

   If you release the clutch pedal too fast at this step, you can "kill" the engine (make it stop running). If it happens on your road test, the examiner will likely fail you.

Do not press on the fuel pedal while you have the clutch engaged! It doesn't matter what you had to do with any other manual transmission vehicles you have ever driven.

4. **Build speed up by giving the engine fuel.** Note when the tachometer hits 1400 RPM (may need 1500 RPM for the higher gears).

5. **Press the clutch pedal in halfway and at the same time, move the gear shift lever into neutral.**

6. **Immediately release the clutch pedal.**

7. **Press the clutch pedal in again and at the same time, slide the gear shift lever into desired gear.**

8. **Release the clutch pedal again but not too fast.**

9. **Repeat Steps 4 through 8 to move the gear shift lever into the next gear.**

Practice the up-shifting steps slowly at first, without the aid of a truck and spectators. Over time, it will start to seem like only two steps because you are pushing your clutch pedal foot in and out and at the same time you are taking the gear shift lever and placing it in neutral.

When you get to fifth gear, get ready for sixth gear by moving the splitter up. It will do the work for you when you shift to sixth gear using the previous steps. You will just have to remember where sixth gear is.

Down-shifting gears

Here's an example for down-shifting gear:

1. **Slow down by using your brake, or simply lose momentum, to 1000 RPM.**

2. **Press the clutch pedal in and at the same time slide the gear shift lever into neutral.**

3. **Immediately release the clutch pedal.**

4. **Press on the fuel pedal to give the engine a shot of fuel, then take your foot off it.**

5. **Press the clutch pedal in and at the same time move the gear shift lever into the next lower gear.**

6. **Let out on the clutch pedal but not too fast.**

7. **Repeat Steps 1 through 6 to move the gear shift lever to the next lower gear.**

When you get to sixth gear, flip the splitter down before you go down to fifth gear.

Practice the down-shifting in your head and in a manual transmission truck. If you have a bad day of practice on your on first day or two, don't worry about it! It's amazing what a good night's sleep does to your mind and coordination. You will be lying in bed one night and you will have a Eureka! moment.

You are required to stay in control of the vehicle at all times, and your examiner will interpret that to mean that you have to keep the truck in a gear. The examiner will allow at least a truck length of driving without having the transmission in a gear. If you mess up here, do not fret. If you look like you are going to freak out about it, that will speak more to the examiner than you missing a gear. Show that you can handle a mistake and learn from it. Knowing how you messed up speaks volumes as well.

Slowing Your CMV Down

There are various ways to slow your CMV down. You can let it happen naturally, or you can use the service brakes. (Service brakes is the term used for the brakes that your brake pedal operates, whether it is hydraulic or air powered.) In a manual transmission, you can downshift. You can also utilize your engine brake if you have one (but I suggest not until you have obtained your license and proficiency of shifting).

The brakes and suspension of large commercial vehicles are made for heavy weights. Heavier vehicles stop faster than light vehicles (this will often be on the written test) because they have more traction on the roads. This is especially noticeable when the roads get slicker. When there is no traction, the heavier your vehicle is, the harder it will be to stop it. The harder it is to stop the vehicle, the more distance you should allow for stopping.

Factoring in distances

The following list contains a few guidelines to consider about braking and distance:

>> **Perception distance.** If you are choosing to get a CDL to see the country, wait until you park your vehicle to do your sightseeing. Sightseeing while driving will take your focus away from being aware of changes or hazards in the road conditions and the distance needed to stop your vehicle. The distance that your vehicle rolls until you realize there is a hazard is your *perception distance*. There are a lot of things you need to be aware of while driving. For example, the more congested your driving environment, the more time it will take to spot a hazard that you must slow or stop for. For this reason, you have to slow down in construction zones, school zones, and when emergency personnel or civilians are on the side of the road.

>> **Reaction distance.** The distance you travel from the time you perceive a hazard to the time you place your right foot on the brake pedal is your *reaction distance*.

>> **Braking distance.** The distance your vehicle will travel once the brakes are applied is called the *braking distance*. At 55 mph (miles per hour) and dry conditions, CDL study guides state that you will travel a minimum of 215 feet to get stopped.

>> **Total stopping distance.** Adding the previous three distances together give you a formula to remember: Perception distance + Reaction distance + Braking distance = Total stopping distance. Figure 4-8 provides a few examples for the total stopping distances for a vehicle with hydraulic brakes and on dry pavement. So if you're traveling at 55 mph, you will need at least 419 feet to stop.

ENGINE BRAKES

An engine brake is a braking system that uses the engine to slow a vehicle down or to restrict its increasing velocity. The engine brake uses the compression ability of the engine by altering the operation of the exhaust valves to reverse the effects of the engine. Engine brakes can be more powerful than what the engine is in normal operation. Also, when the engine brake is used, a truck without a muffler will create a lot of noise, thus many municipalities ban the use of engine brakes in their jurisdiction.

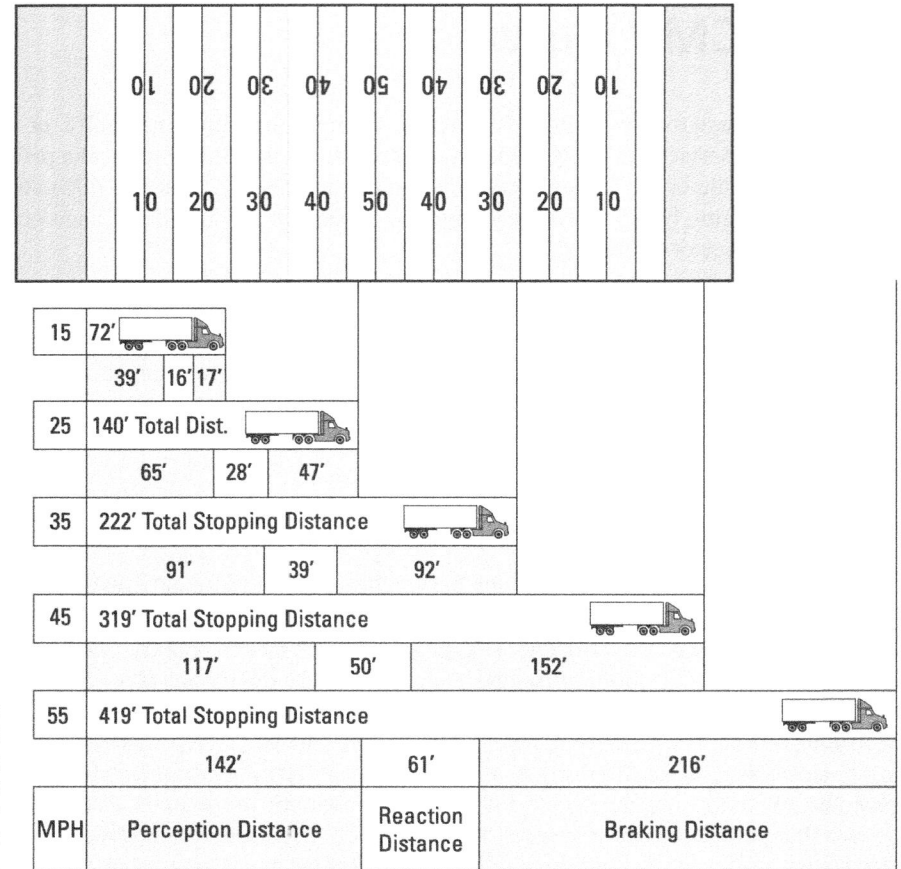

MPH	Perception Distance	Reaction Distance	Braking Distance
15	39'	16'	17'
25	65'	28'	47'
35	91'	39'	92'
45	117'	50'	152'
55	142'	61'	216'

15 — 72'
25 — 140' Total Dist.
35 — 222' Total Stopping Distance
45 — 319' Total Stopping Distance
55 — 419' Total Stopping Distance

FIGURE 4-8: Total stopping distance chart for hydraulic brakes only.

Speed has an effect on your stopping distance too — duh! I will repeat what experts have said over the years — that increased speeds will increase stopping distance exponentially. In the chart below, you will notice how much greater the braking distance is for 60 mph compared to 40 mph compared to 20 mph.

Base speed	Increased speed to	Braking distance increase
20 mph	40 mph	4 times
20 mph	60 mph	9 times
20 mph	80 mph	16 times

TIP

In this chapter, I am referring to hydraulic brakes, which is what your written test will be covering in the general knowledge test. If you are also driving a vehicle with air brakes, you need to remember the difference between hydraulic brakes and air brakes, for total stopping distance. Total stopping distance charts for air brakes add in a short distance for brake lag. Study the air brakes chapters in Part 3 with this in mind.

Driving for good fuel economy

You may wonder why a section on good fuel economy is in the braking section. The tactics for braking gently, for avoiding hard braking, and for that matter, reducing braking, results in better fuel economy. Drivers who are achieving lower fuel consumption are proactive in avoiding hazards and other potential occurrences to use brakes. These drivers look ahead to see what adjustments need to be made, without having to use their brakes (see Chapter 23 for more on this practice).

After receiving your CDL, you can drive for good fuel economy. Driving for good fuel economy sets you up for safe driving. The habits that produce a safe driver are the same habits that produce a fuel-efficient driver. These same habits can be applied to driving on slick roads. You just have to drive more deliberately.

For example, try to allow your vehicle to lose a little momentum as you approach the top of a hill. This practice will not only save fuel but prepare you to stop just a little quicker if you need to. Also, take it easy on your fuel pedal — be soft and gentle. Soft take-offs will improve fuel efficiency and will again decrease your total stopping distance by lessening the inertia because you're driving at a decreased speed.

Looking down the road

Your tests will have questions about how far to look down the road. The answers are you should look ahead 12 to 15 seconds — in town and out in the country. That equates to one or two blocks in town or a quarter mile in the country. However, I say that this isn't enough time. Please do more than what the examiners say to do, and you will be like one of the elite drivers.

Looking as far as possible as you drive down the road will enable you to be proactive at, for instance, timing traffic lights so that you don't have to use up brake pads to stop or fuel to get your vehicle moving again. Looking ahead will help you to spot people who will potentially make a mistake and cause you to make a sudden stop, like the driver who is going to run a stop sign.

Alternatively, you shouldn't get into the habit of *not* paying attention to what is around you. Afterall, if you have an accident, it will be with whatever is closest to you! Be proactive and vigilant, spotting hazards before they become an emergency. Keep a space to your right or left so that you have a way of escape if someone near you makes a driving mistake.

Creating the Proper Space

In my house, if you clear off a countertop or a table, someone will use that space to place something else on it. It can seem like futile effort to clear that space. You may think the same about creating a space while driving a large vehicle because there may be someone who drives into the space you have created. However, you must always create space in front of and behind your vehicle.

Spacing in front of your vehicle

Use the following formulas to determine the minimal amount of space you will need:

1. Calculate 1 second for every 10 feet of vehicle length for a vehicle going under 40 mph.

2. Calculate 1 second for every 10 feet of vehicle length for a vehicle going over 40 mph plus one more second.

These formulas might seem too simple but remember them for your written test and use for real-life driving. Your examiner will also notice if you are too close to the vehicle in front of you during your road test.

So for example, a 50-foot truck traveling 60 mph should have a 6-second space between it and the next vehicle. A 40-foot truck traveling at 30 mph should have 4-second space.

Allowing for space behind your vehicle

Yes, you need to know about creating space behind you as there might be a question about it on your test. First, you don't play games or do tricks by speeding up. It is better to be tailgated at lower speeds than higher speeds. Increase your following distance so that there is ample space in front of you for the tailgater to pull back into should they decide to get around you.

Many experienced drivers have told me that they become a hazard if they slow down. They don't realize that they've unknowingly helped other drivers. If the traffic is so heavy that someone gets stuck behind a big truck driving slow, then their position for safe driving has improved. In an emergency, it is better to react at 55 mph than at 70 mph.

Flowing with traffic

Driving the speed that everyone else is driving is no longer an argument that CDL holders can use in their defense for driving habits. Many municipalities/governments have determined that large trucks are to be driven at slower speeds and, therefore, have set lower speed limits for the truck drivers. Driving above the speed limit is a great risk to you as the driver, and you will assume responsibility for any accidents or mishaps that occur as a result, even if the other driver ran a stop sign!

Although various CDL publications from different states can be confusing because of contradictions among them, you need to know for the written test that:

>> Driving with the flow of traffic is safest.

>> Going faster than the posted limit is illegal.

>> Obeying specific speed limits for trucks and buses is mandatory.

Watching the overhead space

WARNING

Always look at overpasses, railroads that you pass under, and wires strung across the road you're driving on. Your CMV is probably taller than what you're used to driving (13 feet, 6 inches is the maximum legal height). Obviously, you won't be able to create more space above you, so just watch out for any obstacles that are too low. Drivers who hit overpasses cause great grief to many and often get to be a star in a video posted on social media!

Dragging your belly

Low trailers and long trailers have more of an opportunity to get hung up on a railroad crossing or a driveway that has slopes built into it. If you have doubts about making it across a section of road, get out and take a look. If you find yourself in a predicament, where going forward might get you stuck, you can make a call to the local law enforcement officials. They would rather help you get out of your predicament than to fill out the paperwork that is required, if you get hung up on a railroad.

Controlling Your Speed Under Various Conditions

Observing speed limit signs are a good basis for determining the speed you should drive. There are several driving conditions that require big vehicles (and sometimes small vehicles) to be driven at slower than the posted speed limit. In case my stance isn't obvious, the posted speed limit is the fastest you should drive. While Chapter 5 goes into greater detail about driving in hazardous conditions, this section provides some safety guidelines for controlling your speed while driving in various road and weather conditions.

Navigating inclines and curves

Driving down a mountain or any other incline requires prior training. Factors that affect your proper speed decision are the grade and length of the road's descent, whether there are curves in the road, the weight of your vehicle, and the road and weather conditions. (See the section on mountain driving in Chapter 5 for more information.)

Never exceed the speed limit of a curve when your vehicle is heavier and has a higher center of gravity than the traditional car. In fact, those speed limits are usually for cars only, so go 5 mph slower than the posted limit. You can turn your vehicle over if your tires have good traction or slide off the road if they don't.

Barreling down the road

Construction zones are notorious for speeding motorists. It seems harmless to speed where there are no workers in the area. And other drivers may be pushing you to drive faster (at least that is what the long line of cars behind you seems to be saying) but resist the urge to drive faster.

WARNING

Construction workers can be like anyone else and get lost in thought — thinking only about what is directly concerning them. Personally, I've observed a construction worker lose a piece of paper and then chase it into the path of a tanker. Another worker was balancing on a concrete wall separating traffic and construction. And yet another worker moved the long handle of his concrete float in front of a school bus. Due to the excellent driving of three professional drivers, these three workers were unharmed. So remember to keep your speed down as you drive by the traffic barrels in construction zones.

Sliding along the road

Be mindful of identifying the condition of the road that you're driving on. Sometimes this isn't an easy task, but you can recognize the telltale signs of potentially slick conditions, which are provided below.

>> **Shade over a road.** Shady areas can stay slick longer due to the lack of warmth from the sun. Fallen leaves can add to the slickness of the road.

>> **Rain.** When the rain begins, the water can mix with oils on the surface of a road, making it slick.

>> **Melting ice.** Wet ice is possibly the slickest surface. The problem with wet ice is determining whether it is just water, or ice underneath it? If you haven't started driving yet, carefully walk to the road and check it.

>> **Black ice.** Black ice is a thin layer of ice that allows you to see the road just fine. It might look wet, but if it looks wet and there is no spray coming up from tires of other vehicles, you're probably driving on black ice. It might be as slick as melting ice.

>> **Bridges.** Bridges will freeze faster than surface roads, thereby frosting the elevated roads. If your weather app gives a frost warning, don't use it just to make sure to protect your plants. Drive as though any bridge or overpass is frosted and slick. Make no sudden movements with the steering wheel on the bridge. Stay off both the fuel pedal and the brake and just coast over the bridge.

>> **Snow.** It is obvious that when the snow is deep enough to make tracks in it that the road is slick. A surprise comes when the road is clear, snow is on the side of the road, and you come to a stretch where the snow is blowing across the road. The potential for the road to be slick is great. If you are going too fast or you hit your brakes, there is a good chance that your vehicle will go into a skid.

>> **Icing vehicle.** When you see your windshield icing up or ice forming on your side view mirror, do a couple of things: one, turn on your defroster and mirror heat if you have it; and two, drive accordingly. Slow down or even find a safe parking spot if needed. Roads often have some heat retained in them so you might have time to get to that parking spot.

>> **Standing water.** Drive onto some water and you can hydroplane. Tires are made to channel the water, but if you don't have much tread left they won't do a good job. If you start to hydroplane, let off the fuel pedal and don't hit the brake pedal. If your vehicle has a manual transmission, press the clutch down. You want to give your tires every chance to start rolling freely again.

WARNING

Do not use the cruise control when the roads are slick!

REMEMBER

You must be able to stop within the distance that you can see. Obstacles or stopped traffic can appear quickly and close to you in limited visibility. Use this possibility as a determining factor for what speed you should drive in certain weather conditions. For example, driving in fog or blowing snow will require that you drive slower than the speed limit. Add a slick road to the low visibility of blowing snow and now you must drive even slower because it will take longer to stop. At night, you see less with your low beams than your high beams, so you should drive slower than when you are using your high beam headlights.

REMEMBER

Reading this book may cause you to view other drivers in a critical manner. That is okay if you do the same with yourself. Watch what everyone is doing. If you see someone making a mistake, expect them to make another mistake. Stay out of their way and let them go on.

Staying Alert, Focused, and In-Touch

With all the traffic, pedestrians, road obstacles, and other hazards that you will be observing, you must take into consideration all of this gathered information in order to drive safely. In this section, I provide a few important ways to detect driving hazards around you as well as how to communicate conditions to other drivers.

Perceiving hazards

There are hazards everywhere, like a slick road, a deer darting out in the street, or a driver that cuts in front of you and immediately brakes to turn. So you need to identify objects, road conditions, pedestrians, and vehicles that are potential hazards. This will help to limit emergency situations.

CB LINGO

It is good to be warned on the CB of hazards, but not everyone has a CB. What is a CB, you ask? A *CB* (Citizen Band) is a type of two-way radio that truckers use to communicate with each other. Here are three interesting CB phrases and the translations:

- "There's a gator on the zipper just past the 87 yardstick." The gator is a hazard and, no, it is not an alligator, it is a piece of tire in the middle of the road.

- "You got a bear with a customer at the 55 yardstick!" A state trooper has someone pulled over on the shoulder. This is good information as it takes more space for a big truck to move into so that they can be over a full lane from the people on the side of the road.

- "There's a County Mounty on a donut run northbound." A county sheriff is driving at a high rate of speed heading north. CMVs need to stay out of the way.

Joggers and cyclists are often wearing earbuds or headphones, so you need to anticipate that they're not paying attention to their surroundings. Be mindful of watching out for them because they forget to watch out for you. (This comment is not meant to defame cyclists or joggers. I am a cyclist myself and have seen horrifying actions by other cyclists.)

People can walk out from behind delivery trucks, buses, food trucks, and ice cream trucks, which is extremely dangerous. Children, particularly when their playing with toys, can be unpredictable, while teenagers who are texting are usually distracted. Expect that anything can happen and use your horn if it is the only method of helping someone to avoid an emergency situation.

Avoid running over objects, even as harmless as a shopping bag. They have been known to do damage. Avoid chunks of broken pavement and other debris. If your tire strikes a fist-size piece of concrete, it becomes a grenade, propelled in the direction of who knows where.

Communicating to other drivers

Operating your turn signal is an important way of communicating your movements to other drivers, and you will also use other methods to communicate. For example, when you see a hazard ahead and know that people behind you may not be aware of it, you can tap on your brakes or turn on your flashers. Many drivers will get the hint. Also, turning on your flashers when you drop off a passenger or unload cargo is a common practice among truck drivers.

REMEMBER

When you need to make an emergency stop on the side of the road, communicate to other drivers by turning on your four-way flashers. Then you must put out your *roadside warning devices* (usually reflective triangles) within 10 minutes, so that others will know what is going on and what to expect.

Table 4-1 shows three situations where you would need to use warning devices to communicate with other drivers the hazard you have created and where to place them. Remember warning device must be placed within 10 minutes of pulling onto the side of the road.

Driving with minimal distractions

WARNING

Have you ever had to wave your hand in front of someone's eyes to get their attention? If you drive with your eyes or your mind distracted, you are putting yourself and others on the road in danger.

TABLE 4-1 ## Placement for Roadside Warning Devices

Condition or Situation	Warning Device Location (usually three triangles)
One way or divided highway	10 feet, 100 feet, and 200 feet behind your vehicle, facing the traffic traveling towards your vehicle.
Two-lane road with two-way traffic or an undivided highway	100 feet in front of your vehicle, the other two behind your vehicle at 10 feet and 100 feet.
Hill or curve	Place a warning device beyond any hill or curve that prevents other drivers from seeing your vehicle within 500 feet. Move the rear triangle far enough to warn others.

I was driving with my family, playing a road game while heading to Florida one summer. We were driving through Chattanooga and my mind was distracted because I was looking for a 'J" word on a sign. I ended up on I-75 North instead of I-75 South, even though I had driven that route in a big truck dozens of times.

You might be distracted, for example, if you are playing the "talk like Yoda" game, eating a sandwich, observing a GPS, or staring at a yellow 1973 Ford Mustang Mach 1. Cell phones can be distracting, but some states only allow hands-free use while driving.

Combatting your own distractions

Since you will be responsible for many of your distractions while driving, you should consider having a plan of action for your trip and practice some self-discipline.

Here are some ideas for planning your trip:

>> Figure out when and where to stop.

>> Have the directions for each leg of the trip.

>> Know the mile markers and highway numbers.

The following are suggestions for avoiding common driving distractions.

>> Have convenient "no-look" snacks that you don't have to open or look at it, maybe prepared at your last stop by pouring into a wide-mouth bag or a no-spill type bowl. Popcorn was one of my favorites.

>> Prepare your hot or cold beverages in non-slip insulated tumblers with flip lids/straws.

>> Eliminate intense conversations with passengers.

>> Minimize casual conversations.

>> Utilize a Bluetooth headset for your phone.

>> Tell people you're talking to that you will call them back when you're in a safer location.

>> Don't read.

>> Don't watch videos.

Watching out for distracted drivers

Driving a larger vehicle gives you a vantage point for seeing people driving distracted. You will see people eating, texting, shaving, watching a video, reading a book — you name it. Besides seeing the distracted drivers, you should recognize the effects of their distractions — driving at inconsistent speeds, veering off the road, or weaving in and out of a lane. *Give those distracted drivers plenty of space.*

Avoiding aggressive drivers and road ragers

Aggressive drivers are selfish and only care about what they want and nothing about what everyone else needs in order to have a safe trip. Aggressive drivers will speed pass your vehicle to get right in front of you only because they wanted to or thought that they would gain some time advantage.

Drivers with rage, on the other hand, want to do damage, get revenge, do harm. They might want to use their vehicle to intimidate other drivers, or to inflict harm verbally or even physically.

REMEMBER

Avoid confronting someone with road rage. You shouldn't try to confront or try to reason with a person who has road rage. Reasoning with a fool is, well, foolish. Call 911 and get away from that individual.

Don't join their club. Take the high road. Avoid eye contact because they don't need another reason to be enraged.

Preventing driver fatigue

Driving while fatigued is a big no-no. The federal government built a whole set of regulations called *Hours of Service* (HOS). The Federal Motor Carrier Safety Administration (FMCSA) has an HOS guide for drivers on their website. The HOS regulations are for truck drivers to help combat fatigue. But no matter how many rules there are, they can't make you get adequate sleep or rest. It is up to you. (See Chapter 6 for more information on HOS regulations.)

Identifying fatigue

You need to recognize when you are fatigued or sleep deprived. Start by running your sleep numbers. Are you getting 7 to 8 hours of sleep a night, or is it more like 4 to 5? Maybe your numbers look good, so let's look at other identifying factors.

Are you frequently yawning, or are you straining to keep your eyes open? How is your driving? Are you staying in your lane, or is your *departure warning system* (if you have one) going off more often? Are you failing to follow your driving directions? Do you remember what you were doing the last few miles?

AUTHOR SAYS

I was once pulling an implement (a Cultipacker if you must know) in a field, when all of a sudden I stopped, looked around the field, and wondered how I completed all that I did. It took me a little bit to figure out what happened, and I still don't know if I was asleep or what. I am thankful that I can tell the story today.

Sleeping away fatigue

There is only one true way to get rid of fatigue and that is to stop and take a nap. Little tricks like turning up the music, singing loud, rolling down the window (those three together would keep the other motorists awake) but are not effective, safe, or reliable. Caffeine is not a suitable substitute either.

Getting a proper amount of sleep might mean that a short nap of only 5 minutes is all you need to get rid of drowsiness. However, if this is not the case for you, you need to stop for a longer period. The HOS makes it possible for a driver to utilize time to take a nap without always reducing the available time to drive.

WARNING

Accidents due to fatigued driving have killed many people. Get your rest and don't drive fatigued. When it is time to rest, rest! Don't let yourself begin doom scrolling on social media (I was given this term by my son), playing games, or even binge-watching your favorite show. Get some shut-eye!

Practice Questions

1. Why do you inspect commercial motor vehicles?

   (A) For safety reasons

   (B) To comply with regulations

   (C) To avoid a citation

   (D) To get out of doing other work

2. When should you inspect your vehicle?

   (A) At the beginning of your driving day

   (B) Every 3 hours or 150 miles

   (C) At the end of your trip or day

   (D) All these are times to inspect your vehicle

3. Always do the following except:

   (A) Fasten your seat belt when driving.

   (B) Walk around and inspect your vehicle when you get out of it.

   (C) Apply the parking brake when you leave your vehicle.

   (D) Park your vehicle with the four-way flashers on.

4. To prevent a manual transmission truck from rolling backwards when stopped on a hill, you should:

   (A) Let out on the clutch pedal quickly.

   (B) Give the engine more fuel when letting out on the clutch pedal.

   (C) Keep applying pressure on the brake pedal until you feel the vehicle try to move forward.

   (D) Don't stop at stop signs or traffic lights to avoid having to start.

5. Which statement is false?

   (A) It is recommended that you hold on to the steering wheel with both hands.

   (B) Use gradual pressure on the brake pedal to stop your vehicle.

   (C) Push in on the clutch pedal after you have come to a complete stop.

   (D) Avoid backing up whenever you can.

6. Which statement about backing is false?

   (A) Use both mirrors.

   (B) Get out of everyone else's way as quickly as possible.

   (C) Start in a proper position.

   (D) Use a helper whenever possible.

7. Which statement about shifting a manual transmission is false?

   (A) Examiners like you to shift gears without using the clutch pedal.

   (B) If you kill the engine, the examiner might fail you.

   (C) The examiner will expect you to downshift the transmission instead of coasting all the way to a stop.

   (D) You should gently move the gear shift tower into a gear slot.

8. Which statement about shifting a manual transmission is true?

    (A) Shift patterns are all the same.

    (B) Shifting at 2000 RPM is best.

    (C) A splitter can be moved up or down prior to needing to shift into a gear.

    (D) Grasp the gear shift lever like a baseball bat to shift into a gear.

9. Which statement is false?

    (A) If you have trouble shifting into a gear, you can push the shift lever harder into the gear.

    (B) You can use the engine RPMs to determine when it is time to shift.

    (C) You can use your road speed (mph) to determine when it is time to shift.

    (D) You should be able to move the gear shift lever into the gear easily.

10. Why is backing towards the driver's side instead of the right side of your vehicle, better?

    (A) Because the passenger mirror is too far away from the driver.

    (B) Because you can see the spot you are turning into better.

    (C) You can see out the driver's side window.

    (D) Both B and C.

11. Which of the following is an incorrect statement about special shifting conditions?

    (A) Downshift before going down a hill.

    (B) Use the lower range of an automatic transmission for going down grades.

    (C) Downshift before going into a curve.

    (D) There is no problem using an engine brake in any condition.

12. How far ahead should you look as you drive?

    (A) 5 seconds ahead

    (B) 12 to 15 seconds ahead

    (C) One truck length

    (D) One truck length for every 10 mph that you are driving

13. Watching for brake lights, vehicles from side streets and roads, stale green lights, will help you with the following except to determine if you should:

    (A) Slow down.

    (B) Change lanes.

    (C) Increase your speed.

    (D) Readjust your mirrors.

14. Mirrors should be all the following except:

    (A) Clean

    (B) Adjusted continually

    (C) Checked regularly

    (D) Initially adjusted at the pre-trip

15. Which statement about mirror usage is false?

    (A) Convex mirrors make objects appear smaller and farther away than they really are.

    (B) Check your mirrors often and quickly.

    (C) Convex mirrors show a wider area than flat mirrors.

    (D) All these are true statements.

16. Which of the following is a rule for using turn signals?

    (A) Activate your turn signal when you are starting to turn.

    (B) Signal early and continuously for your turn and cancel it after completion.

    (C) Activate your turn signal when you want someone to go around you.

    (D) Signal after you are in a turn lane and stopped to turn.

17. Which is not an aspect of a good lane change?

    (A) Move back into your lane quickly for others to get around you.

    (B) Signal prior to changing lanes.

    (C) Make the move slowly back into your lane.

    (D) Make a lane change smoothly.

18. Which statement about communication with other drivers is false?

    (A) Turning on your hazard lights (four-way flashers) lets people behind you know that there is a potential hazard.

    (B) Hitting your brake pedal prior to a turn is just a way to aggravate people following you.

    (C) Tapping your brake pedal often is good to warn people that you might have to stop due to a bus stopped ahead of you.

    (D) If you must drive slowly, use your emergency flashers if it is legal where you are driving.

19. Don't direct traffic (signal or wave to people to proceed) because:

    (A) You are likely not part of the police union.

    (B) You haven't been trained on the correct hand signals.

    (C) Other drivers will want to do the opposite of what you are directing.

    (D) You can be blamed for an accident and may cost you thousands of dollars.

20. When should you use only your clearance and marker lights?

    (A) At dawn or dusk

    (B) In rain

    (C) In snow

    (D) You should always use your headlights when using your clearance and marker lights

21. Mirrors should be used to check for?

    (A) Traffic to the rear

    (B) Traffic to the side

    (C) Condition of your vehicle

    (D) Mirrors should be used to check all these items

22. When passing a pedestrian or a cyclist:
    (A) Use your air horn to get them to notice you.
    (B) Assume that they know you are there.
    (C) Pass by them as far away as possible.
    (D) Gently alert them by flashing your lights or lightly tooting your horn.

23. If you must park on the side of a divided road:
    (A) Place your triangles (warning devices), out within 20 minutes.
    (B) Place your triangles (warning devices), 10 feet in front of your vehicle, 10 feet behind your vehicle and 100 feet behind your vehicle.
    (C) Place your triangles (warning devices), 100 feet in front of your vehicle, 10 feet behind your vehicle and 100 feet behind your vehicle.
    (D) Place your triangles (warning devices), 10 feet behind your vehicle, 100 feet behind your vehicle and 200 feet behind your vehicle.

24. If you must park on the side of a divided road with a hill or curve blocking the view of your vehicle within 500 feet for other drivers:
    (A) Just place the triangles (warning devices), farther out into the road.
    (B) Place the triangles (warning devices), out as usual but stay with the rearmost device to help warn people.
    (C) Find a box to set the triangles (warning devices), on so they are above the ground.
    (D) Set the rearmost triangle (warning device), beyond the hill or curve.

25. Use your mirrors to:
    (A) Make safe lane changes.
    (B) Know where traffic is behind you.
    (C) Ensure you don't hit a curb on a turn.
    (D) All these are times to use your mirrors.

26. The total stopping distance of a commercial motor vehicle is:
    (A) Equal to perception distance plus braking distance.
    (B) Determined by the type of tire on the vehicle.
    (C) Equal to perception distance plus reaction distance plus braking distance.
    (D) Longer when loaded than empty.

27. Total stopping distance is:
    (A) Affected by road conditions.
    (B) At least 419 feet for a vehicle traveling 55 mph.
    (C) Increased when a driver is fatigued.
    (D) These are all true statements concerning total stopping distance.

28. The effect or impact of speed on stopping distance is:
    (A) 9 times greater at 60 mph than at 20 mph.
    (B) Inconsequential.
    (C) Double at 40 mph than at 20 mph.
    (D) Less with a bus than a delivery truck.

29. Which statement is true concerning the effect of vehicle weight on stopping distance?

   (A) A lighter commercial motor vehicle stops faster than a heavy commercial motor vehicle.

   (B) A heavy commercial motor vehicle stops faster than a light commercial motor vehicle.

   (C) The weight of a commercial motor vehicle is not a contributing factor in its stopping distance.

   (D) A lighter commercial motor vehicle has more traction and thus shorter stopping distance.

30. Which statement is false, concerning slippery driving surfaces?

   (A) A light vehicle performs better than a heavy vehicle.

   (B) If the road looks wet but there is no water spray, the road might be covered with black ice.

   (C) Wet, melting ice is more slippery than ice that is completely frozen.

   (D) Roads can be more slippery right after a rain begins than after a day of rain.

31. Which statement is false concerning speed and curves?

   (A) Vehicles with a high center of gravity can roll over on curves at posted highway speeds.

   (B) Slow to a safe speed while entering a curve.

   (C) Vehicles traveling too fast in a curve can lose traction and go straight.

   (D) Slightly accelerating once in a curve can help you keep control.

32. Which statement is true concerning speed and distance ahead?

   (A) High beam headlights will help increase your safe speed in fog by helping you see further.

   (B) You can always use your high beam headlights at night to increase your safe driving speed.

   (C) Subtract one vehicle length for stopping distance in the fog as a vehicle you see in front of you will be moving as well.

   (D) When you use your low beam headlights, drive slower than when using the high beam headlights.

33. Which is the false statement concerning traffic flow?

   (A) Driving at the same speed as traffic is safer.

   (B) If everyone is driving at the same speed it is hard to crash into someone.

   (C) The posted speed limit for trucks and buses is always the same as cars.

   (D) It is illegal to go faster than the speed limit even if you are going the speed of traffic.

34. Which of the following is not a factor to consider when determining a safe speed to drive down a steep incline?

   (A) Total weight of your vehicle and cargo

   (B) How long a time it will take

   (C) The steepness of the grade

   (D) Road conditions

35. Decrease your driving speed in a construction zone when:

   (A) A construction worker is present.

   (B) When signs state a lower speed limit.

   (C) When you notice your speed creeping back up.

   (D) These are all times to decrease your driving speed.

36. Which of the following is the best philosophy about space and driving a commercial motor vehicle?

    (A) Be aware of space beside you and in front of you.

    (B) Be aware of space beside you and behind you.

    (C) Be aware of space beside you, in front of you, behind you, above you, and below you.

    (D) Be aware of space beside you, in front of you, and behind you.

37. While driving you should find an open spot that is away from other vehicles because:

    (A) You feel trapped if you don't.

    (B) It is a safer position if someone decides to change lanes in a hurry.

    (C) It allows you the freedom to choose any lane.

    (D) You can center your vehicle in a lane better.

38. Which is not a rule for preventing right-hand turn crashes?

    (A) Turn slowly.

    (B) Turn wide to the left prior to making the turn.

    (C) Do not back up.

    (D) When making the turn, you can use the oncoming lane of the road you are turning on to make the turn.

39. Which of the following is a rule for making left-hand turns?

    (A) If there is more than one left-hand turn lane, use the far-left lane.

    (B) Use your right hand mirror the most.

    (C) Wait until you have reached at least the center of the intersection before you start to turn left.

    (D) Politely direct another motorist to move if you need them to.

40. Which of the following is not a hazard?

    (A) White fluffy clouds

    (B) Cyclists

    (C) Pedestrians

    (D) Other drivers

41. Seeing or looking for hazards:

    (A) Allows you see to interesting things.

    (B) Helps you be prepared for maneuvers, whether an emergency or not.

    (C) Means you are being distracted.

    (D) Is synonymous with seeing an emergency.

42. Which of the following is not likely to be a hazard?

    (A) A pedestrian

    (B) A delivery truck

    (C) A house on a corner

    (D) On and off ramps

43. Why is a parked vehicle a hazard?

    (A) A person can suddenly appear to get into or out of the vehicle.

    (B) People can walk out from behind one.

    (C) It can suddenly pull out on the road.

    (D) These are all reasons a parked vehicle is a hazard.

44. Which of the following lists contain an item that is not likely to be a hazard?

    (A) Distracted drivers, children, workers

    (B) Disabled vehicles, ice cream trucks, shoppers

    (C) Confused drivers, slow drivers, drivers in a hurry

    (D) Impaired drivers, traffic lights, accidents

45. Which of the following is a reason for watching for hazards?

    (A) A hazard can turn into an emergency.

    (B) You might see someone you know.

    (C) There might be an item for sale at a garage sale you have been wanting.

    (D) You might have an opportunity to hand out some money to someone.

46. Distracted driving:

    (A) Can be looking at your gauges or mirrors too long.

    (B) Can be caused by changing your CD, cassette tape, 8-track tape, or song on a playlist.

    (C) Can be caused by staring at billboards.

    (D) All these things are true concerning distracted driving.

47. Which is not a way to identify a driver who is distracted?

    (A) Looking down into their vehicle to see what they are doing.

    (B) Noticing a vehicle traveling at inconsistent speeds.

    (C) Observing someone shaving or putting on makeup.

    (D) Seeing a vehicle struggling to keep their vehicle going straight in their lane.

48. Aggressive driving or drivers should be:

    (A) Ignored.

    (B) Reported to the police.

    (C) Viewed the same as a person driving with road rage.

    (D) Treated courteously.

Answers and Explanations

1. **A.** While the other answers might be some people's answer, safety is the best answer.

2. **D.** A through C are all times to inspect your vehicle.

3. **D.** There are no rules or practices that require you to always park your vehicle with the flashers on. Batteries would run down eventually.

4. **C.** Letting out on the clutch quickly will kill the engine. Never give your truck more fuel when you start to drive, and you must stop at stop signs.

5. **C.** You should push in on the clutch when the engine slows to idling RPM. If you wait until you stop, you will probably kill the engine.

6. **B.** Backing quickly will increase your chances of an accident.

7. **A.** Examiners want you to double clutch, push in the clutch pedal twice for each gear change.

8. **C.** Splitters can be moved to another position and even back without moving the gear shift lever, and 1500 RPM is a more optimal shift point. You should be gentle with the shift lever. You should also find the diagram of the shift pattern for the vehicle you are driving and practice before driving the vehicle.

9. **A.** Never force the shift lever into a gear.

10. **D.** You can both see the spot you are backing into and do it through your window.

11. **D.** Using an engine retarder/brake can be a problem in some weather conditions and some towns have ordinances against their use.

12. **B.** Our CDL testers say 12 to 15 seconds.

13. **D.** Mirrors are to be adjusted prior to driving. All the other choices are aided by observing your surroundings.

14. **B.** Mirrors should not require constant adjustment. If they do, they need repair or replacement.

15. **D.** All the choices are true statements.

16. **B.** The other statements are definitely not a stated rule.

17. **A.** Making quick or sudden lane changes is dangerous for commercial motor vehicles as they typically have a higher center of gravity.

18. **B.** Using your brake lights and four-way flashers are good communication devises. The use of them should not aggravate motorists behind you.

19. **D.** You can be blamed for an accident if you direct traffic. You would think that people would look before proceeding, but they don't always.

20. **D.** Don't drive with just clearance lights and marker lights. Always use with your headlamps on too.

21. **D.** Use your mirrors for all these areas.

22. **C.** Flashing lights and sounding your horn are good ways to make someone fall, and you should never make assumptions about whether they're aware of your vehicle.

23. **D.** D is correct and should be done within 10 minutes.

24. **D.** You have to place the warning devices where drivers can see them before they see your vehicle so that your vehicle will not come as a surprise to them.

25. **D.** These choices are all reasons and times to use mirrors.

26. **C.** This formula is for non-air brake vehicles. Loaded trucks stop quicker when loaded due to better traction. Tires would only be a portion of the total stopping distance and would be part of the braking distance.

27. **D.** All the choices are true statements about stopping distance.

28. **A.** See the section, "Factoring in distances," and Figure 4-8 for information on this topic. Expect a question like this on your written test.

29. **B.** Large vehicles are designed to carry heavy weight. If the vehicle is light, it has less traction to stop as quickly as when it is loaded more heavily.

30. **A.** B through D are true statements. Loaded/heavy trucks have more traction, even on slick roads.

31. **B.** You are to slow down prior to entering a curve, not while entering one.

32. **D.** High beam headlights in the fog don't help you see farther. You can't always use your high beam headlights. You can't see as far with low beam headlights as with high beam headlights, so you must drive at a slower speed than posted.

33. **C.** All other statements are true. There are states that have different speed limits for larger vehicles, especially in more highly populated areas.

34. **B.** How long it will take to go down an incline is not a factor for determining safe speed, especially when you consider the other choices.

35. **D.** A through C are all times to slow down in a construction zone.

36. **C.** Be aware of space all around you including above your vehicle for low clearances and below your vehicle to avoid getting hung up on railroad tracks or other uneven road changes.

37. **B.** It's all about safety. If you don't have someone beside you, you can safely make a lane change when someone else makes a dangerous move.

38. **B.** You are not allowed to turn wide to the left prior to making a turn. While making a turn, you are allowed to use the oncoming lane of the road that you are turning onto.

39. **C.** Waiting to make the turn, increases the safety margin in avoiding contact with other vehicles to your left (or vehicles turning with you or sitting on the road in the opposite lane you are turning onto).

40. **A.** White fluffy clouds might be distractions, but they are not hazards.

41. **B.** You might see something interesting, and you might get distracted. Looking for hazards helps you prepare for a hazard to become an emergency.

42. **C.** A house should not be moving around so it should rarely be a hazard.

43. **D.** A parked car is a hazard for many reasons, including all the choices.

44. **D.** Choice D includes traffic lights, which should not be moving or in the way, thus not a hazard.

45. **A.** The best choice again is about safety, watching for potential hazards.

46. **D.** Anything that takes your eyes off driving and the concentration it requires is a distraction.

47. **A.** You can look down into a car to observe a driver, but that may cause *you* to be distracted.

48. **D.** Don't ignore aggressive drivers but watch out for them. However, don't make eye contact as that might be all it takes to turn them into road ragers. Remember, aggressiveness is not the same as having road rage, so you probably don't have enough to report to the police. Acting courteously to an aggressive driver helps you and the other driver avoid becoming enraged.

Chapter **5**

Driving Safely in Hazardous Conditions

D riving a large vehicle is challenging, in normal conditions. When hazardous conditions are present, the driving challenge increases. Pulling off the road every time conditions are hazardous is not an option. Some parts of the country will have several days in a row of hazardous conditions. If everyone who had a Commercial Driver's License (CDL) stopped driving when conditions became hazardous, food would stop being delivered, and children would not be taken to school on buses. Hmmm, I think everyone would be upset about that.

So the alternative is that drivers should know how to drive safely in those conditions. You don't just decide that hope will get you through the day. You must focus on how to drive safely and appropriately in conditions that you will likely encounter.

In this chapter, I discuss how to drive safely when it is difficult to see the road. You will drive down a mountain barely using your brakes and arrive safely at the bottom. You will respect fog and blowing snow, realizing that you must reduce your speed or end up plowing into the trunk of another person's car. Not only will you prepare your driving skills to respond to those conditions, but you will start thinking like a survivalist for the worst-case winter and summer scenarios. This chapter will teach you how to take the curves in a big vehicle and inform you of all there is to know about crossing railroad tracks. You can expect a sizable portion of the CDL general knowledge test to cover information in this chapter.

Minding Visibility

Seeing the condition of roads, the environment and then knowing what to do with that vision is paramount in being a professional driver.

Driving at night

Driving at night is more dangerous. The most obvious problem is the visibility problem. You and I are not nocturnal. You might like driving at night (there are some definite advantages). But to be honest, there are problems that are inherent to driving at night because you are human.

Minimizing the glare

The glare that is a result of bright lights may make it difficult to drive at night. You will have glare from the lights of oncoming vehicles and from streetlights. There will even be glare from your own windows and mirrors. The following suggestions may help you to minimize the glare while you're driving:

TIP

>> **Avoid looking into the headlights of oncoming traffic.** Your eyes might take a few seconds to recover from seeing the bright lights, so don't look directly at them. If you are on a two-lane road and a car is approaching you with bright or annoying lights, look at the white line on the right side of your lane.

>> **Clean your windows.** You can help out the glare of your windows by keeping them clean. Yes, you are to do windows as a professional driver! When you are done cleaning your windows, you shouldn't see any residue remaining or unwiped sections of glass. Try using a lint-free cloth too.

Be aware that certain types of glass cleaners may leave smears even when you thought that you didn't leave any. The type of cleaner I recommend, which is what car detailers use, is typically found in the automotive section of a local retailer. It is a foaming spray that contains no ammonia.

>> **Keep the lighting inside your vehicle to a minimum.** You must see your dashboard information and your controls need to have a little illumination, but beyond that, keep lights off. Lights from inside make glares and reflections on the glass.

>> **Remove any objects on top of your dashboard.** Many items, especially papers, can add to the glare problem at night and even during the day.

Some drivers find that glasses that block certain light rays (such as yellow-tinted lenses) help at night, but scientific studies don't support the claim. Instead, an anti-reflective coating can be applied to your eyeglasses that may help reduce the glare.

Adjusting your body clock

Driving at night because your daytime driving schedule was tossed out the window by events of the day, or by your dispatcher, must be treated differently than if your regular driving shift is at night.

Your number one job is to drive safely and not when you're fatigued. Your second job is to get the delivery(s) made. If you are like me, you can't always simply tell your body, "We are on a different schedule today." Sometimes your body is okay with that, sometimes it is not. When it's not, you shouldn't push yourself to make it happen. When your body is not cooperating while driving, it may be a sign that you must get some sleep. Let it win the battle that it is destined to win.

Your Hours of Service (HOS) should help with this scenario (see Chapter 6). But even when you've had an extended period off-duty before starting your on-duty clock, remember that your body doesn't change its 24-hour clock just because your manager changed your driving schedule. You must drive safely as the laws require. Here are a few things that may help adjust your sleep schedule:

- **Change your sleep environment.** If driving at night, you must train yourself to sleep during the day. But first, you should need a comfortable and quiet space. Ask the people you live with to respect your sleep time. Use blackout curtains or an eye mask and block out any noise with a fan or a white noise machine. These changes can signal to your body that it's time to sleep.

- **Delay your sleep the day before.** The evening before your new nighttime driving shift is set to begin by delaying your normal bedtime by at least two hours. Then take a long nap later the next day to prepare for the night driving.

- **Get some sleep, if needed.** As you are driving at night, get some sleep when you need it. If you are getting sleepy, don't become a danger to yourself and to others. Again, get some sleep because you will be held responsible for the negative consequences. The risk is too great. Lives are more dependent on you getting sleep than on you getting a delivery made by a certain time. Just be sure to communicate (and document). Do what is within your power to be rested to eliminate your fatigue.

- **Stretch your muscles.** You've adjusted your sleep time and 24-hour clock as much as possible so now you are sleeping during the day. Wake your muscles and get them ready to take on the night. Stretch and engage your muscles. Spend 10 minutes getting your muscles awake and ready to go. (Check with your physician first before undertaking any type of stretching routine.) Engage your muscles, stretch all of them. This will send a message to your body that it is time to work. (See Chapter 3 for some stretches you can try.)

Adjust to poor lighting

You probably have plenty of light to drive during the daytime. However, at nighttime, the amount of lighting may vary. Some localities will have good lighting; others will have lots of shadows. Noticing the shadows on the road and intersections will help you determine if a vehicle running blindly down the street is coming.

AUTHOR
SAYS

I was driving my pickup truck one night behind my wife in her car. She proceeded ahead after stopping at a stop sign. I stopped, saw nothing, proceeded on and got hit by a car running without its lights on. My wife saw the car because it was farther down the street under a streetlight. What I saw (besides nothing) was a shadow. Luckily, the officer was able to determine that the other driver didn't have the headlights on because there was damage to the pop-up headlight covers; that type of damage would not have happened if the headlights were on.

TIP

Seeing pedestrians is more difficult at night, especially if they are dressed in dark clothing. You must be on the lookout for that possibility. When there is good lighting in an area, it isn't too hard to do. When the lighting is poor, you may see shadows that are actually pedestrians. Watch out for this hazard.

Switching beams and cleaning your lights

Your headlights can be the only light that you have in many instances of night driving. Use your high beams whenever you can but not when you are within 500 feet of oncoming vehicles. High beams can shine twice as far as low beams. Remember that you have them on and switch to the low beams when other vehicles are within that distance and would be affected by your high beam headlights.

Dirty lights can cut the visibility in half versus clean lights. Headlight lenses that have yellowed over time or developed a film may also diminish visibility. It is worth having the headlights replaced. The cost of new headlights is much cheaper than the downtime that an accident would cause, or the charges of an emergency room visit, or a lawsuit.

Watching for the impaired

REMEMBER

Nighttime brings out drunk drivers (and drunk pedestrians as well) who can appear where they're not supposed to be. Their actions can be predictable if you watch for the signs of intoxication, such as swerving and having issues with keeping a straight line. Drivers may have difficulty keeping a consistent speed and even come to a complete stop for no reason. Failing to observe traffic lights and other traffic control devices will be a clue for you to watch them carefully. Drivers under the influence of drugs or other substances will have similar characteristics.

Dodging the wildlife

"Why did the chicken cross the road?" "To prove to the possum that it could be done." Animals will act like it is all fun and games until one of them gets hurt. Then they all get together to mourn their loss and create a bigger hazard. Watch for the bigger animals like deer to be running from the side of the road. They don't always use the marked deer crossing. Your course of action with wildlife is to apply your brakes. *Do not swerve to miss the animals* as that action increases the possibility of winding up getting hurt (and there is still no guarantee for the animal).

Driving in fog

One of your biggest driving challenges can be fog. Thick fog will limit your visibility and high beam headlights don't cut through the fog to help you. Fog can start to thin out only to become even thicker fog later. Driving too fast increases the chance of rear-ending someone as other drivers might have observed a red traffic light and stopped. However, your vehicle is going too fast and doesn't have enough space to stop, and the traffic in front of it is not moving forward to help with the spacing. Additionally, a driver can decide to pull onto the side of the road, which can be mistaken for a moving car on the road.

AUTHOR SAYS

>> **Limiting your visibility.** I was 18 years old — going to work on a two-lane highway. The fog was thick. I approached a curve (with a warning light) where I was to go straight instead of taking the curve. But I couldn't see the other side of the road. I rolled down my window, listened, and decided to cross the lane to the unseen road. The instant that I got in the other lane, I saw headlights and had a head-on collision. A driver of a semi-truck came along and hit the other car. The semi-tractor driver did not see the car in time to hit the brakes, even though the driver was driving slowly. Fortunately, there were only minor injuries. To give a little bit more of the story, three more vehicles had accidents in the same location that morning.

Solving this problem is not easy. The fog was not as bad where I lived, but it was at that curve! Pulling off the road is not advisable, even if there is a shoulder. Another driver can see your taillights or flashers and think that you are moving and run into you. You just can't determine such things in thick fog. If there is a rest area or a parking lot to turn in to, do so! Avoiding an accident in the fog is best done by being off the road, completely!

Icing your drive. Freezing fog can cause bridges and overpasses to be slick. Don't test to see if the bridges are indeed slick, just assume they are. Stay off the fuel and off the brake pedal in these conditions. Maintain traction and keep the wheels turning.

WARNING

Freezing fog is a very hazardous driving condition, which will cut down your visibility. Droplet will freeze on your windows, your mirrors, and your headlights. Your solution? Get off the road!

Letting other drivers go. I cringe when I see other drivers drive too fast in the fog. I have no interest in seeing an accident. It is good for you to follow other drivers, seeing their taillights, judging the distance that you are following them. But when they start driving too fast, let them go.

>> **Determining the following distance.** In any driving situation, do not drive closer to a vehicle than the distance that you can see *and* stop in. Similarly, do not drive faster than the distance you can see and stop in. To illustrate this: If you are driving behind a car and that car stops, can you stop within the distance that you are following it? Or, if the distance you see is less than your total stopping distance, you are driving too fast. Slow it down! Allow for extra time and space to check your mirrors.

>> **Avoiding cruise control.** In all hazardous driving situations, do not use your cruise control, it will make you lose control. The cruise control maintains constant power to the drive wheels, whereas when your foot is on the fuel pedal, you are controlling the power to the drive wheels. You can instantly release the fuel pedal and control the situation. Cruise control would keep the vehicle moving. By the time you tap the brakes to cancel the cruise control, you might be past the point that you can recover from sliding. With all hazardous driving conditions, cruise control will increase the time and distance it takes to react to an emergency situation.

Adapting for Seasonal Weather

Many of us lay claim to live in a state where if you don't like the weather, stick around, it will change. Preparing your vehicle for the season is much like preparing our body for the season. Think, what does the vehicle need in case . . . happens? (Fill in the blank for any scenario you can think of finding yourself in.)

I can safely say that I don't like the extreme cold as I have had frostbite before, and it wasn't fun. However, I've had heat stress as well, and it wasn't fun either. Both these experiences remind me to prepare, just like when I was in the Boy Scouts, we were to, "Be prepared." This section provides a few examples of preparations for the more extreme weather conditions during the winter and summer.

Driving in the winter

Winter brings snow, freezing rain, extra-slick roads and bridges, power outages, road closures, and just plain surprises if you are not prepared. It is much better to have items you don't need than to need items you don't have! Winter weather driving requires that you and your vehicle are equipped for any weather-related conditions.

Taking care of yourself

It is time for you to be selfish. The most important thing you should do prior to driving in the winter is prepare for the worst-case scenario. The following are standard items you should keep (or wear) during the winter season.

>> **Bring water.** Sure, you can resort to backwoods survival techniques by melting snow or sucking on an icicle for your hydration needs, but there are better ways to "be prepared." Have plenty of water with you. Keep a case of bottled water or a couple of gallon jugs in your truck cab.

>> **Stock food.** Keep an extra week's worth of food with you and rotate your food supply periodically to avoid food expirations. Have some non-perishables like cans of chunky soup, dry cereal, peanut butter . . . whatever works for you.

>> **Wear warm clothing.** Food is your source of energy and helps your body produce heat. Don't let that energy go to waste. Dress to stay warm. There are two aspects for keeping warm. One for when you have been working outside and have become wet. The other for keeping warm while you're sleeping.

>> **Keep a set of extra clothes.** People say layering is good. Do what works for you but you will need to stay warm when your vehicle won't run. Keep some very warm blankets or a good sleeping bag in the cab. Another reason for the extra clothing is when your clothing is wet from working outside and crawling around in the snow. When you get back into the truck, the snow will melt, making your clothes wet. Change out of the wet clothes as soon as possible.

Preparing your truck

Cold winter weather is hard on vehicles. Batteries have less power, diesel engines get harder to start, and improperly maintained vehicles will likely break down. Engine coolant can freeze, and doors with poor seals will bring in the cold. Road tires struggle to get traction. Wintertime will bring out the best in your inspection abilities because you will need to ensure you have all the necessary supplies for your vehicle.

USING A MAINTENANCE CHECKLIST

You should be a driver that believes your vehicle is always well maintained. Take ownership of the vehicle(s) you're driving like it's your own. I don't want to hear you say, "I'm not a mechanic, I'm a truck driver." I am not saying that you have to be the one to change a tire or even change the oil, but I am saying that you can help ensure that it gets done and correctly. Freezing cold weather should be a good incentive to keep your vehicle well maintained. Here are three items that should be on your maintenance checklist:

>> **Diesel fuel additives.** If you have a diesel engine vehicle, ensure that you are adding fuel that has been treated for cold temperatures or putting additives into the fuel to combat what freezing temperatures can do to diesel. When the temperature drops to 15 degrees, the paraffin wax in untreated #2 diesel fuel (the most common diesel fuel) will clump together, giving the fuel a gel-like consistency. Many fuel suppliers will treat fuel in advance. Ask the supplier about their fuel treatment. It might be that they treat the fuel but can only say it's protected from "gelling" down to 0 degrees. You may need to add an additive as well, commonly referred to as anti-gel.

Follow the directions on the anti-gel container as there are different characteristics for the various additives available. Some can be added after you fill your tanks with fuel. Some have to be added prior to filling your tanks because the additive doesn't flow through the fuel, it has to be mixed. If you are driving a big vehicle with large fuel tanks, you will want the higher concentrated stuff that requires you to add it prior to fueling.

TIP

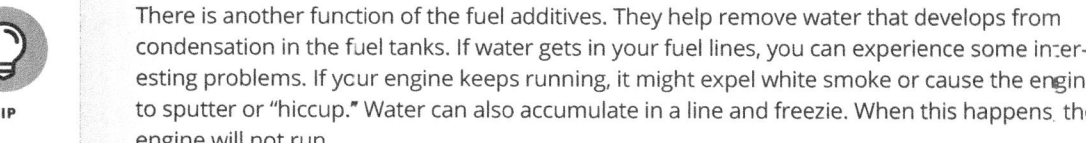
There is another function of the fuel additives. They help remove water that develops from condensation in the fuel tanks. If water gets in your fuel lines, you can experience some interesting problems. If your engine keeps running, it might expel white smoke or cause the engine to sputter or "hiccup." Water can also accumulate in a line and freezie. When this happens, the engine will not run.

>> **Condensation in the fuel lines.** Your vehicle likely has a fuel and water separator. Diesel is lighter than water so somewhere in the fuel system, there should be a holding device where the fuel goes through and the water (or condensation) can stay on the bottom. Drain the water from the separator periodically. How often you should do this will depend on the environment you are in, the fuel you put in the tank, and how much additive there is in the fuel. Ask experts in your area how often you should drain off the water. Diesel fuel with more biomass will have more problems with gelling and developing water condensation.

>> **Tire pressure.** You might have noticed that tires have the maximum tire pressure rating, stated as *cold tire pressure*, on their sidewalls. This means that the pressure should be checked when the tires have resumed the temperature of the weather outside. Tires warm up when you are driving, so don't measure the pressure at that time. When the weather gets cold, your tires will have a lower pressure. Add air to your tires when this happens. When the weather warms up, you will discover that your tires are overinflated when they are "cold." When this happens, let some air out. Remember, don't check the pressure of a hot tire, or you will be attempting to adjust the air in the tires on a daily basis.

STOCKING THE TRUCK

REMEMBER

Winter weather and winter roads are challenging. Be prepared by keeping the following maintenance tools and supplies in your truck.

>> **Windshield wiper blades.** Winter is hard on wiper blades. Don't throw away old ones until you have a replacement set in your vehicle.

>> **Windshield washer fluid.** You will likely use more windshield washer fluid in winter than in the summer. It's best to use washer fluid that is a de-icer or able to withstand freezing temperatures.

>> **Coolant.** Never leave home without extra coolant. However, if you need to add coolant, there might be a problem with your truck. Contact your technician.

>> **Anti-gel.** Don't count finding the brand you prefer at a fuel stop. Keep a few bottles on hand.

>> **Ice scraper/snow remover.** Have an ice scraper that extends for a long reach (unless you are over 7 feet tall) and has a soft pliable edge, which is great for removing snow from your hood that falls during the night (better than a brush which typically leaves residue to blow up on your windshield).

>> **Metal shovel.** You might need to chop up packed snow or ice, and a plastic shovel won't hold up to the task. A camping shovel or a military surplus shovel, which can fold up to store, can be used as a pickax for chopping up that packed snow.

TIP

>> **Granular ice melt.** This type of ice melt has two functions. It will give your wheels some traction while sitting on ice; and it can melt ice and snow, giving you a clearer path to get your vehicle moving. If you know that there will be icy conditions in the morning, sprinkle some ice melt in the path of your drive tires (the tires that the engine powers) in the evening. If your tires are spinning in place, tuck some ice melt *under* the drive tires. When you start to move and the tires start to spin, they will grab the ice melt and pull it under the tires to get traction.

>> **De-icer spray.** If you live in any part of the country that has winter weather, you probably understand the need for de-icer on your windshield. However, spray de-icer can also be used in your door locks and padlocks.

If there is snow or freezing rain on your fifth wheel, spray the de-icer into the locking jaws (see Figure 5-1) when you are starting your pre-trip inspection on the semi-tractor. By the time you are ready to hook to a trailer, all the snow and ice should be melted out of the fifth wheel locking area. Fail to take this step and you can be fooled into thinking that your trailer is securely connected to your semi-tractor.

>> **Chains or other traction devices.** Keep the amount of chains or other traction devices that are required for your vehicle for the state(s) you will be driving in. (See the section, "Chaining tires," for the steps to apply the tire chains.)

Controlling and recovering from skids

The key to driving on the slick winter roads is to keep traction. Spinning your tires does not help with ice and snow. When you start to spin, you must release the fuel pedal so that the drive wheels will stop spinning. Spinning makes heat, which melts the snow or ice, and causes the surface to become much slicker. If you are going up a hill and struggling to keep traction, move the vehicle onto a path that has been less traveled, possibly giving the tires something to grab onto.

There are three types of skids that are possible in icy or snowy conditions: *steer wheel skids* (losing control of steering during a skid), drive wheel skids and the least frequent, trailer skids. All skids are a result of losing traction because all the vehicle's wheels are not spinning.

A *drive wheel skid* is identified by the drive wheel area of your vehicle starting to skid left or right (left is more common due to the physics of powering axles). The following explains how you control a drive wheel skid, which you will most likely encounter at higher speeds. (Higher speeds can easily be as low as 35 mph or lower!)

1. **Take your foot off the fuel pedal.** When you perceive that your vehicle is starting to skid, you don't want to power the drive axle(s).

2. **Don't touch the brake pedal!** Hitting the brake pedal will send you into a greater skid, even with anti-lock braking system (ABS).

3. **Turn your steering wheel in the direction you are intending to drive.** Don't keep turning your steering wheel if your vehicle hasn't responded. That action will eventually whip your vehicle in the other direction, and you will be fighting a *fish-tail* response, hoping your vehicle will stop sliding before you hit someone or something.

Here is how you **prevent** a skid:

1. **Look for a safe place to park.** (The side of the road is not safe.)

2. **Park your vehicle.**

3. **Wait for better road conditions.** Road crews or possibly warmer weather will eventually come along. The only way to absolutely prevent a skid is to park your vehicle off the road and in a safe location.

REMEMBER

You can get into a *front wheel skid* (when the front wheels lose traction) when attempting to turn or are applying the brakes too forcefully or a combination of the two. When you are attempting to turn, *do not apply the brake pedal.* You should have slowed down to your safe speed prior to the turn. Nevertheless, remember, a skid occurs when a tire loses traction. You will have a strong urge to use that brake pedal, hoping to avoid hitting a parked car. But you must avoid the brake pedal so that you can regain steering.

If you ever see the trailer sliding around your towing vehicle, do not touch the brakes but do get off the road as soon as possible! A scenario in which this might happen is when you are descending a mountain or you have a box trailer that is catching wind, and the wind is blowing the trailer off the road. In this case, you made a bad decision to drive that day.

Watching the parade

You are sitting in the parking lot with other drivers when a snowplow spreading salt passes by. All the drivers leave the lot to get started on their driving day. Should you join them? No. It seems to be a good time to start driving as snow has been clear and the salt will help with traction, but you should avoid joining a convoy in the winter, especially a close-knit one. Stopping distances are still greater and if something happens to one vehicle, it will likely invite others to join the party.

Here are some winter driving tips to remember:

>> Be a spectator and pull off the road to park in a safe parking spot when you start to skid or see other drivers' mishaps.

>> Keep greater distances between you and the next vehicle than you would in normal driving.

>> Watch out for the traffic coming from the other direction. They are often the cause of problems on your side of the road (sliding into your lane).

>> Don't attempt to pass another vehicle. There can be snow and ice ruts that can cause a vehicle to slide out of control.

>> Drive no faster than half of the posted speed limit.

>> Approach a turn or curve very slowly, ensuring that you slowed down to the appropriate speed prior to making the turn as your vehicle will want to go straight. When making the turn, remember to take your foot off the brake pedal. Just ensure that you slow down to the appropriate speed prior to the turn.

>> Don't use your cruise control; it will make you lose control.

Chaining tires

Winter driving has the unique feature of precipitation in the form of snow. Delivery trucks to over-the-road trucks are designed to drive on hard flat surfaces, not that soft fluffy stuff. However, winter driving can seem like trucks need to be designed as off-road vehicles. Snow appears as a disguised monster, ready to stop you in your tracks or to slide you off the road.

Although chaining your tires will not be on any of your exams, you might want to understand the following steps before needing to install chains.

1. **Lay out your chains.** Stretch them all the way out (see Figure 5-2).

2. **Remove all the twists and tangles.** Remove these twists (see Figure 5-3) so that all the links of your chain hit the road evenly while driving. If one link hits the ground before other links, that

link will prematurely break and cause some links to flop around while the wheel is turning. (To minimize the need for this step next time, try storing the chains by hanging them on a rack without twists and removed in a reversed order, or hook the ends together if you put them in a bag.)

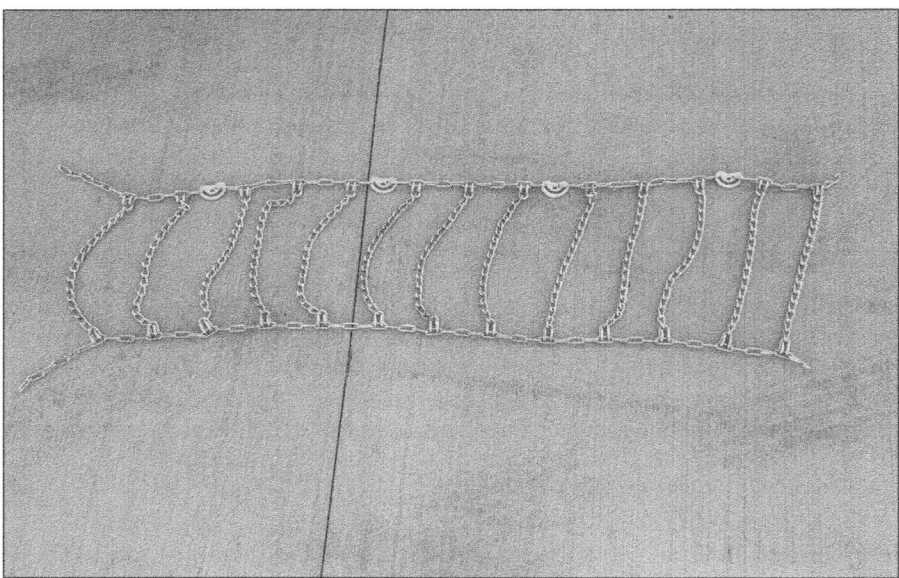

FIGURE 5-2:
Chains
stretched
out.

FIGURE 5-3:
Twists that
should be
removed.

3. **Decide how to pick up the chains.** Pick up the chains as shown in Figure 5-4, ensuring the exposed ends of chain link are away from the tire or in other words, place the chains with the smooth sides of links against the tire. (Figure 5-5 shows a chain incorrectly installed, with the exposed ends against the tire.)

4. **Pick up the chain and throw it on the tire.** Throw the chain over the tire like you are mad at it. This might be how you feel when you have to do this step in the freezing cold. If you have a semi-tractor trailer, you may consider unhooking the trailer to make the chain installations just a little easier, as shown in Figure 5-6.

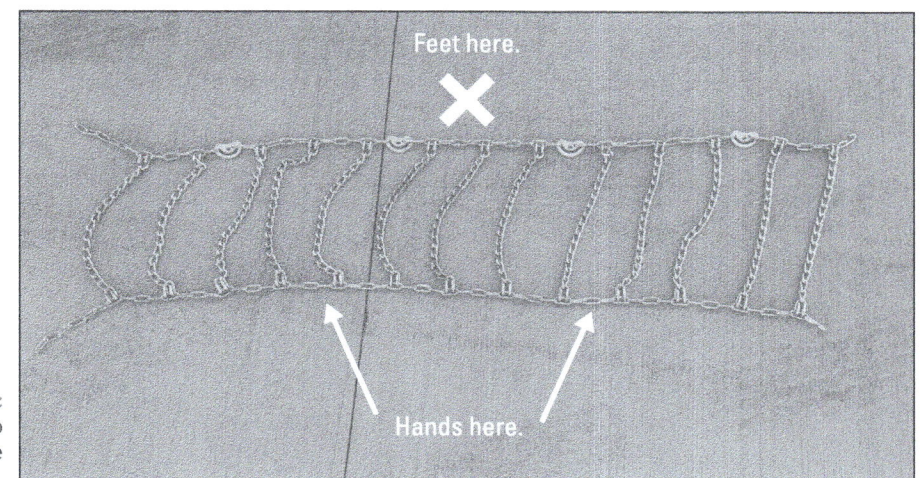

Feet here.

Hands here.

FIGURE 5-4:
How to
pick up the
chair.

FIGURE 5-5:
An incorrect
installation.

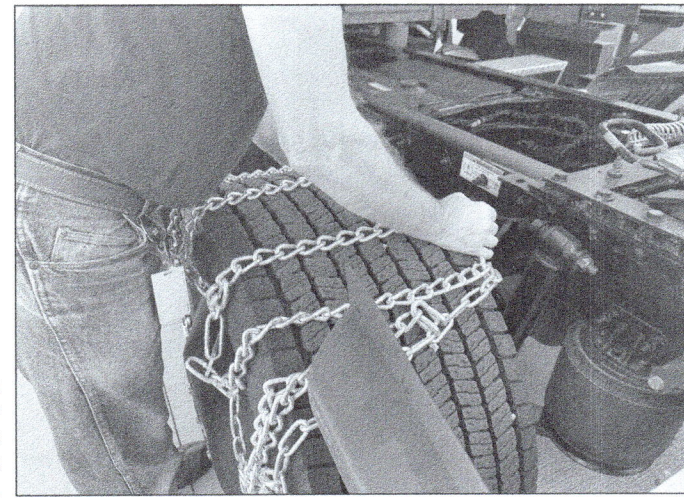

FIGURE 5-6:
Driver
throwing a
chain on a
tire.

5. **Adjust the chain.** The chain should be even from side to side and front to back (see Figure 5-7). Often drivers will install their chains differently from these instructions but for your sake, I will stick with just this one method.

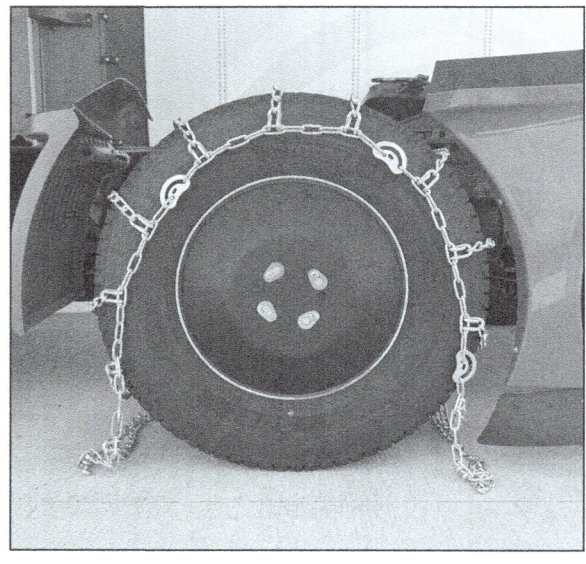

FIGURE 5-7:
A properly
adjusted
chain.

6. **Hook the back side.** You might have to experiment with the fit as chains are made for more than one size tire (see Figure 5-8). A few links may have to be dropped (see Figure 5-9); otherwise, your chain installation will be too loose.

FIGURE 5-8:
Chains in
place to roll
the tires
truck onto
them.

7. **Hook the front side.** It might be a hook (see Figure 5-10) or a lever that hooks the two ends together.

8. **Rotate all the cams.** As shown in Figure 5-11, but the last cams to rotate should be tougher to turn. If it is too tight to turn, it is okay. You might be able to rotate it in the next step.

9. **Roll the vehicle forward.** This step will reveal any chains that are loose. Retighten the links as needed.

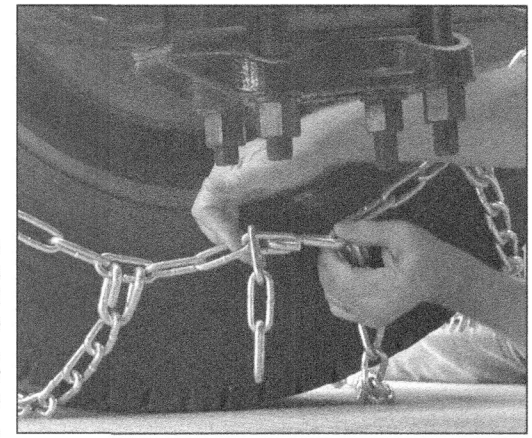

FIGURE 5-9: Chains hooked on the back side, after a few links were dropped.

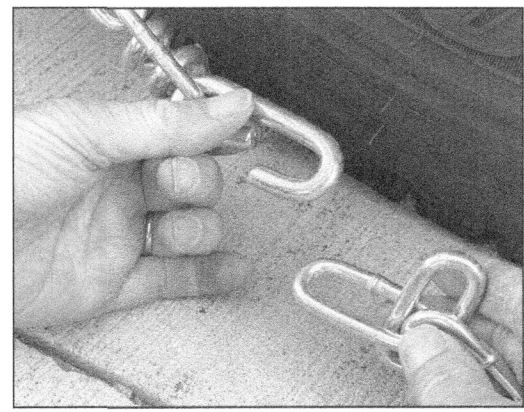

FIGURE 5-10: Hooking the front side.

FIGURE 5-11: Rotating the cams on chains with a chain application tool.

10. Apply the "spider" or a tarp strap (optional). If you are just using the chains to get out of a parking lot, skip this step. The item shown in Figures 5-12 and 5-13 may look like a spider, but it makes the chain stay tight as you are rolling down the road. If you don't have one of them, use tarp straps to attach the opposing points at about six points. Keep the hooks away from the tire to avoid any potential damage to the tire (see Figure 5-14).

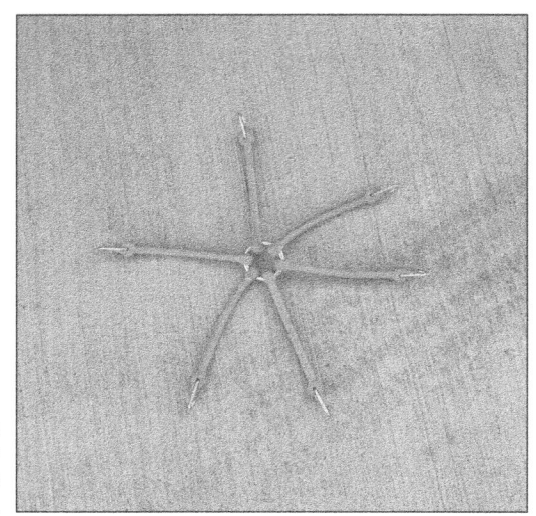

FIGURE 5-12:
A spider
keeps
chains taut.

FIGURE 5-13:
A partially
installed
spider.

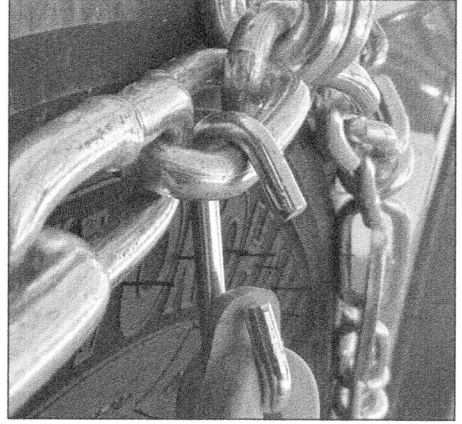

FIGURE 5-14:
Spider
hooks
pointing
away from
the tire.

To remove the chains when you are done with them, reverse all the steps you took to install them and then:

1. **Pull the chains out to the side.** Your vehicle will likely be sitting on the chains. (Figure 5-15 shows the chains removed.)

FIGURE 5-15:
The chains
pulled off to
the side.

2. **Roll your vehicle off the chains.**

3. **Hook the ends of the chain together**. This step (see Figure 5-16) will make it difficult for the chains to get twisted and tangled, regardless of whether you hang them on a rack or put them back in their bag.

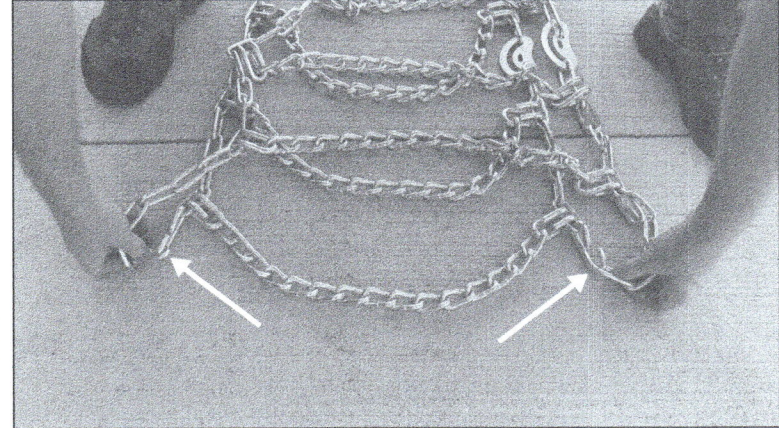

FIGURE 5-16:
Hooking
the ends of
the chain
together.

REMEMBER

Most drivers have the philosophy that if they need to install chains, they need to get off the road. That's not a bad philosophy, but there are times that you don't have a choice. It is better to know how to chain a tire and not need to than to need to chain a tire, while snow is coming down, it's 20 degrees and you don't know how to install chains.

Driving in hot weather

Traveling in very hot weather doesn't take as much preparation as very cold weather, but it is just as important. Don't assume everything will be fine; preparation is the key.

TIP

Now is time for you to be selfish again. Prepare for the worst-case scenario. Have plenty of water (ice cold if possible; that is, if your doctor approves). Unless you have a uniform, wear light clothing — both in color and in weight. Also, make sure you have a hat that will provide shade for your face, ears, and neck. Cooling towels are a good way to beat the heat.

Use the following guidelines for examining your vehicle for summertime driving:

>> **Increase the frequency of vehicle inspections.** One difference for inspecting your vehicle in very hot weather is the frequency. In the winter, your vehicle warms up some, which is a good thing. In very hot conditions, the vehicle warming up adds to the challenge of driving in very hot weather because tires will experience even greater temperatures, exposing them to greater potential for failure. Engines will have a harder time keeping cool and coolant can boil over. Inspect your vehicle every 2 hours or 100 miles in addition to your normal pre-trip inspection.

>> **Checking the oil.** You won't be checking the oil level every couple of hours as you will get false readings. Ensure that your oil is at the proper level at your pre-trip inspection and that the oil is being changed at proper intervals. The oil not only lubricates the engine but also helps to keep it cool.

>> **Checking the coolant.** Most modern vehicles have a reservoir (see Figure 5-17) for the engine coolant, which allows the coolant to be visible from outside, so the coolant level is easy to check. Other vehicles have a sight glass in the pressurized part of the cooling system, typically in the side of the radiator.

FIGURE 5-17:
A coolant
reservoir.

If you have a vehicle that has neither a reservoir nor a sight glass, then you must take precautions in checking the coolant level. Do not ignore the following precautions as severe burns can result if you do otherwise.

This process is only when you don't have a coolant reservoir! When you have a reservoir, you add the coolant into the reservoir, which is a much safer process!

Here's how to safely check coolant levels during a trip, when there is no reservoir or sight glass.

1. **Shut the engine off and wait for the engine to cool.**

2. **Hover your hand over the radiator cap (see Figure 5-18) to test for its temperature.** If it is too hot to touch with your hand, wait 30 minutes before performing the next step. If you don't wait long enough for the engine to cool, hot coolant may splash out and on you.

3. **Use a rag that is folded over a few times or a very well-insulated glove to open the cap.**

4. **Push down hard on the cap and start to turn it left (counter-clockwise).**

5. **When pressure starts to escape, let go of the cap and wait for the radiator to completely depressurize.**

6. **Cautiously turn the cap, while pushing down, all the way to the left where it will come to a hard stop.** If pressure starts to release again, stop and wait. Repeat this process until no pressure or steam is escaping.

7. **Pull the cap straight off.**

8. **Look in the radiator to inspect the level of the coolant.** The coolant should be covering the fins and tubes (the internal parts) or about an inch below the neck. Check with your engine technician to have the best information for your vehicle.

9. **Add coolant, if needed, to the level that your technician advises it should be.**

FIGURE 5-18:
A radiator
cap.

Inspecting the tires

Truck drivers call large pieces of tires that are lying on the road after a blowout, "gators." You know that temperatures are rising when you start seeing them. Tires heat up as you drive down the road in any weather. In very hot weather, tires get much hotter and can become prime candidates for turning into gators or having a blowout.

Inspect your tires by waving your hand in front of all of them. If one of them is giving off more heat that the others, it has a problem or is being affected by another component — other than heat — and therefore needs attention. If you want to get nerdy about checking the temperature of tires and other components, get an infrared thermometer. You can stand safely back and point the thermometer at your tire and read the temperature. Compare that temperature with the other tires.

When you perform your pre-trip inspection, ensure that your tires are properly inflated. Do not check the air pressure of a tire when it is hot as you will get an inflated reading. Then, if you let air out of the tire, it will be low on air when it is back to the "cold" tire pressure. Tires with low air pressure can get hot as well because of the inordinate amount of the tire that is in contact with the road, which increases the tire pressure and might blow.

Inspect the wheel hubs and brakes and keep them well maintained. If you fail to check these and they start heating up due to the improper maintenance, the tire pressure will expand to blowout conditions.

Driving the vehicle

If you are a safe, conscientious driver, there are only a few other items to mention about driving in extreme heat.

Help your vehicle survive the heat by:

>> Avoiding aggressive driving.

>> Keeping your speed down.

>> Watching your gauges.

>> Stopping to make enroute inspections.

>> Watching for tar and oil rising up in the roads.

>> Looking out for roads that have upheavals from swelling in the heat. These can be high enough to cause damage to vehicles.

>> Turning off the air conditioning periodically because A/C makes the engine work harder — just sayin'.

Managing Specific Driving Situations

As you drive across the country or just across town, there are situations where you must apply certain principles to avoid hazardous situations that can become emergency situations.

Crossing railroad tracks

As you approach a railroad track, what do you do? Do you stop or turn around? Do you know what the hazards are? There are rules concerning railroad tracks that drivers of school buses must adhere to as well as drivers of vehicles carrying hazardous material.

Railroad tracks should be marked at crossings with signs that display a *crossbuck* (the X that is formed by two boards or a facsimile of such). Ahead of a crossing, there is often a black on yellow warning sign with crossbucks on it. On multiple lane roads, the pavement should be marked with crossbucks, so that the inside lane has no excuse for missing the warning sign about a railroad crossing. At the crossing, there should also be white and black crossbucks.

Some crossings will have a white painted stop line prior to the crossing. Commercial vehicles that are required to stop at railroad crossings, such as school buses and hazmat trucks, must stop behind the white line. If there is no line, the vehicles must stop behind the white and black crossbucks sign.

There are passive railroad track crossings that have no lights, bells, or crossing gates. There are crossings that have *traffic control devices*, which may be a question on your written test. These can be found in various combinations — lights with bells, lights without bells, either of those combinations with drop arms or literal stopping devices.

It's important that you yield the right-of-way to a train. Did I need to say that? Yes, but unfortunately the people who need to hear it probably aren't reading this book. Yield when the lights begin to flash and wait for the flashing to stop before proceeding. Don't drive around the gates. Wait for them to rise.

Here are points to remember concerning railroad crossings:

WARNING

>> Don't race a train to a crossing.

>> Reduce your speed when crossing a railroad track(s), if you aren't driving a vehicle that requires stopping.

>> Remember: the more tracks there are, the more you must look out for oncoming trains.

>> Note that some towns and cities have ordinances forbidding trains to sound their horn.

>> Don't expect to hear a horn over the noise of your vehicle (or children if driving a bus).

>> Don't rely on railroad crossing signals to always work. Be looking before you get in the vicinity of the crossing, at the crossing, and during the crossing.

>> Lower your windows to listen for an oncoming train can be helpful.

>> Look for sufficient space on the other side of the tracks for your vehicle to fit within if you must stop after crossing the tracks.

>> Search for posted signs warning drivers of the distance between the tracks and the next intersection.

>> Look for posted warning signs of low clearance signs under a railroad trestle.

>> Don't shift gears when crossing a railroad track.

>> Assume it takes 14 seconds for a typical semi-tractor trailer to clear a crossing and 16 seconds to clear a double track. (I haven't checked these figures out, but your written test might ask about these times.)

>> When you are stopping at a crossing, be aware of unaware drivers. Approach your crossing slowly with your flashers on.

When you are driving a vehicle with a low-slung trailer beware! Many livestock trailers, *low-boy trailers* (low platform trailers for hauling taller equipment), removable gooseneck trailers (trailers' kingpin section is removable and looks like a gooseneck, allowing large equipment to drive onto the trailer), car haulers, and moving vans can get stuck on raised railroad tracks. Short tractors that might have only one drive axle rather than two, pulling long trailers get stuck as well as the landing gear will come in contact with raised surfaces sooner. (The *landing gear* is what the front end of a trailer sits on when unhooked from a semi-tractor; see Chapter 12.) There is a longer span between last axle of tractor and first axle of the trailer for this combination.

If you ever get stuck on a railroad track, check for signs that have an emergency number to contact. While calling that number, get away from your vehicle. If there is no number posted, call 9-1-1 immediately! Observe landmarks or identifying crossing numbers to help identify which crossing you are at. If you are driving a bus, see Chapter 14 on driving buses for your responsibilities in this situation.

Taking the curves

I believe Grand Prix-style racing would be fun (based on what little I have driven on go-cart tracks and what I used to do on my bicycle). If you have the urge to take the curves aggressively, I encourage you to purchase a remote-controlled car and have fun with it instead. You have to get serious when driving commercial motor vehicles (CMVs).

The following are tips for dealing with curves:

» **Drifting is not allowed.** Driving a larger truck or a bus involves different dynamics than that of a personal vehicle. When you are still slowing down going into a curve, the weight of the back of your vehicle or the trailer can push you into a skid. You never want the weight of your vehicle to push you but rather you want to be pulling the weight. Slow down to the proper speed for your vehicle before the curve. Use the speed limit signs for determining your safe speed. Subtract 5 mph for your CMV with a lower center of gravity (center of gravity closer to 5 feet) and 10 mph for vehicles with a high center of gravity. If you have a tanker, you might want to cut the speed limit in half (better safe than sorry). This is the maximum speed to drive. Officially, the government guidance will state "well below" the posted speed limit for such vehicles. It is best to be in a gear that would allow you to accelerate in a curve (and turns). This allows you to be in control of the vehicle.

» **Testing Newton's law of motion.** Sir Isaac Newton published a book back in the 1600s about the laws of motion. You learned about those laws back in grade school, or was it junior high? Nevertheless, in spite of people learning about it at an early age, they still want to test the theory.

The common maximum legal weight of a 5-axle tractor-trailer in most areas is 80,000 pounds. Newton stated that it takes some force to change the direction of an object. Can you imagine what force can change the lateral movement of an 80,000-pound object? When you are going around a curve, there is often minimal or no force redirecting 80,000 pounds to make the turn. Assume that no curves are engineered to help a tall, heavy, high center of gravity vehicle to stay upright around a curve. The tires are resisting some force, but if braking doesn't take place prior to a curve, the potential for a rollover or a skid is great.

» **Widening the curve.** The longer the *wheelbase* (the distance from the front/steer axles to the rear axle), the more width that is required for a curve (or a turn). The rear of a vehicle doesn't follow in the same path as the front. This physical scenario is called *off-tracking*. You might have seen drivers with a car run the rear tire over a curb when they have taken a turn too tightly. If it's true of a short vehicle, it's definitely true for a longer vehicle. Add a trailer to the example and you should see that you need a wider lane for a curve.

Here's how you navigate a curve, once you have slowed down to an appropriate speed:

» On a curve to the left, steer so the right front tire that is on the white line on the right side of your lane.

>> Keep glancing at your left mirrors to see how well the left rear of your vehicle or the trailer (if you have one) is staying in your lane.

>> On a curve to the right, keep your left front tire on the white line that is on the left side of your lane.

>> Keep glancing at your right mirrors to see how well the right rear of your vehicle or the trailer (if you have one) is staying in your lane.

Driving in the mountains

Gravity plays a significant role in mountain driving. When you drive up a mountain, gravity slows you down. When you drive down a mountain, gravity pulls you down faster than you should go. Drive down a mountain too fast and you'll only make that mistake once.

In this book, I recommend quite frequently that you should inspect your vehicle at regular intervals. Must be important, huh? Give your truck another inspection before going down a mountain. Check the tires and other items that you check during your enroute inspections. Add brakes to that inspection. Check the brakes to see if they are all doing the same amount of work. One brake or wheel will feel hotter than the others if they are not adjusted evenly. In this section, I provide information to help make driving on mountainous roads more manageable.

Understanding your brakes

REMEMBER

Brakes are designed to take and dissipate a lot of heat. When brakes get too hot, both the drums (on drum brakes) and pads are affected. When the brake pads are too hot, they will lose some of their friction capability and will *glaze* (or crystalize and will have diminished stopping ability even after cooling). When the drum expands (due to the heat), it will pull away from the pads. Put these two problems together and the result is *brake fade*. (This may be on the written test.)

When your brakes have lost their stopping power, you must look for a *runaway truck ramp*. These ramps are designed to stop a truck that is speeding out of control down a mountain through the use of sand, gravel, or other loose aggregate and an upward incline. Your truck will be out of service at that point, even after a tow truck pulls it off the ramp, but you will be safe. Please keep reading because this problem is avoidable.

Examining the lay of the land

Read the road signs. Some mountains have designated areas at the top of the mountain for trucks to stop and check their brakes. Signs will likely show the route, the grade, and speed limits based on the weight of the vehicle. Study this information and picture it in your mind. Pay attention to the curves, the length of the grade, and where the grade percentages change. Note where the runaway ramps are located.

If there is no special speed limit posted for trucks of any weight, ask around (if you have a CB or if you are in a rest area). Otherwise, choose to go down the mountain no more than half the posted speed limit. Go down to one-third of the posted limit if you are carrying a heavy load.

Driving down the mountain

Pull out on the road and keep your vehicle in a low gear or in a low range for automatics. For a manual transmission, choose a gear lower than what you would use to go your chosen speed. Use the manual mode for automated manual transmissions and lock in the gear you want to use once you reach it. When you drive down a mountain once, you gain a lot of information. You know the curves and grades of the mountain. You know how your truck reacts to your choices.

There is an exact science to driving down a mountain. Unfortunately, we don't have all the data necessary to make all the calculations when we need them. Don't despair. You can always go down a mountain slower than you need to.

The engine brake is your best friend going down a mountain. (Most large vehicles have engine brakes, but small delivery trucks and short-haul trucks without a cab may not have them.) An engine brake reverses compression and becomes a powerful brake. While it is being utilized, it is using no fuel. So, when it comes to fuel economy, you use more fuel going up the mountain, but you might not use any fuel going down the mountain. It tends to equalize fuel usage. Just remember that when you go up the mountain, be content to let the engine do its work at lower RPMs. Most engines today have a lot of *torque* (power or force used to create rotation) in the lower RPMs. Depending on your engine, the optimal RPMs might be around 1400.

Your typical engine brake on a 6-cylinder engine has three settings. Number 1 is the weakest and uses 2 cylinders, Number 2 uses 4 cylinders, and Number 3 uses all 6 cylinders and is the strongest.

Use your engine brake to control your speed. When your vehicle gets up to your designated speed, give some light pressure on your brake pedal and slow down 5 mph. Ease up off the brake and when the vehicle hits the designated speed again, repeat with the braking.

Don't try to downshift in a manual transmission when going down a mountain. You might not be able to get it into gear again, and you have lost the ability to use the engine brake.

The engine brake is the main source of braking, which will keep you from going too fast down a mountain.

Handling driving emergencies

Emergencies are easily identified but not always predictable. Emergencies can occur due to mechanical failure or driver failure (yours or other people). Reacting to an emergency correctly in a timely manner is your goal. Think about different emergency scenarios while you are in the classroom and later driving down the road in a semi-tractor (as known as a rig). This section will help you prepare, as much as possible, for an expected event.

Avoiding a crash by steering

You are driving your rig down the road. An emergency occurs. How should you react? Braking is the preferable reaction. Having to quickly steer out of the path of an emergency is more dangerous for a large truck to do than a regular vehicle. However, the choice has more to do with who will get hurt or not get hurt by the driver's actions. If it is an animal emergency, only choose braking. Choose steering as a response to avoiding an emergency when you will likely save a human life or when steering will allow you to move over a lane or to the shoulder.

The safest way to steer in an emergency is to be off the brakes and to make two small, short movements. To accomplish this, make a quick turn with the steering wheel in the direction to avoid the problem and turn it right back. Practice this as a whole movement. The first move of the steering wheel is quicker than the second movement, twice as fast. If you move the steering wheel too much on the first movement, a turnover can result. If you make the second movement too fast, you might be making a whip, or, not succeeding in moving over sufficiently. This maneuver is easier when you are driving with both hands on the steering wheel — on opposite sides — in the upper-half of the steering wheel.

Constantly check your mirrors to watch the traffic around you so you will know what direction to steer when you must move left or right. If you are usually in the right lane beside the shoulder, the shoulder will likely be the best choice since it's likely no one is driving on the shoulder.

When you need to move to the shoulder in an emergency, you should:

>> Hold the steering wheel firmly.

>> Avoid hitting the brakes if there is no peril in front of you.

>> Look out for ditches.

>> Try keeping one side of your rig on the road.

>> If you are completely off the road, return to the road at an angle that your truck will jump back up onto the road, not gradually. Steer back to the direction you should go when both steer tires are back on the road.

Using anti-lock braking system

Anti-lock braking systems (ABS) is a computerized system that uses sensors to prevent brakes from locking up. The process for braking with ABS is to apply the brake with the necessary force required to stop for your situation.

REMEMBER

ABS has made emergency braking a simpler process, at least when it works. Never assume that ABS always works. Perform your inspections and observe your vehicle when you have to use emergency braking.

Now for a little history about ABS. Is it on a CDL exam? Yes, you must prepare to know the information that follows.

The Department of Transportation (DOT) required:

>> Semi-tractors with air brakes, built on or after March 1, 1997, must have ABS. (See Part 3 for more information on air brakes.)

>> Other air brake-equipped vehicles; trailers, converter dollies (used when pulling doubles), buses, trucks, built on or after March 1, 1998, must be equipped with ABS.

>> Hydraulic brake-equipped trucks and buses with a gross vehicle weight rating of 10,000 pounds or more, built on or after March 1, 1999, must be equipped with ABS.

Be among the best drivers by avoiding the need for the ABS to activate. How to operate ABS shouldn't be on your mind very often.

ABS helps you control your vehicle in hard braking by enabling your wheels to keep turning, but here are some points to remember about ABS. It doesn't:

>> Decrease your braking distance on dry roads.

>> Activate until wheels are about to lock up.

>> Help with bad brakes.

>> Affect normal braking.

NEEDING TO STOP QUICKLY WITHOUT ABS

If someone pulls out in front of you and causes a braking emergency, there are two types of braking to know about when the vehicle you're driving doesn't have ABS. The first I will mention is *controlled braking*. In controlled braking, press on the brake pedal as hard as you can without locking up the brakes. If you need to steer, let up on the brakes and reapply them when your maneuvering is done.

The other type of emergency braking is called *stab braking*, which is the following:

1. **Press on the brake pedal all the way down to the floor of the truck.**

2. **When the wheels lock up, release the brake pedal.**

3. **When the wheels start to roll again, press on the brake pedal all the way again.**

4. **Keep repeating, as necessary.**

Driving a truck with a trailer? Be aware that:

>> If you are driving a truck with ABS and pulling a trailer without ABS, you still have steering control. Just watch out for your trailer coming around. If it is let up on the brakes a little to get it back under control.

>> If only the trailer has ABS, it is less likely that the trailer will swing out.

Dealing with a tire failure

Inspect your tires, report problems with tires, keep a watch on them in very hot weather and you will reduce the potential of a tire failure. You need to know what to do in case a tire fails (called a *blowout*) as you are driving down the road.

You will often notice a tire failure, also known as a blowout, by a loud bang — *pow!* — from somewhere near you. If you don't know if it was your vehicle or not, look in your mirrors for any evidence of tires flopping around. If you have a trailer that had a tire blowout, see if the trailer is still tracking straight behind you. If your vehicle has a sudden vibration, you probably have a blowout. If you had a steer tire blow, you will likely feel a drop in the front end of the vehicle and the steering wheel will pull that direction.

When a steer tire blows:

1. **Step on the fuel pedal and don't hit the brake pedal!** The vehicle wants to dip the front end towards the direction of the blown tire. Hitting the brake pedal will send you in that direction with even more intensity, potentially causing an accident. Stepping on the fuel pedal lifts the front end from the engine revving and accelerates the vehicle.

2. **Keep a firm grip on the steering wheel.** When you have the vehicle under control, which should be in just a couple of seconds, let off the fuel and coast.

3. **Slow to a stop in the safest location you can.** Call your employer's preferred roadside service for a new tire.

When you have a rear tire blowout, you won't have much of a problem controlling your vehicle. Don't hit your brakes; slow down and get to the side of the road and a safe place to park.

Failing brakes

TIP

Brake failures with properly maintained hydraulic brakes are rare. When they do fail, it's probably due to a loss of fluid or brake fade going down a mountain. So, when you have tried pumping your brakes and nothing happens, unless you are driving down a mountain, downshift the transmission and continue to downshift the transmission. Use the *emergency brake*, which is a mechanical brake that is separate from the hydraulic system, to come to a complete stop.

If the emergency brake doesn't work, look for an escape. It can be an open field or an alley. Look for an uphill street. Once you do have the vehicle stopped, make sure it doesn't roll into something that it shouldn't. Drive the vehicle into a curb or something that will keep it from rolling more.

If your brake failure occurs when driving down a mountain, look for a runaway truck ramp. I hope that you were watching the signs informing you of where the ramps are as mentioned in previous section, "Driving in the mountains." Once you are aware that you have lost your brakes, do not pass up a runaway ramp. It will only get worse if you delay or hope that a miracle will happen.

If there are no runaway truck ramps, find your own escape.

Practice Questions

1. Which is a false statement concerning driving at night?
   (A) Fatigue is a concern.
   (B) Glare is not a factor.
   (C) More drunk driving occurs at night.
   (D) People cannot see as sharply at night.

2. Which of the following tips is the safest cure for fatigue?
   (A) Get off the road and get some sleep.
   (B) Drink some coffee.
   (C) Turn the radio on loud.
   (D) Get out of the vehicle and stretch.

3. Which of the following statements are true about glare:
   (A) Bothers old people more than young people.
   (B) Can be caused by bright headlamps.
   (C) Can be avoided by looking at the side of the road.
   (D) These statements are all true statements concerning glare.

4. Which is a false statement concerning poor lighting for nighttime driving?
   (A) It should prompt slower driving.
   (B) It makes it harder to see vehicles who are not using lights.
   (C) It may help your headlights show hazards earlier.
   (D) It does not help joggers who don't use reflective material or lights.

5. Which is a false statement concerning headlights?
   (A) Can be out of adjustment.
   (B) Can be dirty.
   (C) Should be kept clean.
   (D) Must be LED.

6. Which is a false statement concerning taillights and brake lights?
   (A) Are more important at night.
   (B) Can be yellow.
   (C) Can be checked for correct operation.
   (D) Can be seen better if they are clean.

7. Which is a false statement about windshields?
   (A) A dirty windshield is more of a problem at night.
   (B) If a windshield is clean during the day, it will not be a problem at night.
   (C) A windshield shows more glare at night.
   (D) It is hard to see anything when driving directly into the sun.

8. Glare isn't caused by:
   (A) Lights inside and outside the vehicle.
   (B) Looking at the white line to the right of the lane.
   (C) Dirty windshields.
   (D) Objects on the dash panel.

9. Turn off your high beam headlights:
   (A) When other vehicles are approaching.
   (B) When vehicles are approaching within 200 feet.
   (C) When vehicles are within 500 feet.
   (D) Never have your high beams on.

10. What is the best thing to do when fog suddenly occurs?
    (A) Pull over to the side of the road.
    (B) Turn off your headlights (if in the daytime).
    (C) Keep a steady speed (don't slow down).
    (D) Pull into a rest area or truck stop.

11. What lights should be used in fog?
    (A) Low beam head and fog lights
    (B) Four-way flashers
    (C) Both A and B
    (D) High beam headlights

12. Which statement is a good driving philosophy for driving in fog?
    (A) It is better not to drive in the fog so park on the side of the road with your flashers on.
    (B) Always stay close enough to the driver ahead to see their taillights.
    (C) Use four-way flashers to help other drivers to see you sooner.
    (D) Use headlights and taillights of other vehicles to determine where the road is.

13. Which of the following is a false statement concerning nighttime driving?
    (A) Fatigue can cause you to not see hazards as readily as in daytime.
    (B) Poor lighting can cause you to not see hazards as readily as in daytime.
    (C) Glare can cause you to not see hazards as readily as in daytime.
    (D) Drivers' eyes adjust to various light conditions in a couple of seconds.

14. Which of the following choices is the best short list of supplies for winter driving?
    (A) Shovel, de-icer, screwdriver
    (B) Rock salt, bottled water, tire chains
    (C) Multi-tool, food, ice scraper
    (D) Anti-gel, hard hat, tow strap

15. Which of the following should you check specifically for winter driving preparation?
    (A) Check coolant and fire extinguisher.
    (B) Check wipers and windshield washer fluid.
    (C) Check tire chains and lights.
    (D) Check mirrors and exhaust.

16. Which of the following is not a recommended for winter driving?

    (A) Practice changing a tire.
    (B) Practice installing chains.
    (C) Put in windshield washer fluid designed for winter.
    (D) Keep an extra set of windshield wipers, even if they are used.

17. Which of the following items should you pay closer attention to in the winter?

    (A) Steps and handholds
    (B) Defrosters
    (C) Tread on tires
    (D) These are all items to pay closer attention to in the winter

18. Check for ice on the roads by:

    (A) Stopping and walking on the road.
    (B) Calling the radio station.
    (C) Identifying a lack of water spray from other vehicles.
    (D) Braking hard or steering quickly.

19. Which is not a good winter driving tip?

    (A) Join other drivers after a snowplow clears away snow.
    (B) Don't use the cruise control.
    (C) Avoid passing (going around in the other lane) other vehicles.
    (D) Drive no faster than half of the posted speed limit.

20. Driving in very hot weather:

    (A) Poses no concern for a well-maintained vehicle.
    (B) Demands the air conditioning be turned off to help the engine stay cool.
    (C) Requires you to drive faster to cool the engine better.
    (D) Causes more tire failures.

21. Checking your radiator fluid (coolant, antifreeze) can be done by looking at the:

    (A) Coolant reservoir.
    (B) Sight glass.
    (C) Level in the radiator after safely removing the radiator cap.
    (D) Can be performed by using any of these methods.

22. Which is the best way to control a skid?

    (A) Let off the fuel pedal and implement stab braking.
    (B) Turn in the opposite direction of the skid.
    (C) Let off the fuel pedal and steer slightly in the direction you are intending to go.
    (D) Step harder on the fuel pedal to counter the skid.

23. How do you prevent a skid?

    (A) Steer in the direction of the skid.
    (B) Drive slower.
    (C) Park your vehicle in a safe place.
    (D) Turn off the cruise control and engine brake.

24. Which of the following is not a warning sign or device for a railroad track?

    (A) A round black on yellow sign with an "RR" and an "X" on it.

    (B) A black and white sign with the railroad DOT number.

    (C) A pavement marking with an "X" and an "RR" on it.

    (D) A white and black crossbuck sign with the words, "Railroad Crossing" on it.

25. If you must stop at a railroad crossing, you should stop behind:

    (A) The "RR" and "X" in the pavement.

    (B) The stop line if there is one.

    (C) The crossbucks sign even if there is a stop line.

    (D) The yellow and black RR crossing warning sign.

26. Choose the best statement concerning railroad crossings.

    (A) A passive crossing is the same as an exempt crossing.

    (B) Railroad crossings must be designed to allow all vehicles to cross without danger.

    (C) When the gates go up you can cross the railroad tracks, even if the lights are still flashing.

    (D) Active crossings have features like lights, bells, and gates.

27. It takes a typical semi-tractor trailer how many seconds to cross a single set of tracks?

    (A) 8 seconds

    (B) 10 seconds

    (C) 12 seconds

    (D) 14 seconds

28. Which of the following is a false statement concerning railroad crossings?

    (A) Never race a train to a crossing.

    (B) Reduce your speed for crossing railroad tracks.

    (C) Expect to hear train horns and signals.

    (D) These are all true statements.

29. When you must stop at a railroad crossing:

    (A) Watch for traffic behind you.

    (B) Turn on your four-way flashers.

    (C) Check for available space on the other side of the tracks for your vehicle to clear the tracks.

    (D) These are all good practices when stopping at a railroad track.

30. All of the following are precautions to take at a railroad crossing except:

    (A) Don't count on hearing a train.

    (B) Don't rely on signals.

    (C) When a train has passed on a double track and the gate is lifted, it is safe to cross.

    (D) Reduce your speed when approaching a railroad crossing to improve your ability to see a train.

31. Which statement is not a correct statement or precaution for crossing railroad tracks?

(A) Do not shift while crossing railroad tracks.

(B) Low slung trailers like low-boys and moving vans can get stuck on railroad tracks.

(C) Dual drive axle tractors are more likely to have a long trailer get stuck on a railroad track than a single axle tractor with the same trailer.

(D) Car carriers can get stuck on railroad tracks.

32. Which of the following choices best answers the question, "When must you come to a full stop at a railroad crossing?"

(A) When the type of cargo makes stopping mandatory by law.

(B) When lights are flashing.

(C) When gates are lowered.

(D) All these are reasons for coming to a full stop at a railroad crossing.

33. The main method or component to keep from going too fast down a mountain is:

(A) The engine brake

(B) The service brake

(C) Stab braking

(D) Controlled braking

34. Which set of criteria is the best set for determining a safe speed to drive down a mountain?

(A) The weight of your vehicle, the size of your engine, the steepness of the grade

(B) The length of the mountain grade, road conditions, total weight of the vehicle

(C) The steepness of the grade, the weather, the speed you drove up the other side of the mountain

(D) The length of the grade, the steepness of the grade, the amount of gears in your transmission

35. Go down a mountain grade:

(A) In a low gear.

(B) In a high gear.

(C) In neutral.

(D) In the gear the transmission selects.

36. Brake fade occurs when:

(A) The brakes are cold.

(B) The vehicle has run out of air.

(C) The brakes get very hot.

(D) The treadle valve starts to leak.

37. Brake fade can occur in the following situations except when:

(A) Brakes are out of adjustment.

(B) One brake is doing more work than the other brakes.

(C) Brakes are used excessively.

(D) The brake pedal goes untouched, and the brakes are cool to the touch.

38. Escape ramps:

   (A) Provide a place for trucks to crash away from other traffic.

   (B) Attach parachutes to runaway vehicles.

   (C) Stop runaway vehicles without harming drivers or passengers.

   (D) Are made of concrete barricades.

39. Accidents occur with the nearest vehicle or object. Emergencies:

   (A) Occur when two vehicles are about to collide.

   (B) Can be mitigated by the driver.

   (C) Can be made less frequently with proper maintenance and inspections.

   (D) All these choices.

40. Which of the following statements is not the most inaccurate?

   (A) Steering to avoid an accident with a large vehicle is generally the safest action to take in emergency situations.

   (B) Emergencies can occur due to mechanical failure.

   (C) Steering to avoid a collision might be the quickest way to avoid an accident, but tall vehicles can tip over.

   (D) If a vehicle comes from the other direction to your side, steering to the right is your best option.

41. Tire failures while driving:

   (A) Require that you realize that you have a failure.

   (B) Demand that you apply the brakes quickly.

   (C) Are handled best by steering in the direction that the vehicle wants to go.

   (D) Only allow you to drive at a top speed of 30 mph.

42. ABS was required to be installed on all truck/semi-tractors with air brakes by:

   (A) March 1, 1997.

   (B) March 1, 1998.

   (C) March 1, 1999.

   (D) March 1, 2000.

43. ABS Systems will:

   (A) Help you stop faster.

   (B) Increase your stopping power.

   (C) Change the way you normally brake.

   (D) Not compensate for poorly maintained brakes.

44. Skids are generally caused by:

   (A) Over braking.

   (B) Over steering.

   (C) Over acceleration.

   (D) All these can cause skids.

Answers and Explanations

1. **B.** Glare is definitely a problem for night driving.

2. **A.** Sleep is the best and only recommended way to get rid of fatigue.

3. **D.** All these statements are true concerning glare.

4. **C.** Poor lighting does not help your headlights, so C is the false statement.

5. **D.** Headlights do not have to be LED.

6. **B.** Taillights must be red.

7. **B.** Headlights and streetlights will often reveal smudges and other cleanliness defects in windshields at night that are not visible in the day.

8. **B.** Looking at the white line to the right of your lane helps with the problem of glare.

9. **C.** The stated distance for switching from high beams to low beams when vehicles are approaching or for following a vehicle is 500 feet.

10. **D.** Pulling over on the side of the road increases the chances of your vehicle getting hit as other vehicles won't realize that you are parked rather than moving. Keeping the same speed usually means that you are driving faster than the space that you can get stopped in. Low beams or fog lights should be used in fog. Get to a safe parking spot.

11. **C.** Low beams and fog lights should be used as they have best chance to shine light on the thinnest fog. Four-way flashers are helpful.

12. **C.** Parking on the side of the road is unsafe, other drivers might be traveling at speeds that are too fast to safely follow, other vehicles might be off the road, so their lights are not helpful. So that leaves using your flashers as a good tip to help others see you.

13. **D.** These are all true statements about night driving except D as people's eyes don't adjust that quickly.

14. **B.** Screwdriver, multi-tool, and tow strap are good items to have, but B is the best list specifically for winter preparation.

15. **B.** Fire extinguisher, lights and exhaust are important to check but are not items for winter preparation list.

16. **A.** Leave the tire changing to the professionals with the proper tools.

17. **D.** Pay attention to all these items in the winter.

18. **C.** If the road looks wet but no water spray is spraying, you have ice on the road. Walking on the road doesn't sound safe and trying to skid isn't any better. The radio station personnel are not sitting where you are.

19. **A.** Stay away from other drivers. Never use the cruise control on slick roads. Passing increases the chance that uneven roads will cause you to lose control and half the posted speed limit is usually a decent speed to choose, definitely no more than.

20. **D.** Indeed, hot weather increases tire failures. Hot weather is a concern even for well-maintained vehicles. I am not recommending that you turn off the air conditioner until you must take drastic measures to keep your vehicle operating. Driving faster will make your car's engine work harder.

21. **D.** Just follow the manufacturer's recommendations for checking the fluid.

22. **C.** To control a skid, you should release and stay off both the brake pedal and the fuel pedal. Steering alone, the right or wrong way, is not as good as steering correctly and staying off the pedals.

23. **C.** The only way to prevent a skid is to not be on the road.

24. **B.** The DOT number sign might be where you must get out of the car to read it.

25. **B.** Stop lines are always the indicator of where to stop in any situation.

26. **D.** Exempt crossings are usually closed tracks that are no longer used. All tracks are not made for low-slung trailers to safely pass over. Do not pass over tracks until the lights are no longer flashing.

27. **D.** The standard answer is 14 seconds is the time stated in CDL study guides for a typical semi-tractor trailer combination to pass over a railroad crossing.

28. **C.** It is not safe to assume that you will hear warnings.

29. **D.** You must watch for other motorists as they might not be able to see the track signals so slow down earlier. Turn on your four-way flashers to help them avoid hitting you. Many tracks have an intersection close to them, which do not have sufficient space for all vehicles to clear the tracks.

30. **C.** There can be another train obscured by the first train on double tracks.

31. **C.** It is the single axle tractor combined with a long trailer that has the bigger problem with space underneath the trailer, not the dual drive axle tractors. Car carriers and other low trailers can get stuck on raised railroad tracks. Shifting the transmission is not allowed on railroad crossings so that is a correct statement.

32. **D.** All these choices are good reasons for stopping at a railroad crossing.

33. **A.** The engine brake offers the safest way to control your speed going down a mountain. Using your service brakes in any manner will help to get them too hot.

34. **B.** The size of your engine and the amount of gears are not helpful in determining the speed to go down a mountain. The other side of the mountain can be a different grade.

35. **A.** Low gears will work to keep your speed down. High gear and neutral do not, and your vehicle generally does not know what you are doing to choose the correct gear.

36. **C.** Brake fade occurs when brakes get too hot.

37. **D.** When brakes go unused, they stay cool. Brakes that get over used, get too hot and brake fade is likely to occur.

38. **C.** Runaway ramps are not designed to cause crashes and are not concrete barriers. It would be neat for parachutes to attach to runaway trucks so if you can invent an effective system . . .

39. **D.** When you are about to collide with another vehicle, it is an emergency. Good drivers work to spot hazards before they become emergencies. Properly maintaining your equipment reduces emergencies caused by equipment failure.

40. **A.** Steering is not the safest way to avoid emergencies as the possibility of a rollover increases. However, steering can be the only effective solution in certain scenarios.

41. **A.** Be aware of when you have a tire failure to help reduce hazards on the road and prevent further damage to your vehicle and other vehicles. Do not slam on the brakes, do not keep driving, do not let the vehicle do what it wants to do.

42. **A.** March 1, 1997 is the correct date for the air brake-equipped truck/semi-tractors (as the government calls them) to be manufactured with ABS.

43. **D.** Poorly maintained brakes are bad brakes, period! ABS does not make a vehicle stop faster, nor does it give your brakes more stopping power. You should brake normally with ABS. ABS does not fix bad brakes.

44. **D.** Over-braking, over-steering, and over-acceleration — especially on slickened roads — can cause skids.

IN THIS CHAPTER

» **Defining Hours of Service regulations**

» **Making preparations for driving**

» **Figuring out what to do during accidents and fires**

» **Knowing the effects of controlled substances**

» **Being a guardian of the roads**

Chapter **6**

Adding the Non-Driving Knowledge

"Dumb truck driver." That is a phrase that has been repeated many times. Truck drivers are neither smarter nor dumber than anyone else. It is just that when they make a mistake, it is very noticeable. Make the same mistake in a car and you might get by with it. Don't choose the career of a truck driver if you think that all you have to do is hold on to a steering wheel. Otherwise, you may end up being the star of a viral video.

Driving a commercial motor vehicle (CMV) will possibly place you in contact with more law enforcement officers than in your previous career(s). It will be beneficial to you to accept that driving a CMV entails much more than holding a steering wheel. The knowledge that you have acquired will place among the best drivers on the road. As an example of the need to have non-driving knowledge is that every year a trucking association conducts a contest for drivers to compete against each other. A significant portion of this contest is a written test!

In this chapter, you examine Hours of Service regulations and how to: log your on-duty, driving, and off-duty hours, prepare for your trip, and avoid the use of drugs and alcohol. You also discover which task to do first when an accident or fire occurs.

Following Hours of Service Regulations

Transportation dispatchers and managers have a lot of pressure on them to get the cargo shipped to the customers. They will often pass that pressure on to you. Ultimately, no one can make you drive; it's up to you to make the right decision. But believe it or not, you have a friend in regulations called Hours of Service. *Hours of Service (HOS)* sets limits and parameters for when you can drive so that you can legally refuse to drive when someone is trying to force you to drive. The HOS regulations were created to reduce accidents — to protect you and those around you. The rules for HOS are not perfect, but they are there for you when you need them.

When you are taking your written exam, you might not find any questions about hours of service, but you should find a healthy dose of HOS training in your Entry-Level Driver Training (ELDT) class. Every business that has a position requiring a driver with a Commercial Driver's License (CDL) is to comply with HOS. Some employers might demand that your HOS records be logged continually (as the regulations mandate), while other employers invisibly take care of your HOS for you (where the HOS exceptions allow). In this section, I will give you just some fundamental rules and exceptions because there are far too many to cover them all in this book. The Federal Motor Carrier Safety Administration (FMCSA) website has the HOS guidelines for CDL holders if you want or need to go deeper into the regulations (www.fmcsa.dot.gov/regulations/hours-service/summary-hours-service-regulations).

When examining regulations, you will often read a statement that will sound restrictive. As you keep reading, you will find *exceptions* (or exemptions) to that restrictive statement, which are sometimes difficult to interpret. The FMCSA, who publishes these rules and exceptions has been known to interpret them incorrectly as well. Do not try to use AI (artificial intelligence) to interpret the rules and exceptions (nor should you search for answers in online forums or on social media).

It may be difficult to remember all the important rules and regulations for driving a CMV, so take this book with you on the road and refer to it often — when you're not driving, of course!

Understanding your status

You might land a job where you are not required to keep a complete record of your activity, but you are still obligated to comply with the regulations. There are federal HOS regulations for inter-state drivers (drivers operating state to state or hauling freight that originated in another state or is headed to another state). A few states have unique variations for their intrastate HOS when compared to the federal regulations, but most have adopted the federal rules.

You must follow the HOS regulations if you drive a CMV that weighs 10,001 pounds or more, including the load, or if your vehicle has a gross weight rating or a gross combination weight rating of 10,001 pounds or more, or you are transporting hazardous materials (also known as *hazmat*) in quantities that require placards.

On duty

As a CMV driver, you are in one of four duty statuses all the time, on-duty, off-duty, sleeper berth, and driving. It can be tricky to determine which status you should be declaring — so careful attention to the details of the regulations is important.

You cannot declare when you are on duty or off duty just whenever you feel like it. There are regulations that help you determine what is off-duty time or on-duty time. Generally speaking, you're on duty when you are working and off duty when you're not.

Here is a general list of what is *on duty* status:

>> All time spent driving your CMV.

>> All time signing paperwork, loading or unloading cargo, or supervising the same activities involving your vehicle.

>> All the time you are waiting on assistance on your vehicle when it has broken down.

>> All the time you're maintaining your vehicle — inspecting, servicing, cleaning, washing, or fueling.

WARNING

You must be on-duty all the time at the terminal or any property of your employer, or public property when you are ready and waiting to be dispatched. This is possibly the most falsified record of duty status. Falsifying a log sheet can be a severe violation. Don't get in that trap, any extra money that you think you will make isn't worth it. If you are relieved of duty, you are exempted from this rule for now.

Here is a list of what is considered exceptions to on-duty status:

>> Time spent *resting* in or on a parked vehicle. This includes time spent resting in a sleeper berth.

The *sleeper berth duty* status is fairly straightforward. If you are in the *sleeper berth* (a compartment, in your semi-tractor cab, where you can lay down and sleep) you should choose the sleeper berth duty status. You should not choose the sleeper berth duty status any other time. If your vehicle does not have a sleeper berth, you are not allowed to choose the sleeper berth duty status — duh!

When you're driving as a team, up to 3 hours resting in the passenger seat of your CMV immediately before or after a period of at least 7 hours in the sleeper berth.

>> Taking a random or non-random drug screen, including the travel to and from the place of the screening.

>> All the time spent training.

>> All the time spent driving a company car.

>> All the time spent performing compensated work for anyone else, whether driving related or not.

Off duty

If I explained on duty well enough, you probably have a good idea of what is off duty now.

You should choose "off duty" as your duty status:

>> If you are relieved of all duties.

>> If you are not being paid to work.

>> If you are free to pursue activities of your own choosing.

>> If you are able to leave your vehicle and go elsewhere.

Limiting your driving time

All the limits that are in the HOS are about driving. When you have reached a limit, you are not allowed to drive. You can work but not drive. (Refer to the on-duty list in the previous section.) This is a common misconception partly because the 14-hour rule is often called the *14-hour on-duty rule.*

The 14-hour rule

One basic rule you should remember is the 14-hour limit. When you begin your work, your clock starts. You have 14 consecutive hours in which you can drive *no more than 11 hours*. Once you have reached the end of the 14 hours, you shouldn't drive any more until you have a break of 10 hours or more that resets some drive time. The 14 hours is unaffected by the various duty status' that you will be switching to during the day.

The 11-hour driving rule

REMEMBER

You have a maximum of 11 hours of driving that can cumulate within your 14-hour clock. After driving 11 hours, you must take a sufficient break of at least 10 hours before you can start driving time again. Your 14-hour clock and 11 hours of driving starts over at that point.

The 30-minute driving interruption break

Another rule that the FMCSA has established for drivers to avoid fatigue is to make it illegal to drive more than *8 cumulative hours without a consecutive 30-minute break*. This time period can happen often without much planning as drivers have to stop during the day to pick up cargo, deliver cargo, have a meal, or sleep off some drowsiness.

You may use any duty status other than driving for the 30-minute break. This break from driving gets the driver away from staring down the road for hours on end — even getting out of the vehicle to move some cargo can be refreshing.

The 60- and 70-hour rules

To help CMV drivers avoid being fatigued from an accumulation of driving/working, day after day, there is a cumulative limit that is spread over several days.

If your employer has employees driving 6 days a week or less, they would use a 60-hour, 7-day rule. This rule means that you cannot drive after you reach 60 hours on duty in any 7 consecutive days.

If your employer has drivers operating vehicles every day of the week, the 70-hour, 8-day rule would apply, which limits driving to 70 hours in any 8 consecutive days.

Protecting your time

A dispatcher says to you, "I don't care about you being tired. Get this load delivered by 5 in the morning if you want to keep this job!" This type of *coercion* occurs when someone in position to threaten to take work from you or take employment action against you because you refused to operate in violation of the HOS rules. This act can be reported to the FMCSA or the Occupational Safety and Health Administration (OSHA). And you might consider being on the lookout for a good honest employer or to find an honest broker.

In a similar situation of a potential HOS violation, a manager says, "If you get this load delivered for me, I will make sure that your sister-in-law gets the job that she applied for here." Although this doesn't seem as bad as coercion, this type of "bargaining" is still against the law and can lead to long-term negative consequences for you.

AUTHOR SAYS

I insist that you always use your HOS properly and not falsify your log sheets to avoid work. You should do what it takes to be prepared, rested, and ready when it is time to work. Be a professional! When you regard the HOS rules as important and encourage other drivers to do the same, customers may better appreciate that philosophy. After all, they want their cargo delivered safely.

Operating under exceptions

I am not teaching you how you can cheat on your logs (people tend to think of ways to do that on their own — shame on them!). As I mentioned in an earlier section, there are many *exceptions* in the HOS rules. But you should utilize the exceptions you are familiar with when it is to your advantage.

Yard moves

So you have to drive around your employer's terminal, which is using your HOS driving time. That's not fair! Fortunately, there is an exception to the rule in this case. My interpretation of this exception is that any time you are driving on private property where public four-wheelers are not allowed; for the purpose of doing business, you can use the *yard move* exemption (which puts you on-duty and not driving). However, you are not allowed to use yard move as the time spent driving at a public truck stop.

Another yard move exception is when you are at a facility to have your vehicle repaired. You are allowed to use the yard move exception for that driving.

At the time of this book's publishing, the FMCSA is working on the definition of yard move, though they officially started in January 2021. Once they decide on the definition, which can be called a "finalized guidance," they are supposed to publish it. After 5 years, the FMCSA will re-examine the guideline and decide to withdraw it or reissue it for another 5 years. Then at that point, they have the same options as before, or they can add it to the official safety regulations.

Personal conveyance

You've run out of time to drive at a customer's location. The customer says you can park there, but you really want to head to a restaurant and take advantage of what they have to offer. In this case, you are allowed to use an exemption called *personal conveyance* (which is off-duty) to go do something personal, like go to a restaurant, do some shopping, or play a game of pickleball. You simply aren't allowed to conduct business — no fueling the vehicle, no washing it, nor just advancing to your next stop. As a general rule, you should go back to the location where you were already parked. The regulations state that you can only use personal conveyance if your company allows it.

REMEMBER

Let's say that the customer who said you can park overnight there came out and said, "We're sorry, but we forgot that we have people coming in to resurface the parking lot tonight and you will have to move your vehicle." Wow, that messes up your logs because that will interfere with the break needed to be consecutive. Good news! The regulations also allow you to drive to the nearest safe parking spot if you are *forced* from a parking location. Just go back to the duty status you were in prior to using personal conveyance (probably sleeper berth).

Adverse driving conditions

You have a daily route that you drive, which gets you back to the terminal every day in under 14 hours. But today, a freak unpredicted snowstorm occurred, and you had to drive half the speed you usually do in order to be safe. Fortunately, you don't have to be in violation of the driving limits. You can use the *adverse driving conditions* exception. That exception will allow a driver to drive two more hours and have two more hours added to the 14-hour clock when a condition occurs that keeps them from completing the run within the legal hours.

Split sleeper berth

When you have completed a day of driving and your truck has a sleeper berth, you can use it to sleep and rest in. After completing a day of driving, you must have a break of 10 hours, which can be taken in the sleeper berth or off duty, or a combination of the two. However, there is an exception to that 10 consecutive hour rule, which is called the *split sleeper berth* exception.

The following rules make up the split sleeper berth exception:

>> A 10-hour break can be split into two segments.

  ● The longer segment must be at least 7 hours and must be in the sleeper berth duty status.

  ● The shorter segment must be at least 2 hours and can be in the sleeper berth or off duty.

>> Together, the two breaks must total at least 10 hours.

>> Both of the breaks suspend the 14-hour clock.

>> When the driving time immediately before and after each rest break are added together, the total must not exceed the 11-hour driving limit.

>> The duty status segments immediately before and after each rest break must not exceed the 14-hour limit in which to drive.

WARNING

Unless you have a firm understanding of this exception, and have a specific need to use it, don't try using it.

The 34-hour reset

TIP

You are at home for the weekend. Wouldn't it be nice to start at zero again to calculate your 60- or 70-hour clock? There's an exception for that too; it's called the *34-hour reset*. Remain off duty for 34 hours consecutively, and you can reset your accumulated hours to zero. You can use off duty and sleeper berth, in any combination, as long as it is a consecutive 34 hours. There seems to be a little-known fact among drivers that this actually an exception. However, I don't know anyone who doesn't take advantage of it.

Recording your activity

Your activity must be tracked. Usually this will be accomplished with an electronic logging device (ELD). A few drivers are allowed to keep their activity recorded on paper. In 2015, when the FMCSA released their decision to mandate ELD, they used a different term for logs; they were called Record of Duty Status (RODS). I believe that most CMV drivers and law enforcement officers use the term ELD logs instead of RODS, which I use in this section as well.

Logging manually

In some states, a CMV officer doesn't need a reason to stop you and then conduct a safety inspection. In other states, they must have a reason (which they'll easily find, like going 1 mile over the speed limit). When a CMV officer asks you for documents, they usually ask for your blank stash of paper log sheets. You must have at least 8 days worth of blank log sheets. If your ELD malfunctions, you are to start using paper logs to record your activity and report the malfunction to your office within 24 hours. Your office, even if it is you, must get you back on ELD within 7 days.

The following items are required to be filled on a log sheet. Figure 6-1 corresponds to the numbers in the list. (The grid at the bottom of the figure is filled out for a full 24 hours.)

1. **Date.** The date that a 24-hour log period begins.

2. **Total miles.** Record only the number of miles you drive during the driving day.

3. **Equipment used.** Add every piece of equipment you use during the day (truck, trailer, bus, and so on).

4. **Shipping information.** List the number that identifies your load/assignment with your employer. This can be an order number, *pro number* (a freight carrier's tracking number), or bill of lading number. In lieu of a number, you can use the shipper and the commodity, but you must use both the shipper and the commodity, not just one or the other. Include all the different assignments that you do during the workday.

   Not sure about the definitions in the previous paragraph? Here's a quick reference:

   - **Shipper:** The business facility from the cargo is picked up.

   - **Commodity:** The type of load being carried.

   - **Carrier:** Transports the cargo to be delivered.

   - **Bill of lading:** A contract between a shipper and the carrier.

5. **Start time of the log period.** A company can establish a different time for the logging day to begin other than the traditional midnight start time. Use the time zone where your employer's terminal is located.

6. **Name of company or carrier.** Record the name of the company you are working for.

7. **Address of company.** Include the address of the company.

8. **Driver's signature.** Sign your log to certify the entries are correct.

9. **Name of co-driver.** If you have a co-driver, fill in this space.

10. **Total hours.** Add the hours for each duty status line and the total of those hours.

11. **Remarks.** Document the location of each duty status change by listing the town where it occurred. Record any information that will explain unusual events that would otherwise be unclear.

Any other fields on log sheets are there to use if you so desire. Additional information about keeping logs can be found in the regulations.

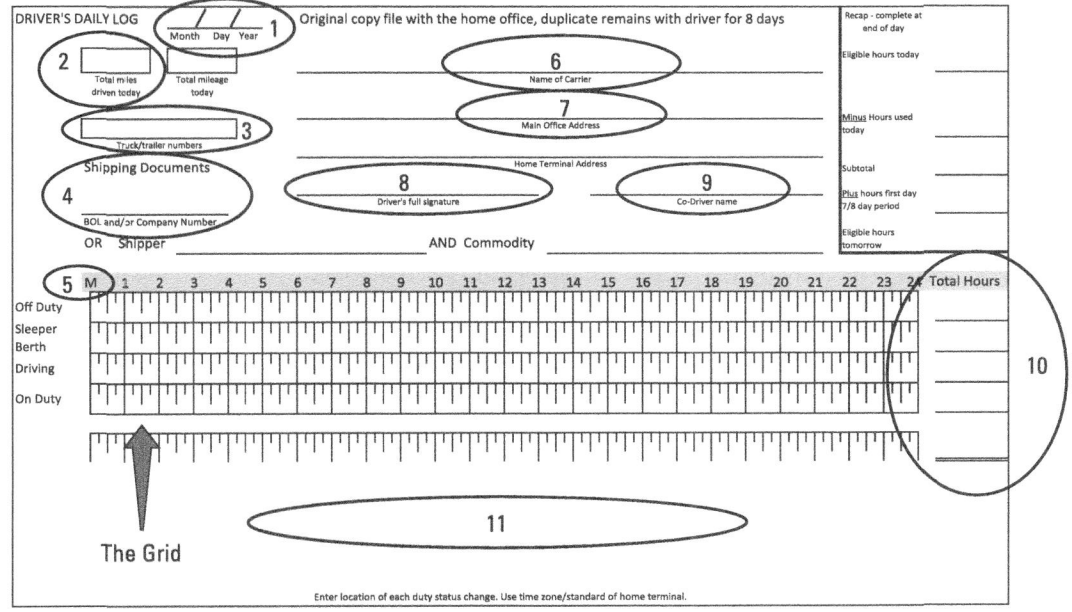

FIGURE 6-1: A blank log sheet with required fields circled.

Reviewing a sample log

One day you may need to keep a paper log, so here is an example that can be used for reference. Figure 6-2 shows a simple log sheet for a fictitious but realistic day. The following list highlights the required log information.

>> AC begins the day at 06:00 at Cisne, IL.

>> AC performs a pre-trip inspection, procures the paperwork, secures the cargo on a preloaded trailer, and gets left at 6:45.

>> AC drives to Simpsonville, KY and stops for fuel at 11:15.

>> At Simpsonville, AC purchases fuel and leaves there at 11:45.

>> AC drives to the destination, Erwin, TN. At Erwin, AC's trailer is unloaded. AC is given permission to stay overnight on the property, so AC performs a post-trip inspection and stays the night in the sleeper berth.

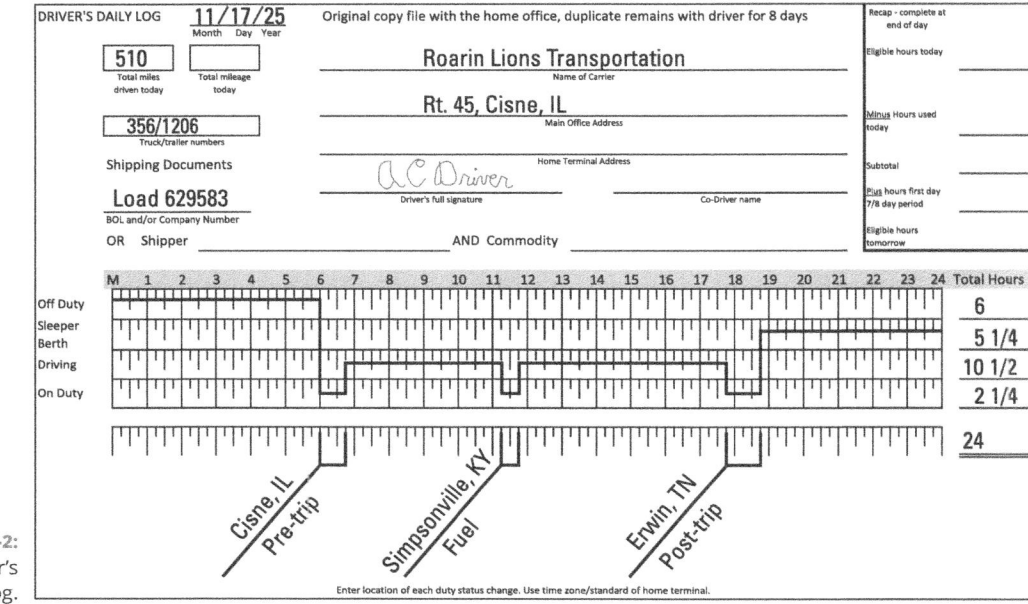

FIGURE 6-2:
AC Driver's
log.

Going high tech with ELD

Once upon a time, not really that long ago, there were electronic logs that were called Automatic On-Board Recording Device (AOBRD). These devices were able to be edited by a driver's office, but not necessarily by the driver. I have heard that there were people who would actually change a driver's log in order for the driver to have more hours to drive.

Obviously, this practice can have had catastrophic results. Drivers can be driving when they were unfit (fatigued) to drive, and they didn't have much power to do anything about it. The ELD mandate fixed this problem by placing full control in the hands of the driver.

A few of the items that were mandated with ELD:

>> Locations are automatically recorded.

>> All movement of the truck is recorded.

>> The device must place the driver in driving duty status by the time the vehicle reaches 5 mph.

>> Driving time is not editable.

>> Employers can only make suggestions for correcting a log entry. A driver can choose to reject the edit or accept it if it is true.

>> Edits require an explanation.

>> Drivers are allowed to edit their logs without the help of their employers in order to get their logs correct and legal.

>> It must show a graph. A graph gives a picture of a driver's log record.

>> It must allow a driver to transmit the logs to a CMV officer.

Planning Your Trip with HOS in Mind

You are driving down the road and then realize that you are supposed to be taking a break. But you don't see a place to do so. Your GPS isn't helping, and you didn't check your route beforehand and now you see a "no trucks allowed sign" at the intersection ahead. This is going to be a bad day.

The best way to avoid this situation is to plan your trip. This step will be easier as you gain more driving experience. But in the beginning of your career, you can help yourself by making a little form or checklist, organizing all the parts of your trip.

There are many truck driving jobs that are constructed in such a manner that you don't have to remember how many hours you have to drive or when you should be taking a break. I am going to address drivers who do need to plan their trip keeping the HOS in mind.

REMEMBER

You have limits in the HOS and mandatory breaks that you must incorporate into your plan for your trip. You have an 11-hour driving limit for the day, and you must do that driving within a 14-hour window. At some point, you must take a solid 30-minute break from driving before you accumulate 8 hours of driving. And it will behoove you to plan your week out further by including your 60 hour/7-day or 70 hour/8-day limit.

Checking the map

TIP

Acquire a copy of Rand McNally's *Motor Carriers' Road Atlas*. This guidebook shows truck routes, important state-to-state information for truck drivers, and maps — lots of 'em. It will be your most valuable tool and one of your best teachers. If you use a GPS only, you may eventually be referred to as the "dumb truck driver" in a viral video. The road atlas will help you retain more information. When your brain has to go through a problem-solving process, it remembers more details than when it is just waiting for a new instruction to follow. Read the road atlas as you would read a magazine. Look at the fine print. It contains the following features that might be very important for you:

>> **Truck routes.** Some roads are not meant for trucks. Truck routes are marked in yellow.

>> **Toll roads.** You get the privilege of paying (on top of road use taxes) to drive on these roads, which are marked in green.

>> **Weigh stations.** Weigh stations will weigh your vehicle to verify you are driving legally. They also inspect trucks as the inspector's time allows.

>> **Rest areas.** Rest areas are marked by little blue huts. May the one you want to stop at accepts trucks and isn't closed.

>> **Restricted routes.** Restricted routes are listed in one of the front sections of the road atlas. There are various reasons for a route to be restricted.

>> **Low clearances.** State and national roads with overpasses may have heights below 13 feet, 6 inches, which is considered low clearance.

>> **Important phone numbers.** Numbers for state police and other agencies are included. Every once in a while, you may need some non-emergency help from an officer.

>> **Time zones.** Time zones can be confusing in some states. The large North American map shows the time zones.

>> **Mileages between towns.** There is a large list of 200 cities, including the mileage between them. There are also small charts accompanying each state map with mileages.

>> **Mileages of interstates within a state.** There is a section with each state, noting the mileage for interstates in the state.

>> **Index of towns.** A convenient index helps you locate a town on a map.

>> **Counties.** Counties are shown for each state. Counties can have curfews for oversize loads, or there might be quarantines for invasive insects — which is important if you're hauling produce or live plants.

>> **Legal weight charts.** Legal weights change with the number of axles and the distance between them so refer to these charts as needed.

>> **Size limitations.** There are various restrictions for size of vehicles on the federal roads and even more restrictions on state roads.

Reading your assignment

You are sitting waiting for a load assignment, and you finally get a load to pick up that goes to St. Louis. You make the pickup, quickly sign the paperwork, and head to St. Louis. You receive a call from dispatch asking where you were going. It turns out that the load was to go to St. Louis Park, Minnesota not Saint Louis, Missouri. No matter how rushed you feel, do not rush checking paperwork and other instructions.

REMEMBER

Paperwork (or bills of lading) have traditionally been prepared by the carrier, but truckload shipments are usually completed by the shipper. This makes the paperwork process better for both the shipper and the carrier. Make no assumptions about paperwork, read it through carefully prior to signing anything.

Here are the items to check on a bill of lading and assignments:

>> **Address of stop(s).** This is obviously important for both driving to the correct location and for verifying that the paperwork matches the assignment.

>> **Special instructions.** These instructions are just special. Read them.

>> **Delivery and pick up times for each stop.** These are more likely to be on the assignment and not a bill of lading. Nevertheless, you need to incorporate this into your trip plan.

>> **Weight.** A necessary item for ensuring legal loads and cargo securement.

>> **Pieces.** The *consignee* (the customer to whom the cargo is being delivered) and the shipper are both interested in verifying all the shipment made it to its destination. And you, the carrier want protection when the consignee states they ordered more than what you delivered.

>> **Hazmat.** If there is hazardous material in the shipment, you need to ensure certain tasks are performed.

>> **Shipper signature.** If nothing else is stated on a bill of lading, the shipper's signature means that they have placed the items on the bill into your custody. It does not mean that everything is there and loaded correctly.

>> **Shipper's Load and Count (SL&C).** An act of Congress back in the first quarter of the 1900s allows carriers to sign bills with SL&C when picking up a shipment that they cannot verify is all there or that it has been shipped correctly. Without SL&C, you are saying everything is loaded and loaded properly.

>> **Driver's signature.** If the paperwork isn't carbon copies or on NCR (carbonless) paper, *sign* all copies along with the *date* and the *SL&C*.

>> **Carriers name.** Whoever you are driving for, even if it is your own company, should have their name on a bill of lading. Don't allow any other name to be stated as the carrier.

When you have verified the bills, assignments, and any other documentation, process the paperwork as your employer directs. Don't take shortcuts!

REMEMBER

Bills of lading become receipts of delivery. When you have someone sign for the shipment you delivered, have them print their name on the bills or you print it.

Documenting and Processing an Accident

I hope you are never in an accident or even near an accident. But if you are, I want you to know what to do and what *not* to do when it happens. Don't bother panicking. Just think of the logical steps you're about to read. This section can also be useful for you while driving, for passing your exam, or to render aid or help at an accident that you weren't involved in. If you are driving a bus, you have a responsibility to your passengers (see Chapter 14).

Calling the authorities

You are involved in an accident. Turn on your four-way flashers. Park where your vehicle will be out of the way, if possible. Don't be the cause of another accident.

TIP

As a common practice, know where you are at all times when driving. Read out the mile markers as you drive down the road. Be aware of what road you are on. It will be important to know your location when you make a 9-1-1- call. If you don't know, perhaps your phone will provide the location. The operator may be able to find your location via your cell phone if you stay on the line long enough to transmit that digital information.

If you have no cell phone signal, try your CB (citizen band) radio. If you don't have one, find a driver who has one. Some good driver will roll down their window and ask if you need anything. They will probably have a CB to get hold of a Local Yokel, County Mountie, or a Smokey Bear (all CB slang for the local, county, and state law enforcement officers).

Next, take your reflective triangles (roadside warning devices) and place them to help alert other motorists that they should slow down and expect that there's something to watch out for.

Caring for the injured

Chances are you don't have any medical license, but there are still some tasks that you can do that don't take a doctor or an EMT (Emergency Medical Technician) to perform.

>> First, various state CDL study guides advise to not move a severely injured person unless there is a danger of fire or passing traffic makes it necessary. I am not so sure that you should move a person even if they aren't severely injured, except for safety reasons of course. Encourage an injured person to move to a safe location under their own ability.

>> If the injured or simply a person in the accident is wandering around, try to get them to sit in a safe place.

>> Keep the person who is injured or in shock warm.

>> If there is severe bleeding, apply pressure on the wound to stop the loss of blood.

>> Stay out of the way of trained medical personnel as soon as they arrive; keep quiet and assist only when asked.

Taking pictures

If you are in an accident, regardless of whose fault it is, take pictures! It is okay to take more pictures than needed.

TIP

Make your pictures tell an accurate story. Take the pictures from *every angle* from many *varying distances.* Take a picture of *all vehicles* that were involved in the accident, again from every angle and varying distances. Be sure to take pictures of their *license plate, insurance card, driver's license,* and any other identifying information, like the name and numbers on the side of a CMV. Take pictures of the *people involved* in the accident as well as *witnesses* and any *law enforcement* (especially the officer interviewing you); take pictures of their badges with their numbers as well.

Also take pictures of the area. Make sure you can tell the whole story with your pictures. If you say that something happened 200 feet back, take pictures 200 feet back. Be careful when taking the pictures (for safety's sake), but if you can take them from your point of view as a driver, that will be good too.

Talking at the scene

REMEMBER

Some people talk too much, especially when they are nervous. Think about the following list to prepare yourself:

>> When an officer talks with you, give the officer the facts, just the facts.

>> Give no speculations.

>> Don't admit to any guilt; however, cooperate with officers and tell the truth!

>> Call your safety department/person when the law enforcement officers are done talking to you. Your safety representative will inform you of who else you can talk to.

>> Do not talk to any insurance company until your employer's safety person has told you who you can talk to.

>> Do not talk to other people's insurance companies. You will probably be given a name as to who you can talk to next.

Reacting to Fires

Truck fires can occur in and around accident sites. Tires, brakes, and other components — due to poor maintenance — can catch fire. Faulty wiring has been known to cause fires and even cargo can start a fire.

Preventing fires

"Only you can prevent forest fires!" This has to be one of the most well-known ad lines in the United States, especially among Baby Boomers. I had the privilege of playing Smokey Bear a few times for schools, nursing homes, and day care centers, encouraging people to help prevent fires and what to do if there is a fire. While I am not wearing a Smoky Bear costume, I am still asking you to help prevent CMV fires and diminish their impact if one does occur.

>> Conduct a good pre-trip inspection. Inspect wiring, tires, cargo, fuel systems, and exhaust systems.

>> Don't neglect the enroute inspection. Feel the air around items that have a capacity to get hot. See if a component is hotter on the other side of the CMV.

>> Be attentive while driving down the road. Do you have a gut feeling that something is wrong? Check it out.

>> Verify the safe loading of hazmat loads and check for any incompatibility of products.

>> Keep a watch on mirrors for smoke and gauges for a component overheating.

Fire extinguishers

When you are conducting your pre-trip inspection, include to look for and at your fire extinguisher. It is one item that when you need it, it needs to be where it belongs and ready to work.

Your fire extinguisher is to be:

>> Properly mounted and accessible.

>> Marked with a current inspection date.

>> Properly rated for the cargo that you haul.

>> Fully charged.

>> Found with the pin in place.

Fire extinguishers have different ratings, which means they have different capabilities based on the type of fire (see Table 6-1).

TABLE 6-1 Class and Type of Fires

Class	Type of Fires
A	Wood and paper
B	Gasoline and petroleum products
C	Electrical
D	Combustible metal

Fire extinguishers can be effective against more than one type of fire, such as a BC fire extinguisher that is widely available.

Protecting people

TIP

As soon as you spot smoke, move your truck off the road and to a location that is away from buildings and people. Do not stop at a fuel station. Avoid areas with dry vegetation. Call the authorities.

If you have an engine that is on fire, turn off the engine. Don't open the hood. The less oxygen it gets, the slower it burns. Attempt to put the fire out around or through any opening of the hood.

WARNING

If you have a fire in a van trailer, do not open the doors as the oxygen that gets sucked into the trailer will increase the intensity of the fire.

Take your fire extinguisher and stand as far away from the fire as the extinguisher will reach, with the wind in your back, and spray the base of the fire, not the flames but where the actual object is that is burning.

Avoiding Alcohol and Drugs While Driving

There are many things that I can say about alcohol and drugs and the CDL holder, but I only have a few hundred pages to devote to you passing your exam and most exam questions will not be about drinking. In this section, I discuss how alcohol affects the body and how being impaired by alcohol and drugs works against your CDL.

Drinking and CDL holder

Most of the following information about alcohol in this section is from various state's CDL study guides. Although there seems to be some conflicting information, here's what you need to know for the written test.

Alcohol obviously goes to your stomach and into your intestines. But some of it will go straight into your bloodstream, which takes it directly to your brain, in 30 seconds. Some of the alcohol will be removed in your urine, through your perspiration, and through your breathing. The remaining alcohol gets carried to your liver. The liver only processes one-third to one-half an ounce of alcohol an hour. The more alcohol you consume, the higher your Blood Alcohol Concentration (BAC) is.

The effects of higher BAC in a driver are:

>> Bad judgment.

>> Using more than one lane.

>> Fast starts.

>> Passing when they shouldn't.

- » Weaving.
- » Driving in the wrong lane or direction.
- » Running over curbs.
- » Running stop signs and stop lights.
- » Failing to use lights.
- » Failing to use turn signals.
- » Driving erratic speeds.
- » Slow to react to hazards and traffic control devices.

A person weighing 240 pounds can drink twice as much as a 100-pound person and have the same BAC. One drink is equal to a shot of whiskey (1.5 ounces, 80 proof), or 12 ounces of beer, or 5 ounces of table wine.

Disqualifying yourself

REMEMBER

When you obtain your CDL, you imply that you consent to random drug and alcohol tests. Don't jeopardize your job or other people's lives by being impaired from drugs and alcohol while driving. Here are some ways to disqualify yourself:

- » If you fail a test or even refuse a test, you are disqualified for a minimum of 12 months.
- » If you are convicted of a DUI, you are disqualified for a minimum of 12 months, even in a non-CMV.
- » If either violation mentioned above was done while hauling hazardous materials, you are disqualified for a minimum of 3 years.
- » If you commit two of the above violations, you are banned (disqualified) from holding a CDL for life.
- » If you are convicted of driving a CMV with any amount of drugs, including cannabis, you will be disqualified for 12 months.
- » If you are found to have any amount of alcohol in your system, you are put out of service for a minimum of 24 hours.

Here is what you need to know for as a CDL holder: Drivers are forbidden to consume or be under the influence of alcohol within 4 hours of going on duty or operating a CMV.

Saying no to drugs

I am talking about prescription, over-the-counter, and illegal drugs. Drugs that are legal for most people to use, may not be legal or right for you to use as a professional driver. Any drug that has you under the influence or makes you drowsy or otherwise makes you unfit to drive is prohibited. Cannabis, though legal in some states, is illegal for a CDL holder to use. If you are sent for a random drug screen and you have been using a CBD product, you will test positive for using a banned substance. Your career is jeopardized.

Assessing Hazardous Materials

You should not skip this section, no matter what you are planning on using your CDL for, even for driving buses. There will likely be a hazardous materials question on the written test. Plus, you need to know a few things about hazmat for any driving job.

TECHNICAL STUFF

Hazardous materials mean any material that has been designated as hazardous under *49 U.S.C. 5103* and is required to be placarded under subpart F of *49 CFR part 172* or any quantity of a material listed as a select agent or toxin in *42 CFR part 73*.

In English, this means that the powers that be have declared that not all hazardous materials need to be defined as hazardous materials for transportation on the road. For the purpose of transportation by any road vehicle, the quantity and class of the material determines if the cargo is classified as hazmat.

For transportation by truck, materials in Figure 6-3 require a placard and an endorsement (they go hand in hand) no matter the amount. With the exception of bulk packaging (a container has a capacity greater than 119 gallons) hazardous materials in the hazard classes listed in Figure 6-4 need placards and an endorsement if the material is 1,001 pounds or more. Never placard a load if you don't have a hazmat endorsement (see Chapter 2), nor should you haul a hazmat load if an endorsement or placards are needed.

Some material that can be shipped by truck without placards have to be treated as hazardous material when it gets shipped by plane or boat.

REMEMBER

For bus drivers: The federal government has a Hazardous Materials Table that shows which materials are hazardous materials. Hazardous materials are to be marked on their packaging with a diamond-shaped label that contains the name and an identification number. There are nine different labels. While you are allowed to transport some specific hazmat, *don't allow any hazardous materials on your bus if you are not sure the rules allow you to do so.*

Placard Any Amount	
IF YOUR VEHICLE CONTAINS ANY AMOUNT OF......	PLACARD AS...
1.1 Mass Explosives	Explosives 1.1
1.2 Project Hazards	Explosives 1.2
1.3 Mass Fire Hazards	Explosives 1.3
2.3 Poisonous/Toxic Gases	Poison Gas
4.3 Dangerous When Wet	Dangerous When Wet
5.2 (Organic Peroxide, Type B, liquid or solid, Temperature controlled)	Organic Peroxide
6.1 (Inhalation hazard zone A & B only)	Poison/toxic inhalation
7 (Radioactive Yellow III label only)	Radioactive

Placard 1,001 Pounds or More	
Category of Material (Hazard class or division number and additional description, as appropriate)	Placard Name
1.4 Minor Explosion	Explosives 1.4
1.5 Very Insensitive	Explosives 1.5
1.6 Extremely Insensitive	Explosives 1.6
2.1 Flammable Gases	Flammable Gas
2.2 Non- Flammable Gases	Non-Flammable Gas.
3 Flammable Liquids	Flammable
Combustible Liquid	Combustible*
4.1 Flammable Solids	Flammable Solid
4.2 Spontaneously Combustible	Spontaneously Combustible
5.1 Oxidizers	Oxidizer
5.2 (other than organic peroxide, Type B, liquid or solid, Temperature Controlled)	Organic Peroxide
6.1 (other than inhalation hazard zone A or B)	Poison
6.2 Infectious Substances	(None)
8 Corrosives	Corrosive
9 Miscellaneous Hazardous Materials	Class 9**
ORM-D	(None)
* FLAMMABLE may be used in place of a COMBUSTIBLE on a cargo tank or portable tank.	
** Class 9 Placard is not required for domestic transportation.	

Buses are allowed to carry small-arms ammunition, emergency shipments of drugs, hospital supplies, and some other material if there is no other way for the shipper to send it. There are a significant amount of restrictions and exceptions in the regulations, but you will not need to know that information for your written test.

Appreciating Roadside Inspections

You are driving your CMV, and you see a sign that says weigh station. Should you pull in? Most likely yes. The rules are different state to state, but generally speaking, any CMV over 10,000 pounds is required to pull in. While the people at the weigh station will most likely just weigh your vehicle, they can have you pull around to the back to inspect your vehicle.

REMEMBER

Don't get nervous unless you are doing something illegal, or you didn't conduct your pre-trip inspection. The officers, usually CMV inspectors due to their special training, are checking to ensure that the largest vehicles on the road are safe to be out on the road.

When an officer has chosen to give you and your vehicle an inspection — yes, they inspect drivers too — stay in your seat with the seat belt on until you are told to do otherwise. Be nice and cooperative but don't get too chatty; you might make yourself look guilty about something.

These inspections can occur on the side of the road as well, which is most likely as a result of something you did to trigger the inspection. Some states have laws that state an officer can only pull you over and perform an inspection when there is a reason, like speeding, driving in the incorrect lane, or any number of minor (or major) infractions!

KEEPING IT CLEAN

Early in my over-the-road career, I was pulled over for an inspection by a CMV officer in North Carolina. The officer said, "I can usually tell if a driver is taking care of the vehicle or not." The officer simply checked my log book and then checked that all my lights were working and sent me on my way with a paper stating there were no violations.

My truck was clean and well-maintained, the chrome was shining, the load of damaged racking that I was hauling was properly secured. (As always, I had performed a pre-tip inspection.)

When the officer looked at my dashboard, there was nothing to see. When my door was open, there was no debris on the floor, just a carpet remnant catching any dirt that came off my boots. The name of my company was straight on the door, along with the proper tags. There was no diesel residue around the fuel cap. Extra grease was not sitting on the catwalk.

Keeping your vehicle clean gives you a good feeling, better than treating yourself to a specialty coffee (which you can do after giving your vehicle a good cleaning). Give yourself a good day, clean your CMV!

Practice Questions

1. At an accident scene, what is not a step you should take?

    (A) Park close to the accident.

    (B) Set reflective triangles out quickly.

    (C) Put on your four-way flashers.

    (D) Call emergency service (911).

2. Name causes of truck fires.

    (A) Spilled fuel in an accident

    (B) Low tire pressure

    (C) Dual tires touching each other

    (D) These are all causes of truck fires

3. What kind of fire is a BC fire extinguisher good for?

    (A) Electrical

    (B) Gasoline

    (C) Gasoline and electrical

    (D) Wood gasoline and electrical

4. Care for the injured:

    (A) Only if no fire is present.

    (B) Whenever it is convenient.

    (C) After you call dispatch.

    (D) When they are cold and no medical personnel are present.

5. If your vehicle is on fire:

    (A) Pull into a truck stop.

    (B) Open the doors to a van trailer if the fire is in it.

    (C) Use a Class A extinguisher on a diesel fire.

    (D) Turn off your engine if it is an engine fire.

6. Prevent fires by:

    (A) Checking tires and wheels during an enroute inspection.

    (B) Inspecting all electrical, fuel, and exhaust systems during your pre-trip inspection.

    (C) Monitor gauges and mirrors for any indications of overheating or smoke.

    (D) These are all ways to help prevent fires.

7. Which of the following are consecutive limits for Hours of Service?

    (A) 11-hour driving limit

    (B) 14-hour limit

    (C) 70-hour limit

    (D) These are all consecutive limits

8. Which of the following is not a part of planning a trip?

   (A) Your lunch menu.

   (B) Remembering Hours of Service.

   (C) Checking your map.

   (D) Reading the load assignments.

9. The sleeper berth duty status:

   (A) Should be used when you are home and on a 34-hour restart.

   (B) Should be used when you are splitting your 10-hour break and want to extend your day.

   (C) Should only be used when you are in the sleeper berth.

   (D) Can be used if your vehicle doesn't have a sleeper berth, but you stay in a hotel.

10. When using a fire extinguisher, which is the best process?

    (A) Aim at the flames but stand as far away as possible.

    (B) Stand upwind and spray at the base of the fire.

    (C) Stand downwind and spray at the base of the fire.

    (D) Get close to the flames and aim at the base of the fire.

11. Use water to put out a:

    (A) Tire fire.

    (B) Electrical fire.

    (C) Diesel fuel fire.

    (D) Use water for all these fires.

12. Drivers who have been drinking alcohol:

    (A) Must exercise greater care when driving.

    (B) Must drive slower than they usually do.

    (C) Have diminished judgment and self-control.

    (D) Have smoother starts.

13. Drugs that are okay for drivers to use while driving are:

    (A) Cannabis.

    (B) Controlled substances.

    (C) Cold medicines.

    (D) Drugs prescribed by a doctor ensuring they will not affect safe driving.

Answers and Explanations

1. **A.** You should set out your reflective triangles, put on your flashers, and call emergency service; but you should get your vehicle out of the way!

2. **D.** All these items can cause fires.

3. **C.** A BC fire extinguisher is good for B-type fires (gasoline) and for C-type fires (electrical).

4. **D.** If a fire is present, you need to get the injured away from it. Dispatch can wait until the injured are being taken care of by medical personnel.

5. **D.** Get away from petroleum products. Don't open the doors on a van as this will just give a fire its desired oxygen and a Class A fire extinguisher is good for wood and paper, so that leaves choice D as the best answer.

6. **D.** All these are ways to prevent fires.

7. **B.** The 14-hour limit is a consecutive limit, but the 11-hour limit and the 70-hour limit are cumulative limits.

8. **A.** What food you are going to eat is something you should plan, but it wouldn't be part of planning your trip. Do plan for when you should eat though.

9. **C.** You can only use the sleeper berth duty status if you have a sleeper berth in your cab and only when you are in it. You can't use the sleeper berth duty status when you're not in your sleeper berth.

10. **B.** You should stand upwind, letting the spray be carried by the wind as well as the smoke and flames away from you.

11. **A.** Tires need lots of water to get them cooled down. Never use water on electricity, you can get electrocuted. Water will just spread diesel.

12. **C.** Drivers who have been drinking *should not* be driving, and they also have less control of their faculties.

13. **D.** Cannabis is illegal for a driver, controlled substances are illegal for everyone, and cold medicines make people sleepy so choice D is the best answer.

IN THIS CHAPTER

» **Taking a look at the cargo**

» **Considering how weight affects securing cargo**

» **Understanding what securement devices can do**

» **Placing your cargo**

» **Satisfying the regulations**

Chapter **7**

Loading and Securing Your Cargo

There doesn't seem to be too many jobs where you have a greater responsibility than when you are a commercial driver. Driving safely and defensively are obvious responsibilities. Inspecting your vehicle is a constant task requiring responsible habits. In this chapter, I address another of your responsibilities as a commercial driver — loading and securing your cargo.

The Federal Motor Carrier Safety Administration (FMCSA) has rules for the proper securement of cargo. The rules are the minimum requirements for general freight, but there are additional rules for specific types of cargo, like steel coils and concrete pipes. In addition to these requirements, special vehicle types have their own regulations, including tankers and buses, which have their own chapters in this book.

Be forewarned: The word *minimum* implies that there is likely more that can or even should be done. That is especially true for securing cargo. For example, your cargo may require more than the minimum for it to be safely secured. If you like to use shortcuts, stop! This is an area where shortcuts will cut short someone's life, and it might be yours! A good commercial driver will not only drive safely down the road, but they will also ensure that what they are hauling stays safe, intact, and away from the rest of the motoring public.

Performing Your Inspections

What? Another pre-trip inspection? Well yes, but this one is a little different. This one includes you checking on all your *cargo securement devices*.

All your devices should be in good shape and not out of service. Devices wear out and must be replaced. Don't ever use a device that is by its condition, out of service as it is against the regulations to do so. Throw it away! Figure 7-1 shows how to determine if a strap is deemed out-of-service.

Web Strap Defect (Out-of-Service)

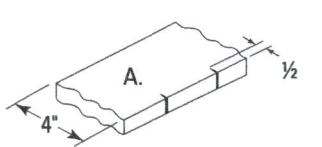

A. Cuts on the same side are not added together.

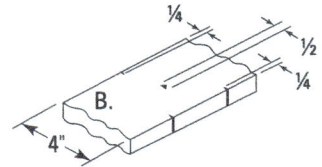

B. Cuts across the width of a strap are added together.

FIGURE 7-1:
The criteria
for straps
that are out
of service.

Web strap size	Defective at—
4"	Larger than 3/4"
3"	Larger than 5/8"
2"	Larger than 3/8"

You should have a list of cargo securement supplies from your company of what you should stock in your truck. Note that you cannot plan for every commodity as you have only so much room in your storage compartments.

When you arrive at a shipper, check to see what they are loading in or on your truck. You will decide where to place the cargo in order to secure it and be legal on your weights. (More on weights in the next section.)

When you are given a loaded vehicle, you are responsible for checking the following:

>> Inspect the cargo.

>> Ensure your cargo is secured properly and that your view to the sides and rear are not obstructed.

>> Have access to your emergency equipment.

>> Examine the load for overweight or oversized loading.

>> Look for poorly balanced loading.

>> Perform official inspections:

- When picking up or just after the cargo has been loaded.

- Within the first 50 miles.

- Every 150 miles or 3 hours, whichever comes first.

- At every duty status change.

Knowing Your Weights

In order to make good decisions about the cargo you're carrying, you need to know various weight limitations. Both the states and federal government have weight limits on trucks for driving on US highways and interstates.

Here are various weights to verify and to remember for your written test:

- **Axle.** This is the weight allowed on just one axle. Some states will have a different limit for the steer axle than other axles.
- **Tandem.** A tandem is two axles together, probably less than 10 feet apart. Together they have a weight allowance of 34,000 pounds.
- **Spread tandem.** The distance that two axles are apart changes the weight they are legally allowed to carry. Commonly a 10-foot spread (at least 10 feet from center of axle to center of the next axle) has a 40,000-pound limit.
- **Gross.** The maximum weight allowed for your whole vehicle including cargo. The most common gross for any vehicle is 80,000 pounds. This would require at least five axles.

Here are a few definitions and abbreviations you need to know:

- **Gross vehicle weight (GVW).** The *total weight* of the vehicle and the cargo.
- **Gross vehicle weight rating (GVWR).** The *maximum weight of a single vehicle* including the cargo as determined by the vehicle's manufacturer.
- **Gross vehicle weight rating (GCW).** The *total weight of a combination vehicle* — towing (powered) vehicle, plus the towed/connected vehicle, plus the cargo.
- **Gross combination weight rating (GCWR).** The *maximum weight of a combination vehicle* — towing (powered) vehicle, plus the towed/connected vehicle, plus the cargo as determined by the vehicle's manufacturer.

TIP

Commercial vehicle manufacturers have maximum limits for their axles, suspensions, tires, the coupling system (the components of the vehicles that are hooked together when in combination), and the whole vehicle. The limits are usually on a decal or plate, inside the door on a truck or semi-tractor, on the side of a tire, and on the frame or on the front of the trailer. These limits are legally binding; you also find the legal weight limits in Rand McNally's *Motor Carriers' Atlas*. (See Chapter 6 for more information about the atlas.)

TECHNICAL
STUFF

There is a federal bridge formula used to determine the maximum allowable weight of a vehicle and each axle of a vehicle, which is based on distances between axles and the number of axles. The formula is: W = 500 * (LN/N-1 + 12N + 36) where:

- W = the maximum weight in pounds that can be carried on a group of two or more consecutive axles (to the nearest 500 pounds).
- L = the distance in feet between the outer axles of any group of axles.
- N = the number of axles in the group.

There are two reasons why you don't need to memorize this formula:

1. The actual formula will not be on the written test, but you might need to know what the formula does.

2. There is a chart located in *Motor Carriers Atlas* (and in federal publications) that has all the computations listed.

Understanding Your Limits

You can only do so much work, you have your limits. Maybe you can push yourself to do one more repetition on the weight machine or one more lap on the track. When you are determining how to secure your cargo, you also have to determine what the limits are of your devices that will hold the cargo in place.

Let's discuss some terms first.

>> The devices that secure the cargo are *tie downs*.

>> The locations where they attach are called tie down *attachment points*.

>> The limits that the tie downs have are called *working load limits (WLL)*.

>> When you combine the WLL of two or more devices, you are now talking about the *aggregate working load limit* or the *aggregate WLL*.

Determining your cargo securement devices limits

Examine the device to see if it is marked with its WLL (see Figure 7-2).

>> If the device is not marked, you can refer to the manufacturer's table of working load limits for the type of tie down you are using. I recommend throwing away web strapping (a very common tie down device) when it is no longer marked with its WLL. It is probably worn out.

>> Attachment points don't have to be rated, but some manufacturers do rate the attachment points on their equipment — flatbeds, for example.

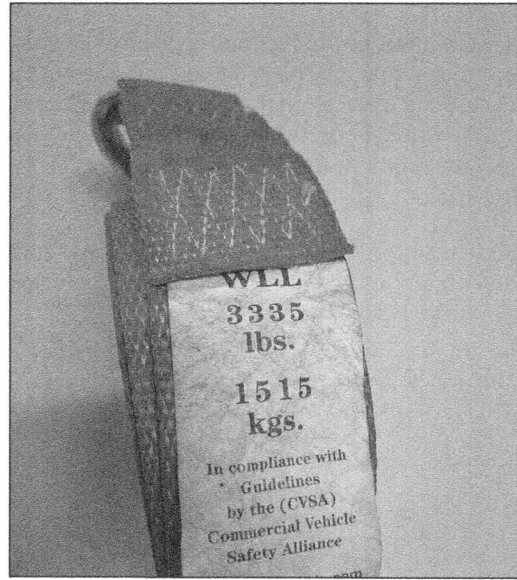

FIGURE 7-2: A marked strap.

Chains that are marked might have a G and a number designating their grade as shown in Figure 7-3. (Note in the photo that one of the links is marked, not just the hook.)

You have to know the diameter of the links to determine the WLL. Once you know both, you can use that information to determine your chain's WLL. The National Association of Chain Manufacturers (NACM) Welded Steel Chain Specifications developed this information, which is used by chain manufacturers, the FMCSA, and the Commercial Vehicle Safety Alliance (CVSA). A partial listing of an NACM table is shown below.

Chain size (inches)	Grade 30	Grade 43	Grade 70
1/4	1,300	2,600	3,150
5/16	1,900	3,900	4,700
3/8	2,650	5,400	6,600
7/16	3,700	7,200	8,750
1/2	4,500	9,200	11,300

FIGURE 7-3: A marked chain.

Attaching makes a difference

REMEMBER

You can attach a tie down directly to your cargo. This is called a *direct tie down.* Direct tie downs pull on the cargo in one direction, which means it needs to be countered with a tie down pulling the other direction. A direct tie down is thus considered to be doing half of what it needs to be doing. The direct tie down method cuts in half the WLL of your securement device. Figure 7-4 is an example of a direct tie down.

You can attach a tie down to the truck or trailer on one side of your cargo and have it go over the cargo, and attach it to the truck or trailer on the other side. This is called an *indirect tie down.* An indirect tie down is pulling your cargo down in two directions, thus working at its full potential. An indirect tie down is rated at its full WLL. Figure 7-5 is an example of an indirect tie down.

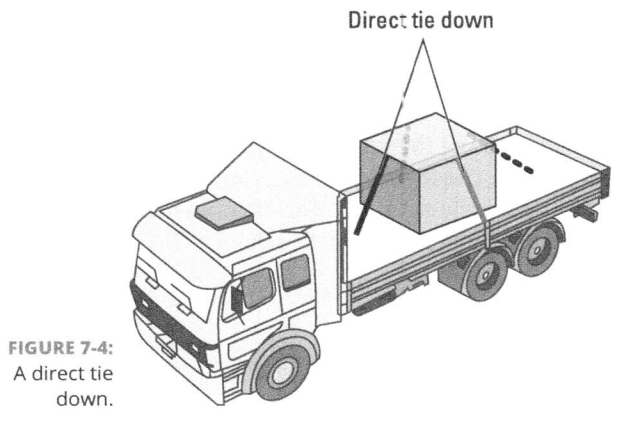

Direct tie down

FIGURE 7-4:
A direct tie
down.

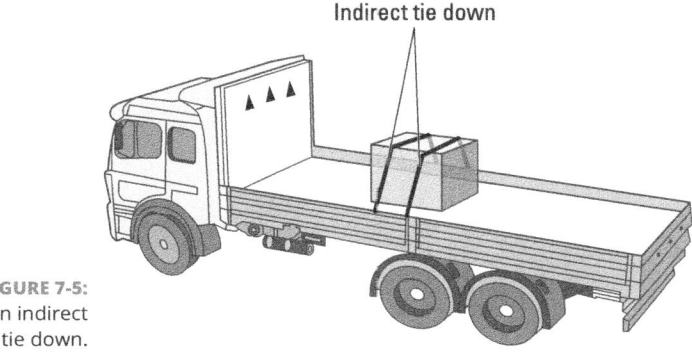

Indirect tie down

FIGURE 7-5:
An indirect
tie down.

Figuring Out the Minimums

REMEMBER

You must use enough tie down devices to satisfy the minimum requirements published by the FMCSA, but you might need more than what the regulations state. Each type of load can create different challenges.

You must prevent your cargo from moving in order to keep the cargo from becoming damaged; this is in addition to keeping yourself and everyone around your vehicle safe. Stopping forward momentum is the first and most important aspect of load securement. I have heard shippers say, "It weighs 20,000 pounds. It's not going anywhere." I am guessing that they were daydreaming when Newton's laws of motion were introduced back in grade school science class. In case you were daydreaming that day as well, the law goes something like this, "An object in motion tends to stay in motion until acted upon by another force." Cargo must be restrained, be deprived of the possibility of movement, especially forward movement.

If you don't restrict the potential for movement of cargo, you risk damaging it when a car pulls out in front of you and you must slam on your brakes. Any cargo that has the ability to move will move forward as it was moving at the same speed as the vehicle it is in. As much as is feasible, cargo securement needs to be looked at as making the cargo an attached part of the vehicle.

When determining the amount of securement devices you need, there are some criteria you must consider.

By g-force (weight)

I knew a driver who once picked up a load of forklifts. One forklift had a tall mast that was so tall that it had to be laid down in the semi-trailer. (A unique thing about forklift masts: for them to extend up, hydraulics must be used, but gravity returns it to the lowered position.) The driver had to stop fast. The mast was in a position that gravity would let it move forward, which it did — through the front of the trailer and into the cab of the truck! The driver and the driver's spouse were not physically hurt. After that incident, the shipper started placing the masts in the trailers in the opposite direction and blocking them. This is an example of g-force on an object.

Here are the forces that cargo securement systems must withstand:

>> 0.8 g *deceleration* (or braking) in the forward direction

>> 0.5 g in the rearward (or backward) direction

>> 0.5 g in a lateral direction

REMEMBER

In other words, you must have enough cargo securement devices to have an aggregate WLL of 80 percent of your cargo's weight to prevent forward momentum. *Structures in your truck or trailer will help out with this requirement.*

For the side movement, you need cargo securement devices with an aggregate WLL of at least 50 percent of your cargo's weight. It's the same requirement to stop rearward movement — 50 percent.

The regulations use the term g-force, but you might find it's easier to think in terms of weight and percentages. For example, to stop the lateral movement of a 10,000-pound crate, you need cargo securement devices that have a minimum aggregate WLL of 5,000 pounds (50 percent or 0.5 g).

To summarize, you can usually take 50 percent of your cargo's weight and ensure that you have an aggregate working load limit of that amount or greater.

By length

Once you have determined how many devices you need based on the weight, you have to figure out how many devices you need based on the length of the cargo.

Use the following rules for cargo *without anything* preventing its forward momentum:

>> If the item is less than 5 feet and weighs less than 1,100 pounds, one device is the minimum.

>> If the item is less than 5 feet but it weighs more than 1,100 pounds, two devices are the minimum.

>> If the item is longer than 5 feet, no matter how much it weighs, the minimum is two devices.

>> If the item is longer than 10 feet, add a device for every 10 feet or part of 10 feet.

For example, you have a 35-foot-long pipe. You must have two tie downs for the first 10 feet, one tie down for each successive 10 feet (two more) and one for the remaining 5 feet for a total of five tie downs (minimum). (see Figure 7-6).

FIGURE 7-6:
A 35-foot
piece of
cargo
secured but
doesn't have
its forward
momentum
blocked.

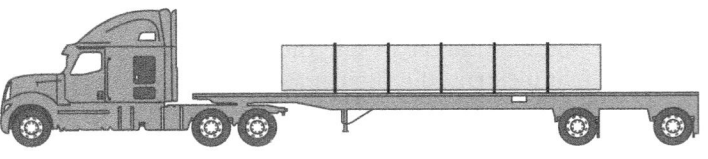

For cargo that *is prevented from* forward momentum:

> ▶▶ The regulation is one tie down for every 10 feet or part of 10 feet.

This minimum is when the potential for forward movement is prevented by a header board, bulk-head, other cargo (see Figure 7-7), or specially placed tie downs. In the illustration, notice the change in the number of straps on the piece of cargo (B) in the previous figure.

FIGURE 7-7:
A 35-feet
piece of
cargo
secured with
its forward
momentum
blocked by
other cargo.

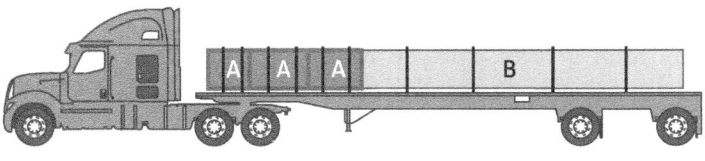

The front ends of box or van trailers, and bulkheads on flatbed trucks are often used for prevent-ing the forward movement of cargo. Bulkheads, *headache racks* (metal structure separating a cab to protect the driver from forward shifting cargo, often doubling as a storage rack) and header boards must be in good condition. They should be rated sufficiently for the load you are hauling.

When you allow any cargo a chance to move forward (because it's not adequately secured), you have given it potential energy. Take away that potential energy.

WARNING

Do not haul steel coils unless you have been trained! There are special securement regulations for safely hauling coils that must be adhered to for the safety of the driver and anyone around the driver. Coils can weigh up to 50,000 pounds and since they are round, have enormous potential energy.

Exploring Cargo Securement Devices

Okay, you probably don't buy your own cargo securement devices if you are working for a com-pany, but you might have some input on their purchases, for your personal preferences. Never-theless, I want you to have some knowledge about a few cargo securement devices. I will be surprised if this information is on the written exam, but you should know how each of the fol-lowing devices work to secure cargo.

Stopping rearward movement with load bars

If you are driving a box trailer or truck, the most common securement that you will be using contains the cargo on the backside (stopping that rearward movement), keeping it from traveling rearward. Cargo that is stacked is especially vulnerable to falling backwards. Regulations state that if the cargo is all the way back to the door, you are not required to put restraints behind the cargo because the cargo can be covering the attachment points. The doors will be the securement for the rearward motion. But if you can, put a securement device behind your cargo. In case the load does move, it won't be against the door, thus preventing you from opening it safely.

There are two different types of load bars: one presses against the side walls of the trailer and the other hooks into special posts or tracks in the wall (see Figure 7-8). The load bars that press against the sides are prone to fall to the floor as you drive because the sides of commercial vehicles will flex.

FIGURE 7-8: The top load bar presses against the walls; the bottom bar hooks into a track on each side.

Straps are also used to stop the rearward movement in a box vehicle. These straps have more versatility as they can "bend" around cargo. They can attach to the side of the box, forward from the rear of the cargo, pulling the cargo towards the front. Edge protection might be needed to protect the cargo from the strap or the strap from the cargo. (See the section, "Loading the Cargo," for more on edge protectors.)

Chaining and binding the cargo

Chains are the main securement used for many steel products, vehicles, and other heavy items. A device must be used to tighten the chain. Most of the devices used are called *binders;* the most common are *snap binders* and *ratchet binders.* Binders that are operated with a drill are more expensive but allow a person with less strength to properly secure a load with chains.

When tightening a chain with a snap binder, you must be careful. First, pull down, utilizing your weight and presenting less potential for injury. Use a bar that has a safety end on it. That end allows the "connection" of the binder and bar to hinge, instead of sending the bar flying. Ratchet binders don't have this issue, but they take more time. Ensure that chains are not twisted when you are tightening them. If you tighten them when they have a twist, the binder can be forced/twisted into a position that is difficult or dangerous when releasing the ratchet or snap binder.

Strapping down the load

Straps are popular cargo securement devices. They are lighter than chains and will do less damage to cargo. Straps come in a variety of connections, including a flat hook, wire hook, and chain with hook. There are straps that have no special connections on either end but are designed to be tightened and wound onto reels (on both ends) that are mounted on the trailer or truck. They can also be tightened using a portable ratchet.

Here are a few rules you should adopt for using straps. The first three are FMCSA regulations.

>> Don't place more than one-half twist in a strap.

>> Don't tie a knot in a strap.

>> Don't use an out-of-service strap.

>> Strive to attach the strap at a 90-degree angle whenever possible.

>> Keep your straps tight.

>> Know that getting a strap extremely tight does not make it stronger or more effective, just more easily cut.

>> Avoid attaching a strap to a *rub rail*, which is rail on the side of a flatbed to protect the strap and other securement devices.

Blocking and bracing the load

Blocking and *bracing* cargo is the process of positioning wood, usually 2x4s, to stop the movement of cargo. The wood is typically nailed to the floor and against the cargo. The more nails that are used, the stronger the block is.

The wood floor in box trucks and box trailers, and the wood nailing strips in flatbeds are a durable, dense, strong wood — stronger than the wood that you would use for blocking. The wood boards assembled in the floor of flatbeds are for the purpose of nailing blocks to help stop movement of cargo. Framing hammers or powered nailers work best for getting nails into the wood. And for the same reason, you will need a substantial prybar to remove the nails.

Bracing cargo takes blocking to an extreme. A more elaborate system of 2x4s are used to not only block the bottom of the cargo but to prevent the cargo from tipping over the block (See Figure 7-9). A strap should be added to complete this securement.

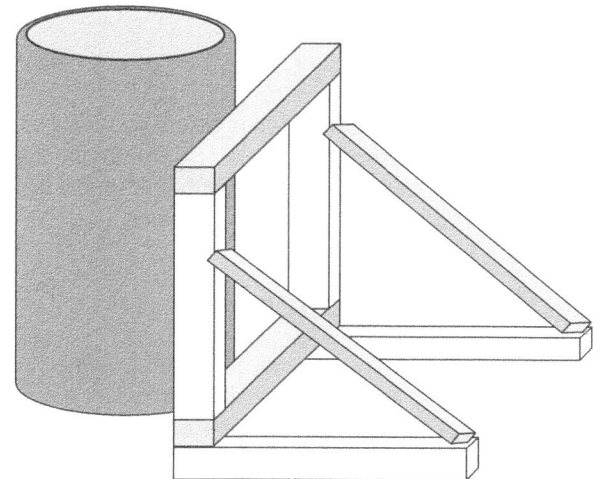

FIGURE 7-9:
A drum held
in place by
bracing.

Examining the Bill of Lading

When you arrive at the shipper or even your own company, find out what you will be hauling. Ask to see the shipping papers or *bill of lading* (a contract between a shipper and the carrier). Besides confirming the destination(s) you were told, you will begin devising a plan for where and how to place the cargo. You will need to consider the weight restrictions of your vehicle, the legal restrictions, and the requirements of the *commodity* (the type of cargo you're carrying). Some of your decision-making will be based on which customer is to be unloaded first. Each stop you have you will need to resecure the remaining cargo.

Here are a few items to check on a bill of lading when you are considering how to secure your cargo:

>> **Commodity.** Examine the bill of lading for the commodity or product being shipped. Are there special rules for securing the cargo you are picking up, or will the general rules of cargo securement suffice? There are commodities that have specific securement requirements, such as boulders, logs, concrete pipes, intermodal containers (shipping containers that are designed to be used in ships, on trains, and on special chassis), metal coils, tiered building materials, paper rolls, light vehicles as well as heavy and crushed vehicles.

>> **Hazmat.** Check the shipping papers for hazardous materials, especially if you do not have an endorsement to haul hazmat. If you have that endorsement, you will need to follow the placard guidelines and ensure that the hazardous material is loaded and secured correctly. (See Chapters 6 and 16 for more information on hazmat requirements.)

>> **Weight.** Determine your load weight and ask yourself how it can be placed in or on your truck. In a box trailer, you will typically place it in the nose (location farthest away from the doors that are in the back) of the trailer or van. However, you can't place it all in the nose as you have weight considerations (legal axle weights).

>> **Adequate cargo securement devices.** The weight and size of your cargo, and the type of vehicle you have, are all considerations in determining whether you have an adequate type and number of securement devices. Heavy machinery is generally set up to utilize chains. Building materials generally need straps. Several individual pallets on a flatbed will require several straps. But if the same load is placed in a box trailer, you might only need a couple straps behind the cargo.

Loading the Cargo

Since you are responsible for the load and the securement of your cargo, you need to be as active as much as the shipper will allow. If you have a flatbed truck, you will usually be able to be very active in the loading process, whereas when you have a box trailer, you don't have nearly as much opportunity as many shippers will force you to stay off the loading dock.

Placing the cargo within the space

When you have a tank or a hopper bottom trailer, your liquid or granular cargo can generally move around and not be able to be contained by straps and chains. (A *hopper bottom trailer* has gates or doors at the bottom of the hopper that open, and the cargo flows out into a pit for transferring to a storage location.) When you have a flatbed truck or a box truck or trailer to load, you have some planning to do.

Gapping

When you leave a gap between pieces of cargo, you create potential for cargo to move while you are driving. This is important when you have a box trailer or truck, or if you have a flatbed trailer or truck.

If you have a flatbed truck with a gap from side to side (see Figure 7-10), after securing the cargo and driving down the road, the force from the tie downs pressing in on the sides will cause the cargo to move towards each other. This will cause the tie downs to loosen. The tie downs then have a possibility of becoming detached and becoming a road hazard. When the gap is front to back, there is an increased potential for forward movement, giving you a chance to test Newton's first law of motion.

Gap-looking at the cargo from the rear.

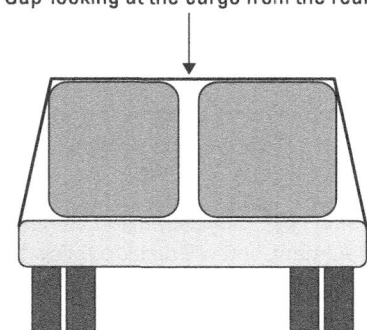

FIGURE 7-10: A gap was left in the loading process, creating potential for the freight to move, causing straps to get loose.

I need to note that some cargo isn't supposed to touch. When you have that scenario, you will need to add extra securement or *dunnage* (material used to fill space and prevent movement) between the pieces of cargo that are allowed to touch the cargo.

For a flatbed, if you aren't the one loading, communicate with the loader as you stand at the end of the bed, because the loader is seeing what they are doing from just their viewpoint while you can stand (out of the way) at 90 degrees to where they are and inform them of when the cargo is in contact with the next piece.

In a box truck or trailer, you generally place your cargo all the way to the nose with the pieces of cargo touching each other, front to back. If you have cargo that is to be spread out, then you will need to place extra tie downs in front of your cargo, or you will need to have blocking and bracing holding the cargo in place.

Another alternative is to creatively place the cargo in a pattern that spreads the weight but -keeps the pieces of cargo intact with each other, Figure 7-11 compares how two trucks are loaded differently.

The drive axles are overloaded in truck 1. In truck 2, the weight has been spread out more evenly between the drive axles and the tandem axles (axles of the trailer) to avoid being overloaded.

FIGURE 7-11: Two trucks loaded with the same amount of cargo. The second truck has the weight spread out more evenly.

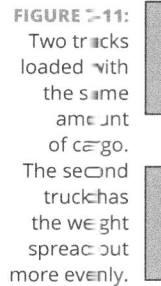 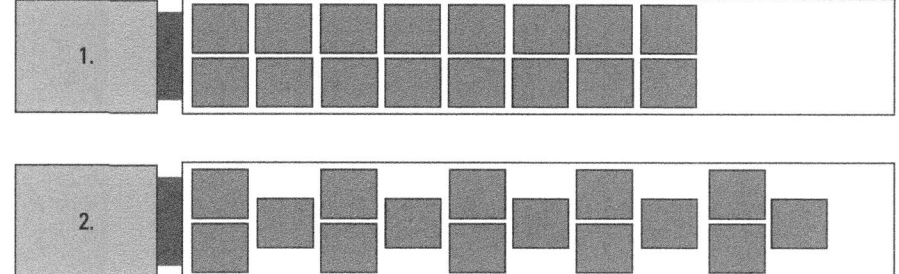

When there are gaps from side to side in a box truck or trailer, there is potential for your cargo to shift, especially if it is stacked. A shift in the cargo can result in a fall or cause damage to the cargo by awkwardly coming in contact with other cargo. Additionally, you can have a problem when unloading the cargo. When pallets are no longer level or if the product is sitting precariously, there is potential for the cargo to be damaged. If the consignee is supposed to unload the shipment, they might refuse due to the unsafe, unlevel pallets.

Sticking over the edge

If your flatbed is already at the maximum legal width, you cannot load cargo nor allow someone to load cargo on your truck bed with any of the cargo sticking out over the edge, unless that is how wide the piece of cargo is. Then of course, you will need to procure a permit to haul a load that is oversized (See the section, "Specializing your hauling," for more information about oversized loads.)

Considering the type of vehicle

Although cargo can be placed anywhere in the trailer, you need to remember some guidelines based on the type of commercial vehicle. For a flatbed truck, keep the cargo low and towards the middle (remember this for the written test). However, that setup is challenging for a box or van trailer. In a box trailer, you are limited in how and where to place cargo. When you place items in the middle of a box van trailer, it's your responsibility to prevent the cargo from moving sideways, forward, and rearward.

Using tie downs

When you are examining your cargo, you are thinking about the best type of tie downs for your cargo and where to place them. Generally speaking, you spread your tiedowns evenly. However, when the integrity of the cargo you are securing can be compromised, you will need to place the tie downs where they will not do harm to the cargo. You also need to protect the cargo from the tie down device for cosmetic reasons, and you need to protect your devices from the cargo by using edge protection. (See Figure 7-12 for an example of an edge projector.)

FIGURE 7-12:
The orange
piece
between the
strap and
the cargo
is an edge
protector.

Squeezing out the cargo

One day you secured your load, for example a stack of steel frames with more straps than the minimum requirement. But, as you drive down the road, they start moving. So you stop to tighten the straps, but the frames just seem to move from side to side even more. What is going on?

There is a dynamic to hauling stacked (tiered) cargo that demands that you secure it a little differently. When you have a stack of a commodity, in tiers, and you secure the stack according to the minimum requirements for general cargo, the bottom tier is held securely against the bed of your vehicle. Your straps are squeezing down on the load. In the previous example and in Figure 7-13, the middle frames are waiting for the opportunity to shift because there is no resistance to the sides. So when you hit a bump or drive around a curve, an action occurs against the frames in a direction that encourages them to move away from the force of the securement. Figure 7-13 shows the cargo and one direction that it is inclined to move.

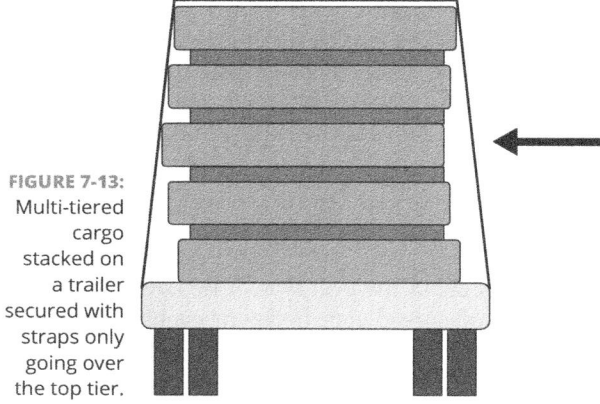

FIGURE 7-13:
Multi-tiered
cargo
stacked on
a trailer
secured with
straps only
going over
the top tier.

You need to take away the side-to-side potential that is caused by the straps that are only going over the top piece. This is done by putting straps over the other layers, not just on the top layer. (See Figure 7-14 for an example.)

FIGURE 7-14: Tiers of cargo secured to avoid the side shift.

The regulations offer options on how to secure building materials and related material (or I'd say anything with tiers). In my experience, the effective option is to put straps over each layer except the bottom one.

Sealing the load

If you drive a box truck or pull a box trailer, you might be asked to *seal a load*, or the shipper might place a seal on its doors. Either way, a seal will be placed on the latch of the door. The seal is made in such a way that it can be used one time only. Each seal is unique, having a sequential number. It must be cut to be removed. The number will be recorded on the paperwork that is signed by the shipper and the driver. The consignee who receives the load, verifies that the number on the paperwork matches the number on the seal and that the seal has not be cut. Then it can be removed. Obviously, this does not stop theft, but it identifies whether there was a possibility of the door being opened. Some food or food-related loads will be rejected if the seal has been broken. I encourage you to use a high security padlock in addition to putting a seal on it, it is worth the investment by the company you work for.

Covering the cargo

Covering the cargo is easy when you have a box truck or trailer. Flatbed trucks are not so easy unless you have a *covered wagon*. These are flatbeds with removable sides and a specially designed tarp that makes covering cargo simpler to do. There are also flatbeds that have curtain sides or sides and tops that move like an accordion to the front or back.

For the written test, you need to know that there are two basic reasons for covering cargo:

>> The cargo needs protection from the weather.

>> People need protection from falling cargo.

WARNING

Some states have laws that require certain cargo to be covered. Open-top vehicles like dump trucks and refuse haulers may need a cover to keep loose debris from falling off. Similarly, a flatbed hauling bricks might need a cover to prevent loose bricks from escaping.

Using a tarp to cover the cargo is an artform to many drivers. Take time to learn from other drivers who take pride in tarping their loads. Watch their techniques and tricks. It is similar to wrapping a present. While I am not going to teach you how to tarp in this book, I will give two tips:

>> Have a forklift place the tarp on the cargo or have the tarp on the cargo as the forklift is placing it on the flatbed.

>> If it is going to take more than one tarp to cover the load, work from the back to the front. This will help to keep the wind from taking the tarp off the cargo.

Remember to check on the coverings, or tarps, periodically by checking your mirrors. Coverings that are getting moved a lot by the wind have a good chance of tearing and becoming a hazard.

Specializing your hauling

You need to give special attention to some unique cargo:

>> **Livestock.** Livestock can move around if they are given enough space. Even when they don't have space, they can lean into your turns, moving your vehicle's center of gravity towards the outside radius of your curves and turns. This creates more potential for a rollover. Utilize the adjustable panels and compartments to keep the livestock safe and still.

>> **Oversized loads.** Any load that cannot fit legally with the confines of a flat bed or is over any weight limits, requires a permit in order to be out on the road. There can be a variety of requirements that a driver must abide by. Special equipment like flags, banners and flashing lights can be required. Some larger loads require a licensed escort, and some require police escort. There might be specific routes to take and only certain times of the day to run as well. If a load can be divided into two or more loads and hauled within the legal weight, length, and width, then it is not allowed to be hauled as an oversized load. This means that you cannot haul ten pieces of cargo that puts your vehicle over the weight limit when eight of those pieces would have your vehicle under the weight limit.

>> **Hanging meat.** Meat can be hung in a refrigerated van, making the center of gravity very high. As you turn, that center of gravity (the meat) will swing towards the outside of the turn, moving your center of gravity towards that side.

>> **Dry bulk containers.** Besides requiring special training to load and unload these trailers, they require special driving attention as their center of gravity is high. There is a possibility of load shift as well. Be sure to drive slowly around curves, turns, and ramps.

Practice Questions

1. If you have cargo that is 33 feet long and is not kept from having forward momentum, what is the minimum number of tie downs with a WLL of 5,000 pounds each?

    (A) 3

    (B) 4

    (C) 5

    (D) 6

2. You have a 45,000-pound load to secure. What is the minimum number of tie downs rated at 4,000 pounds WLL each are needed to secure the load?

    (A) 4

    (B) 5

    (C) 6

    (D) 7

3. You are picking up a piece of construction equipment (a backhoe), which has a loader attachment on the front and a backhoe attachment on the rear. It weighs 24,000 pounds and has attachment points near the four wheels. How many tie downs, at 5,000 pounds WLL each does this piece of equipment require, at a minimum?

    (A) 4

    (B) 5

    (C) 6

    (D) 7

4. Which of the following is not a way to stop forward momentum?

    (A) Blocking

    (B) Friction mats

    (C) Temporary bulkhead

    (D) Dunnage filler

5. When is a 4-inch strap out of service?

    (A) When it has a ¼ inch cut on one side.

    (B) When it has two cuts on opposite side of ¼ inch each.

    (C) When it has a cut in the middle of an inch.

    (D) These are all out-of-service scenarios.

6. Which is the best answer? Federal regulations require you to inspect your cargo and/or securement:

    (A) The beginning and end of the day.

    (B) Every two hours.

    (C) Beginning of your trip, within 50 miles of the start of the trip, and every 3 hours or 150 miles.

    (D) The shipper is responsible for cargo securement.

7. Working load limit refers to:

(A) The gross weight rating of the vehicle.

(B) The maximum weight a device is rated for.

(C) The net weight your vehicle can legally hold.

(D) The maximum stress your cargo can have placed on it.

8. You find a cargo strap that has an inch-long cut half way to the end of it:

(A) You can use it as long as you have enough good straps to hold your cargo.

(B) You can tie a knot at the cut to continue using it.

(C) Throw it away.

(D) Repair it by cutting out the cut area and resewing it.

9. For a 43,000-pound load, using cargo securement straps rated at 5,400 pounds WLL, the minimum of securement devices are:

(A) Four straps.

(B) Five straps.

(C) Six straps.

(D) Seven straps.

10. What is the best reason to be concerned about cargo securement?

(A) It can cost the company money if the cargo gets damaged.

(B) The inside of a trailer can get damaged if cargo is not secured.

(C) I, the driver, am responsible for the securement.

(D) Safety of everyone around me.

11. What is not a consideration for securing a large heavy piece of cargo?

(A) The length of the cargo

(B) The distance to the receiver

(C) The weight of the cargo

(D) How to attach tie downs to the cargo

12. What is the best advice to secure multiple tiers of cargo?

(A) Strap down each layer.

(B) Place a tarp on the cargo.

(C) Place the same quantity of straps over the top of the cargo as you have tiers.

(D) Strap each tier to the tier above it.

13. To determine the WLL of a chain:

(A) You must know the weight of the cargo.

(B) You must know the diameter and grade of the chain.

(C) You must know the length and grade of the chain.

(D) You must know the length and diameter of the chain.

14. What is the difference between the Gross Vehicle Weight Rating and the Gross Combination Weight Rating?

    (A) The Gross Vehicle Weight Rating is the manufacturer's cargo limit, rating on a single vehicle whereas the Gross Combination Weight Rating is the manufacturer's limit/rating for the cargo on a combination of vehicles.

    (B) The Gross Vehicle Weight Rating is the maximum legal weight allowed on a road while the Gross Combination Weight Rating is the maximum legal weight allowed by a combination of vehicles.

    (C) The Gross Vehicle Weight Rating is the manufacturer's limit/rating including the load, on a single vehicle whereas the Gross Combination Weight Rating is the manufacturer's limit/rating on a combination of vehicles (truck/semi-tractor and trailer) including the load.

    (D) The Gross Vehicle Weight Rating is the maximum weight for a vehicle without a load while the Gross Combination Weight Rating is the maximum weight, including the load for a vehicle.

Answers and Explanations

1. **C.** The weight is unknown, but the cargo has nothing to stop its forward momentum. So, in this example, two straps should be used for the first 10 feet plus one for every 10 feet or part thereof, making the answer 5 straps.

2. **C.** Divide 45,000 in half to obtain 50 percent of your weight. Now take your answer of 22,500 and divide it by 4,000 and round your answer up to a whole number.

3. **C.** This is a trick question that won't be on your written test but will get you thinking about weights and tie downs. This piece of equipment requires the tie downs to be attached directly to the equipment, so that means cutting the tie down rating in half. Divide 24,000 by two to find the 50 percent that is required for the minimum tie downs based on weight alone. You can only use half of your tie downs' rating so that takes down your figure to 2,500 pounds WLL. Dividing 12,000 by 2,500 and rounding up gets us five tiedowns needed. So why did I say six tie downs were required? There is a regulation that states all four corners of heavy equipment must be attached and that any attachments must be secured as well. So that is how we have six as the minimum number of tie downs to secure the backhoe. By the way, always separate steel and aluminum. Place dunnage between the backhoe attachments and the bottom of your flatbed.

4. **D.** Dunnage filler just fills gaps. Everything else can stop forward momentum.

5. **C.** According to the illustration of out-of-service straps, to be declared out of service, the cut or addition of cuts must be over ¾ inch across the width on a 4-inch strap.

6. **C.** The regulations rightly assume that tie downs can loosen and thus need to be checked often.

7. **B.** Working load limit is the rating for the maximum load a device is designed to handle.

8. **C.** You can't repair a strap, tie it into knots, or even use a damaged one that you think is simply an extra tie down.

9. **A.** Four straps meet the minimum regulations, but any good driver will use more.

10. **D.** Being concerned about others and your own health and well-being is paramount.

11. **B.** The distance that you must drive makes no difference for securing a load properly.

12. **A.** Strapping every tier is the best way to keep this type of load from shifting around. Tarps are no guarantee to keep anything in place or to even keep something big on the bed. Cargo is to be strapped to the bed not to each other and putting more straps across the top may result in the various tiers wanting to shift.

13. **B.** The diameter and the grade of the chain are the criteria used for determining the WLL.

14. **C.** Gross vehicle weight ratings include the load — everything — the meaning of gross.

3

Exploring Air Brakes

IN THIS PART . . .

Understanding and knowing all about air brakes is vital when using an air brake vehicle. Name the parts of air brakes and explain how the air system functions.

Inspect and test brakes to ensure a safe trip, to provide peace of mind, and satisfy regulations.

Chapter **8**

Discovering How to Work with Air Brakes

F red Flintstone used the friction of his feet to stop his prehistoric car. The driver of covered wagons pushed on a pedal or operated a rod to apply friction against a wheel for stopping forward motion. Modern vehicles still use friction to stop. Although the conduit of power in your personal vehicle is likely a fluid traveling through lines that press some pads against a disc or a drum, most large vehicles — including trains — use air as the conduit of braking power.

Air has proven itself as an effective conduit of the driver's foot on a pedal to the brake pads against a brake drum or disc. When you apply pressure on a brake pedal in a vehicle equipped with air brakes, you are controlling a valve that channels air pressure through air lines. This pressure is powerful, so if you are a person who is challenged in leg strength, you will still be able to effectively stop a truck that weighs 80,000 pounds.

Have you ever watched a murder mystery in which a person intent on murdering the victim cuts a brake line so that brake fluid is lost as the brakes are applied? Their intended target won't be able to stop when driving towards Dead Man's Curve. When the brakes don't work, the car crashes down a cliff. If the murderer tried this on a vehicle with properly maintained air brakes, they would be completely unsuccessful. You can drive with assurance that you will have brakes, knowing that your vehicle is constantly producing the air pressure used for controlling the brakes. The other important aspect of air brakes is that the air pressure keeps brakes from *setting* (being applied so that the vehicle will not roll or stop randomly as you drive down the road). There are powerful springs that must be held back by air pressure in order for your vehicle to roll down the road.

In this chapter, you explore various types of air brakes in large commercial motor vehicles (CMV) and how to use them effectively. You also examine the components of an air brake system.

Understanding Different Types of Air Brakes

My intention in this section is to remove confusion about all the different types of brakes that get mentioned in Commercial Driver's License (CDL) exam study guides. First, you should know that there are brakes at each wheel. These are referred to as *foundation brakes*, which can be s-cam brakes, disc brakes, or wedge brakes. Any brakes that I or anyone else refers to use the same physical components.

Foundational brakes

I advise reading this paragraph carefully as it explains a confusing concept. Foundation brakes are at the end of each axle with brake components attached to each wheel. They are the same brakes that are used when someone mentions emergency, spring, parking, or service brakes, just different names for the different ways that the brakes are applied. The same physical components are being used, no matter what brake is being discussed. The terms are different, but the components are the same. The difference is in how the brakes were applied. Your personal vehicle works the same way. It also has foundation brakes (disc or drum) that can be applied by using the brake pedal (service brakes), by pulling up on a handle when parking (parking brake), or by pulling up on a handle when the brake pedal fails (emergency brake). You don't have different types of brakes on each wheel, just different needs or ways to apply the same brakes.

The following list provides an overview of foundation brakes:

REMEMBER

>> **S-cam brakes.** Known as the most common brakes used in CMVs, I will go into detail about them in this chapter because the brake questions in the written test will mostly be about them. The s-cam pushes brake pads into a brake drum.

>> **Disc brakes.** Gaining popularity because some vehicles have them as standard equipment, disc brakes cost more than drum (s-cam) brakes but are lighter. Commercial Learner's Permit (CLP) exam might have a simple question about disc brakes. Know that they consist of a rotor (disc) that gets squeezed or clamped by pads on both sides of it to operate.

>> **Wedge brakes.** These brakes can be found on very old vehicles, so you might never see a wedge brake. However, you might see it referenced in a question in your written exam. Know this for your exam: a wedge pushes brake pads/shoes into the brake drum to cause the brakes to apply.

Dual air brake system

Most large vehicles have a dual air brake system. The first (or primary) system might operate the rear axle brakes, and the second (or secondary) might operate the steer axle brakes and the other rear axle's brakes — if there is more than one rear axle. If there is a trailer, both systems will operate the brakes on the trailer.

Each of these systems have their own air lines, supply tanks, and so on. However, there is only one brake pedal, compressor, governor, and air dryer (more on these components later in the chapter). You don't change the way you drive the vehicle when you have dual brake systems. The only difference is to observe two gauges or one gauge with two needles and wait for the air pressure to build up in both of them. Once air pressure is built up, you can perform the tests discussed in Chapter 9. When you determine that your air brake system is functioning properly (and everything else passes your inspection) you may drive your vehicle.

Utilizing Air Brakes

The CDL study guides will have most students confused about how to use air brakes, so I'll give you some helpful information. The written exam will likely have more questions that were developed with the mindset that commercial motor vehicles (CMV) don't have anti-lock brake system (ABS) when the last CMV made without ABS was before the turn of the century.

Stopping your vehicle in normal circumstances requires you to simply apply normal pressure on the brake pedal. The braking methods described below (stab and controlled braking) need to be understood for the written test, but as long as you use properly maintained equipment (after acquiring your permit and license), you should brake as you would your personal vehicle. Stopping your vehicle fast when using a manual transmission requires just a little more thought and action.

The following three braking application points are all about you using your foot on the brake pedal, also known as using the service brakes.

>> **Braking in an emergency.** Sooner or later, someone will pull out in front of you and then decide to stop. Your animal instincts will tell you to ram into the rear of that vehicle. But your angelic side will tell you to have compassion, ignore the obliviousness of the other driver, and step on your brake pedal — listen to your angelic side!

   If there is enough distance to stop your vehicle, slamming on your brakes is the right way to avoid the accident. However, always attempt to keep proper spacing between you and any other vehicle in front of you to avoid having to slam on your brakes. People will always take up that cushion you have created between other vehicles, which may drive you crazy. Don't take it personally, just know that they are being selfish and ignorant of the physics of a large vehicle. Resist the urge to get right on the tail of their vehicle. You will be the big loser if they wind up under your front bumper! (Refer to Chapter 4 for safe driving practices.)

>> **Controlled braking.** One way to safely stop fast is by using controlled braking. Here is the process: press your foot on the brake pedal as hard as you can without locking up the brakes. I know what you are going to ask, "How do I know when the brakes are going to lock up?" I have two answers for you. The first is "Experience." The second answer that you will like better is to read the section, "Applying anti-lock brakes" in the next section.

   You can do light steering while you are performing controlled braking, but if you need to steer more aggressively, let up some on the brake pedal. If the brakes lock up, let up off the brake pedal until the brakes release and the wheels are rolling again. Then attempt controlled braking again.

>> **Stab braking.** You can master stab braking more easily than controlled braking. Here's the process: Apply your foot as hard as you can on the brake pedal. When the wheels lock up, release the brake pedal. When your wheels start rolling again, apply the brake pedal as hard as you can and repeat the steps again.

BRAKING WITH A MANUAL TRANSMISSION

For a truck with a manual transmission, press your right foot firmly and hard on the brake pedal. When your RPMs (rotations per minute) reach idle speed (most likely around 600 RPMs) press your left foot on the clutch pedal, disengaging the transmission. You do not want to try downshifting when stopping hard and fast. Also, remember to press in on the clutch pedal because failure to do so will kill the engine. Failing to do this on a road test will result in a failed test.

You will likely see questions about controlled braking and stab braking on the exam to receive your CLP. I hope you won't have to implement either of these emergency braking methods in a real-world situation but being prepared to use them can prevent a collision.

Calculating stopping distance

Be prepared for questions surrounding the braking distance of air brakes on your air brake test. There is one difference between air brakes and hydraulic brakes, which is the lag time described below. Remember the following components of braking distance for air brakes:

>> **Perception distance.** Perceiving a hazard is part of stopping your vehicle. Driving more cautiously in construction zones, school zones, and anywhere where there is more activity or objects is paramount. Driving slower in such areas gives you more time to perceive a hazard. Driving slower equals covering less distance, which in turn means you will see the person who is walking dangerously close to your path much sooner.

>> **Reaction distance.** You perceive the hazard, and brain sends a signal for your foot to step on the brake pedal. The time from perceiving the hazard to stepping on the brake pedal is the *reaction distance.*

>> **Brake lag distance.** Air brakes have an additional component to factor in the stopping distance formula. The time it takes for the air to pressurize in the air brake line from your brake pedal to the brake chamber is called *lag time*. Remember for your written test, brake lag can take a half second or more. In a well-maintained vehicle, you will not notice the lag as it happens quickly, but you will still drive a longer distance. The faster you drive, the more distance you cover.

>> **Braking distance.** After lag time, your brakes are applied. When your vehicle comes to a stop, your braking distance is established.

REMEMBER

>> **Total stopping distance.** For air brakes, the stopping distance formula is Perception distance + Reaction distance + Brake lag distance + Braking distance = Total stopping distance. Figure 8-1 provides a few examples for the total stopping distances for a vehicle with air brakes and on dry pavement. So if you're traveling at 55 mph, you'll need at least 451 feet to stop.

Using parking brakes

Use your parking brake any time you are parking your commercial vehicle. Pull the yellow knob and pull the red knob when you have an air brake trailer attached. If your brakes are wet and it is freezing weather, park on level ground and use a *wheel chock* (a wedge that prevents a wheel from moving and thus your vehicle from rolling away). Drum brakes can freeze in such conditions. If you descend a mountain too fast or in too high a gear and your brakes get hot, don't set the parking brakes until they have cooled down.

Using emergency brakes

In the previous section, I told you how to brake in an emergency, like when someone pulls out in front of you. In your personal vehicle, the emergency brake is what you utilize when your normal brake pedal fails to operate. In an air brake-equipped vehicle, the air system decides when there is an emergency. That emergency would be a loss of air in the brake/air system. The catastrophe that the emergency brakes avoid is a runaway vehicle.

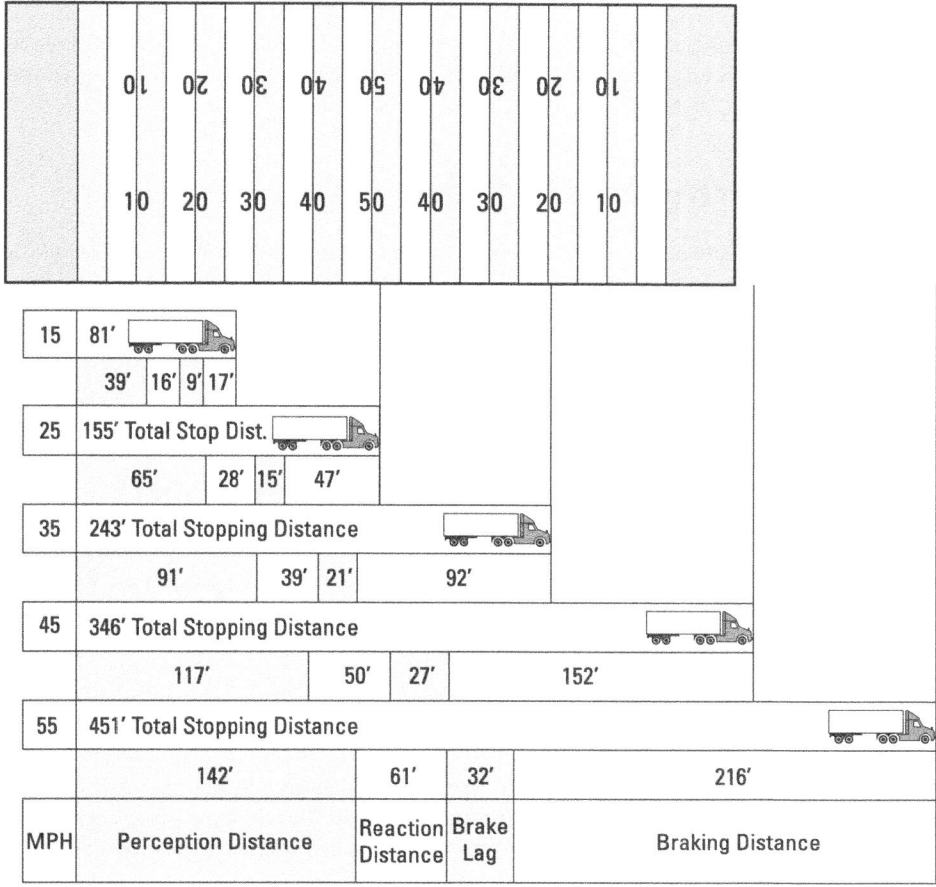

FIGURE 8-1: Total stopping distance diagram for air brakes.

Here is how it works: when an excessive amount of air is lost, a valve(s) release the remainder of the air in the trailer (when pulling an air brake-equipped trailer) and then the semi-tractor or simply the truck if there is no trailer. Instantly the springs that were being held back by the air apply the brakes (now called emergency brakes).

Setting all your parking brakes while loading or unloading is a must.

REMEMBER

Stopping with anti-lock brakes

When your wheels lock up, your tires skid on the pavement. When your tires skid on the pavement, you don't have control of your vehicle. Only when your tires are gripping the road do you have control. You want your tires to keep traction (rolling) even when you are making an emergency stop. ABS prevents wheel lock-up.

When you attempt to use controlled braking or stab braking in a vehicle with ABS, the brakes should not lock up. The ABS controller should sense when your brakes are about to lock up and keep them from doing so. ABS is more helpful on wet and slick roads than dry roads. It will also help you maintain control of steering. However, ABS will not necessarily stop your vehicle faster than if it did not have ABS.

You should remember (at least for the test) that ABS is required on all air brake-equipped truck/semi-tractors manufactured on or after March 1, 1997 (except for vehicles engaged in driveaway, towaway operations, which for the most part is transporting a vehicle with at least one set of wheels on the ground to a repair facility, or say from a manufacturer to a dealer). For all other air brake-equipped vehicles like trailers (again, except for vehicles engaged in driveaway, towaway operations) that manufactured date is March 1, 1998. Can you believe that they would have a history question on a CDL test?

Remembering brake fade

Air brakes have no advantage over hydraulic brakes when overheating, or *brake fade*, is concerned. If the brakes are constantly or excessively used, they will overheat (like going down a mountain without the use of an engine brake). Brake pads will glaze, and drums will expand and possibly deform. For more information, review Chapter 5, which addresses the proper way to descend a mountain and keep brakes cool and effective.

Looking Inside of an Air Brake System

You probably don't have to know as much about any part of your commercial motor vehicle as you do with your air brake system. Understanding how your air brake system works and knowing the components that make up the system will make you a safer, more professional driver.

Brake chamber

I am introducing you to the brake chamber before other components in the air brake system because it actually uses the air (see Figure 8-2). You will find that the other components are operated mechanically first by the brake chamber or are instrumental in compressing the air.

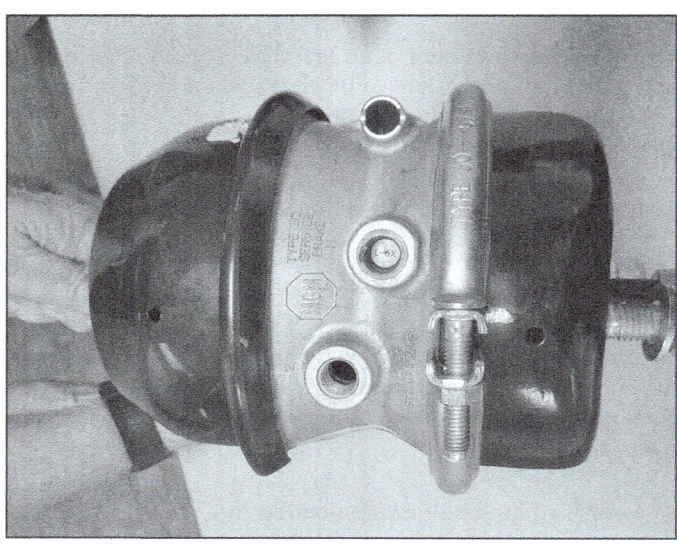

FIGURE 8-2:
A brake
chamber.

Figure 8-3 shows the two spaces inside brake chambers. Look inside chamber (1), and you will see a larger colored spring (2) that is quite powerful. The large spring is referred to as the emergency and parking brakes and mechanically operates or sets the brakes when no air is preventing it from applying the brakes.

Looking in the other chamber (3), you should see a smaller, less powerful spring (4), which is simply a return spring that helps return the diaphragm and the push rod to the non applied position (brakes are not being used for stopping or parking).

You can also see in the photo the thin edge of two diaphragms (5). They are what the compressed air pushes against to activate the brakes or to release the brakes. Air lines (not shown) are attached to individual chambers of the brake chamber.

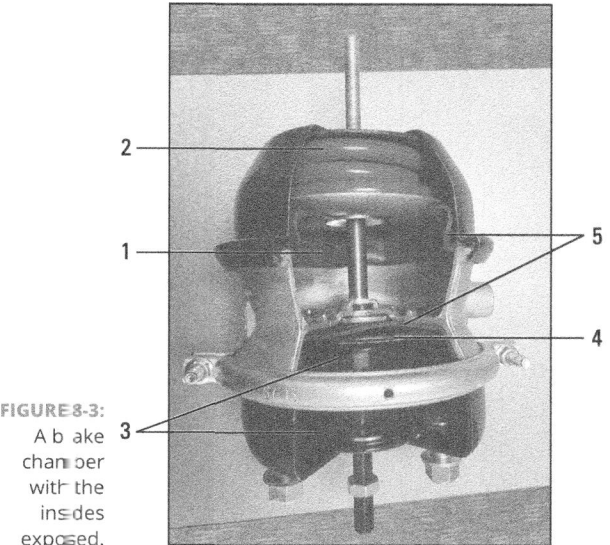

FIGURE 8-3:
A brake
chamber
with the
insides
exposed.

Air compressor

To manufacture the air pressure that is needed for the brake chamber, you need to have an air compressor (see Figure 8-4). You might have an air compressor at your home for some shop tools or a little one in your personal vehicle for airing up your tires. The one for your commercial vehicle is similar to these tools but is powered by the engine and thus is under the hood and mounted to the engine. On the day that you are doing your pre-trip inspection test and a license examiner wants you to inspect under the hood, you might be asked to identify if your air compressor is belt-driven or gear-driven. Your CDL instructor will tell you which it is well in advance of the test. You will find air lines attached to the compressor (assuming you can find your air compressor as it could be hiding behind a lot of other components).

FIGURE 8-4:
A new air
compressor.

Governor

Your air compressor will just keep compressing air if you let it, but to do so will supply too much air pressure in your air and brake system. So, something has to control it, like a governor (I don't know why it wasn't called a mayor). The governor (see Figure 8-5) can be mounted near the air compressor). Nevertheless, it tells the compressor when to stop compressing air so that it doesn't damage your system with too much pressure.

FIGURE 8-5:
A governor mounted to an air dryer.

AUTHOR SAYS

In case you want to know, there is a *thingamajig* in the compressor that gets told by the governor to just channel the air to go back and forth within the compressor, which just keeps running. You won't need to know this bit of technical jargon for any test.

Air storage tanks

There is no way an air compressor alone can keep up with the immediate demand for air pressure when you decide that your vehicle must stop. You need the pressurized air to be stored in tanks, which are shown in Figure 8-6), so that it's ready for use when you step on the brake pedal. You will find air tanks in a variety of places and in varying sizes. If you are pulling a trailer equipped with air brakes, you can find a couple of air tanks under the trailer or in between frame rails.

FIGURE 8-6:
Air storage tanks.

© TMR Aluminum

Air storage tank drains

You might recall from a grade school science class, that when air is compressed, moisture forms due to the rise in temperature and the humidity in the air. When there is more moisture than what the air can hold, condensation results; and in this case, condensation runs to the bottom of the tank. If you let your tanks fill up with water, you will have problems getting your brakes to work properly, especially when the temperature drops below freezing!

You need to get rid of the moisture in your tanks. One way this is done is with a valve or an air storage tank drain (see Figure 8-7). You need to drain the tanks daily. There will be a cord or cable for you to pull, which is called a manual drain valve. Be sure to stand back as water, air, and a little oil will spew out of the tank. The oil will be from the air compressor that uses the oil from the engine for lubrication. When oil and water are mixed together, you will get a darkish milky-like substance.

There may be a chance that the vehicle you will drive has an automatic drain, as shown in Figure 8-8, that — believe it or not — drains automatically because there's a hole in the bottom.

FIGURE 8-7: An air supply tank with a manual drain valve.

FIGURE 8-8: Air supply tank with an automatic release.

Air dryer/evaporator

You might be glad to hear that someone created a component that removes some of the moisture prior to accumulating in the air storage tanks. One device that was installed in older trucks was the alcohol evaporator. While you might never see an alcohol evaporator, you might still find a question about them on your written test. Alcohol will damage air lines and the ABS.

Most trucks are equipped with air dryers that take out the moisture that builds from compressing the air (see Figure 8-9). The governor sends signals to the air dryer, which is sometime located near it, at the same time as the compressor, so the governor does double duty (no political jokes are allowed in this paragraph).

FIGURE 8-9:
An air dryer.

Air pressure gauges

The main air pressure gauge that you need to know about for your exam is the air pressure supply gauge(s) (see Figure 8-10). One gauge can show the air pressure for both the primary and secondary system. However, you can have two gauges or one for each system.

Looking at a big truck's dashboard may reveal other gauges. While these gauges are useful, they will not be on your exam for your leaner's permit, nor do you need to mention them on your pre-trip inspection test. For that matter, they are not on every vehicle equipped with air brakes.

AUTHOR SAYS

However, if you really want to know, I will introduce them to you: application air gauge, tracking how much air pressure is being applied to the brakes and air suspension gauge(s), showing the air pressure used for the vehicle's air suspension(s).

Safety valve

Your air compressor is compressing the air, and the air is getting stored in tanks. The governor tells the compressor when to stop compressing, but what if it fails? You have a safety valve on a tank that will open at 150 PSI. Your vehicle is now out of service because there can't be an audible leaks, but your vehicle's air system is saved from damage. You will need to have your brake technician fix the problem.

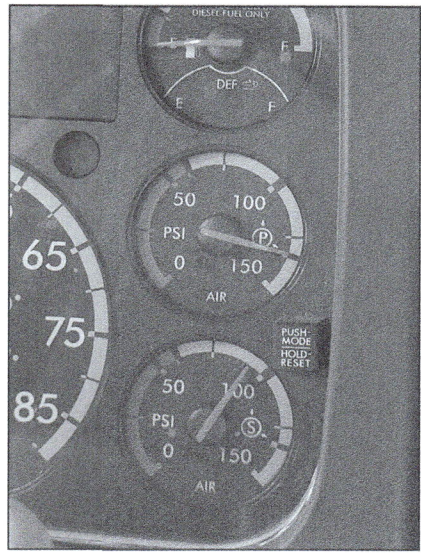

FIGURE 8-10:
An air
pressure
gauge.

Applying the Pressure Components

Developing air pressure is a critical operation for a CMV; the brakes have to be functional and in good working order. Department of Transportation (DOT) officers consistently find brake components as one of their top three vehicle components that fail their safety inspections (tires/wheels and lights/reflectors being the other two). Study this section, examining the figures, to gain an understanding of the brake components, so you will know what you are looking at when you are inspecting your CMV.

>> **Brake pedal.** You have all this air built up and ready to use. Stepping on the brake pedal sends air pressure into the brake chambers and starts a mechanical process. The brake pedal is also referred to as a *treadle valve*. The reason you can call it a treadle valve is because the pedal is directly connected to a valve.

   You might have seen antique sewing machines that were powered by the sewers' feet; those machines are called *treadle* sewing machines because the sewer's foot would tread (press) on the pedal and that energy or motion was converted to a motion that the machine can use. Similarly, pressing your foot on the treadle valve releases air from the tanks to go to the brake chamber. Your foot controls the amount of pressure that is used to stop your vehicle through the treadle valve.

>> **Brake chamber (again).** Your operation of the brake pedal sent air pressure to the brake chamber (see the previous section, "Looking Inside of an Air Brake System." The air pushes on a diaphragm, which pushes on a rod.

>> **Push rod.** As the diaphragm pushes on the push rod (see Figure 8-11), the push rod is pushing on a slack adjuster. At the end of the push rod and connected to your slack adjuster is simply a stirrup, which is attached to the slack adjuster with a pin and a cotter key (see Figure 8-12).

>> **Slack adjuster.** The slack adjuster is a magnificent device that keeps the brakes adjusted. As you use your brakes, the pads (that are described below) wear down. The slack adjuster, under the right conditions, will adjust to keep maximum braking power. While you won't need to know this much information when you test for your learner's permit, it will help you be a good professional driver.

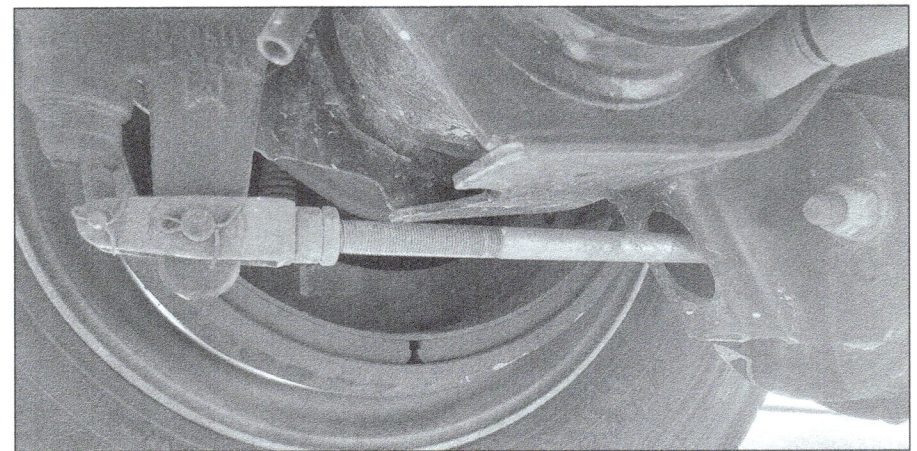

FIGURE 8-11:
A push rod.

FIGURE 8-12:
A slack
adjuster.

Here's how to make your automatic slack adjuster "automatically" work: apply 90 PSI or more pressure to the brakes. You do this by looking at the application air gauge while pushing on the brake pedal. Reach more than 90 PSI and then release the pedal. The brake adjuster adjusts one click when you do this. Repeat this process for the adjuster to fully adjust. When you continue to do this process after the brakes are fully adjusted, you are just exercising your leg.

>> **S-cam shaft.** You have an s-cam shaft connected to the slack adjuster with the s-cam at the other end of the shaft (see Figure 8-13). The s-cam shaft changes the horizontal force of the push rod to a rotational force that operates the brakes.

>> **S-cam and s-cam rollers.** Your s-cam might be hard to see in real life, but it is pressing against the s-cam rollers. The s-cam rollers are part of the brake shoe (see Figure 8-14). The rollers roll as the s-cam rotates. The rotation of the s-cam pushes the cam outwards against the rollers.

>> **Brake shoe/pads.** The shoes and the pads are one assembled unit (see Figure 8-15). When you step on the brake pedal, the result is the brake pads pressing on the brake drum.

FIGURE 8-13:
S-cam shaft.

FIGURE 8-14:
S-cam
pressing
against
S-cam
rollers.

FIGURE 8-15:
New brake
shoes and
pads.

>> **Brake drum.** The brake drum is a big heavy piece of metal that is bolted to the wheel (see Figure 8-16). When the brake pads are pressed against the drum, the wheel is slowed and eventually stopped.

FIGURE 8-16:
New brake
drum.

>> **Front brake limiting valve.** Air brake-equipped vehicles made prior to 1975 can be found with a valve that limits the brake air pressure that is sent to the front axle (steer wheels). After 1975, some vehicles were made with an automatic valve. These valves, which cannot be controlled by the driver, reduce the amount of air pressure sent to the front brakes, except under hard braking (when the air pressure is over 60 PSI).

Front wheel braking is good under all conditions.

REMEMBER

Dual parking control valve. When you lose air pressure in an air brake-equipped vehicle, the spring brakes automatically apply (remember that spring brakes are referred to as the brakes when they are applied by the big blue spring in exposed brake chamber photo earlier in the chapter, and in this instance are called emergency brakes). If the spring brakes apply due to a loss of air pressure while driving a bus full of people, on a railroad track or in an intersection, you will need help. Some buses and other vehicles have an extra parking brake system (basically another tank and a valve) that is in place for such an emergency. Push in the button to this valve to release the spring brakes and make it to a safe location. Use this valve carefully and wisely as there is only enough air pressure to use this valve a few times.

DRUM BRAKES VERSUS DISC BRAKES

When the components of brakes are mentioned in the tests, the references will be all about the s-cam drum brakes. Disc brakes are gaining in popularity so here is a little bit of information on the differences between disc and drum brakes.

- **Rotor.** The big brake drum is replaced by a rotor or disc. Looking at the disc brake rotor in first figure, you might see that there is a lot less steel and less weight than a drum brake, which is one of their selling points. Like the brake drum, the rotor is attached to the wheel.

- **Brake chamber.** There is still a brake chamber for air disc brakes as shown in the second figure, but you won't see a slack adjuster — nor will you see anything related to an s-cam. You can see the brake pads (difficult on some brands of disc brakes), but not the inner workings. As in s-cam drum brakes, when you press on the brake pedal, air enters the brake chamber. The brake chamber operates the calipers that press the pads against the rotor.

Practice Questions

1. The parking brake should be applied except when:
   (A) They are hot from coming down a mountain.
   (B) You are backed up to a dock for loading/unloading.
   (C) Parked on a flat surface.
   (D) The truck is at a fuel stop.

2. Brakes can fade when:
   (A) Air pressure is too low.
   (B) Air pressure is too high.
   (C) Brakes are too cold.
   (D) Brakes are too hot.

3. Brake fade can occur because of all the following reasons except for:
   (A) Low air pressure.
   (B) Some of the brakes are out of adjustment.
   (C) Excessive use of the service brakes.
   (D) Failing to use the engine brake going down a mountain.

4. You should have your truck in the proper gear for going down a mountain because:
   (A) The clutch won't operate going down a mountain.
   (B) The truck can pick up speed if you try shifting while going down a mountain.
   (C) Too high of a gear makes the vehicle go too slow.
   (D) Too low of a gear makes the vehicle go too fast.

5. The dual parking control valve is:
   (A) Used as a supplement to the regular parking brakes.
   (B) A valve for the extra set of parking brakes some vehicles have.
   (C) Used for emergencies to release spring brakes.
   (D) Used for the trailer in a combination vehicle.

6. Air tanks should be drained:
   (A) Daily.
   (B) When they are full of water.
   (C) Weekly.
   (D) Only in cold weather.

7. When brakes fade:
   (A) The slack adjusters have maladjusted.
   (B) The engine brake was overused.
   (C) The brake pads have frozen.
   (D) The brakes have overheated.

8. Stab braking is necessary:

   (A) On vehicles with ABS.

   (B) For vehicles with ABS in an emergency stop.

   (C) On vehicles without ABS.

   (D) For vehicles without ABS in an emergency stop.

9. Controlled braking is all of the following except:

   (A) Good for maintaining control of steering.

   (B) Good for vehicles with ABS in an emergency stop.

   (C) Applying your brakes all the way until the wheels lock up, releasing them until the wheels roll again, and then applying your brakes fully again.

   (D) Applying your brakes all the way without locking the wheels.

10. A dual air brake system:

   (A) Has two brake pedals.

   (B) Has two separate air tanks and lines.

   (C) Is for combination vehicles only.

   (D) Has a primary system and a backup system.

11. Air tanks are drained to:

   (A) Protect the air brake system from having to contain pressure all the time.

   (B) Lubricate the brake mechanism.

   (C) Let excess air out.

   (D) Let water out.

12. Which is not a type of air brake?

   (A) Wedge

   (B) Coaster

   (C) S-cam drum

   (D) Disc

13. Which statement is not true about the air supply gauge(s):

   (A) Shows the pressure that is applied when the brake pedal is applied.

   (B) All vehicles with air brakes are to have an air supply gauge.

   (C) Shows the pressure that is in the air tank(s).

   (D) One air supply gauge can have two needles.

14. Which statement about front wheel or steer wheel brakes is true:

   (A) Are good in any weather if they have properly working ABS.

   (B) Should have at a minimum of ⅛-inch wear left on their pads.

   (C) Are optional.

   (D) All trucks with air brakes are equipped with front brake limiting valves.

15. The air pressure warning signal must warn a driver:

   (A) If the pressure reaches as low as 30 PSI.

   (B) If the pressure reaches up to 150 PSI.

   (C) If the air pressure reaches 150 PSI or down to 30 PSI.

   (D) By the time the air pressure drops to 60 PSI.

16. Which statement is true about automatic slack adjusters:

    (A) You are to adjust an automatic slack adjuster using a wrench and a screwdriver.
    (B) Automatic slack adjusters connect the brake pads with the brake chamber.
    (C) Automatic slack adjusters need no maintenance as they are automatic.
    (D) Automatic slack adjusters need to be seen by a certified technician if they have to be adjusted daily.

17. Set your parking brakes:

    (A) When your vehicle is being loaded or unloaded.
    (B) When your brakes are hot.
    (C) When your brakes are wet and there are freezing temperatures.
    (D) When at a stoplight.

18. Which is not true of brake linings (friction material or pads):

    (A) Must be free of grease.
    (B) Must not be loose.
    (C) Must not be dangerously thin.
    (D) Must be made of ceramic.

19. Total stopping distance for air brakes is:

    (A) Reaction distance and braking distance.
    (B) Perception distance, brake lag distance, reaction distance, and braking distance.
    (C) Perception distance, reaction distance, and braking distance.
    (D) Perception distance, reaction distance, distraction distance, and braking distance.

20. Which sentence is false? If your vehicle has low air pressure:

    (A) The engine needs to just run at higher RPMs.
    (B) You should find a place to pull over and park.
    (C) After the alarm sounds, you might have just a little time before the spring brakes come on.
    (D) The spring brakes can be automatically applied making it difficult to control your vehicle.

21. When parking a vehicle for a short time, a driver should:

    (A) Set the service brakes.
    (B) Set the parking brakes.
    (C) Should use the engine brake.
    (D) Park on level ground.

22. Which statement about air brakes with ABS is false:

    (A) A vehicle with air brakes and ABS, should be operated normally (as vehicles without ABS).
    (B) You should not operate a vehicle when its ABS is malfunctioning.
    (C) A semi-tractor with ABS combined with a trailer without ABS requires normal brake applications.
    (D) If you have ABS on even one axle of a vehicle, you have more control over the vehicle when braking.

Answers and Explanations

1. **A.** When you overuse the air brakes while driving down a mountain, you heat up the drum to extreme temperatures. Setting the brakes will possibly deform the brake drum into a non round shape, which is a real problem to smooth braking. Remember to use the engine brake when descending a mountain or steep incline.

2. **D.** Brake fade is when the brakes begin to fail due to overuse/overheating. When the brake drum gets hot, it expands and the brake pads don't make proper contact with the drums.

3. **A.** Low air pressure doesn't cause a brake to fade, but it might cause the spring brakes to set on your vehicle.

4. **B.** Although the clutch will still operate, too high a gear will cause you to go too fast down the mountain and too low a gear will simply cause you to go slower than you need to. (You can never descend a mountain too slow.) But if you try to shift going down a mountain, it can be challenging — too challenging for a novice.

5. **C.** The dual parking control valve is a valve to release the spring brakes when air pressure has been lost.

6. **A.** Air supply tanks should be drained daily because water can enter where it does not belong.

7. **D.** When brakes overheat, they become less effective as the drum expands and pads don't contact the drum sufficiently. That is the definition of brake fade.

8. **D.** Stab braking shouldn't be necessary with ABS-equipped vehicles. Even if your vehicle doesn't have ABS, stab braking is for emergency stops. (A strange and tricky question, like some CDL exam questions.)

9. **C.** Choice C is the exception because it's the definition of stab braking not controlled.

10. **B.** Having two tanks and accompanying air lines is a characteristic of a dual brake system.

11. **D.** Draining air tanks is to get rid of the water (or condensation) that forms from the compression process.

12. **B.** Coaster brakes are on some bicycles but are not air-operated.

13. **A.** Choice A is the definition of an application gauge not the pressure gauge.

14. **A.** Brake pads should have a minimum of ¼ inch of wear left. You should have brakes on your steer wheels. Front brake limiting valves are not on all vehicles.

15. **D.** The air pressure warning system is required to warn a driver when air pressure is dropping by the time it reaches 60 PSI.

16. **D.** Automatic slack adjusters should be worked on only by certified brake technicians.

17. **A.** Don't set your brakes when they are overheated, or when the conditions are right for freezing them (chock the tires!). Don't park at a traffic light, just use your service brakes.

18. **D.** Brake linings are made of various materials.

19. **B.** The four factors that make up total stopping distance are perception distance, reaction distance, brake lag distance, and braking distance.

20. **A.** There is a problem with the air system. It is too risky to continue to drive.

21. **B.** While parking on level ground is nice, it is not always possible, but your parking brakes should always be working correctly.

22. **B.** A vehicle with a malfunctioning ABS can be safely operated. However, an officer can cite you for the ABS working incorrectly and then send you on your way, with the ABS still malfunctioning.

Chapter **9**

Testing Air Brakes

Testing your air brakes and the air system of your vehicle is possibly the most important part of the vehicle inspection. You must know how to perform this check on your vehicle's air brakes and air system before you can safely take your commercial motor vehicle (CMV) or rig out on the road.

Many drivers are diligent about checking their vehicle's lights and tires before they start their driving day, probably because those items are more visible and easier to inspect. Perhaps drivers never learned how to efficiently check their brakes and air system or think that they don't have the time. But I'm letting you know that when you understand how to correctly inspect your braking system, you will drive down the road with confidence, knowing that your brakes are in good working order.

In this chapter, I describe the process steps for testing your vehicle's air brakes and air system for various configurations of CMVs. You must be able to properly demonstrate this skill to qualify for your Commercial Driver's License (CDL).

Testing the Air System

Air is the conduit of power in the air brake system of most commercial vehicles; air makes the brakes work. In your personal vehicle, the conduit of power is a fluid. So when your car has a leak in the brake system (which can cause the brakes to fail), you see a puddle of the fluid on the ground.

But with air brakes, a compressor works behind the scenes to keep up with the demand you put on the system when you apply the brakes. So, you won't always know whether the air brake system has a leak that can cause it to fail unless you do the tests I describe in this section. (And you definitely won't be warned by a puddle of brake fluid on the ground if it does.)

Air systems vary from vehicle to vehicle, and you can and must ensure that safety devices (such as the emergency brakes) are working properly. As discussed in Chapter 8, spring brakes, which are also the parking and emergency brakes, are released with air. Without air (should the system fail), the brakes are *set* (meaning the emergency and parking brakes are being applied to stop the vehicle or keep it in place), even when you're driving down the road.

Pressurizing the system and testing the air system governor

The first part of the process for testing your vehicle's air system involves starting the vehicle to check the air system's pressure. Follow these steps to get ready to safely start the truck for this check:

1. **Secure the wheels by placing *chocks* (as shown in Figure 9-1) in front and back of the rear tires (as shown in Figure 9-2) to prevent the vehicle from moving.**

   When you are learning this process in a school, the facility might provide a way to safely start the air system checks without chocks, and that is okay.

2. **Make sure that the transmission is in neutral by moving the gear shift lever left and right (with a manual transmission) and simply verify the gear shift lever indicates N for neutral on automatic and automated transmissions.**

3. **Place the key in the ignition and turn the key to start the engine.**

   If your vehicle has a manual transmission, press and hold down on the clutch pedal before you turn the key.

FIGURE 9-1:
Wheel chocks.

FIGURE 9-2:
A wheel that is chocked.

4. **Observe the air pressure gauge to determine the air supply reading.**

   The air pressure gauge reads in pounds per square inch (PSI). The air pressure needs to be above 100 PSI (as shown on the middle gauge in Figure 9-3) for a valid test. I recommend that you let the pressure build until you observe that the *governor* (which tells the compressor to stop compressing air) "cuts out" or tells the compressor to stop compressing air.

FIGURE 9-3:
Reading the air gauge.

Testing the governor cut out and cut in

When you are inspecting your air system, using a logical, efficient process is important. At the end of the process described in the preceding section, you examine the air gauge and observe when the governor cuts out, which tells the air compressor to stop building air pressure.

The air pressure gauge should read at least 120 PSI for a fully functional air system. Normal cut-out pressure for the governor is 120 to 140 PSI. If the air pressure doesn't get as high as 120, you have less air to operate the brakes and other items that use the air pressure built by the air compressor. Here are other considerations regarding the air pressure system and governor:

>> **If the air pressure fails to reach 120 PSI,** you should inform your mechanic that you need a new governor installed. (Unless you want to replace it yourself; it's not that difficult to do.)

>> **If the pressure continues to build (after 140 PSI),** a safety valve in the system will release the pressure (blow) at 150 PSI.

TIP

Having the safety valve blow will put the vehicle out of service, but it will avoid a bigger repair. In this situation, just the safety valve — and most likely the governor — will be all that you need to replace.

REMEMBER

When your vehicle uses up air pressure, the governor must tell the compressor to start building pressure well before pressure gets dangerously low. For most vehicles, this low figure will be 100 PSI. The dangerously low figure would be 90 PSI.

Follow these steps to know the point at which the air compressor governor cuts in:

1. **Release the brakes by pushing in on the yellow parking brake knob (see Figure 9-4), and the red trailer air supply knob if you have a trailer that has air brakes (see Figure 9-5).**

2. **Step on and off the brake pedal repeatedly to use up some air pressure.**

3. **Watch the air pressure gauge and slow down the frequency of stepping on the brake pedal when the air pressure reading nears 100 PSI.**

4. **Slow down stepping on the brake pedal when the pressure is below 100 PSI so that you can see whether the compressor has started building pressure or not.**

If pressure is not rising, release a little more pressure until you can determine when the compressor starts building air pressure again.

WARNING

The absolute lowest reading at which the compressor must start building pressure again is 90 PSI. (There can be an exception to this, as is the case in some buses.) If you reach a reading any lower than that, you will need to have work done on your vehicle; the governor probably needs to be replaced.

FIGURE 9-4:
A straight truck or bus parking brake knob.

FIGURE 9-5:
A trailer air supply knob in a combination vehicle.

Note: On some vehicles with air brakes, you risk bursting a diaphragm in a brake chamber if you press on the brake pedal while the brakes are set. Other vehicles have a protection system that will keep you from damaging the brake chamber. So don't press on the brake pedal when the parking brakes are set. See Chapter 8 for more information on the brake chamber.

Conducting the tests for leaks

You need to know that there are no or at least minimal leaks in your air and brake system. So you will conduct two tests to determine if or how much leakage you have. The first is called a *static test*. It is called that because you just sit there, not applying the brakes, seeing if your vehicle loses any air pressure. The second test you conduct is the *applied test*; you apply the brakes for this test.

REMEMBER

Various tests listed here are specific to the vehicle size or configuration, so a reminder of definitions is in order. A *straight truck* is a vehicle that is normally without a trailer. Examples of a straight truck (for testing purposes) would be a bus, a two-axled delivery truck, or a concrete mixer truck. A *combination vehicle* is a two-part vehicle — a towing unit and a trailing unit — joined together (or coupled). A trailer is considered a vehicle. Semi-trailer is the most common example of a combination vehicle. Again, for testing purposes, a *semi-tractor* that is not connected to a trailer is tested as a straight truck.

The static test

After the governor cuts in test, follow these steps to test for air pressure leakage:

1. **Allow the compressor to build air pressure again until the governor cuts out, which should be at least 120 PSI (100 minimum PSI for the test).**

2. **Turn off the engine.**

3. **Turn the key back on so that the gauges operate.**

4. **Wait for 1 minute.**

   When the license examiner is testing you so that you can obtain your CDL, they will most likely tell you when a minute is up (even if it has only been 7 seconds). (A minute is the official time to determine if an air system is holding air pressure sufficiently or not.)

5. **Observe the gauge to watch for air pressure leakage.**

   The maximum amount of air pressure that is allowed to be lost is

   • *2 pounds when testing just one piece of equipment* such as one truck or semi-tractor, or just the trailer.

   • *3 pounds when testing a combination* of a trailer with the truck.

The applied brake test

You need to know whether any leaks occur when the brakes are applied because more components of the braking system use the air pressure when the brakes are applied. This test is called the applied test, ingenious, right!? You hopefully see the importance of conducting this test — you don't want to have air leaking when you apply the brakes.

After you complete the static break test (see the preceding section), follow these steps for the applied brake test:

1. **Begin with the vehicle engine off and the key turned on so that the gauges are operating.**

    You probably finished the static test with this configuration (engine off, key on).

2. **Press and hold down the brake pedal for 1 minute.**

3. **Observe the gauge with the brakes applied.**

REMEMBER

Because your vehicle uses air in more components (double the equipment) when you perform the applied brake test, your vehicle (straight truck or semi-tractor) is allowed to lose a bit more pressure:

- *3 pounds when testing just one piece of equipment* such as one truck or semi-tractor, or just the trailer.

- *4 pounds when testing a combination* of a trailer with the truck.

The following mini-table shows the maximum air pressure loss allowed for static and applied brake tests.

Test/Vehicle	Single Vehicle	Combination
Static	2 PSI	3 PSI
Applied	3 PSI	4 PSI

Testing emergency systems

To avoid having your vehicle become an uncontrolled monster truck and roll over cars, is the reason that you have emergency systems, including the low pressure alarm and the emergency brakes. You don't want to get out on the road without knowing that these systems are in good working order.

The low pressure alarm

If your vehicle's air pressure drops to dangerous levels, your low pressure alarm should warn you so that you can take action. The warning must happen by the time an air system drops to 60 PSI. (**Note:** Some buses might have low pressure alarms that come on at 80 PSI.)

You can test this safety warning system by reducing the air pressure, pressing the brake pedal like you do when testing the governor (see the section "Testing the governor cut out and cut in" earlier in the chapter).

The visual alarm, whether a *wig-wag* (an old-fashioned device that drops in front of your face; see Figure 9-6) or a light that turns on you reduce the pressure enough (see Figure 9-7). Your vehicle is likely to have an audible alarm as well. If the visual alarm fails to appear before going down to 60 PSI, you have a defective alarm. Report it and get it fixed — it isn't the governor at fault in this situation.

TIP

In spite of the wig-wag being an old-fashioned device, a question about it might still appear on your CDL written test.

FIGURE 9-6:
A wig-wag,
the low air
pressure
warning
device in
older trucks
and buses.

FIGURE 9-7:
A modern
warning
light.

Pick up the vehicle conditions in which you ended the applied brake test: brakes released, wheels chocked, key on, engine off. Then test your low pressure alarm by performing the following steps:

1. **Press on and release the brake pedal repeatedly.** Doing this lets air pressure out of your system.

2. **Observe your air pressure gauge to watch the pressure.** Your air pressure will be dropping on your gauge.

3. **Watch for your vehicle's low air pressure alarm to come on.**

If your vehicle's low air pressure alarm came on by the time the pressure dropped to 60 PSI, your vehicle passed the low air pressure alarm test. If the alarm didn't go off, have your vehicle repaired.

The automatic spring brakes

The spring brakes are the brakes that function both as parking brakes and as emergency brakes. If your truck's air system failed while you were traveling down the road, in order to keep the truck from rolling freely into anything, the emergency brakes should come on.

Follow these instructions for testing that your spring brakes come on automatically.

1. **Press on and release the brake pedal, repeatedly.** Doing so will let the air pressure out of your system.

2. **Observe your air pressure gauge to watch for low pressure.** Your air pressure will be dropping on your gauge.

3. **Watch for your vehicle's spring brakes to come on automatically.**

The knob or knobs for your vehicle's spring brakes should pop out (or set) somewhere between 20 and 45 PSI, with 20 PSI being the absolute lowest. If you do have a trailer with air brakes hooked to your vehicle, the red trailer knob will pop out first — maybe by only a fraction of a second — and then the yellow tractor parking brake knob will pop out.

Testing the buildup rate

Your air system must build at a sufficient rate. *Typically, a system should build to 85 to 100 PSI in 45 seconds in a dual air system* (the engine speed is usually 1000 RPMs for this test). Vehicles with larger air tanks will take longer to build to these pressures. Trucks built prior to 1975 are expected to build from 50 to 90 PSI in 3 minutes with the engine running at 600 to 900 RPMs. The important item for you to know is what the manufacturer of your vehicle says is acceptable. Your driving instructor should have this information or might make up figures for you.

RECAPPING THE AIR SYSTEM TESTS

These are the actions and conditions you use to test the air system on your vehicle for the CDL exam.

- Safely start the vehicle (chock wheels)

- Place vehicle in neutral and release brakes

- Build air pressure

- Observe when the air pressure quits building: *governor cut out test*

- Release air pressure observing when the compressor begins to build pressure again: *governor cut in test*

- With pressure over 100 PSI, turn engine off, key on

- Observe air pressure gauge for a minute for the *static test*

- Apply the brakes and observe the air pressure gauge for a minute for the *applied test*

- Release air pressure to *test the alarm*

- Release more air pressure to *test the emergency brakes*

- Build air pressure again, observing the *rate of build up*

Testing the Brakes

After you know that your vehicle has a properly functioning air system, you can test the brakes to see whether they work properly. Remove the chocks that you put in place for testing the air system from the tires before performing any tests on your vehicle's brakes.

REMEMBER

Every time you climb out of your vehicle, ensure that the parking brakes are on, turn off the engine and take the key. You may now get out of the vehicle and remove the chocks. An inspector can fail you for leaving the engine on or even leaving the keys in the ignition. It is permissible to ask the inspector if it is okay to leave the keys in the ignition, but I recommend that you get in the habit of turning the engine off and removing the keys.

REMEMBER

Every time you get in and out of your vehicle, use what the safety experts refer to as three points of contact. Either two hands and one foot or two feet and one hand should be in appropriate contact with the vehicle. (Your hands should be grasping a bar or steering wheel and your feet stepping on a step or floorboard.) *Always* exit and enter the vehicle with your body facing it. If you don't do this on your test, the license examiner will tell you that you can leave and come back another day. After you pass your test and have your license in hand and you fail to exit the vehicle this way, you might get to meet an emergency room doctor.

AUTHOR SAYS

I have information in this book for both straight vehicles and combination vehicles. After you pass your written tests, it might be best for you to study just the portions of this book that pertain to the vehicle and systems (like combination vehicle or not, and, air brakes or not) that you will be using for your next tests, the behind-the-wheel skills test and the road test. Look for headings that describe the type of vehicle that you will be driving for the test. The license examiner won't test you on the process for a vehicle that you don't bring with you. (Just in case you are wondering, whoever is conducting the Entry-Level Driver Training, ELDT, should supply the vehicle you are to test in.)

Testing the semi-tractor, straight truck, or bus's spring brakes

REMEMBER

An *automatic transmission* is like the transmission in most personal vehicles, and the *automated manual transmission* is a manual transmission that is shifted by the vehicle's computer, but you drive it like an automatic transmission.

Testing with an automatic or automated manual transmission: semi-tractor with trailer (combination vehicle only)

Follow these steps to test the spring brakes of the semi-tractor, truck, or bus, which is pulling a trailer with air brakes:

1. **Release the trailer brake (press in the red knob).**

2. **Set the semi-tractor, truck, or bus spring brake (the yellow parking brake knob should be in the "out" position).**

3. **Place the transmission in drive or in forward gears.**

4. **Gently press on the fuel pedal. When you meet resistance, remove your foot from the fuel pedal.**

5. **Place the transmission in neutral.**

Your semi-tractor's spring brakes pass the test. However, if your semi-tractor moves, the spring brakes have failed, meaning your emergency brakes will fail and your parking brake will fail. Take your foot off the fuel pedal and place it on the brake pedal. Chock a wheel and report this failure to your favorite brake technician. Do not take this semi-tractor out on the road.

Testing with an automatic or automated transmission: straight vehicle or semi-tractor only

This test is simple and short because there is no trailer and no clutch pedal!

1. Set the parking brake (yellow knob).

2. Place the transmission in drive (or in the forward gears).

3. Gently press on the fuel pedal. When you meet resistance, remove your foot from the fuel pedal.

4. Place the transmission in neutral.

Your truck or bus's spring brakes pass the test. However, if your vehicle moves, the brakes have failed. Take your foot off the fuel pedal and place it on the brake pedal. Chock a wheel and report this failure to those in charge of the maintenance of your vehicle. Do not take this vehicle out on the road.

Testing with a manual transmission: semi-tractor with trailer (combination vehicle only)

This test verifies that your truck, semi-tractor, or bus with a manual transmission has working spring brakes. The only difference in this test is for you to ensure the trailer brakes are released so that the semi-tractor's spring brakes can be isolated and tested.

Follow these steps to test the spring brakes of a manual transmission vehicle pulling a trailer with air brakes:

1. Release the trailer brake (press in the red knob).

2. Place the yellow parking brake knob in the "out" position.

3. Press on the clutch pedal.

4. Place the transmission in first gear.

5. Slowly start to release the clutch pedal. When you meet resistance (the semi-tractor is attempting to move but doesn't), *push the clutch back in*.

6. Place the transmission in neutral.

Your semi-tractor's spring brakes pass the test, and you are ready for the next test. However, if your semi-tractor moves, the brakes have failed. Press on the clutch pedal, placing the transmission in neutral and taking your other foot and place it on the brake pedal. Chock a wheel and report this failure. Do not take this semi-tractor out on the road.

Testing with a manual transmission: straight vehicle

This test will verify that your vehicle has working spring brakes, but there is no trailer to contend with.

Follow these steps to test that your vehicle with a manual transmission has properly working spring brakes:

1. **Set the parking brake (yellow knob out).**

2. **Press your left foot on the clutch pedal.**

3. **Place the transmission in first gear.**

4. **Gently start to release the clutch pedal. When you meet resistance, *push your foot back down on the clutch pedal*.**

5. **Place the transmission in neutral.**

Your truck or bus's spring brakes have passed the test, and you are ready for the next test. However, if your vehicle moves, the brakes have failed. Press down on the clutch pedal and place your other foot on the brake pedal. Place the transmission in neutral. Chock a wheel and report this failure. Do not take this vehicle out on the road.

Testing the trailer's spring brakes (for combination vehicle only)

Like all brake tests, you must isolate the trailer's spring brakes that you are testing, if possible.

Testing with an automatic or automated transmission

With an automatic transmission or automated transmission, you don't have to worry about using the clutch so there are less steps in testing the spring brakes.

Follow these steps to test your vehicle's spring brakes:

1. **Place your transmission in drive.**

   With the automatic and automated transmissions, this can be as simple as rotating a knob, pressing a button, or moving a lever to the drive or forward gears.

2. **Release your semi-tractor parking brake (push in the yellow parking brake knob) and leave the trailer brake set.**

3. **Gently press on the fuel pedal (or accelerator).**

   You want the semi-tractor to attempt to pull the trailer, not dragging it so that the tires leave rubber on the concrete.

4. **You should feel the trailer stop the semi-tractor, when it does, let off the fuel and step on the brake pedal.**

You have successfully tested the trailer's spring brakes and they have passed. However, if the trailer starts to roll during your test, the trailer spring brakes have failed and need repair. Don't take this trailer out on the road until the repairs are complete.

Testing with a manual transmission

The main extra component when testing the trailer's spring brakes with a manual transmission is the use of the clutch. Using finesse when operating the clutch pedal will help with your success.

Follow these steps to test your trailer's spring brakes when using a manual transmission:

1. **Press your clutch pedal down.**

2. **Place the transmission in first gear.**

3. **Release your semi-tractor parking brake (push in the yellow parking brake knob, leaving the red knob out).**

4. **Slowly start to release the clutch pedal.**

5. **When you start to feel the semi-tractor attempt to pull the trailer, press the clutch pedal back down and hold your foot there, preparing for the next test.**

The trailer spring brakes pass the test. However, if the trailer starts to roll during your test, depress the clutch pedal and take your right foot off the fuel and step on the brake pedal. The trailer spring brakes have failed and need repair. Do not take this trailer out on the road until the repairs are complete.

Testing the trailer's service brakes (combination only)

AUTHOR SAYS

By this point you might be thinking, why don't we do all these tests on personal vehicles? While I don't have the answer, it is good that we do it for the heaviest vehicles on the road!

This test is for the trailer service brakes, the brakes that help stop your rig as you are rolling down the highway. However, you can only perform this test if your semi-tractor is equipped with a trailer brake handle (see Figure 9-8).

FIGURE 9-8:
Trailer service brake handle.

Testing with a manual transmission

Follow these instructions for testing your trailer's service brakes:

1. **Press on the clutch pedal.**

2. **Place your transmission in first gear.**

3. **Release all your parking brakes (push in both the red and yellow knobs).**

4. **Pull down on the trailer brake handle (or whatever direction your trailer parking brake should go when being applied).**

5. **Slowly start to release the clutch pedal. When you start to feel the semi-tractor attempt to pull the trailer, but failing, press the clutch pedal back down.**

6. **Release the trailer brake handle, ensuring that it moves back into the original position and press on the brake pedal.**

Your trailer's service brakes pass the test. If the trailer starts to roll during your test, depress the clutch pedal, take your right foot, and step on the brake pedal. The trailer's service brakes have failed and need repair. Do not take this trailer out on the road until the repairs are complete.

Testing with an automatic or automated transmission

Follow these instructions for testing your trailer's service brakes when your vehicle has an automatic or automated transmission:

1. **Place your transmission in drive or forward.**

2. **Release all your parking brakes (push in both the red trailer and yellow parking brake knobs).**

3. **Pull down on the trailer brake handle.**

4. **Gently press on the fuel or accelerator pedal. When the truck attempts to pull the trailer, but is stopped by the trailer, pull your foot off the fuel pedal and place it on the brake.**

Your trailer's service brake successfully passed the test. If the trailer starts to roll during your test, the trailer service brakes have failed and need repair. Do not take this trailer out on the road until the repairs are complete.

Testing the semi-tractor, straight truck, bus's service brakes

You cannot isolate the service brakes of your straight truck, bus, or semi-tractor when you are pulling a trailer. As a result, there are less variations to testing the truck's service brakes. However, there is a different observation that you must make when conducting the test — watch the steering wheel for movement.

Testing with an automatic or automated transmission

Follow these instructions for testing the truck's service brakes:

1. **Place the transmission in drive.**

2. **Put your foot on the fuel pedal and get the vehicle going about 5 mph.**

3. **Take your hands off the steering wheel (yes, I said take your hands off the steering wheel).**

4. **Press firmly (but try not to do it fast) on the brake pedal, bringing your semi-tractor/truck/bus to a complete stop.**

5. **Observe the steering wheel as you stop.**

   If you see your steering wheel move to the left or the right, your truck has a maintenance problem that must be resolved. It can be the brakes, but it can also be some other mechanical problem. Also, if your brakes seemed to be hesitant, mushy (technical term for being soft like a marshmallow), your brakes need to be attended to by a brake technician. If your steering wheel stays straight, you can declare that your service brakes are in good working condition.

Testing with a manual transmission

Follow these instructions for testing the truck's service brakes but with a manual transmission:

1. **Press on the clutch pedal.**

2. **Place the transmission in first gear.**

3. ***Slowly* let out on the clutch pedal and when you feel the transmission take hold, let all the way out on the clutch pedal, and give the engine enough fuel to get up to 3 to 5 mph.**

4. **Depress the clutch pedal.**

5. **Take your hands off the steering wheel (yes, I still say to take your hands off the steering wheel).**

6. **Press firmly (but try not to do it fast) on the brake pedal, bringing your semi-tractor/truck/bus to a complete stop.**

7. **Observe the steering wheel as you stop.**

   If you see your steering wheel move to the left or the right, your truck has a maintenance problem that is to be resolved. It can be the brakes, but it can also be some other mechanical problem. Also, if your brakes seemed to be hesitant, mushy (you know, like a marshmallow), your brakes need to be attended to by a brake technician.

REMEMBER

You cannot place too much importance on testing your brakes. Whether you drive the same truck every day or switch trucks and/or trailers a few times a day, test the brakes. You will learn to do it quite efficiently. Remember, federal and state laws prohibit driving an unsafe vehicle.

RECAPPING THE BRAKE TESTS (IN NO CERTAIN ORDER)

Test the trailer's spring brakes (combination vehicle only).

Test the semi-tractor, truck, or bus's spring brakes.

Test the trailer's service brakes (combination vehicle only and only if there is a trailer brake handle).

Test the semi-tractor, truck, or bus's service brakes.

Practice Questions

1. The air pressure warning signal must warn a driver:
   (A) If the pressure reaches as low as 30 PSI.
   (B) If the pressure reaches up to 150 PSI.
   (C) If the air pressure reaches 150 PSI or down to 30 PSI.
   (D) By the time the air pressure drops to 60 PSI.

2. You can check your spring brakes:
   (A) By setting your parking brakes and gently trying to move the vehicle.
   (B) By moving your vehicle at 3 to 5 mph and pressing on the brake pedal.
   (C) By looking at the gap between the spring and diaphragm.
   (D) You can't check your spring brakes.

3. Maximum air pressure leakage for a static test in a non combination vehicle is:
   (A) 2 PSI.
   (B) 3 PSI.
   (C) 4 PSI.
   (D) 5 PSI.

4. Which of the following is not part of the applied brake test?
   (A) Watching for the low pressure alarm to come on
   (B) Applying pressure to the brake pedal
   (C) Waiting for a minute
   (D) Watching the air supply pressure gauge

5. The low pressure warning can best be tested by:
   (A) Removing the air line to the front left brake.
   (B) Releasing water from the air tanks.
   (C) Operating the low pressure test lever.
   (D) Using up air pressure by continually stepping on and off the brake pedal.

6. The spring brakes can be tested for automatic operation by:
   (A) Releasing the brakes and lowering the air pressure by pressing and releasing the brake pedal repetitively.
   (B) By pulling out on the brake release knobs and attempt to pull forward.
   (C) By pulling forward and stepping on the brake pedal.
   (D) By utilizing the spring brake test button.

7. Which of the following is not part of testing the low air pressure alarms?
   (A) Observing the application air pressure gauge
   (B) Releasing air pressure from the air supply tanks
   (C) Observing the air pressure supply gauge
   (D) Watching for the visible low pressure alarm/warning

8. To conduct an air system leakage test, the air pressure in the supply tanks should be at least:

(A) 40 PSI.

(B) 90 PSI.

(C) 100 PSI.

(D) 120 PSI.

9. Which of the following is part of testing the governor cut-in and cut-out pressures?

(A) Chocking a wheel

(B) Releasing the parking brake

(C) Observing the air pressure supply tank gauge

(D) Waiting 1 minute

10. Maximum air pressure leakage for an applied brake test in a non combination vehicle is:

(A) 2 PSI.

(B) 3 PSI.

(C) 4 PSI.

(D) 5 PSI.

11. If you take your hands off the steering wheel during any part of the brake tests:

(A) You will automatically fail.

(B) You can be testing the spring brakes of a semi-tractor or bus.

(C) You can be testing the service brakes of a semi-tractor or bus.

(D) Nothing would happen.

12. Which of the following is not part of testing the air pressure build-up rate?

(A) Checking to see how much time has passed.

(B) Observing the air pressure gauge.

(C) Know at what rate your truck builds air pressure.

(D) These are all part of testing the air pressure build-up rate.

13. Which of the following is not part of testing the service brakes?

(A) Move or attempt to move the vehicle.

(B) Chocking a wheel.

(C) Have the engine running.

(D) Have a sufficient amount of air pressure built up.

14. Maximum air pressure leakage for an applied brake test in a combination vehicle is:

(A) 2 PSI.

(B) 3 PSI.

(C) 4 PSI.

(D) 5 PSI.

15. Which of the following is part of testing the parking brakes?

    (A) Release the spring brakes.
    (B) Chock a wheel.
    (C) Pull out on the yellow parking brake knob.
    (D) Engage the transmission and get your truck moving 5 mph.

16. Maximum air pressure leakage for a static test in a combination vehicle is:

    (A) 2 PSI.
    (B) 3 PSI.
    (C) 4 PSI.
    (D) 5 PSI.

17. Which of the following is not part of testing the static air leakage rate?

    (A) Observing the air pressure supply gauge.
    (B) Observing how much time has passed.
    (C) Applying pressure to the brake pedal.
    (D) Build air pressure until the governor cuts out.

Answers and Explanations

1. **D.** The regulations state that there is to be an alarm by the time the pressure goes down to 60 PSI.

2. **A.** The spring brake is also the parking brake so you can test it by setting the parking brake and gently try to move the vehicle.

3. **A.** You conduct the static test by just having your vehicle just sit still. There is no trailer, so you have a minimum of brakes and brake components using air pressure; so thus, it is the lowest figure that you memorized for the static and applied brake tests.

4. **A.** You are looking for the step that is not part of the applied brake test. You don't want your vehicle to be losing any air (4 PSI at the most if you are testing a combination vehicle). So you definitely aren't looking for the low pressure alarm to come on, but you are watching the gauge to see if there is any drop in pressure.

5. **D.** You don't remove any air lines for testing the brake system. You will find that using the valve to release water an inefficient way of testing, and you won't find a low pressure test lever. So that leaves Choice D, using up air pressure by using the brake pedal.

6. **A.** When you pull on the release knobs, you might be attempting to test the spring brakes but not the automatic operation of them. When you move your vehicle forward and step on the brake pedal, you are testing the service brakes. And you do not have a spring brake test button.

7. **A.** The application gauge measures the air pressure when the brakes are being applied. Your vehicle might not have one.

8. **C.** You build the pressure in your air brake system until the governor cuts out, which should be around 120 to 140 PSI. The minimum for the brake test is 100 PSI.

9. **C.** Chocking one of your wheels and releasing your parking brake are not part of testing the governor cut-out and cut-in pressures. You are just testing the pressure at which the cut in and cut out occurs.

10. **B.** When you are conducting the applied test the maximum amount of air pressure that can be lost is 3 PSI. (See question 3.)

11. **C.** When you are testing the service brakes of your straight vehicle or semi-tractor of a combination vehicle, you take your hands off the steering wheel to observe its reaction.

12. **D.** When you are checking your vehicle's air pressure build-up rate, time and the pressure are factors, so the answer must be all the choices.

13. **B.** Service brakes are the brakes are used when you are rolling down the road. So when you are chocking a wheel, you are preventing your vehicle from rolling and thus preventing a valid test of your service brakes.

14. **C.** When you are testing the air pressure leakage for a combination vehicle, you know that the allowed loss is more than a straight vehicle and a static test result on a combination vehicle. None of the tests you perform have 5 PSI as a test figure.

15. **C.** The spring brakes are parking brakes, and the test isn't checking a chock for its ability to stop the vehicle. If you roll the vehicle, you are not testing the parking brakes but maybe the service brakes.

16. **B.** The static test for a combination vehicle will have a higher air pressure loss limit than a straight vehicle but less than the maximum air pressure loss in an applied brake test for a combination vehicle. The table of maximum air loss amounts in this chapter has the information for you.

17. **C.** You are conducting a static test; thus, you do not apply pressure to the brake pedal.

4

Combing Through Combination Vehicles

IN THIS CHAPTER

» **Turning a combination vehicle correctly**

» **Avoiding a vehicle rollover**

» **Remembering to drive safely year-round**

» **Stopping skids**

» **Examining railroad crossings**

Chapter **10**
Driving a Combination Vehicle

D riving a big rig (semi-tractor) has been your dream for a long time. You have 18 wheels under you and 18 gears to match. Life seems just right. Then you suddenly see a sign that says, "NO TRUCKS OVER 5 TONS," and you see another sign that says the truck route takes a right turn. You quickly take the turn but your trailer rolls over the curb, the back of your trailer hits a light pole that falls onto a sidewalk. Now you've had your worst nightmare, becoming an Internet star of idiot truck drivers.

When you step up into your truck, sit in your seat, and look around you, there is a very important switch in your mind that you should flip. It is called "Driving Mode," specifically the one that is for a semi-tractor combined with a trailer. That switch in your mind should permeate your whole body and, if you are really geeky about it, your soul.

In this chapter, I take you through the process of safely turning your big combination vehicle without becoming an Internet star. You will look like a driver who knows what to do instead of someone who thinks that taking a fast turn will make them look like a professional — wrong! And of course, you will receive the information you need to pass the knowledge test for combination vehicles.

Turning Your Big Rig

The switch in your mind, the one that says, "Driving Mode — Combination Vehicle" should be on now. You must block your nightmares from your mind and replace them with thoughts of proper turning. You must remember that your goal is not the goal of the impatient driver behind you. Your goal is to make the turn safely, not quickly.

Tracking your tracking

Look in your mirrors (especially the ones to the inside of your turn) as you make a turn. You will see that your trailer is not taking the same path as the truck that you are sitting in. This phenomenon is called *off-tracking*. Forgetting that your trailer does this sort of thing will bring on the nightmares. Checking your mirrors will help you know how your trailer is off-tracking. The diagram in Figure 10-1 shows how a trailer takes a different path than the semi-tractor that it's attached to.

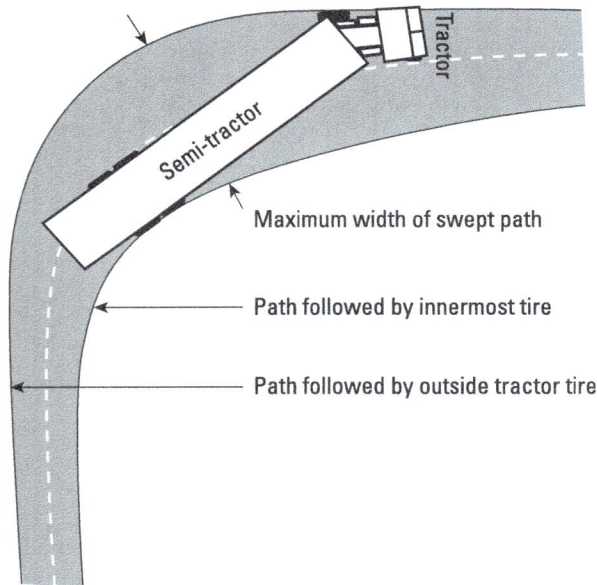

Maximum width of swept path

Path followed by innermost tire

Path followed by outside tractor tire

FIGURE 10-1:
How a trailer takes a different path or off tracks.

Plan on taking a lot more room to turn than you would in your personal vehicle. When you come to an intersection and there is not enough room to turn because there are other vehicles sitting there, remember this:

>> You must wait until traffic has cleared before you make a turn.

>> You must not direct traffic. That is to say, do not motion for people to move on. The license examiner will define your motion as directing traffic. This is likely an automatic fail.

>> You must not go ahead and turn, wishing for the best. It is like throwing a ball up in the air, and this time, hoping it defies gravity and doesn't fall back down.

>> Patience, you must have!

Preparing to turn

Turning to the left and to the right require different processes or tactics. You need a secondary switch in your mind that is labeled left turns and right turns. Program your brain to recognize the differences between the two turns. Remember that you have a trailer behind you, possibly as long as 53 feet.

Before making any turn, look for any signs that are warning you not to do what you're about to do — like a low clearance, no trucks allowed, or even being the wrong street according to your carefully planned directions.

Turning Left

REMEMBER

As you prepare to turn left and there is more than one left turn lane, you need to choose the lane farthest to the right (see Figure 10-2). When you turn to the left, the *blind spots* (areas that you can't see) increase. On your right side, especially with a box trailer, you have no idea what is there. You need to eliminate the possibility of someone driving around on your right side, as much as is in your power to do. So your concern is to eliminate the space where other vehicles can drive. That drives your motive for this process (pun intended). It is for the other driver's sake as much or more than for yours.

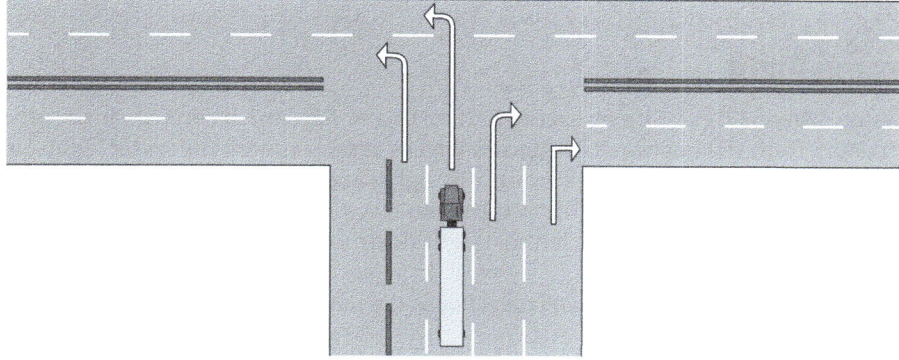

FIGURE 10-2:
Use the farthest lane to the right when there are multiple left turn lanes.

Follow these steps to make a left turn:

REMEMBER

1. **As you approach your intersection — prior to getting to the intersection — signal your intentions (turn on the left turn signal).**

2. **Slow down, way down.**

   There are plenty of things that need to happen and driving too fast at this point will make you miss out on a step or two, resulting in dire consequences.

3. **Shift your manual transmission to the gear that you want to take the turn in, even if you are not driving a manual transmission.**

   You want your transmission to be in a lower gear so that it won't go too fast during the turn. To make your transmission do this, perform the prior step of slowing down until you see that your transmission has shifted to a lower gear or that you have to give the engine more fuel to speed up.

4. **Drive past the middle of the intersection.**

   You don't want to go so far that you run your right steer tire into a ditch, a curb, or anything else that is not part of the road. That would be too far past the middle.

5. **Turn your steering wheel to the left, placing one hand over the other hand as you turn and turn back, gripping the steering wheel as you go.**

   This method gives you better control of a commercial vehicle. You are ready for any pothole or other road imperfection that tries to steer you away from your path. When you use the hand-over-hand method, you can make a very smooth turn. People riding with you will notice and say, "Wow, that was really smooth!" Indeed, this technique makes you a more professional driver.

6. **Watch mirrors on both sides.**

   Never leave anything to chance. On your right, watch for any vehicles, or a cyclist who seem to come from nowhere. On your left, watch to clear any obstacle (other vehicle, the median, signs, light poles). You can insert this step of watching your mirrors in between any of these steps.

7. **Start turning back to the right, remembering which lane you are turning into.**

   If you have more than one turn lane, it should be the far-right lane if you chose the correct left turn lane when you were preparing to turn.

8. **If you are turning from a road that has just the one turn lane, block the turn lane with your trailer.**

   Your trailer will off track: your semi-tractor will be farther to the right, but your trailer will be farther to the left. Blocking the lane to the left, or any space to the left, helps to protect other drivers that may want to foolishly attempt to drive in that space. *Now you are in the left-hand lane!*

Turning Right

The main difference in failing to execute left turns and right turns correctly is the type of accident that results from the mistake. Left-turn mistakes result in more rollovers. Right-turn mistakes result in knocking down streetlights or traffic lights and running tires into curbs, which result in tire and wheel damage. Incorrect right turns can also result in hitting a pedestrian standing on a corner. Both incorrectly executed left and right turns result in hitting other vehicles too.

If there is more than one right turn lane, choose the farthest left or outer turn lane when turning right as shown in Figure 10-3.

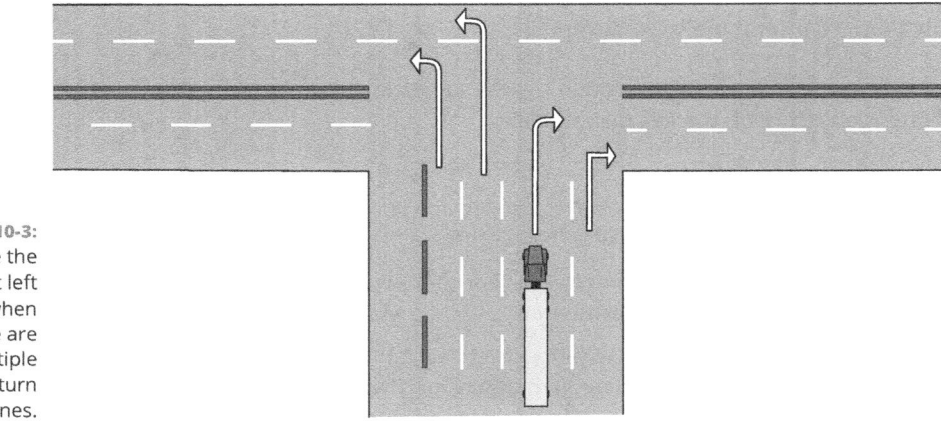

FIGURE 10-3: Choose the farthest left lane when there are multiple right turn lanes.

Follow these steps to make a right turn:

REMEMBER

1. **As you approach your intersection — prior to getting to the intersection — signal your intentions (turn on the right turn signal).**

2. **Slow down, way down, even more than for the left turn.**

   There are plenty of things that need to happen and driving too fast will make you miss out on a step or two, resulting in dire consequences.

3. **Shift your manual transmission to the gear that you want to take the turn in, even if you are not driving a manual transmission.**

   You want your transmission to be in a lower gear so that it won't go too fast during the turn. To make your transmission do this, perform the prior step of slowing down until you see that your transmission has shifted to a lower gear or that you have to give the engine more fuel to speed up but don't. (Do these steps sound familiar?)

REMEMBER

4. **Drive far enough into the intersection, possibly half or farther, so that your tandems stay within 4 feet of the curb or shoulder (even farther if trying to avoid a ditch).**

   Your *tandems* (the rear wheel/tire area of the trailer) do not follow the semi-tractor's path but it tracks off to the side on turns.

5. **Check your mirrors, left and right, right more than left but don't neglect the left mirror and continue checking through these steps.**

6. **Turn your steering wheel to the right, using the hand-over-hand method.**

   As you are driving slowly to make this turn and checking your trailer's wheels in relation to the side of the road, adjust your steering to keep within 4 feet of a curb, sidewalk, and so on.

7. **Turn back your steering wheel, gauging how much to adjust as you make the turn.**

   Plan to be in the outer lane if you are turning from an outer lane. Turn back into the right lane if there was only one turn lane. Focusing on your trailer's position as much as you do your semi-tractor's will help you make a successful turn.

WARNING

Do not make a jug handle turn. A jug handle turn is when you cross over into other lanes (especially the oncoming direction of traffic) prior to turning onto another street or a driveway. Instead, you should perform a *button hook*.

While I said that you shouldn't use the other lanes to turn, that instruction is for the street that you are coming from, not the one you are turning onto. It is permissible to use the lane(s) of the oncoming traffic of the road that you are turning onto. You might have to wait on other vehicles to move out of the way, but whatever you do, do not direct them to do so. See Figures 10-4 and 10-5 for illustrations of the jug handle turn and the button hook. Remember that the goal is to prevent creating space on your right so that a vehicle can't drive into that space.

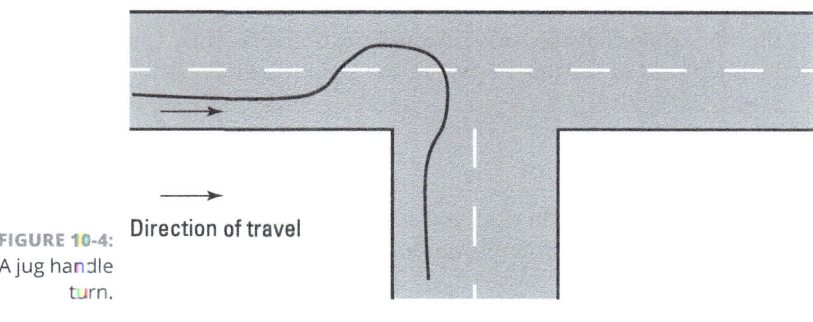

Direction of travel

FIGURE 10-4: A jug handle turn.

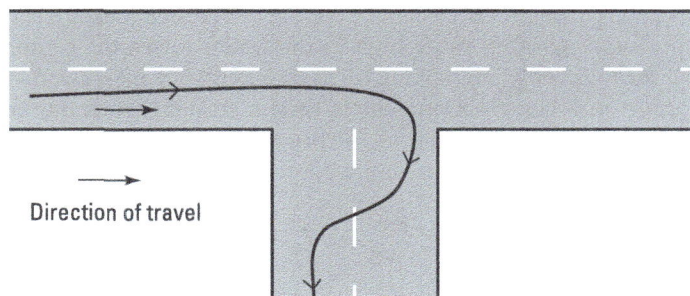

Direction of travel

FIGURE 10-5: A button hook turn.

Preventing Rollovers

Rollovers are generally the most serious accidents for commercial vehicle drivers as rollovers account for more than half of driver deaths. Commercial vehicles, including buses, usually have a much higher center of gravity than personal vehicles and get loaded with more cargo, which raises the center of gravity. The combination vehicle presents more factors affecting rollover potential. Drivers of combination vehicles must use more skill, awareness, and safe handling of the vehicle than when driving a straight truck or bus.

Cracking the whip

AUTHOR
SAYS

Take a whip, like Indiana Jones, and make it crack. Here's how you do it: make the whip fly in one direction, like behind you, and then change the direction with a snap of your wrist and forearm, before it has reached its farthest point. You probably cracked the whip! That can be fun with a whip. The second direction that the whip took was the one that created the crack — the little sonic boom.

You can have a similar "crack-the-whip" effect with a combination vehicle. It occurs when you have to make a sudden lane change and then a second one to get back into a safe place. The second turn of the wheel causes the "crack." Now obviously that movement isn't fast enough to make a crack sound like Indiana Jones' whip, but it can produce a rollover.

REMEMBER

There is another physical factor affecting rollovers called *rearward amplification*. Rearward amplification produces the crack-the-whip effect or rollover.

As you can see in Figure 10-6, different types of combination vehicles have different effects on rearward amplification. Note that the conventional double combination has a rearward amplification effect of 2.0. This means that the rear trailer is two times more likely to turn over than the semi-tractor. You can see that the triples have a rearward amplification effect of 3.5, meaning the rear trailer has 3.5 times the likelihood of turning over than the semi-tractor.

Preventing rollovers

Yes, you can prevent rollovers! Don't let anyone rush you into taking shortcuts or driving irresponsibly. On the other hand, work with intentionality so that you are not distracted.

Loading correctly

REMEMBER

Load your cargo low and centered whenever possible. Loading to one side makes the vehicle lean, increasing the rollover potential. Loading cargo high in the trailer raises the center of gravity, creating greater potential for rollover when making turns or emergency maneuvers. Loading the cargo low is more important in a combination vehicle than a straight truck due to the added physical characteristic of the vehicles' coupling or hitching. Fully loaded semi-tractor trailers have 10 times the likelihood of rolling over than empty ones.

Slowing down

REMEMBER

The real reason rollovers occur is because a driver is driving too fast. The high center of gravity simply makes a rollover occur more easily when driving too fast. In the previous section I talked to you about slowing down for turns. However, curves and ramps are where I have seen the most truck rollovers.

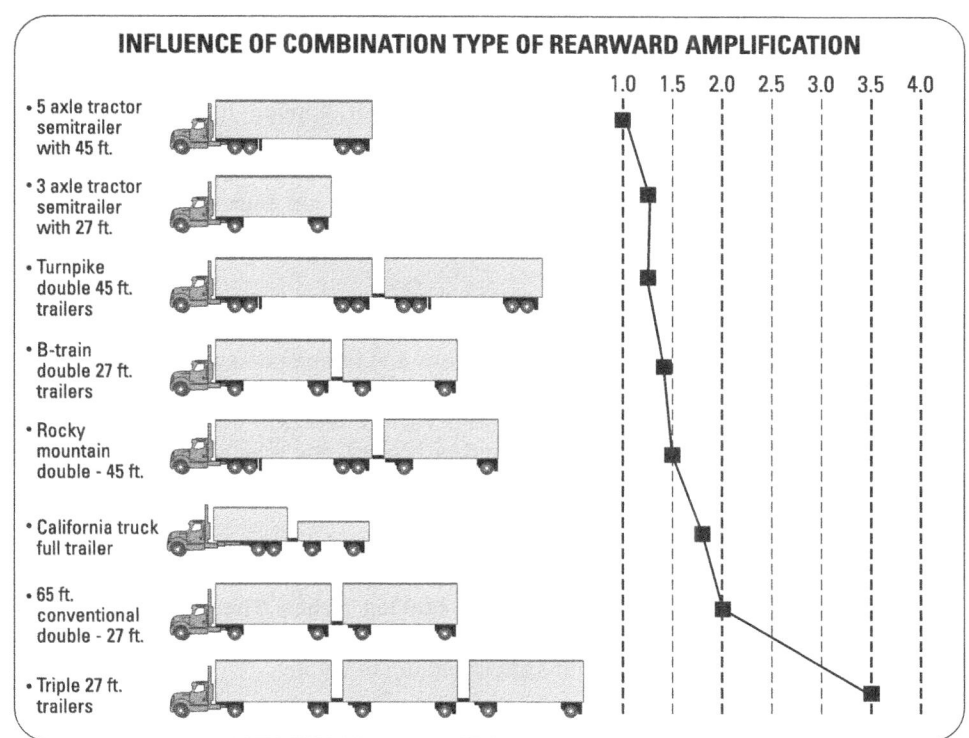

INFLUENCE OF COMBINATION TYPE OF REARWARD AMPLIFICATION

- 5 axle tractor semitrailer with 45 ft.
- 3 axle tractor semitrailer with 27 ft.
- Turnpike double 45 ft. trailers
- B-train double 27 ft. trailers
- Rocky mountain double - 45 ft.
- California truck full trailer
- 65 ft. conventional double - 27 ft.
- Triple 27 ft. trailers

FIGURE 10-6: Rear amplification in combination vehicles.

The speed limit posted for ramps *is not* for big combination vehicles. Those speed limits are for cars. Many trucking companies have a policy that you must drive half the speed of the posted limit on ramps. Your philosophy for your speed on ramps should be the same as driving down a mountain. You might drive around the curve slower than you need to, but you will never go around a curve too slow. However, you need only to drive around a curve or ramp too fast just once.

Driving Like You're on a Snow-Packed Road

When you drive aggressively — like you are angry — you use more fuel, you increase chances of an accident, and you will feel more drained at the end of the day. I want you to adopt a philosophy for driving safely — especially when you're driving a combination vehicle — like you're driving on snow-packed roads all year long. This mindset will increase your safe-driving habits, allowing you to get better fuel mileage, and help you avoid hazards that may become emergencies.

When you drive all year long like you are driving on slick winter roads, you are looking for cars and trucks that are barreling down a side road, appearing as if the drivers won't stop at the upcoming intersection. You must observe people, anticipating what they are preparing to do. You recognize what other drivers are going to do because you cannot stop quickly on the "slick" roads. You also shouldn't take off as though you are in a race because that will raise your fuel consumption. The section presents three more points to consider.

Steering carefully

TIP

Always steer your vehicle smoothly and deliberately. When you drive on a snowy road, you must do so with as little movement in your steering as possible. You realize that steering sharply or quickly can result in an accident, and you try to avoid situations where you must alter your steering.

Braking early but not often

When you drive on hard-packed snow, you know that stopping quickly can be a challenge. You don't know where it will happen, nor do you know when your vehicle will actually stop. So you drive accordingly by trying to avoid situations where you must stop. For example, you can adjust your speed to time traffic lights because you might not get your vehicle stopped fully for a red light. And if you do, you might have difficulty moving again.

When you are driving a commercial motor vehicle, you are encountering physical problems you don't have in a personal vehicle. One oddity is that an empty vehicle takes longer to stop than when it is loaded. This is due to stiff suspensions and strong brakes. Modern *air ride trailers* (trailers that use air bags for suspensions rather than steel springs) and properly maintained equipment have improved this situation, but your written test will only reference stiff suspensions (like how many springs can be missing and/or broken, and which vehicle stops faster — empty or loaded).

When you are *bobtailing* (driving your semi-tractor without a trailer), you have greater control problems, even with modern, properly maintained equipment. You will have more weight on your steer axle than your drive axle(s), causing braking issues. The Federal Motor Carrier Safety Association (FMCSA) reports that it can take longer to stop a bobtail tractor than a fully loaded semi-tractor trailer. I believe it, but I am not going to try it.

Accelerating

TIP

There is an important tactic in winter driving that helps the successful combination vehicle driver. Do not spin, maintain traction. Accelerating too fast on slick roads can send you into a ditch. Spinning your tires only gives you the opportunity to buy more tires and fuel. So in the same practice, take off slowly instead of using all the fuel you can to get up to the speed you want.

Putting a Stop to Skids

If you listen to some old-time drivers talking about winter driving experiences, you might hear one of them say, ". . . my trailer was coming around . . ." If their story was true, and it probably was, they were talking about their trailer skidding. The wheels on the trailer locked up. When the wheels on a trailer lock up, the tires do not have the traction needed to stay behind the semi-tractor. The trailer will want to slide left or right. This is the start of a short-lived event called a *jackknife*. You don't have to experience it.

REMEMBER

You should recognize when you are in a skid. When your mirrors are set correctly, you see only a sliver of your trailer in each mirror (when your semi-tractor and trailer are straight with each other). When you see more of the trailer in one mirror than the other, your trailer is moving in that direction. When you step on your brake pedal hard, you can expect a jackknife scenario, especially if you are pulling an antique trailer or a poorly maintained one.

After recognizing the trailer skid, take your foot off the brakes. When the trailer wheels start to roll again, the trailer will start to track behind the semi-tractor again. Do not use your trailer hand brake (also known as a Johnny bar) because being hard on the brakes caused the problem in the first place.

TIP

If you are on a rain-slick road or even a dry road when this happens, get your brakes and anti-lock brake system examined afterward. If they are in good working condition, you need to examine your driving habits and change them. Put a cup of water on your dashboard and then drive in such a manner that it doesn't spill.

AUTHOR SAYS

If you are on a slick winter road and driving a combination vehicle, you should have made the decision to stay safe by parking your truck and trailer. Don't risk damaging cargo, equipment, and most of all, people's lives.

Crossing Railroad Tracks

I hope you will be the type of commercial vehicle driver who looks up and down railroad tracks prior to crossing them, and I also hope that you conduct other cautionary procedures.

First, know whether you should come to a complete stop at railroad crossings. If you have a hazmat endorsement or a passenger endorsement, you should know the requirements you must observe. (See Chapters 14 and 16, respectively, for information on driving with passengers and hazardous materials.)

REMEMBER

Check the clearance underneath your vehicle. Low-slung trailers can get stuck on tracks that are raised. Also, if a fifth wheel is set far back on a semi-tractor or the semi-tractor has just a single drive axle, a long trailer's landing gear has an increased chance to get stuck on a railroad crossing. (The *landing gear* is what the front end of a trailer sits on when unhooked from a semi-tractor; see Chapter 12.)

If you ever get stuck on railroad tracks, get out of your vehicle, call 911, look for any identifying marks or US Department of Transportation (DOT) numbers of the crossing. Report your location and any landmarks that help identify the crossing.

Practice Questions

1. Which of the following will help prevent a rollover?

   (A) Pull a longer trailer and stay in the right lane.

   (B) Keep the cargo close to the ground and drive slowly around turns.

   (C) Place cargo as close to the front as possible.

   (D) Make your turns sharper.

2. Rearward amplification is:

   (A) A trailer tracking the opposite of a semi-tractor when backing.

   (B) Greater when pulling a long trailer.

   (C) Greater when pulling doubles over a single trailer.

   (D) Only a problem in the mountains.

3. Which of the following will help make a rollover likely?

   (A) Stacking cargo high.

   (B) Going fast around a turn.

   (C) Make a quick lane change while pulling doubles.

   (D) All of the above will help make a rollover occur.

4. Fully loaded rigs (semi-tractor and trailer) are:

   (A) 2 times more likely to rollover than with an empty trailer.

   (B) 5 times more likely to rollover than with an empty trailer.

   (C) 10 times more likely to rollover than with an empty trailer.

   (D) Going to stay on the road better due to their weight.

5. The rearward amplification of truck pulling conventional doubles (two 27-foot trailers) is:

   (A) 1.0.

   (B) 2.0.

   (C) 3.0.

   (D) 3.5.

6. Which statement is true?

   (A) A bobtail tractor will stop more quickly than a fully loaded semi-tractor trailer.

   (B) A fully loaded semi-tractor trailer will stop more quickly than a bobtail tractor.

   (C) A semi-tractor trailer combination will stop faster because it has more brakes.

   (D) Stiff suspensions decrease stopping distance.

7. Which of the following statements is true concerning safe braking?

   (A) You should brake early.

   (B) You should give yourself more space between you and the vehicle in front of you.

   (C) Look far ahead for potential stops.

   (D) All these are true statements for safe braking.

8. Which of the following statements is true concerning railroad crossings and combination vehicles?

(A) There is less of a problem for a single axle tractor than a dual axle tractor pulling a long trailer over a raised railroad crossing.

(B) If you get your trailer stuck on a raised railroad crossing, stay with the vehicle until authorities arrive.

(C) If you get your trailer stuck on a raised railroad crossing, walk down the track to warn trains to stop.

(D) Low-boy trailers and car carriers are more likely to get stuck on raised railroad crossings.

9. The rearward amplification of truck pulling triples (27 ft. each) is:

(A) 1.0.

(B) 2.0.

(C) 3.0.

(D) 3.5.

10. Which of the following is part of a proper procedure when you get your trailer stuck on a raised railroad crossing?

(A) Check to see if there are any DOT numbers identifying the crossing.

(B) Look for nearby landmarks.

(C) Call 911.

(D) All these are parts of a proper procedure for when you get your trailer stuck on a raised railroad crossing.

11. Which of the following is a false statement?

(A) A trailer skids when it loses traction.

(B) A trailer will more likely skid when loaded.

(C) A trailer skids when the brakes lock up the wheels.

(D) A trailer will stop skidding when the brake pedal is released and the brakes release.

12. Which of the following is a true statement?

(A) A trailer skid is when the trailer is pushing the semi-tractor around.

(B) You should stop a trailer skid by using the trailer hand brake.

(C) Once your trailer skids out of your lane, you have a better chance to prevent a jackknife.

(D) Recognize a trailer skid by checking your mirror when you brake hard.

13. Identify the false statement concerning turning:

(A) Swing wide to the left to make a right turn.

(B) When making a right turn, encroach onto the opposite direction of traffic on the street you are turning onto, if you need the space.

(C) Keep the rear wheel close to the curb on the right side of the trailer.

(D) When a trailer follows a different track than the semi-tractor, it is called off tracking.

14. On right turns, keep other vehicles from entering between your trailer and the curb by:

    (A) Keeping your tires close to the curb.

    (B) Swinging wide to the left first.

    (C) Jumping your tires over the curb.

    (D) Performing a jug handle turn.

15. Why wouldn't you use the trailer hand brake to control a trailer skid?

    (A) The trailer hand brake only works when testing brakes.

    (B) The brake chambers will burst with the extra pressure.

    (C) The brakes need to be released for the skid to stop.

    (D) You can use the trailer hand brake to control a trailer skid.

16. The trailer hand brake:

    (A) Is sometimes called the Jenny bar.

    (B) Should only be used for testing the brakes.

    (C) Should be used for parking.

    (D) Should be used to control skids.

17. Which statement about rearward amplification is false?

    (A) Is also known as surging

    (B) Causes the crack-the-whip effect

    (C) Is greater with two trailers than with one trailer

    (D) Is greater in a three-axle tractor trailer combination (27 ft. trailer) than a five-axle combination.

Answers and Explanations

1. **B.** Turning sharp does not help and can contribute to a rollover. Longer trailers and staying in the right lane and putting the cargo up front isn't much help. Keeping the cargo low and driving slowly around curves and turns are the best way to avoid rollovers.

2. **C.** Rearward amplification has nothing to do with backing and is not limited to mountains. Doubles have greater amplification than a single trailer as does triples over doubles.

3. **D.** All these scenarios can contribute to a rollover.

4. **C.** According to government sources, a fully loaded rig is 10 times more likely to rollover than an empty one.

5. **B.** According to the rearward amplification chart, it is 2.0.

6. **B.** Empty trucks and bobtails and stiff suspensions all have problems keeping their wheels on the road whereas a loaded truck will keep traction on the road and thus have shorter stopping distances.

7. **D.** All these items are true for safe braking.

8. **D.** Short single-drive axle tractors have more distance from the back of the tractor to the landing gear. Always get away from the railroad tracks.

9. **D.** According to the rearward amplification chart, it is 3.5.

10. **D.** You should look for ways to identify which crossing you are stuck as you call 911.

11. **B.** With more weight pushing the tires down on the pavement, it gets harder for a trailer to skid.

12. **D.** A trailer skid is when the trailer is skidding around the tractor. You never use the trailer brake handle for getting out of any skid. Choice C makes no sense, but you should check your mirrors for a possible trailer skid in hard braking occurrences.

13. **A.** Steering wide to the left will open up space on the right for a car to get pinch between your truck and some other object. It will also fail you on your behind-the-wheel road test.

14. **A.** Ultimately your goal is to keep your tires close enough to the curb to make it impossible for a car to get in between your vehicle and the curb.

15. **C.** The trailer brake handle will work even though it's not to be used for anything other than testing. However, to stop a skid, the wheels need to start rolling again.

16. **B.** It's Johnny bar not Jenny bar. It should be clear that the trailer brake handle is only for testing the trailer service brakes.

17. **A.** Surging is a term involving liquids in a tank.

Chapter **11**

Backing a Combination Vehicle

The physics of backing a combination vehicle is the same, for the most part, whether you have a car with a little utility trailer or a semi-tractor with a 53-foot-long trailer. There is a difference in how fast the two parts of the combination react based on how long the sections are. So the speed changes, but the direction you turn your steering wheel and the direction that the trailer turns doesn't change. In this chapter, I use a toy truck and trailer, a "long" set to illustrate backing a combination vehicle. After all, besides watching my dad, playing with my toys is how I initially learned how to back up a combination vehicle. And if you played with me, you had to drive correctly, none of this scooting vehicles sideways. When you backed a trailer, you were not allowed to cheat. By the way, in case you missed it, I couldn't play with trucks, cars, and tractors with other kids — they didn't "drive" right.

This chapter explains how a combination vehicle works when backing up to take the mystery out of it and get your mind wrapped around backing such a vehicle. Then I walk you through, step by step, how to be more successful in backing any size basic combination.

TIP

In a later section, I give you a physics lesson on a commonly unexpected maneuver that is required when backing a trailer. Unless you have been playing with the toys or have experience with backing a camper or boat trailer, you might find it strange that you turn the steering wheel in the opposite direction of where you want your trailer to go. In short, you turn the steering wheel right to make the trailer go left.

Preparing for Backing

AUTHOR SAYS

I have a friend who tells a story about an older carpenter who was installing vinyl flooring, the kind that comes in one roll, in the kitchen of his parents' house. The carpenter would measure and then he would go outside to mark the vinyl and back inside measure again, taking "forever" to get the vinyl cut for that kitchen. Finally, the carpenter took the vinyl and laid it out in the kitchen — perfectly. This example demonstrates how you can accomplish your goal by performing the right steps before and during your backing process.

Setting your mirrors

TIP

If you didn't properly set your mirrors during the pre-trip inspection, do it before backing. First, position your semi-tractor or truck straight with the trailer by pulling straight ahead first. This sets your trailer straight with the towing unit so that mirrors can be adjusted properly. Adjust your mirrors so that you see only a sliver of the trailer in each mirror — the same amount of trailer in each mirror. By setting your mirrors this way, you can see which direction your trailer is going. If you see more trailers in the right mirror, your trailer is moving to the right, whether that is your intention or not.

Practicing WATER and GOAL

REMEMBER

GOAL is a well-known acronym in the trucking industry that stands for Get Out and Look. Like the carpenter who repeatedly went in and out of the house measuring again, you should get out and look at your backing path and at the objects in your *blind spots* (the areas you can't see). You are limited during your behind-the-wheel test how many times you can get out and look before the license examiner starts giving you points (that you don't want). After you get your license, you have no limits on how many times you can GOAL. "But it's not professional to get out and look," you say. Do you think it's professional looking to hit an object?

WATER is a lesser-known acronym, probably because it came after the GOAL acronym and drivers realized that GOAL was effective. WATER stands for Walk Around the Entire Rig. WATER adds an aspect of GOAL where not only do you get out and look, but you must look all around the vehicle. Many commercial drivers go to the back end of the trailer and stop there. They fail to inspect the right side or the blind side of the vehicle. Failure to WATER often results in a backing failure.

Finding a spotter

It can save time, and anxiety, when you use a spotter that you can trust. It likely won't happen often. But when you use a spotter, be sure to agree on signals, especially for the one that means stop. Your spotter should not tell you how to back up or steer — just how much room you have. Your spotter should always see you in your mirror and should never pass behind the trailer where you can't see them. By the way, you can't use a spotter on your behind-the-wheel test. The time you will most likely use a spotter is at a customer location that is difficult to back into, meaning the customer is well aware of the issue and thus is probably accustomed to providing a spotter.

Setting Yourself Up for Success

A carpenter will set their arm in a specific position to effectively hammer a nail into a board. You position your hands in a specific position at your keyboard when you want to type a message or composition effectively. As a driver, you will set your vehicle in a position to effectively back it into the desired location.

The best setup is the one where you can back straight into the parking spot or the dock. However, there will be many locations where you won't be given enough space to back straight. This would be the case for truck stops and most warehouses. So in this section, I address primarily backing at an angle, like a 45-degree angle, the similar scenario you will find at the truck stops and warehouses.

Know that the distances over which you perform backing steps are determined by lengths of the towing unit and trailer. How long or how soon you start to turn will depend on these dynamics. I am not going to give you a formula to accomplish this every time. It is impossible to do that. However, I will tell you how to do this successfully — no matter the size of the vehicles.

Seeing the path of success with a proper setup

Figure 11-1 shows there is a path for the trailer to roll into the parking location. To arrive at this *setup* (the term used for placing your vehicle in a position to back up), you typically drive past your spot with the spot on your left. How far you drive past your spot depends on your equipment. If you are pulling a 53-foot trailer with a semi-tractor with a sleeper berth, pull up beside the second space past the desired space. Keep moving and make a hard right turn (when I say hard right or left turn, I mean turn the steering wheel all the way left or right). Keep moving. When the semi-tractor has moved 90 degrees (parallel with the parking spot) steer all the way back to the left. Again, keep the rig moving. Stop when you see both the left rear of the trailer and the spot that you want to back into. (This "formula" is shown at the end of this chapter and will vary slightly, depending on the equipment.)

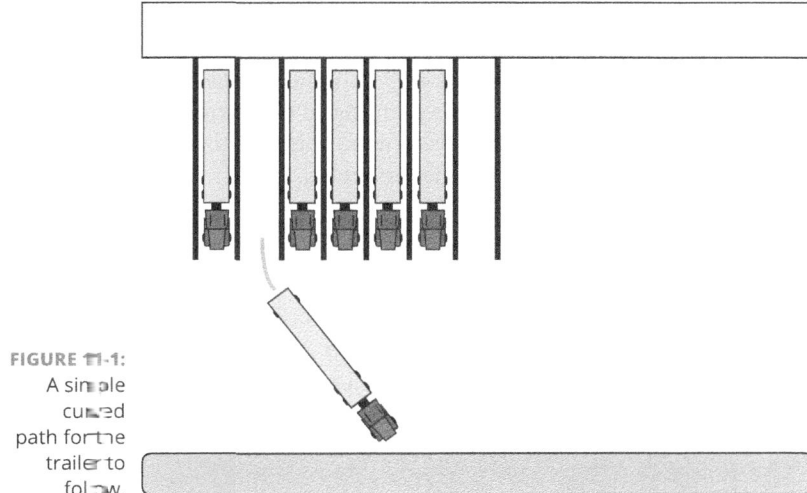

FIGURE 11-1: A simple curved path for the trailer to follow.

"Why can't you just give us a formula?" I can give you a formula, but it won't be what you are thinking. The one that most people want isn't possible because the degree of steering is different from vehicle to vehicle. The distance from the steer tires to the pivot is different, the position of the drive axle in relation to the connection of the trailer and towing unit is different. The trailer can be hooked behind the axle, or it might be over the axle. The distance between the trailer/towing unit connection and the trailers axle(s) is different. There are just too many variables to produce a formula that works in every backing situation.

Making it hard with an improper setup

I am being emphatic when I say don't bother attempting to back a trailer when the trailer is not facing the correct direction. To say it another way, don't attempt backing when the path that you would have to steer the trailer is in the shape of an "S" (see Figure 11-2). You are not ready to back the trailer. Don't bother trying! The trailer's path should be straight or a simple curve.

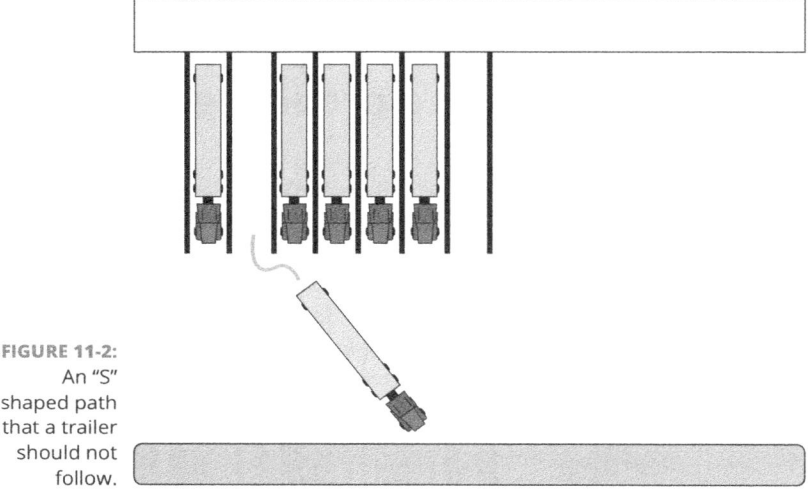

FIGURE 11-2:
An "S"
shaped path
that a trailer
should not
follow.

So you ask, "What do I do then?" There are two basic things to do when you would have to steer in an "S" instead of a simple curve or straight line. One is to pull up farther away from the spot you plan to park the trailer, until the rear of your trailer is pointing in the correct direction. The other is to try again, starting over. It will be quicker and less frustrating than to make an attempt at backing a trailer in a situation that experienced professionals would avoid.

Being the tortoise instead of the hare

Backing a combination vehicle is not a race, it is an accomplishment — a task. A task that has a couple of goals at the end. The goals are to place your trailer straight in the center of the parking spot or squared up with a dock (where cargo is unloaded, with a floor that meets at the same height as your trailer). The actual first goal is to not hit anything in the process of backing your trailer to the desired position.

You need to take the process slow because there is too much to do and to verify. When you cover ground too quickly, you likely fail in the actual first goal listed above. As you are backing, your head should be on a swivel, swiveling back and forth checking your mirrors.

Visualizing the back

See in your mind what should be happening as you back into a spot. Anticipating is preparing or attempting to make steps occur at the proper time. You can also refer to it as timing. Recognizing is visually checking your position and then understanding what you need to do. When you get the opportunity to observe someone backing, take advantage of it. Whether they are experienced or a brand-new student, it makes no difference as you can learn from the observation. These are both critical skills for you to develop.

Anticipating alignment

TIP

Anticipate when the semi-tractor will come in line with the trailer. Anticipating too late will result in going past the squaring up mentioned in the main goals above. But that is okay, I still do it some to this day. It is no big deal as I will show you what to do in just a little bit. With successful anticipation, the trailer is progressively moving into the center of the parking spot, with the semi-tractor moving towards being in line with it. The semi-tractor's steer wheels are turned in a direction that is moving the front of the semi-tractor into the same line as the trailer. This is anticipating when the trailer is going to become straight and attempting to have the semi-tractor become straight at the same time.

Now, you will often mistime this part of backing. Again, this is okay. When you mistime this event, watch the far end of the trailer (I hope you have been watching it all along). If the trailer is going back to its left, stop and pull forward, turning your steering wheel to the right. This maneuver more quickly straightens the trailer and gets the semi-tractor closer to being straight with the trailer. There is no need to pull up far. Just pull up far enough that your trailer is again pointing in the right direction. Don't pull up too far and undo all your hard work.

Recognizing movement

REMEMBER

In an earlier section, I instructed on mirror adjustment and usage. Their adjustment is very important now. When you are backing into position, use both mirrors to see your semi-tractor's position relative to the trailer. Recognize at this point what is happening, remembering that if you see more of your trailer in one mirror than the other, the trailer is moving that direction. If you don't want the trailer to move that direction, turn your steering wheel in that direction. Yes, I said that correctly. If you look in your mirror and your trailer is moving to the right a little bit, move your steering wheel to the right a little bit, moving the steering wheel back to center as your trailer starts going the right direction again.

You should constantly swivel your head back and forth looking in both mirrors. As you do, react immediately to any drift of the trailer by making slight adjustments with the steering wheel. If you are not making little tweaks constantly, you will probably have to make bigger tweaks, like stopping completely and moving forward until your trailer is set up again where you can see a simple path for your trailer to be steered into the desired position.

TIP

Not all "pull-ups" are the result of bad decisions, sometimes pulling up is just part of the backing process.

Studying Physics

The basic combination vehicle has one pivot point, which is the setup I discuss in this chapter. It is usually at the fifth wheel or where the trailer is coupled to a hitch. There are more complicated vehicle combinations with extra pivot points. One example is *doubles* (two trailers). When you have both of your trailers and the dolly (see Chapter 15) all coupled together, you have three pivot points. Don't bother attempting to back this combination. While it is possible to back a vehicle with two pivot points, I am not going to address that scenario either, and you will not be required to do a behind-the-wheel test with such a setup, nor should you even think about trying (unless you grew up on a farm backing hay wagons).

Seeing the path of the wheels

TIP

One way to determine the path of the trailer is to observe the *tandems* (the two axles that you commonly see under a big semi-trailer). Which way are they heading? Which way would they go if you reversed direction? How far off are they from the intended target? When you ask yourself these questions, look and picture in your mind what will happen when the trailer is moved. The more you do this, the better you will be at assessing your situation.

Seeing the path of the trailer

TIP

Something bigger (sometimes) to watch is the rear of the trailer. When you have a box trailer, there is a good chance that there is trailer sticking out several feet behind the rear axle. You must watch this path for three reasons.

>> To know if the trailer is about to hit another trailer, a building, or anything else.

>> To know where the trailer is going at all times.

>> To guide you in the backing process.

When you are backing a trailer, you are sitting in a remote position, guiding and steering the back of the trailer. You are steering the trailer with your semi-tractor. So when the trailer is headed the wrong direction, go back to where you were and do the opposite.

Steering left to go right

Steering to the left to go right, "That makes no sense," says the rookie. If it doesn't make sense that you turn your steering wheel to the left to make the trailer go right, it is time for you to play with the toys. When you are starting to back your trailer and need it to go right, you turn the steering wheel to the left which pushes the front of the trailer to the left but the trailer pivots on the tires. By pivoting on the tires, whatever is behind the tires points in the opposite direction . . . in this case, it is the right side of the trailer — vice versa for turning the trailer to the left.

At some point (soon) after steering the trailer in the desired direction, the steering wheel must be steered in the opposite direction in order to not perform a *jackknife* (describes the situation where the towing unit strikes the trailer).

Picturing it all together

I mentioned earlier that one of the ways I learned to back was by playing with my toys as a kid. You can do the same thing. Find a semi-tractor with a steering wheel or a truck that steers and attach a trailer. Experiment and learn the physics of backing by using the toys. Seeing the bird's eye view of backing can put a new perspective on how backing works for you.

In Figure 11-3, I used toy trucks in a series of backing photos to illustrate how a real truck would back up. Read the descriptions below and look closely at the photos because there are subtle differences. It might be worth replicating the backing maneuver by borrowing some toy trucks from your kids or grandchildren (or maybe find toy trucks at a garage sale).

1. Driving past with the spot on the left.

2. Turning the steering wheel to the right. This semi-tractor doesn't have a very tight turning radius so the driver must turn earlier than I mentioned previously in this chapter.

THE COMMON MISTAKES NEW DRIVERS MAKE WHEN BACKING

One common mistake that a new driver makes when backing is turning the steering wheel too far. Another mistake is holding a turn of the steering wheel too long. Even worse is turning the steering wheel too much for too long, which can really complicate things.

Making these mistakes results in placing your trailer in a worse position. Remember the anticipating section earlier in the chapter? It takes longer for a long semi-tractor or a long trailer to react — both for correcting a mistake and for making the correct maneuver. If you recognize that the trailer is in the correct position and then at that point begin trying to get your semi-tractor in line as you back up, the trailer will continue to turn, moving out of position.

There will be occasion to turn the steering wheel a lot but remember that it is just for a brief moment that you hold the steering wheel in this position.

I need to mention one more common mistake. New drivers can forget about part of their vehicle when backing. They fail to Get Out and Look and don't see the part of their vehicle that is out of sight, like the right rear corner of the trailer or the front right corner of the semi-tractor.

3. Moving right . . .

4. Still moving to the right.

5. Steering left and still moving . . .

6. Still steering left and still moving. Driver does not have a view of the left rear of the trailer nor of the space to back into.

7. Driver stops. Driver now has a view of the left rear of the trailer and of the space to back into.

8. After Getting Out and Looking (GOAL) our driver puts the semi-tractor in reverse and steers to the right. Turning the steering wheel to the right while backing steers the trailer to the left.

9. As the trailer continues to turn, the angle that the semi-tractor and trailer forms gets tighter. The driver is steering the trailer and determines the angle of the semi-tractor with the trailer needs to remain the same for a bit (for the trailer to hit the parking spot).

10. Since the driver determined the angle the semi-tractor and trailer need to remain the same for a bit, the driver returns the steering to center for the steer tires to be straight. The driver will *alternate* between the steering being straight *and* to the left a little to keep the same correct angle.

11. Still moving, the driver is alternating between the steering being straight and to the left a little to keep the same correct angle. Here the steering wheel is to the left.

12. As the trailer gets farther and straighter into the spot, the driver knows that the semi-tractor is not going to be straight with the trailer. The driver does not need to pull completely out to make adjustments — maybe several little adjustments — but each time making progress in moving the semi-tractor straight with the trailer. The driver should have performed another GOAL or two by this point.

13. The driver must stop at this point and pull forward a little, steering to the right. The driver will observe the trailer and how it will straighten up prior to the semi-tractor getting straight with the trailer.

14. After pulling forward a little and the trailer straightening up with the spot, the driver is backing up, turning the steering wheel to the left to gain ground on getting the semi-tractor straight with the trailer. The driver will repeat this back-and-forth procedure as many times as necessary.

15. After a few up and backs, the driver has the semi-tractor straight with the trailer and will back the trailer all the way into the parking spot.

16. But alas, the driver has the semi-tractor and trailer a little over to its left side. That is okay as the driver will make one last pull-up to straighten and center the trailer when backing in the spot. Centering the semi-tractor and trailer helps with anyone who arrives or leaves in the spaces next to that driver. It will also help dock operations to work correctly.

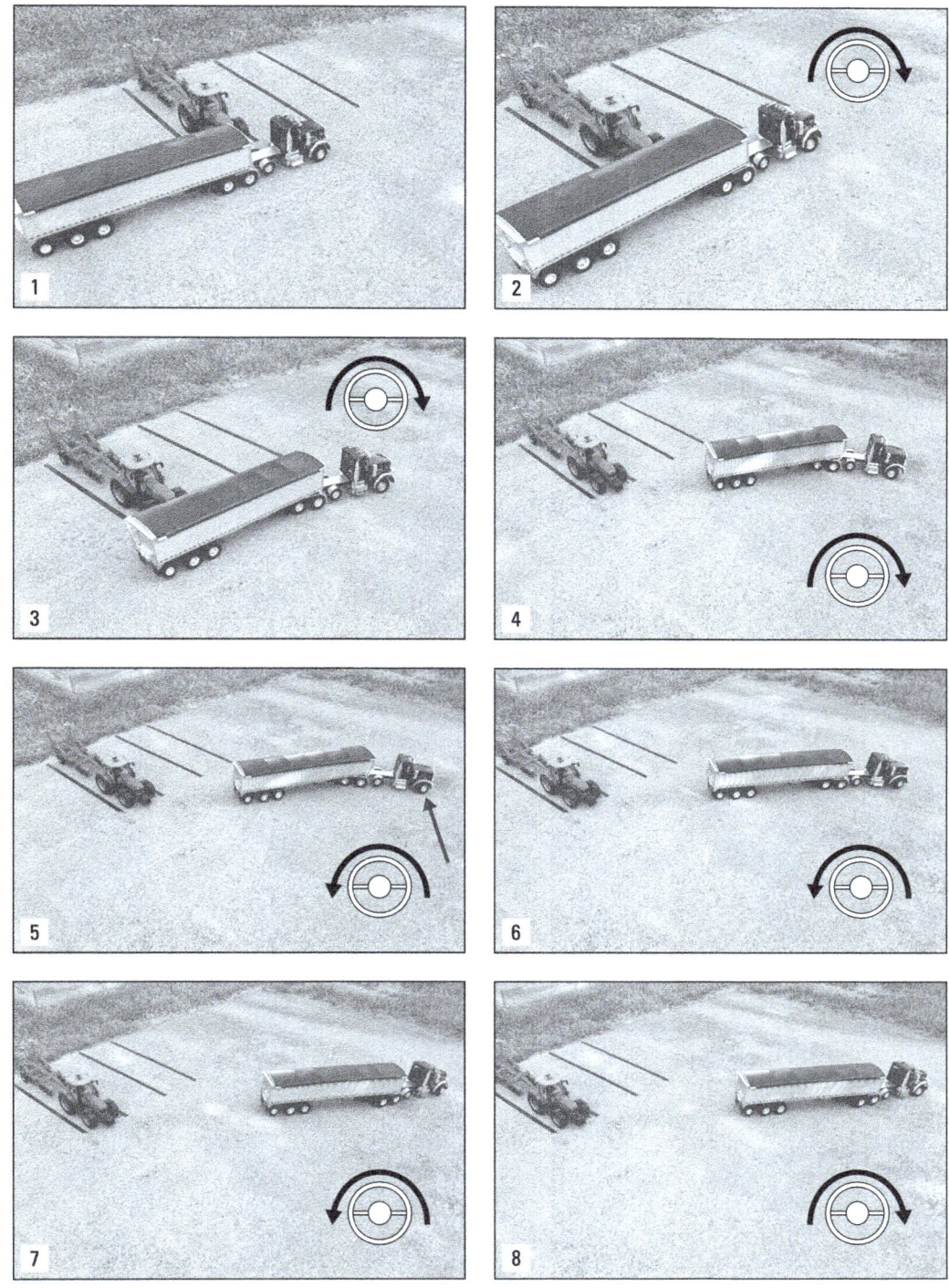

FIGURE 11-3:
A backing
sequence.

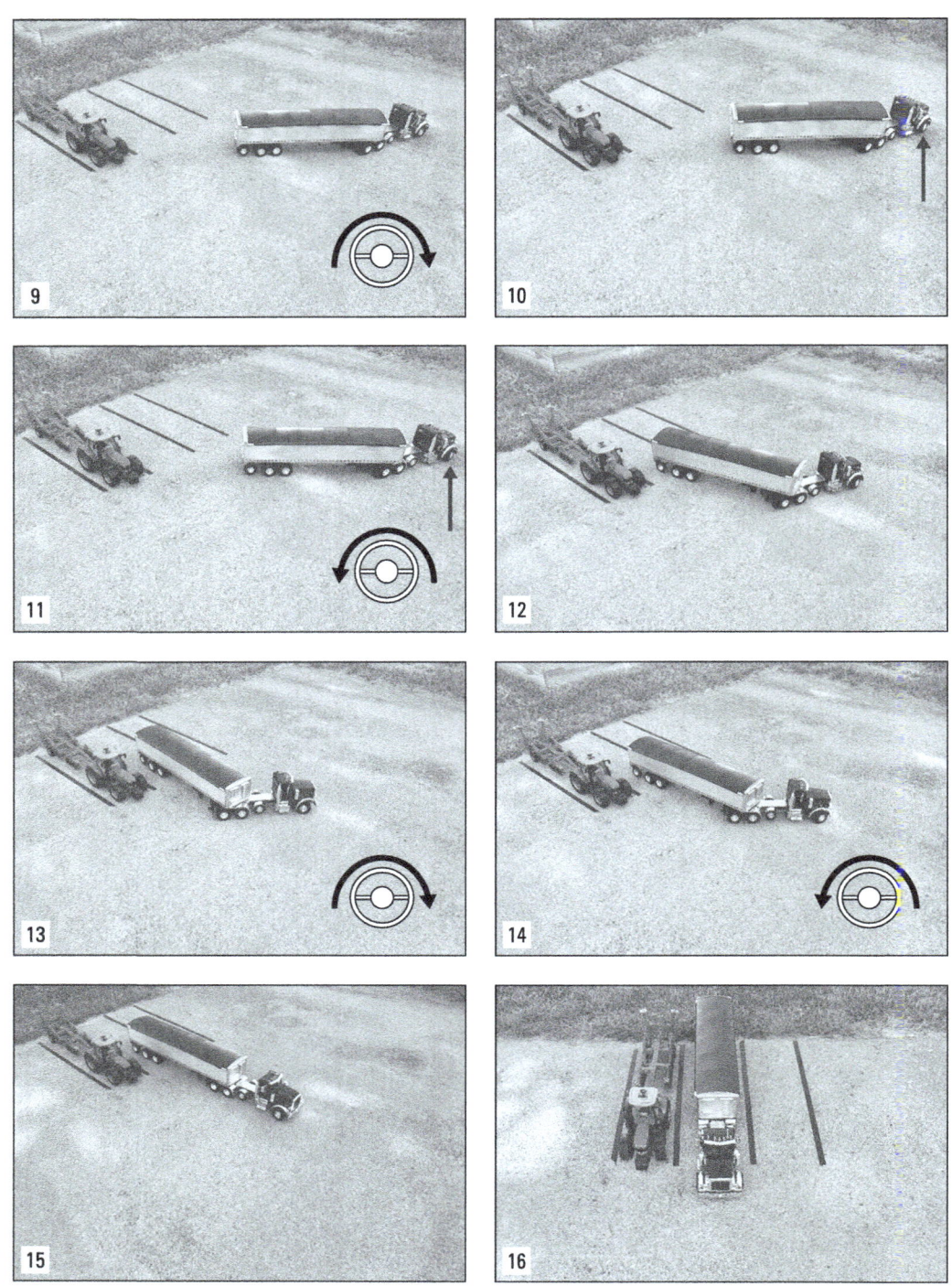

FIGURE 11-3: continued

Practice Questions

There are no questions on the written test for backing. However, there might be a question or two on backing in the combination vehicle test, so here are a few practice questions:

1. Which of the following is the best position for backing?
    (A) Straight line
    (B) Curved line
    (C) An "S" path
    (D) A 90-degree angle

2. When backing, which is better?
    (A) Have the parking spot on your right.
    (B) Have the parking spot on your left.
    (C) Standing on your step and steer the truck from the outside.
    (D) Remembering the formula.

3. Which of the following helps to be more successful at backing?
    (A) Adjusting your mirrors properly.
    (B) Move slowly.
    (C) Getting out and walking around the entire rig.
    (D) These are all helpful in backing.

4. When your trailer is starting to drift to the left, which of the following is the best tactic?
    (A) Keep the course, it will straighten itself out.
    (B) Turn the steering wheel to the right.
    (C) Turn the steering wheel to the left.
    (D) Stop, pull up, and start all over.

Answers and Explanations

1. **A.** Always choose to back straight when you have a choice. Backing straight eliminates the blind spots on the sides.

2. **B.** The best choice is to have the parking or dock spot to the left. If it is on the right, you have a bigger blind spot. Any specific formulas will fail you from time to time. Every situation is likely to be different.

3. **D.** These are all helpful in backing.

4. **C.** When your trailer is drifting to the left, steering to the left pushes the front end of the semi-tractor to the right, which pushes the front end of the trailer to the left, which causes the rear of the trailer to point more to the right, thus correcting the left-hand drift.

Chapter **12**

Understanding the Parts and Functions

I n your test for a combination vehicle (Class A), there will be questions on the different aspects of driving combination vehicles and on the uniqueness of combination vehicles. While you might be getting a Commercial Driver's License (CDL) for combining a *straight truck* (which is designed to be used by itself without a trailer but optionally with a trailer, like a dump truck that one day pulls a flatbed trailer with a loader on it), all the questions will be on the traditional trailers that are combined with semi-tractors. Additionally, questions will be on air brakes and fifth wheels but not on *pintle hitches* (a common hitching mechanism for a straight truck with a heavy-duty trailer).

The written tests also assume that trailers have air brakes. If you will be driving a straight truck and pulling a trailer occasionally in real life, you are more likely to have electric, hydraulic brakes, or *surge* (brakes that are mechanically activated when the towing vehicle has its brakes applied, and the trailer pushes into the towing vehicle). I am guessing that the reason for the snub of these type of brakes is that there is less to know or do with those brakes. The assumption might be that air brakes require more unique knowledge than other brakes because once you have air brakes connected properly you don't have to do any additional steps. (I personally know pulling trailers with other types of brakes don't mean you aren't a professional driver.)

In this chapter, I discuss how to couple and uncouple (hookup and unhook) a semi-trailer to a semi-tractor, using the method that states (collectively known as the State Departments of Transportation or State DOTs) use as there will be questions on their written tests. However, I also provide my way of coupling/uncoupling, which is different from the State DOTs method, yet it's effective. Most professional drivers perform this task close to if not the same way that I do it.

Getting Familiar with Unique Components

In this section, I want to acquaint you with unique components that are found in combination vehicles. The uniqueness of coupling two or more vehicles together requires more safety considerations and components to learn. The components that couple a semi-tractor and trailer together are addressed later in this chapter. Connecting and checking the air brake system has its own requirements as well.

Lining up the connections

A combination vehicle literally combines two vehicles. One of them supplies the power — air, electrical, and "muscle." Lines or cords connect between the two vehicles to the supply the towed vehicle (trailer) with operating brake lights and taillights, and air for brakes and suspensions. Some more specialized trailers will have more uses for the air and electrical. Dump trucks will utilize hydraulic pressure from the semi-tractors, but these functions and applications are not on the tests nor will I address them in this section.

Service air line

REMEMBER

The *service air line* (also called the control line or the signal line in books) is the conduit to communicating with the trailer's brakes. It is controlled by the brake pedal or the trailer hand valve. You control the braking power by how hard you press on the pedal, the harder you press on the pedal, the harder the brakes are applied. The service line is connected to relay valves that allow the trailer brakes to be applied more quickly. This line can be blue or have a blue end to it called a *gladhand* (see Figure 12-1).

FIGURE 12-1:
A service air line.

Emergency air line

REMEMBER

The *emergency air line* can also be called the supply line as that is its main function, at least what it is doing 99.9 percent of the time (that's my unofficial estimate). This air line supplies air to the trailer, which has one or more tanks to fill.

When there is a loss of air in the trailer's air supply, usually sudden or at least a substantial loss, the emergency air line replenishes the air needed for the emergency brakes on the trailer. The emergency air line is red or has a red gladhand at the end (see Figure 12-2).

FIGURE 12-2:
An emergency air line.

The sudden loss of air can be from a trailer coming uncoupled or a hose air line bursting or getting damaged. My personal observation has been that it's always due to someone failing to couple a semi-tractor to a trailer correctly or forgetting to remove the air lines after uncoupling.

Gladhand

REMEMBER

There are components of commercial motor vehicles whose inventors had no creativity in naming their invention. However, that is not true with gladhands. Gladhands are the ends of air lines that couple with other gladhands. They can be the end of another air line that they attach to or to a solidly mounted coupler mounted on a trailer. Gladhands provide a connection, like a firm hand-shake, but do not require tools to accomplish it. There are rubber seals that meet up with each other to provide a leak-proof connection (see Figure 12-3).

TIP

Clean the seals on two gladhands and place the seals together forming a 90-degree angle with the gladhands (see the photo in the section, "Trying my method" later in the chapter). The rubber seals should rotate on each other as you rotate the gladhand(s) to form a straight line. If the glad-hands don't seem to be in line with each other, try again; but this time, moisten the rubber seals just a little bit — just don't get water into the lines.

You don't want water or dirt in your air lines so store unused gladhands on dummy couplers (or holders) as shown in Figure 12-4, or couple them with each other in the same manner that you would couple them with the trailer's connections.

Seven-way cord

REMEMBER

The *seven-way cord* is the electrical cord that connects between the semi-tractor and trailer or other similar combinations. The seven-way cord plugs tightly into a receiver. Dielectric grease is a waterproof, nonconductive lubricant that should be used on these connections. It will extend their life by reducing corrosion and providing lubrication for easier connecting and disconnect-ing. There is a lid to the connection box where the cord is plugged into that doubles as a "keeper" for the plug. The lid must have a spring to keep the lid down so that the tabs of the two compo-nents work to keep the cord in the receiver (see Figure 12-5).

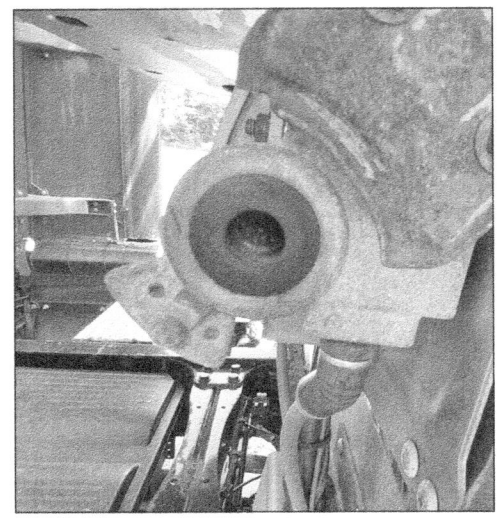

FIGURE 12-3:
A gladhand seal on the trailer gladhand (the round black rubber).

FIGURE 12-4:
Gladhands on a dummy coupler.

FIGURE 12-5:
A lid with its tab keeping a seven-way cord in place.

Identifying the air valves and tanks

Your typical semi-tractor and trailer is equipped with air brakes, and thus your exams will have its questions constructed assuming the same. The other brake systems do not require as much knowledge to operate. There was not a lot of imagination used when naming the following components, so try using their names to help you remember their function.

REMEMBER

>> **Trailer air supply control valve.** This valve is what the eight-sided, red knob (located in the semi-tractor cab on your dashboard) is attached to. When you push it in, it allows air to pressurize the trailer's air lines, air supply tanks, and air bags. It also controls the parking brakes on the trailer. When you pull out on the knob, air is released from the brake lines that were keeping the spring brakes from being applied; take away the air and the spring brakes are applied.

When the air pressure drops, somewhere between 20 and 45 PSI, the red knob pops out, spring brakes (which function as parking brakes and emergency brakes) get set.

>> **Tractor protection valve.** Also controlled somewhat by the same red knob mentioned above, this valve, located likely at the rear bottom of the semi-tractor's cab, protects the air supply in the semi-tractor in the event of a substantial air loss in the trailer's air system (like the air lines becoming disconnected or the trailer itself disconnecting). When there is that type of air loss from the trailer, this valve will shut off the air supply to the trailer, protecting the air supply for the semi-tractor. The spring/emergency parking brakes will be set on the trailer, the same as when the trailer air supply control valve is pulled out.

I have found conflicting information on the pressure at which the valve should pop out, but it was always 20 to 45 PSI. I don't think that anyone will miss a question if they remember that it is in this basic range. The valve should never pop out below 20 PSI!

REMEMBER

>> **Tractor parking valve.** Controlled by the yellow knob on the dashboard, this valve will close (pop out) when air pressure is too low, 20 to 45 PSI, causing the semi-tractor emergency brakes to come on.

>> **Shutoff valve.** Gladhands from a *converter dolly* (the chassis looking device that enables a semi-tractor to pull two or more trailers or doubles) can hook to these valves, which are generally located at the end of a trailer, so that air can be supplied to an additional trailer. Shutoff valves should be open if there are lines hooked to them. They should be closed if there are no lines connected to them.

>> **Trailer air tanks.** Trailers — like trucks, buses, and semi-tractors — need to have air pressure stored and ready to be used for braking applications. You will have one or more tanks on your trailer. Like the tanks on the powered vehicle, they need to be drained of water accumulation (condensation) by an automatic drain valve or by draining them manually.

Pressure in the service line (controlled by the driver on the brake pedal) tells how much pressure the relay valves (components that speed up the application and release of the brakes) should release to the brakes.

>> **Trailer hand valve.** CDL study guides and most likely written tests will refer to a trailer hand valve, which is what you use for testing the trailer brakes; but it's also known as the trailer hand brake, Johnny bar, Johnson bar, or trolley valve. Do not use it for driving purposes or to attempt to get out of a skid. When you apply the brakes with your foot on the brake pedal, it sends air to the towing vehicle and the trailer. Using the trailer hand valve may cause a dangerous situation in which you go into a skid.

AUTHOR
SAYS

Your written test might have a question about using the trailer hand valve for parking, which will cause you to lose all your air and then have no spring brakes. This is a true statement for trailers built prior to 1975. These antique trailers have emergency air brakes that work as long as there is sufficient air supply. Once air runs out, there is no emergency brake or parking brake. So if you are driving one of these trailers, be sure to *chock* (block) the wheels so it won't roll away.

For a vehicle built before 1975, you have emergency brakes for as long as there is air in the trailer's system. But if there is a substantial leak, you can end up with no brakes for the trailer.

Using ABS

You don't have to know a lot about anti-lock brake systems (ABS), but there will likely be questions about ABS on more than one written test. ABS is a component of the general knowledge test, the air brake test, and the combination vehicle test, and oh yeah . . . it is in the pre-trip inspections as well. I cover a few basics in this chapter, just like you might see on your test.

Regulating the ABS

All trailers and converter dollies are manufactured with ABS as of March 1, 1998. You aren't likely to pull a trailer older than that because many companies will not allow their freight to be hauled with trailers older than 10 years. However, the date is important to remember for the written test.

Trailers with ABS should have a yellow ABS malfunction lamp on the left side (which would be in the view of the driver's side mirror). It can be located on the front or rear of the trailer (in real life, you will only find the yellow lamp on the rear corner by the red marker lamp). Converter dollies are to have the ABS lamp simply on the left side.

These lamps are to come on when the key/ignition is turned but go out in a few seconds, in which time, your ABS performs a self-diagnostic test. If your lamp stays on, the ABS has a malfunction. If your lamp didn't come on at all, you might have a bad bulb, bad wiring, or another problem. In either of these cases, if the light stays on or never comes on, have a repair performed as soon as possible. Your brakes will still function normally but you do have a violation.

If ABS fails (malfunctions), drive normally, but get the ABS repaired soon. There's no reason to have roadside service come and make a repair but do prioritize getting to a shop.

Applying ABS

ABS is a system added to your brake system, but it does not make your brakes more powerful or increase your brakes capacity, nor does it allow you to drive faster or closer to other vehicles. ABS doesn't even activate until it senses that your brakes are about to lock up.

ABS helps prevent your wheels from locking up. When wheels lock up, a vehicle can skid. When you have a skid, you are out of control of the vehicle because the tires are not rolling. You can control where your vehicle goes when your tires have a grip on the road.

If there is ABS only on your trailer, or only one axle, you still have greater control when you are braking. Your trailer is less likely to swing out in hard braking events. If you lose control of your steering, you need to let off of the brake pedal until you resume control (wheels are no longer locked up but rolling).

When you drive a vehicle with ABS, brake normally. This means:

>> Only use the amount of braking force for you to brake safely and stay in control.

>> Brake the same way whether you have ABS on just your semi-tractor or just your trailer or on both.

>> Monitor your semi-tractor and trailer as you slow down to stay in control, easing off the brake pedal to stay in control if it is safe to do so.

Coupling and Uncoupling the Trailer

Coupling to a trailer is the action of hooking a trailer to a semi-tractor. To couple a trailer and a semi-tractor together is like making them one unit. When they are properly coupled they generally don't come apart, even in accidents. The engineering and strength of the kingpin and fifth wheel is truly incredible.

I propose that there are two ways to successfully couple a semi-tractor with a trailer — the method that State DOTs say the coupling should be done and my method (as well as many other drivers').

In this section, I introduce you to a few components that are unique to combination vehicles. You need to understand the function of these components, which will be helpful for passing tricky written tests and the pre-trip inspection test.

Satisfying the state

REMEMBER

This section about coupling is the one to study in preparation for your written test. The CDL written tests and the study guides are written as if all the trailers in use today were made before 1975. As of January 1, 1975, all trailers manufactured with air brakes must be equipped with spring brakes. Spring brakes are synonymous with parking brakes. So, to recap, use this section to pass the written test for your Commercial Learner's Permit. I will follow up with a modern version of coupling with photos to boot.

1. **Inspect your fifth wheel and kingpin (see Figures 12-6 and 12-7) to ensure that:**

   - It is greased.
   - The locking jaws are open.
   - The fifth wheel is tilted down in the back.
   - The safety lock/unlock handle (see the figure with Step 16) is in the automatic lock position.
   - Kingpin is not bent or broken.
   - If your fifth wheel is a sliding fifth wheel, make sure it is locked.

2. **Chock the wheels or ensure that the spring brakes are on. Any cargo should be secure.**

3. **Position your semi-tractor directly in front of the trailer, backed up evenly from side to side.**

4. **Back slowly until the fifth wheel touches the trailer.**

5. **Put the semi-tractor's transmission in neutral, set the parking brakes, and turn off the engine.**

FIGURE 12-6:
A fifth
wheel.

FIGURE 12-7:
A kingpin.

6. **Check the trailer height and alignment with the truck.**

- The trailer should lift off the ground slightly when the semi-tractor is backed under it. Adjust as necessary to make this happen. If the trailer is too high, it will not be coupled correctly. If the trailer is too low, the fifth wheel or semi-tractor frame can hit the trailer.

- The kingpin and the opening in the fifth wheel should be aligned with the path of the semi-tractor.

7. **Inspect your air lines and their seals.**

- Connect the red emergency air line to the trailer's emergency gladhand.

- Connect the blue service air line to the trailer's service gladhand.

- Ensure the lines will not get pinched or damaged when the semi-tractor is backing under the trailer.

8. **Supply air to the trailer.**

   - Push in the trailer air supply knob.

   - Wait for the trailer's tanks and air lines to fill.

   - Shut engine off.

   - Listen for leaks.

   - Test the trailer brakes by listening for the air being applied and released and the brakes applying and releasing.

   - Check the air pressure supply gauge for normal air loss.

9. **Set the trailer brakes by pulling the red air supply knob.**

10. **Put your semi-tractor in the lowest reverse gear and back under the trailer, slowly, stopping when the kingpin locks in the fifth wheel.**

11. **Check for a secure connection.**

    - Raise the landing gear with the dolly crank handle (see Figure 12-8) to be just an inch or slightly more off the ground.

    - Tug on the trailer by gently pulling forward. The trailer should resist the movement and keep the semi-tractor from dragging it. If the kingpin uncouples from the fifth wheel, immediately stop the semi-tractor! Assess what went wrong. Get help if you don't know.

FIGURE 12-8: Landing gear that has its pads an inch off the ground.

12. **Secure the semi-tractor.**

    - Set the parking brakes.

    - Put the transmission in neutral.

    - Turn off the engine and take the keys.

13. **Inspect the coupling (kingpin and fifth wheel connection).**

    - There should be no space between the fifth wheel and the apron of the trailer.

    - Look through the back of the fifth wheel. The fifth wheel locking jaws should be securely locked around the kingpin.

- The locking handle or release handle should be in the lock position (all the way in).

- The safety latch is in position over the locking lever.

- If the coupling is not correct, it must be fixed before driving with a trailer.

14. **Connect the electrical cord and inspect.**

- The electrical cord (seven-way cord) should have the safety latch/cover in place securing the cord.

- Check for damage on air lines and the cord.

- Ensure the air lines and electrical cord will not be contacting any moving parts nor rubbing on other parts of the semi-tractor.

15. **Raise (crank) the landing gear all the way up, stowing the crank handle in its holder (see Figure 12-9). Ensure that the clearance is sufficient between:**

- The landing gear and frame/tires/mudflaps to avoid contact in tight turns.

- The trailer *apron* (or upper fifth wheel) and semi-tractor tires. The apron is the surface of the trailer that contacts the semi-tractor's fifth wheel. This would be the area that has to be sufficiently lubricated, greased, or a Teflon-plated fifth wheel.

- The front of the trailer and any part of the cab to avoid contact in tight turns.

Note: Landing gears can have different configurations of high gear or low gear (sometimes pushed in is high gear or pulled out is high gear and vice versa for low gear). The dolly handle can crank clockwise or counterclockwise to raise or lower the landing gear.

16. **Remove the trailer wheel chocks.**

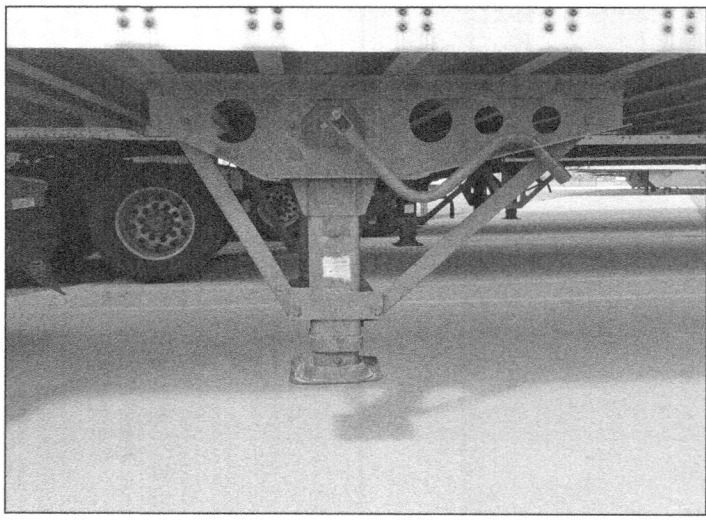

FIGURE 12-9:
A stored dolly crank handle.

Trying my method

TIP

This is my method, but I have observed that I'm not the only person who has figured out this process. If you couple to a trailer using this method, you will be treating components of your truck gently. Drivers who treat their truck this way have less maintenance issues than those who are rough (slamming the semi-truck into the trailer) with their truck.

1. **Inspect your fifth wheel and kingpin (see the photos with Step 1 in the previous section) to ensure that:**

   - The big flat surface of the fifth wheel is greased or has a Teflon plate.

   - The locking jaws are open.

   - The wheel is tilted down in the back.

   - The safety lock/unlock handle is in the automatic lock position.

   - Kingpin (part of the trailer) is not bent or broken.

   - If your fifth wheel is a sliding fifth wheel, make sure it is locked.

2. **Position your semi-tractor directly in front of the trailer, backing up evenly from side to side. Keep using both mirrors to keep tweaking your semi-tractor's position as you back up (see Figure 12-10).**

3. **Put the semi-tractor's transmission in neutral, set the parking brakes and turn off the engine. Get out using three points of contact — always!**

   The *three points of contact* is the phrase for always having a combination of three of your hands and feet in contact with the truck when exiting or entering the cab. Your body should always face the interior of the cab as well.

4. **Check the trailer height and alignment with the truck.**

   - The trailer should be lifted off the ground slightly when the semi-tractor is backed under it. Adjust as necessary to make this happen. If the trailer is too high, it will not be coupled correctly. If the trailer is too low, the fifth wheel or semi-tractor frame can hit the trailer. The height isn't as difficult as I just made it sound, but it is very important. (See the photos with Step 11 in the previous section.)

   - The kingpin and the opening in the fifth wheel should be aligned with the path of the semi-tractor.

FIGURE 12-10: Use both mirrors to keep semi-tractor centered in front of the trailer.

5. **Lower your suspension if you have that option. Many semi-tractors with air ride suspensions have a control in the cab where you can lower your suspension and raise it again.**

    This step and the following step are different from the process of most drivers as most do not lower and raise the suspensions. This prolongs the life of the various components.

6. **Slowly back your tractor under the trailer, stopping to raise the suspension when the front of the trailer is just past the pivot pin of the fifth wheel (see Figure 12-11). You should get out and look to ensure that you don't go too far.**

7. **Continue backing slowly until you hear the locking jaws in your fifth wheel lock around the kingpin.**

8. **Perform two of three checks for a secure connection.**

    • Get out and confirm that the release handle is all the way in (locked position) as shown in Figure 12-12. If it is not, push the truck into the trailer with a little more force or simply try again.

    • While you are out, go under the trailer and look at the fifth wheel to ensure that the jaw and locking bar are in their proper position (see Figure 12-13).

FIGURE 12-11:
Pivot pin of fifth wheel just past the front of the trailer.

9. **If you have a trailer brake handle, raise (crank) the landing gear all the way up, stowing the crank handle in its holder. If your semi-tractor does not have a trailer brake handle, raise the landing gear to have no more than 2 inches of clearance with the ground. Ensure that the clearance is sufficient between the:**

    • Landing gear and frame/tires/mudflaps to avoid contact in tight turns.

    • Trailer apron (upper fifth wheel) and semi-tractor tires. The apron is the surface of the trailer that contacts the semi-tractor's fifth wheel. This would be the area that has to be sufficiently lubricated, greased, or has a Teflon plate.

    • Front of the trailer and any part of the cab to avoid contact in tight turns.

    This is a controversial process. To raise or not to raise the landing gear all the way up at this point is the question. When you have a trailer brake handle, my process will catch a trailer that becomes uncoupled faster than other methods (see Step 12 below). This process ensures that you don't bend the landing gear by dragging it on the ground.

FIGURE 12-12:
Release the
handle all
the way
in and the
jaw and
locking bar
in proper
position
around the
kingpin.

FIGURE 12-13:
When the
connection
is correct,
you will see
the back of
the locking
bar only.

10. Connect the air lines (red to red and blue to blue) and the seven-way cord. To connect gladhands, hold the semi-tractor gladhand up at a 90 degree to the trailer gladhand and rotate down to 180 degrees (see Figure 12-14).

Inspect the parts as you connect (see Figure 12-15). The hoses should not touch the catwalk, (the walking plate spanning the frame or parts of the frame. Your vehicle might have a cord wrap that keeps the lines from touching the frame and other parts.

11. Perform this third secure connection check if you *have* a truck with a trailer brake handle; otherwise, go to Step 12.

- Push in all brake/air knobs.

- Wait for the air to stop filling brake and air system components (listen for the air to stop moving).

- If your truck and trailer start rolling, step on the brake pedal. You have just confirmed that all your brakes are free (no brakes are stuck).

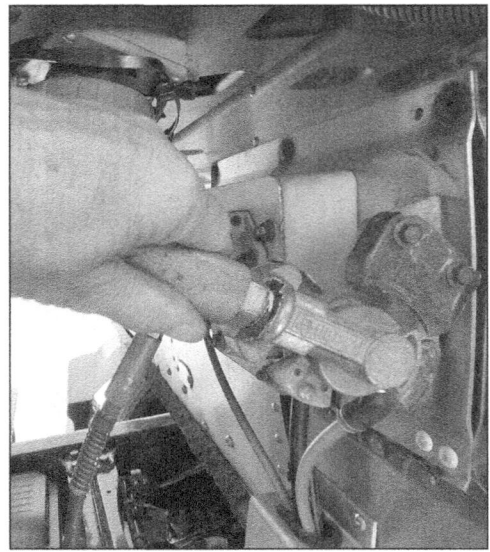

FIGURE 12-14:
Connecting
the
gladhands.

FIGURE 12-15:
Connected
air lines and
the seven-
way cord.

REMEMBER

Always ensure that your brakes are free, unstuck, not frozen. Drum brakes can be stuck in the middle of July. Dragging a tire down the road will ruin it in a very short time. At that point, you saved no time.

- Put your truck in gear, start rolling the truck at 3 to 5 mph.

- Remove your foot from the fuel pedal and hover your foot over the brake pedal.

- Pull down gently on the trailer brake handle. (If you have a manual transmission, push in on the clutch pedal at the same time.) This action should stop the whole rig, but if not and the trailer is disconnected, slam your foot on the brake.

If the trailer is still connected, but the tires are skidding on the ground, that means you likely have a manual transmission and didn't push in the clutch pedal, or you have an automated transmission that wants to keep going. Press on the brake pedal. There is nothing mechanically wrong in this scenario.

If the trailer is connected and the tires are rolling, the trailer has bad brakes or needs a brake adjustment. Get them fixed!

12. **Perform this secure connection check if you *don't have* a trailer brake handle. With the trailer brakes set (red knob out), put the transmission in low gear or drive, start to move the truck.**

- **If you have a secure connection,** the trailer should resist, and you should stop tugging. (The unofficial terminology for checking for a secure connection is "tug test.")

- **If the connection is not secure,** the trailer will stay in its place as the truck moves forward. Quickly press your right foot on the brake pedal and simultaneously push the clutch in with your left foot (if you have a manual transmission). The goal is to catch the trailer before it falls; however, this is why you leave the landing gear close to the ground.

- Raise the landing gear all the way up.

Uncoupling the trailer

When you uncouple a truck from a trailer, you don't just reverse the steps of coupling, at least not exactly. One of the most important steps you take is choosing where to drop the trailer. Sometimes parking spots will be marked so you won't have to make that decision. (*Drop* is the common term used in the industry for uncoupling from a trailer and leaving it at a location.)

AUTHOR SAYS

Years ago, someone dropped a trailer that I was going to hook to at a later date. The ground was too soft and over time, the landing gear sunk in the ground to the point where the front of the trailer was lower than the frame of my semi-tractor — way lower than my fifth wheel! Many drivers with this scenario have had to have a wrecker come out and lift the trailer up. Fortunately, I was able to let the air out of my suspension and move the semi-tractor frame under the front edge of the trailer. Then I put air back into the suspension, raising the trailer, and through a repetition of this process and improving the ground support under the landing gear, was able to connect to my trailer.

Following the state's process

Here are the steps you need to know for the State DOTs written tests.

REMEMBER

1. **Choose a spot that will support the weight of the trailer. The critical consideration is where the landing gear will be sitting. There can be a lot of weight placed on one small area.**

2. **With the semi-tractor and trailer in line (straight) with each other:**

- Set the brakes on the trailer.

- Back the semi-tractor gently into the trailer. This relieves pressure that might have been against the kingpin and locking jaw.

- Set the semi-tractor brakes.

3. **For your written exam, and for any trailers without air brakes, chock the trailer wheels. For all the trailers with air brakes, go to Step 4.**

4. **Lower the landing gear.**

- For empty trailers, lower the landing gear until it makes firm contact with the ground.

- For loaded trailers, lower the landing gear until it makes firm contact with the ground and then switch to low gear and turn a few more times. This will make it easier to disconnect from the fifth wheel and to hook to the trailer next time.

5. **Disconnect the air lines and the electrical line.**

   - Stow them on the dummy coupler or hook the gladhands together.

   - Ensure the lines will not touch any moving parts.

   - If there is not a holder, stow the seven-way cord plug side down to help prevent rain getting inside it.

6. **Unlock the fifth wheel by pulling the handle out to the locked-out position.**

7. **Drive the semi-tractor forward/out for the fifth wheel to be clear of the trailer but stop with the frame under the trailer. This is to ensure that the landing gear is not collapsing or sinking.**

8. **Place the transmission in neutral and set the parking brakes.**

9. **Inspect the trailer supports — the landing gear and the ground.**

10. **Pull the semi-tractor clear of the trailer.**

Considering my uncoupling process

TIP

My process for uncoupling the trailer from the semi-tractor has a couple of subtle different aspects, from a State DOT process, that takes into account the differences between semi-semi-tractors today and those made sometime prior to the turn of the century. Today's semi-tractors (and trailers) have ABS, spring brakes, air ride suspensions, and *leveling valves* (a valve combined with a simple mechanical process that keeps the fifth wheel at a designated height.

1. **Choose a spot that will support the weight of the trailer. The critical consideration is where the landing gear will be sitting. There can be a lot of weight placed on one small area.**

2. **With the semi-tractor and trailer in line with each other:**

   - Set the brakes on the trailer.

   - Back the semi-tractor gently into the trailer. This relieves pressure that might have been against the kingpin and locking jaw.

   - Set the semi-tractor's brakes.

3. **Lower the landing gear. (For many trucks, performing the actions in Step 4 of the State DOTs' process can cause a problem because they have a leveling device that attempts to keep the fifth wheel and frame at a specific height. You can end up having more difficulties unhooking the trailer!)**

   - Lower the landing gear until there is firm contact with the ground.

   - Reverse the direction you were cranking and crank three revolutions. This will leave the landing gear off the ground almost an inch. I used to tell people to leave it an inch off the ground, but I discovered that people didn't know what an inch was, or they were looking from the wrong angle to perceive the inch, or the two legs of the landing gear are uneven.

4. **Disconnect the air lines and the electrical line.**

   - Stow them on the dummy coupler or hook the gladhands together.

   - Ensure the lines will not touch any moving parts.

   - If there is not a holder, stow the seven-way cord, plug side down, to help prevent rain getting inside it.

5. **Unlock the fifth wheel by pulling the handle out to the locked-out position. (Some semi-tractors will have the feature of an in-cab release button.)**

6. **Drive the semi-tractor out from under the trailer.**

    *   Pull just about one foot and stop.

    *   If you can lower your suspension, do so. The landing gear should be fully supporting the trailer now. If your landing gear collapses, you performed a poor inspection earlier in the day or you damaged it during the day — just sayin'.

    *   When the suspension is lowered, pull out slowly. Even if you can not lower your suspension, pull out slowly, allowing the trailer's landing gear to sit softly on the ground.

REMEMBER

Always keep feet out from under tires in case the vehicle moves a little.

Practice Questions

These questions are based on what can be on your CDL written test, not on my personal methods, which I mention are different from State DOTs' methods.

1. Why wouldn't you use the trailer hand brake to control a trailer skid?

    (A) The trailer hand brake only works when testing brakes.

    (B) The brake chambers will burst with the extra pressure.

    (C) The brakes need to be released for the skid to stop.

    (D) You can use the trailer hand brake to control a trailer skid.

2. Which is the best choice for the order of coupling a semi-tractor and trailer together?

    (A) Line the semi-tractor with the trailer, connect the air lines, set the trailer brakes, back under the trailer.

    (B) Line the semi-tractor with the trailer, drive under the trailer, connect the air lines, raise the landing gear.

    (C) Move the semi-tractor under the trailer, raise the landing gear and connect the air lines.

    (D) The order in which a trailer is coupled with a semi-tractor makes no difference as long as all the steps are conducted.

3. Which statement is false concerning the emergency air line?

    (A) It supplies air to the trailer tanks.

    (B) It is blue.

    (C) Loss of air pressure in the line causes the emergency brakes to come on.

    (D) When the emergency air line loses pressure, it causes the semi-tractor protection valve to close.

4. The red trailer air line is:

    (A) The emergency air line.

    (B) The service air line.

    (C) The seven way.

    (D) A back up to the blue line.

5. Which statement is false concerning gladhands?

    (A) Gladhands are often color coded.

    (B) Gladhands have rubber seals.

    (C) If gladhands are connected to the wrong connection, they will not allow you to release the trailer brakes.

    (D) On trailers without spring brakes, you can connect the gladhands to either gladhand and always have braking power.

6. Which statement is false about trailer air tanks?

    (A) Trailer air tanks are on all trailers and converter dollies.

    (B) Trailer air tanks are optional as semi-tractors have tanks of air.

    (C) Trailer air tanks must be drained to avoid water buildup in the lines.

    (D) Pressure in the service line tells how much pressure the relay valves should send to the brakes.

7. Which statement is true concerning shutoff valves?
   - **(A)** Should be open when not in use.
   - **(B)** Should be closed when a gladhand is connected to one.
   - **(C)** Control the oil supply to the trailer chassis.
   - **(D)** Should be in the off position when they are located on the last trailer.

8. Which of these steps should be first (of the four choices) in coupling to a trailer?
   - **(A)** Raise the landing gear.
   - **(B)** Connect the air lines.
   - **(C)** Back under the trailer.
   - **(D)** Ensure the fifth wheel handle is in the locked (in) position.

9. Which is not a consideration when preparing to uncouple a trailer?
   - **(A)** How much weight is in the trailer?
   - **(B)** Do you have enough time left on your 14-hour clock?
   - **(C)** Is the ground solid where the trailer will be dropped?
   - **(D)** Will the trailer be secure?

10. What should you do with the air lines after uncoupling a trailer?
    - **(A)** Stow them on the dummy coupler.
    - **(B)** Stow them on the trailer.
    - **(C)** Hang them off the frame of the semi-tractor.
    - **(D)** Hook them to the seven-way cord.

11. Which is not a safety check for coupling?
    - **(A)** Ensuring the release handle is all the way out.
    - **(B)** Ensuring the jaw and locking bar are locked around the kingpin.
    - **(C)** Ensuring the seven-way cord is kept in place by the receiver cover.
    - **(D)** Ensuring there is no space between the trailer apron and fifth wheel.

12. If the ABS malfunctions:
    - **(A)** Law enforcement can put your vehicle out of service.
    - **(B)** Your brakes can be used normally.
    - **(C)** You must drive at half speed to a repair shop.
    - **(D)** Brakes can lock up without warning.

13. Gladhands
    - **(A)** Connect to electrical lines.
    - **(B)** Secure a trailer to a semi-tractor.
    - **(C)** Connect two air lines.
    - **(D)** Hold air lines off the frame.

Answers and Explanations

1. **C.** The trailer hand brake will work anytime. However, using the trailer hand brake will likely create a skid, rather than control one. Use the trailer hand brake only for testing the service brakes of the trailer.

2. **A.** Hooking the air lines and setting the brakes on the trailer prior to moving the semi-tractor under the trailer, is the State DOTs' way of connecting the two together.

3. **B.** The emergency air line is red, so all the other statements are true.

4. **A.** The red line is the emergency air line and has a different function than the blue service air line.

5. **D.** The absence of spring brakes did not change the operation of air brakes. They were still to be connected to the correct lines.

6. **B.** Trailers and converter dollies must still have tanks to store pressurized air. Without them, air brakes would not be as effective.

7. **D.** Shutoff valves should be shut when no lines are attached and open when gladhands are connected to them. They are part of the air system.

8. **B.** On the written test, the state wants you to couple to a trailer the way that you had to when trailers had no spring brakes, which means that you need to connect the air lines first and charge the trailer system with air. Then set the brakes on the trailer before backing under it. The fifth wheel handle should be in the out position. The landing gear can't be raised until the semi-tractor is under the trailer.

9. **B.** The weight of the trailer and where it will sit is important for both security and for physical ground support. Even if you don't have time left on your 14-hour clock (see Chapter 6), you can drop a trailer but don't go driving out on the road!

10. **A.** The gladhands stay with the semi-tractor and must be stowed safely to avoid damage occurring to them. So, connect them to a dummy coupler when one is mounted on the semi-tractor.

11. **A.** You check for the release handle on the fifth wheel to be all the way in whenever you have coupled to a trailer.

12. **B.** Law enforcement can only cite you for a violation when ABS is malfunctioning. Your brakes will work normally, so you will be safe to drive to the repair shop at normal speed.

13. **C.** Joining the gladhands is how two air lines connect.

5
Examining Other Endorsements

Drive trucks safely with both portable tanks and permanently mounted tanks.

Know how to provide a safe bus ride for passengers — whether for adults or children.

Pull two or more trailers at the same time with confidence.

Keep the public safe when hauling hazardous materials.

Chapter **13**

Hauling Liquid: Tanker

P ulling or hauling a tank presents the most challenging of driving skills. When adding the sloshing around of liquid and how it constantly changes its center of gravity, to any other aspect of driving a commercial motor vehicle (CMV), you can have a potential hazard within your vehicle. This is the reason you need a tank endorsement.

Drivers deliver products of all sorts using tanks every day. Milk, water, and syrup are some food items that you might think of first. Tanker trucks also deliver gasoline and diesel to the fuel stations, medical supplies such as oxygen, nitrous oxide, and nitrogen; and bulk quantities of chemicals and other ingredients to manufacturing plants.

Most tanks are more sophisticated than simply having a port for filling and a valve for unloading. Some are more sophisticated simply by their construction where they can be made of special materials or liners to avoid corrosion of some chemicals to materials that are easily cleaned as in food grade trailers. Many petroleum tankers have multiple compartments to allow delivery of a variety of products. Some tankers are heated to keep the product at a precise temperature. Cryogenic tankers haul chemicals that are as cold as 300 degrees below zero Fahrenheit.

Dry bulk tankers can unload their product to another holding tank that is higher than it is by pressurizing the trailer and aerating the product, making it act more like a liquid. One of the most important features that some tankers have are their safety features. Safety valves would be one that people can guess that they have but many tankers have a fire suppression system.

In this chapter, I provide you with the information you need to know to prepare to drive a tank vehicle, explaining how to drive a tank vehicle safely and whether you need to get an endorsement.

However, I'm not going to train you or give you the information you need to operate the various types of tank trailers and tank trucks. It will be the responsibility of your company to ensure that you receive proper training to operate the tank you will be pulling or hauling. Your company should also give you training for any hazardous materials that you might haul.

Recognizing the Need for a Tank Endorsement

You have seen the bright shiny tanks being pulled by semi-tractors or on a straight truck. Tanks are easily identifiable, even if they are not the shiny kind. But you are reading this chapter to find out if you can drive one, right? Commercial Driver's License (CDL) holders who drive trucks, vans, or semi-tractors/trailers may need a tanker endorsement.

There is a regulation (of course there is!) that specifically defines who needs a tank endorsement. You must have a tank endorsement if you haul liquids in a quantity of more than 1,000 gallons in containers larger than 119 gallons. Many manufacturers will transport liquids in containers larger than 200 gallons in a box or van trailer. So if you pick up a load of vegetable oil that weighs a total of 40,000 pounds and is in 22 containers that hold 256 gallons each, you will need a tank endorsement. Why? Because each container is larger than 119 gallons and cumulatively, there is more than 1,000 gallons. The weight of the shipment had nothing to do with whether you need a tank endorsement or not.

Let's say that you have a load to pick up and this time it is vinegar. The vinegar weighs 42,000 pounds and is in 1,000, 5-gallon containers. Do you need a tank endorsement? While it is more than 1,000 gallons, the containers are less than 119 gallons, the minimum individual container size portion of the requirements for a tank endorsement. The weight still doesn't matter.

Inspecting a Tank Vehicle

When it comes to inspecting a tank vehicle, your written test will only address the vehicles that have a tank attached, either by mounting to the truck or the trailer is a tank, not the smaller containers that sit in your box truck or trailer. The smaller containers can be inspected by using the general rules, which include looking for leaks and ensuring that the cargo is properly secured.

Your employer should give you proper training on operating and inspecting your tanks. If they do not, make it a priority to find another employer! The training to operate tanks safely is paramount. For this section on inspecting a tank vehicle, I cover the items you need to know to pass the written test for the tank endorsement.

In case, you are wondering, tank vehicles are washed out when a different product is to be loaded next in the tank (and maybe even when it is the same commodity). You'll need to obtain the documentation (ticket or receipt) for the washout. The next customer will likely ask for it.

The following is a list of items to inspect:

REMEMBER

>> **Checking for leaks.** Your number one reason to check for leaks is safety. The liquid or gas that you are hauling can harm the environment, or a leak can present more of a danger to you or those around you. Further reason for checking for leaks is more selfish — that is, you can be cited for having a leaky tank. If that isn't motive enough, fines or fees for cleanup easily runs into the thousands of dollars. You should check:

- For leaks when you couple to a trailer.

- Every cap and ensure there is a gasket or seal.

- The manhole cover; it should be closed and have a gasket or seal.

- Every valve is in the closed position, ensuring that no leaks are coming from them.

- For dents or damage that might produce leaks.

When you pick up a trailer from a facility that conducts washouts, don't assume that they close everything back up. It might be part of their process to leave valves open.

>> **Ensuring the functionality of special equipment.** Depending on what type of tanker you are inspecting, there are different pieces of equipment to inspect. There are pumps, compressors, built-in fire extinguishers, grounding and bonding cables, vapor recovery kits, and emergency shutoff systems. All these items require special training but at the same time, anything on a CMV is to be properly secured. It should not be broken. If at all possible, have the operating manuals (either in hand or on your phone or tablet) of these items and get geeky about reading them.

>> **Remembering the normal inspections.** It seems that every aspect I address in operating a CMV is of the utmost importance. And inspecting a tanker is no exception. You still inspect all the basic components of the vehicle just like any other CMV. See Chapters 4 and 17 for more on inspecting your vehicle.

Driving a Tank Vehicle

Being a CDL holder means that you have acquired more skills than are needed to drive your personal vehicle. If you want a bigger challenge, drive a tank vehicle. The high center of gravity and liquid moving around requires specific skills in addition to driving with determination and attentiveness. And while you should never be driving distracted, being distracted while driving a tank vehicle can be disastrous.

Remembering the physics

Take away the flavoring and carbonization of a cola and all you really have left is water. Take away the two main characteristics of liquid in tanks (high center of gravity and surging) and all you have left is another general commodity to haul. These two main physical characteristics are what prompted the government to require an endorsement for operating tank vehicles. Understand what to do with these two characteristics and you will pass your written test and become a safe tank driver. Without these critical characteristics, the rest of this information would be in the general knowledge section for obtaining a CDL.

High center of gravity

REMEMBER

"The bigger they are, the harder they fall." Having a high center of gravity means that the weight and load of a tanker is carried higher off the ground other vehicles as demonstrated in Figure 13-1. This means you have a greater potential for rollover. When the center of gravity is high, there is less room for error. Ramps and curves cause the center of gravity to change (see Figure 13-2). When it changes to a point outside its base, a rollover results.

WARNING

If you drive your tanker around a curve at the posted speed limit, there's a good chance of turning the vehicle over. The posted speed limits are for automobiles. You must slow down far in advance of the curve or ramp and reach the speed you want to go prior to the curve starting.

Your written test can contain a question that might say something like speeding up in a curve. If you choose to agree with this on the test, you will probably get it right. If you choose to do it in real life on a ramp, you may find yourself lucky to remain upright and still on the road.

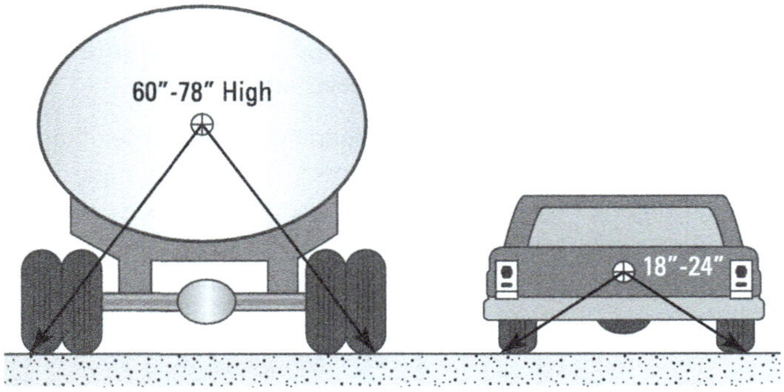

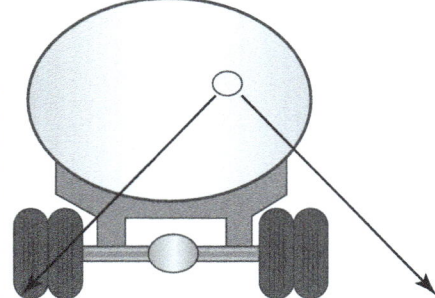

FIGURE 13-1:
The center of gravity difference between a tanker and a passenger vehicle.

FIGURE 13-2:
When the center of gravity moves past the edge of stability, a rollover results.

Here are my two suggestions for choosing a speed for a curve or ramp:

>> Drive at one-half the posted speed limit.

>> Talk to some drivers who have operated tankers for years and have never turned one over. Find out their decision-making process for determining a safe speed.

Just remember to have the same philosophy as going down a mountain: You can drive down a mountain slower than you need to a thousand times, but you only go down a mountain too fast once. You might just get one chance to go around a ramp too fast. If you survive it, ask yourself if it was worth being concerned about the motorists behind you getting held up for a few seconds.

Surging

In Chapter 7, I discuss how to eliminate the potential for forward movement. Talk about your challenges of stopping liquid in a tank! Surge is the second physical characteristic of driving a tanker that you must know about. Merriam-Webster defines *surge* as "swelling, rolling, or sweeping forward like that of a wave," For a tank vehicle, surge happens when attempting to stop.

When you are coming to a stop, all the liquid is pushing forward as it wants to keep moving. When you finally stop, the liquid will go backward, and then it moves forward again — pushing you forward. Surge can push you into an intersection, especially if you are not prepared for it. If you are at a slippery intersection, it can push you right on into the intersection.

SEEING SURGE IN ACTION

A great way to observe surging in action on a small scale is to take a partially full gallon of water or milk and push it across a countertop and see what happens. It slows, maybe stops, and then it moves again. Multiply this by 5,000 or so and that is what happens in a tank vehicle.

A partially full tank will exhibit more surge than a full tank. However, you are not to load a tank to full.

The following are some key points to consider when driving a tank vehicle:

>> **Keeping balanced.** Bulkheads divide tanks into smaller compartments, allowing for different products to be hauled in the same tank vehicle. However, you have to be careful because you don't want too much weight on one end of the vehicle than the other. Having an imbalance can occur at loading or unloading the vehicle. Whether it is you or someone else, ensure at loading that the cargo is in compartments compatible with your delivery route and proper weight distribution. Consider the amounts of product in each compartment to prevent the back half of the trailer from being substantially heavier. Load the tanker according to the safer levels.

>> **Baffling the liquid.** Surge can be reduced by placing bulkheads with holes in a tank, which are called baffles. Baffles will slow down surge but do not eliminate it and are ineffective for side-to-side surge, which can cause rollovers.

>> **Smoothing the tanks.** Imagine cleaning and rinsing milk out of a 5,000-gallon tank with lots of compartments or nooks and crannies. How about rinsing out syrup? There are public health laws that prohibit hauling products such as milk in baffled tanks for the same reasons. Therefore, unbaffled tanks are required, which are also called *smooth-bore tanks*. Be extremely cautious when hauling product in the smooth-bore tanks. I address a few safe driving guidelines in the next section.

>> **Knowing the outage of your product.** You might be one of those people who continue to pump fuel into their gasoline tanks after the pump handle clicks off (most people probably are). Never do that in a cargo tank! You must allow some space or room for expansion, which is called *outage*. Different liquids require different outages, so you must find out what the outage is when hauling any liquid in bulk.

>> **Weighting your product.** In addition to outage, you must consider weight. Some liquids, due to their density, will put you over the legal road weight limits if you load them to your tank's capacity.

The amount of liquid that you can haul in your tanks will depend on:

- The weight of the liquid.
- The legal weights for the roads you will be driving.
- The amount your liquid will expand during transit.

Applying the physics

I might have made operating a tank vehicle sound dangerous or risky. If I have, then I will have done part of my job. You can take away some of the danger and risk by driving professionally. This section provides a few ways that you can reduce potential risks of driving a tank vehicle.

Controlling the surge

Surge occurs when you are slowing down and stopping. You can plan on it. When you come to a stop at an intersection in your personal vehicle, you basically sit there and relax a bit, waiting for your turn. When you are driving a tank vehicle and you come to the same stop, and relax a bit, you get slammed into, or so it seemed as the liquid came forward a second time and slammed into the front of the tank. You must not relax on the brake pedal at an intersection. The force of the liquid coming forward again will push you into the vehicle in front of you or into the crosswalk or intersection. Here are a few suggestions for stopping a tank vehicle safely.

>> Anticipate the stop. Slow down earlier than normal.

>> Remember that your stopping distance has increased with a tank vehicle.

>> Wet roads double your stopping distance.

>> Plan your full stop well behind the next vehicle.

>> Leave an exaggerated amount of space between you and the next vehicle. Expect someone will move into that space so prepare for that to happen as well.

>> Know that if you have that extra space, when the liquid comes forward after stopping, you can allow the truck to move forward with the rush of the liquid, absorbing the liquid's force.

>> Avoid taking your foot off the brake pedal too soon.

>> Remember if you must make a sudden stop — for the test use *controlled* or *stab braking* (see Chapter 5) — but in real life your ABS should keep your wheels from locking up.

>> Do not steer quickly while braking or you might have a rollover.

>> Keep steady pressure on the brake pedal when you stop.

Taking the curves

REMEMBER

Driving a tank vehicle around curves will require a thick skin to ignore the vehicles line up behind you. Here are some helpful suggestions to accomplish the task:

>> Slow down prior to the curve.

>> If you have a manual transmission, choose a gear that will allow you to accelerate.

>> Ignore the drivers behind you; they will just have to wait on you to get around the curve or ramp.

>> Choose to cut the speed limit in half for your safe speed.

>> Accelerate slightly in the curve. You want the semi-tractor to pull the trailer, not the trailer pushing the tractor.

Skidding

If you oversteer, overbrake, or you over-accelerate, you can place yourself in a skid, and your vehicle can start to jackknife. When any of your tires start to skid, you must react and restore traction to those tires. Until you do so, you are not in control.

Practice Questions

1. A surge is:

    (A) A military rank above private and corporal.

    (B) The rush of liquid that will push a tank vehicle forward.

    (C) The expelling of liquid from the unload pipe in a tank vehicle.

    (D) The expansion of liquid as it is compressed in a tank.

2. Which of the following is not a physical characteristic of hauling liquids?

    (A) Liquids can expand.

    (B) Liquids can rush forward.

    (C) Liquids can push to the sides.

    (D) Liquids cannot be loaded in rubberized tanks.

3. Which of the following is the best list of items to inspect during your pre-trip inspection of a tank vehicle?

    (A) Valves for leaks, manhole covers for seals, and the tank for dents.

    (B) Valves turned off, vents are clear, and chains are tight.

    (C) Manhole cover closed, fire extinguishing system has proper pressure readings, and the flamjam is closed.

    (D) Pipes for leaks, the turbo for leaks, and the tank for leaks.

4. Which of these choices doesn't help with controlling surge or the effect of surge?

    (A) Give the vehicle a little fuel after the first push of liquid.

    (B) Use more distance to slow down.

    (C) Keep firm pressure on the brakes.

    (D) Plan to stop with extra space between you and the next vehicle.

5. Which is the best reason to use a smooth-bore trailer?

    (A) A smooth-bore trailer unloads faster.

    (B) A smooth-bore trailer is easier to clean out.

    (C) Certain commodities require it by regulation.

    (D) Surge is greater with smooth-bore trailers.

6. What will a leak cause?

    (A) A citation from an officer.

    (B) A fine from the EPA.

    (C) An out-of-service order.

    (D) All these things can be the result of a leak.

7. Which of the following is the best safe speed philosophy for curves while driving a tank vehicle?

    (A) Stay under the posted speed limit.

    (B) Stay 5 mph under the posted speed limit.

    (C) Cut the posted speed limit in half and stay under it.

    (D) As long as you are able to accelerate through the curve, any of these options work.

8. What criteria should you consider when determining how much to load in your tank?

   (A) Legal weight limits.

   (B) How much the liquid expands.

   (C) How much the liquid weighs.

   (D) All these are criteria in determining how much liquid should be loaded in the tank.

9. Which of these terms are defined incorrectly?

   (A) Surge: The expansion of liquid as it is compressed in a tank.

   (B) Baffle: A bulkhead with holes to limit the effect of surge.

   (C) Bulkhead: A divider in a tank for the expressed purpose of creating another compartment.

   (D) Outage: The space in a tank allotted for liquid expansion.

10. What are reasons that make it necessary to take extreme care when driving a tank vehicle?

   (A) Surge will push a vehicle an extra distance when stopping.

   (B) Outage will cause a tank to burst.

   (C) Tank vehicles have a higher center of gravity.

   (D) Both A and C.

Answers and Explanations

1. **B.** A surge is not the same thing as Sarge in the military. Surge is the force of liquid rushing into the front of the tank, pushing the tank forward.

2. **D.** All these are characteristics of liquids that you should remember except that there are rubber-sided trailers for some specific liquids.

3. **A.** Most of these items are areas to check when conducting an inspection. But chains should not be used with tankers. I don't know what a flamjam is, and the turbo has nothing to do with your tank.

4. **A.** All the answer choices help with surge or the effect of surge except when you give the vehicle some fuel after the first surge. This will amplify the second surge.

5. **C.** This is a tricky one. A smooth-bore trailer is easier to clean out, and it might unload faster. But controlling surge is more important than those other reasons. However, food products like milk must be hauled in a smooth-bore trailer by regulation.

6. **D.** A leak, if detected by an officer, can result in all of these problems for you.

7. **C.** Tank vehicles can turn over at the posted speed limit for curves and ramps so even 5 mph under can be dangerous. Accelerating when going through a curve helps to keep the load from pushing you around and causes the truck to be pulling instead of being pushed. But if you are going too fast, rollover can still occur. Take it slow!

8. **D.** You must keep within the legal weight limits and allow for outage (the liquid to expand). You also need to know how much the liquid weighs to keep within the legal limit.

9. **A.** Surge is the rush of liquid as a tank vehicle is attempting to stop. Surge can occur repeatedly.

10. **D.** Both surge and tank vehicles, having a higher center of gravity, are reasons for taking extra care when driving a tank vehicle. If B is a true statement, it isn't an actual driving concern.

Chapter **14**

Transporting Passengers

D riving a bus is one of the more unique applications of a Commercial Driver's License (CDL). Your cargo is completely different than, say, concrete blocks that sit calmly and quietly with no complaining. If you haul 15 or more passengers, regardless of getting paid or not, you need to have a CDL with a passenger endorsement.

In this chapter, I examine the requirements for inspecting all buses along with the special items for a school bus. I also explain different driving practices that are peculiar to hauling passengers. Some practices will be about your driving and others will be concerning your cargo, er, passengers.

A school bus endorsement is usually an additional requirement to the passenger endorsement. It is likely that you will have background checks conducted as part of your certification.

Recognizing Your Responsibilities

There aren't too many types of cargo that loads itself. Drivers often have cargo loaded onto their trucks for them, but they should receive shipping papers stating what is loaded. When you drive a bus, you are likely to have cargo that loads itself, and not only that, brings additional items. It is your responsibility to observe the passengers and what they bring with them.

The responsibilities I give you in this section are for any bus you may drive — city, school, tour, or party. Buses operated by limo services have the same expectations for the drivers, in spite of the lighthearted mood of the passengers. All these tasks are important and required. School buses are not the only buses that a lot is expected out of the driver, they are simply at the top of the list.

CDL drivers don't usually talk to their cargo, but bus drivers can, giving them some special responsibilities along with duties that normal driving doesn't require a thought. In this section, you discover operational differences from other CMVs like fueling your bus and crossing railroad tracks. Additionally, you explore what to do when you stop the bus and what you can allow passengers to carry on board with them. You will inspect the bus with a slightly different philosophy.

Inspecting your vehicle

One of the unique aspects of driving buses is that, for the most part, your cargo loads and unloads itself. This is helpful when it is time to inspect your bus. Inspect the bus while it is empty, and for that matter, don't allow passengers to board the bus until it is loading time. You must ensure that the bus is safe for passengers.

REMEMBER

Inspect everything the same as you would on any other commercial motor vehicle (CMV). However, there are a few differences when you have a passenger-carrying vehicle. A Driver Vehicle Inspection Report (DVIR) is required to be filled out by drivers regardless of defects present or not. Drivers much check the seats, exits, and for a school bus, a first aid kit and a body fluid clean up kit.

Additionally, for school buses, you must inspect the school bus-specific items like the stop arm (stop sign), safety arm, student lights (flashing hazard lights and strobe light if so equipped), and the student mirror.

Carrying hazardous material

Your first thought might be that no hazardous material (hazmat) would be allowed. However, it is legal for some hazmat to be hauled on a bus. A bus company can choose to prohibit all or most hazardous materials. Watch what your passengers bring on board with them. There are some hazardous materials that are forbidden, which are outlined below:

>> Division 2.3 poison gas

>> Liquid Class 6 poison

>> Tear gas

>> Irritating materials

>> Class 6 poisons in quantities greater than 100 pounds

>> Explosives in the space occupied by passengers (small arms ammunition is the exception)

>> Labeled radioactive materials in the space occupied by passengers

>> More than 500 pounds of total hazardous materials

>> More than 100 pounds of any one class

Communicating with riders

Both you and your passengers want to have a safe trip, but some of your passengers don't realize that the best way for them to have a safe trip is to leave you alone, to not be a distraction to you. I want you well with those types of passengers.

The time to communicate with passengers is while boarding and preparing to depart. Announce pertinent information like your destination and safety protocols. When you arrive at a stop, inform your passengers where you are and why you stopped. Have them gather all their belongings. It might be appropriate to announce a departure time. Remind them to watch their step and get clear from the bus after departing. Many buses have all this information automated or can be activated by a touch of a button. So, if public speaking isn't your thing, one of these buses might be for you.

When passengers are bringing items onboard with them, ensure that aisles are kept clear. Any baggage should be stored in appropriate areas. Standing should only take place on buses made for standing.

Knowing a montage of imperatives

Your cargo has the ability and even the permission to move, at times, unlike the cargo that you secure with chains and cargo straps. Keep an eye on your passengers by checking your mirrors with regular frequency. Watch for unruly passengers. If you have an unruly passenger, maybe one that is under the influence, you are not to discharge them just anywhere. If your state or company allows, drop the passenger off in a well-lit area or at the next scheduled stop. If you must, call authorities to assist sooner in removing the passenger.

As you are driving, you must be as attentive as possible, just like in any other CMV. But with passengers, you should have a never-ending reminder of your driving responsibilities. The suspension on many buses is like riding on marshmallows. The bus will seem to rock side to side on turns. Take your time to navigate intersections and curves. Recall that a wet road is a slick road.

Due to your special cargo, you have increased responsibilities and different processes from hauling general cargo. These all make perfect sense once you have your mind wrapped around your new passenger-carrying philosophy. The following checklist are items you will need to be aware of while driving a bus:

>> **Driving defensively.** Ensure that other traffic sees you. Yes, people fail to see big buses, yellow ones, black ones, ones with 17 flashing lights. They also have a hard time seeing a big truck pulling a 53-foot-long trailer that is over 13 feet high.

As you drive, attempt to always have a place to move the bus just in case that type of maneuver is necessary. In other words, have space to your right or to your left to immediately move into should someone perform an unthoughtful stunt in front of you.

>> **Standing.** If your bus has a *standee line* (a 2-inch line signifying where to stand), no passengers are to be standing on the driver's side of the line. Otherwise, the aisles should be clear.

>> **Fueling.** When it is time for you to fuel the bus, have the passengers unload. Don't fuel the bus with passengers aboard. If at all possible, do this where the passengers can walk around, shop, or eat. This will make your job easier. Inform the passengers what time to return to the bus, where it will be, and what number it is if that is a concern.

>> **Waiting on drawbridges.** Stop at any drawbridge that doesn't have a traffic control device or a traffic control attendant at least 50 feet before the draw of the bridge. If a drawbridge has a traffic control light showing green or there is an attendant or traffic officer, obey their instructions. Don't automatically stop, but slow down while ensuring that it is safe to proceed.

>> **Using brake door interlocks.** City buses often have what is called an *interlock system*. When the rear door is open, the brakes are applied and the engine is set to idle. When the door is closed, the interlock is released. The interlock is not to be used as a parking brake.

>> **Towing guidelines.** The only time to tow a bus with your passengers on it is to get them to a safe place to unload. Otherwise, don't tow a bus with passengers on it. You unload them when it is safe to do so and to wait for the next bus. If it isn't safe to wait outside, have passengers wait on the bus until the substitute bus arrives.

>> **Considering high winds.** Strong winds are to be highly respected. There doesn't have to be a tornado to take a high-profile vehicle, like a bus, off the road. Controlling a bus is more difficult in high winds, especially if your bus has the marshmallow suspension. Here are some best practices for driving in high winds.

>> Slow down. This lessens the effects of wind.

>> Keep a firm grip on the steering wheel.

>> Find a safe parking spot and contact your company and/or school for consultation.

Crossing railroad tracks

I expect you can identify a railroad crossing when you see one. If not, I will give more information in the school bus section. Here is what you do at a crossing:

>> You must stop your bus between 50 and 15 feet before a railroad crossing.

>> Look and listen, in both directions, for trains. Open your door and window if it improves your ability to see or hear an approaching train.

>> If there is more than one track, ensure that all tracks are clear, especially if a train just passed on one of the nearby tracks. You will need to wait a bit longer until the first train is far enough down the track to verify that a second train isn't on another track.

>> I haven't seen a manual transmission bus in a few decades, but you need to know that you aren't allowed to shift gears on the tracks. Knowing this also means that crossing the track in a manual transmission bus takes longer than the automatic transmission buses.

You don't have to stop at a crossing if a police officer is directing traffic there (lights might be errantly flashing) but do slow down. You don't have to stop at *exempt crossings* (are no longer in use *and* are marked as "exempt") and streetcar crossings.

Braking with ABS

REMEMBER

An anti-lock brake system (ABS) will work the same in buses as in any other CMV. However, there can still be questions on your written test about ABS. So, remember the following facts about ABS:

>> It helps to avoid wheel/brake lock up when braking, keeping you in control.

>> The brakes will work normally if ABS malfunctions. It should not change the way you brake.

>> It does not shorten stopping distance or increase nor decrease stopping power.

>> ABS does not mean you can drive faster.

>> It does not increase nor decrease stopping power.

>> Your brakes still need to be maintained because it doesn't prevent "bad brakes."

>> An ABS malfunction lamp that remains on after starting to drive indicates that ABS control is lost on one or more wheels.

>> It does not work on skids while turning.

Driving Children to and from School

When I was in school, our bus drivers were responsible, mature drivers. That was typical of any schools that I was familiar with. I went to college and one of my classmates there was a bus driver at his school, when he was in high school! Since the CDL was created, and with the Entry-Level Driver Training (ELDT) requirement, that practice has changed. However, the license or endorsement and the qualifications to drive a school bus still are different from state to state. Regardless of whether a given state has high standards or not for being a school bus driver, what I present in this section is a good set of practices to build on. Check with your State Department of Transportation (DOT) to learn about their qualifications and requirements.

Generally speaking, you need to have a passenger endorsement to have a school bus endorsement. For full-size buses, you need to have a Class B license. ELDT is needed now to get a Class B license and to get the passenger and school bus endorsement. (See Chapter 2 for more information on the ELDT and endorsements.) Most, if not all, states require a school bus endorsement to drive a school bus with passengers. Don't be surprised if you have to submit fingerprints for a background check. Many school bus companies and school districts have registered ELDT training. Drivers with passenger endorsements must have DOT physicals.

TIP

There might be a reference in a written test about tape players or even the more modern CD players, possibly as an example of what is or is not allowed on a bus. For younger readers, these fabulous pieces of technology are the predecessors of MP3 players and iPods. (Yes, I know about streaming music players on phones, but your written tests will probably act like kids are still walking around with Walkmans or boomboxes.)

Watching out for your passengers

You are the earthly guardian angel for the school children. Yes, I believe that you, if you become a school bus driver, are your passengers' earthly guardian angel. You watch out for the children before they get on the bus. You watch out for them while they are on the bus — for what can occur inside and outside the bus. And you keep your eye on them after they leave the bus.

REMEMBER

In case you didn't know, it is much more dangerous for a student outside the bus than inside!

Removing danger zones

There are dangerous areas around the bus, and around the school parking lot. Since you aren't a full-fledged guardian angel with powers to move faster than Super Man, you can't control all areas of danger, but you can control what you do and how you do it. And, you can continually educate your students. In this section, I identify potential blind spots and explain how to adjust your mirrors accordingly.

REMEMBER

Danger zones are the areas around the bus where students are most likely to get hit, either by another bus or by personal vehicles. The worst danger zone is to the left of the bus where other traffic is passing by. There is also potential for you or other drivers to be distracted by the passengers in both vehicles. Since the left side is the most dangerous side, always endeavor to drop students off where they do not have to cross where other traffic is. This problem is usually planned out for you on a school bus or city bus route, but what about the special events that you drive for? You might need to be the one who plans the loading/unloading location beforehand (or on the fly).

Adjusting your mirrors

TIP

Adjust your mirrors as part of your pre-trip inspection each day, and then, each time you get in the bus. Verify that the mirrors haven't been moved. Use all your mirrors to ensure no students are in the danger zone.

Here's a list of mirror adjustments you should make:

>> **Outside right and left mirrors.** There are big flat mirrors at the sides of the windshield. Your mirrors need to be adjusted to see the following:

- The sides of the bus, but just a sliver for both sides; you don't need to see what your bus looks like

- The rear tires touching the ground

- 200 feet behind the bus

>> **Outside right and left convex mirrors.** The convex mirrors are located just below the big mirrors at the sides of the windshield. These mirrors are to help see a wider angle than the larger mirrors. They do not accurately reflect the size of objects, but they do give a view of the lanes on either side of the bus.

>> **Outside right and left crossover mirrors.** The big partial sphere mirrors at the front corners of the bus give a view of the danger zones and blind spots in front of the bus as well as behind the bumper on either side of the bus. These mirrors help fill in the view that the other two mirrors do not show. Adjust these mirrors to try to eliminate any space left undetected by mirrors. Like the other convex mirrors, objects in the mirrors are not depicted accurately in size or distance from the bus.

REMEMBER

>> **Overhead inside rearview mirror.** This is the mirror that I looked at when I was a kid sitting in the back seat of the bus to see if the driver was looking at what I or my friends were doing. This mirror is great for seeing all the students and will sometimes give you a glimpse of traffic and surroundings through the windows at the back of the bus. Adjust it so that you see the top of the rear windows and *all* the students.

Picking up and dropping off students

Kids can be unpredictable. They can do things that make no sense. A teacher or parent may ask them, "Why did you do that?" And their response is invariably, "I don't know." The kids are probably telling the truth, even if there was a smidgen of reason, like they were dared. Envision that one of the darling children will do the unexplainable, so follow the precautions that a school bus driver must take to avoid a catastrophic event.

Approaching and completing a stop when picking up students

As you approach a stop, you must watch (and expect) for the kids to come running up to the bus. They are not thinking about the dangers that you know exist.

1. **Go slow, looking for any pedestrians and other traffic. Continue looking and observing throughout the stop.**

2. **Continually check all your mirrors.**

3. **Use your right turn signal.**

4. **Activate your amber flashing lights at least 200 feet prior to the stop or in accordance with your state's law.**

5. **Move over to the right as far as possible.**

To complete the stop:

6. **Bring the bus to a full stop with the front bumper at least 10 feet away from the students.**

7. **Attempt to count the children while they are still outside.**

8. **Activate the red lights and extend the stop arm.**

9. **Put the transmission in park or neutral and set the parking brake.**

Loading passengers and leaving a stop

Don't expect children to calmly take a seat, at least until you have them thoroughly trained. Protect students from bullying and from themselves when they might be showing off. If arguing over which seat to sit in occurs, seating arrangements might be in order.

1. **Allow the students to board when it's safe to do so (open door).**

2. **Count the students.**

3. **Account for any missing students. It's helpful to know the students' names.**

4. **Keep monitoring the mirrors.**

5. **Ensure that all students are seated with their backs to the back of the seat and their bottoms seated on the bench or seat cushion.**

REMEMBER

If for any reason you must move out of your seat, turn off the engine and remove the keys.

To leave the stop:

1. **Close the door.**

2. **Engage the transmission and release the parking brake.**

3. **Turn off the flashing lights and retract the stop arm.**

4. **Signal your intentions to pull away from the curb or equivalent.**

5. **Check your mirrors.**

6. **Move properly and safely into the lane.**

Unloading your passengers

Your first and utmost responsibility is for the students on your bus. Just a smidge behind that is for students and others anywhere around your bus. For another aspect of examining other people around the drop-off area is to watch for suspicious characters. When the unloading area is safe, follow the guidelines listed here.

AT A ROUTE STOP

At the designated stop, conduct the stop the same as described in the previous sections on approaching and leaving a stop, where students can step off the bus safely.

1. **Direct the students to remain seated until the bus is fully stopped, and you say they may leave the bus (opening the door conveys they can leave the bus).**

2. **Count the students leaving the bus to confirm the correct number are leaving the bus.**

3. Instruct the students to move at least 10 feet away from the bus to a spot where you can see them and will be able to move the bus safely away from them.

4. Leave the stop as described in the previous section.

AT THE SCHOOL

Students may want to exit the bus all at the same time or rush to be the first off, even before the bus is stopped. So remember to keep them safe, including safe from their own devices.

1. Perform a safe stop as I stated for the other stops.

2. Turn off the engine.

3. Instruct the students as to when they can stand and exit the bus (you might need to have an unloading order like front seats first, working towards the back).

4. Follow any state or local instructions specific to you as the driver.

5. Observe that students depart the bus orderly, safely, and clear the confines of the bus.

6. Check the bus for any students and student belongings still on board.

7. Account for the whereabouts of students. None should be next to the bus nor under the bus.

8. Leave the stop safely, including all points that I previously mentioned.

WARNING

Watch for students to do the unexpected, like drop something and attempt to retrieve it. This can occur at any time.

Directing students who need to cross a roadway

Here is where you, the bus driver, must exercise great care and responsibility.

1. Direct the students to walk at least 10 feet to the right front corner area of your bus, far enough away that you can see their feet.

   If they were to fall at that spot, you still should be able to see them.

2. Have the students stop at the edge of the road.

   The students should look for the bus lights to still be on and to look for your signal.

3. Make sure after you signal (for it being safe for them to cross), students are to:

   • Stay far enough away from the bus for you to see their feet.

   • Look for traffic in both directions.

   • Proceed across the road, continually looking in both directions.

AUTHOR SAYS

Your school bus might have the added feature of a *strobe light on top of the bus*. This light helps other drivers notice you in low-visibility situations. Follow any state rules for these lights.

Managing your students

When you are having problems with your cargo staying secured, you can attempt to fix the problem by adding more straps or chains. You are not allowed to do this with students. You are not even allowed to demonstrate what happens if they are not sitting in their seats like they were told to and you have to stop the bus abruptly. I truly think that the students would learn the lesson, but again, you are not allowed to teach in this manner.

But seriously, you need to gain some skills in handling unruly students. This might not be a natural thing for you. If it is not, it is even more imperative that you follow your school or company's policies for handling bad behavior. Here are some rules and best practices for handling serious problems.

REMEMBER

>> Stop the bus in a safe location, performing safe stopping procedures (place transmission in park, set the parking brake, and take the keys).

>> Speak to the student, calmly, in a quiet voice, directly making eye contact but not menacingly.

>> State the policies and repercussions for failing to follow the rules.

>> Never put the student off the bus except at the school or at the designated stop. If the situation is serious enough, call for a school administrator or a police officer to come and remove the student.

Understanding evacuations

You will need to quickly assess an emergency situation to determine whether an evacuation is necessary. Is there a safer action to take? What is the potential outcome if students stayed on the bus? Generally, the safest place to be is on the bus. But if the bus stalled on a railroad crossing, staying on the bus is a terrible place to wait.

Considerations for determining if an evacuation is in order or not:

>> Is there fire?

>> Do you smell fuel leaking?

>> Are there downed power lines?

>> Is there speeding traffic all around?

>> Is there hazardous materials spilled in the area?

>> Is there a tornado in sight or is water rising?

REMEMBER

You must evacuate if:

>> The bus is on fire.

>> There is an immediate danger of collision.

>> There is a hazardous material spill that necessitates it.

>> The bus is stalled on a railroad crossing.

Training students on how to help

TIP

Train your students as if you *know* there will be a need for an emergency evacuation of the bus. While all your students should know what to do in an emergency, select a couple of older responsible students for specific duties. Instruct them on either to assist you in the following or to be completely in charge should you be incapacitated:

>> Where to go in the event of an evacuation:

· Away from traffic, away from the road, away from a railroad track, away from the bus — at least 300 feet.

- Upwind from the bus (in case of fire).

- In the event of a tornado, to a ditch or culvert (if no appropriate building is available), generally to the southwest of the bus.

To evacuate the bus:

- Use the appropriate emergency exits: the roof or windows when the bus is no longer on its wheels, the rear exit, and the normal service door(s).

- Assist smaller and weaker students.

Preparing for evacuation

Having yourself and your students prepared for worst-case scenarios will help reduce panic. When training kicks in, the mind and body can react to the training and delay an emotional response.

REMEMBER

Always secure the bus when you encounter or execute an emergency stop by shutting down the engine, setting the parking brake, and removing the key. If you fail to do this, another emergency can result.

If there is time, or at least when there is time, notify authorities (911) and your bus company or school officials. This action can also be delegated to a responsible student or aide as you are handling other matters. Here are some guidelines you should follow in an evacuation:

>> Give clear instructions to the students.

>> Ensure that all students have left the bus.

>> Deploy emergency triangles when students are safe and if it is appropriate.

>> Don't move a student who might have suffered a broken neck or a spinal cord injury unless their life is in immediate danger.

>> Join your students as soon as possible. Be a calm presence for them and thank them for their excellent execution of the evacuation.

Crossing railroad tracks

REMEMBER

You must adopt a new habit when you drive buses. Stop, look, and listen prior to proceeding to cross railroad tracks. Official CDL study guides state that there might be different rules in some states that include not having the requirement to stop at railroad tracks. But since regulations say that passenger buses in general are to stop at active railroad tracks, I would say that it is just as important for school buses to stop as well.

Railroad track warnings are usually easy to see. There should be nice black on yellow signs (see Figure 14-1), with an X and two Rs, warning everyone that they are approaching a crossing. Often, a similar image will be painted on the pavement prior to the crossing (see Figure 14-2). Along with this image, on the pavement, there might be a "No Passing Zone" sign.

Railroad crossings with no lights or gates are called *passive crossings*. When the crossings have lights and maybe gates, they are called *active crossings*. Treat these crossings the same and get your bus stopped. *Exempt crossings* are crossings that are marked with the word "exempt," meaning that they are closed down. Trains can't be on them. Don't stop at exempt crossings.

FIGURE 4-1:
The advanced warning railroad crossing sign.

FIGURE 4-2:
A pavement sign.

The final warnings are at the crossing. It might have a stop line, but there has to be a *crossbucks sign* (the traditional railroad crossing sign) at the tracks (see Figure 14-3). If there is more than one track, the sign should state how many tracks there are to cross.

FIGURE 4-3:
The traditional railroad crossing sign with the number of tracks.

REMEMBER

Stop behind the stop line if there is one and if not, stop behind the sign. The distance stated for other types of buses to stop is 15 to 50 feet prior to the crossing. Be sure to conduct the procedure that your state has for school buses stopping at railroad crossings. Here is one procedure:

1. Start slowing down, and downshifting if you are driving a bus with a manual transmission (although they are extremely rare).

2. Turn on your four-way hazard lights approximately 200 feet prior to the crossing. Using the hazard lights earlier is fine with me if you think the driver behind you needs an extra warning.

3. Scan your surroundings, including behind you (watch for inattentive drivers).

4. Stay to the right.

5. Have an escape route planned in case there is any emergency (brake failure, inattentive driver behind you).

6. Stop between 15 and 50 behind the stop line or before the crossbucks sign if there is no stop line. Be sure to get the best view of the tracks.

7. Place the transmission in park or neutral and set the parking brake.

8. Turn off all radios and noisy equipment. Ask the students for silence.

9. Open the service door and the driver's window, looking and listening for any trains.

10. After determining that there is no train coming, close the door and proceed across the tracks (releasing the parking brake and engaging the transmission).

   - If you have that rare manual transmission, choose a low gear and stay in it. *You are not allowed to shift gears as you cross.*

   - If a gate comes down as you are crossing, keep going! Don't worry about the gate. Clear all tracks.

   - If you had to wait on a train at tracks with multiple tracks, allow the train to make it far enough down the track to ensure there are no other trains coming. One train can hide a second train.

Tracks often have additional warnings with flashing red lights and gates. These safety devices should not bother you if they deploy because you have already determined, when you see a train somewhere down the tracks, that it wouldn't be prudent to take a busload of students across the tracks. So you were going to wait on the train anyway, right?

WARNING

Before crossing railroad tracks, ensure that nothing will prohibit you from driving the entire bus all the way clear of the tracks, like a traffic light at the intersection just on the other side of the tracks.

REMEMBER

If for whatever reason, *your bus stalls or gets trapped on a railroad track,* evacuate the bus immediately. Move far away from the bus and if there is a train approaching, move in that direction as well. (The train will send bus parts flying, and you and the students should move in a direction away from the flying parts.)

Figuring out bus maneuvers

The physical size of many buses makes them a challenge to drive, especially when it is time to maneuver them in other than a straight line. Keep an awareness of the following topics in your mind to avoid, if possible, or to perform safely.

Backing up

REMEMBER

Backing is always a dangerous maneuver, and you should always avoid it when possible. But when you must do back up, remember these practices (or call them rules):

>> Always have your students on the bus — pick up students prior to backing and drop them off after backing. Never have your students outside the bus while backing.

>> Utilize a spotter. The spotter should inform you of obstacles, people, and vehicles. They are to leave the driving maneuvers up to you.

>> If there is no spotter, stop the bus, put the transmission in park or neutral, set the parking brake, and take the keys. Walk to the end of the bus to verify that the path is clear.

>> Use your mirrors.

>> Back slowly.

>> Never guess or hope, *know* what is behind you or in your path.

Tail swing

REMEMBER

Have you noticed stop signs, located near curbs on narrow streets, that are bent over? Buses, or their drivers, are often the cause of such curiosity. Buses, especially school buses can have a long tail swing. This is the part of the bus that is behind the rear axle, which swings in the opposite direction of the way you are turning the bus. You need to know how much tail swing is possible with the bus you are driving. Here's how you do it:

1. **Park the bus next to a curb on your right, giving room for your steer tires to turn while sitting still (or you can use a straight line in a parking lot).**

2. **Turn your steering wheel all the way to the left.**

3. **Put the bus "in gear" and move slowly forward.**

4. **Stop the bus when the rear bumper has crossed over the curb (or line) at the greatest distance possible.**

   You might need to get out a couple of times to verify when the bus is extended over the curb the farthest distance.

5. **Measure (visually or literally) the distance the bumper is past the curb.**

   This is the minimum distance (plus a few inches) that you should be from a curb or any obstacle sticking out over the curb, like a stop sign, when making left-hand turns. It is possible for this distance to be 3 feet!

With this information you know how far away from curbs and signs you must be in order to make turns without the risk of hitting the stop or street signs. Use the minimum distance that you came up with in Step 5 and add a few inches to it. Write it down, maybe on a sticky note and place it in a convenient location as a reminder of how far to stay away from curbs. Remember that a stop sign sticks out farther than the post it is on, so the sign might stick out past the curb!

Practice Questions

Some questions on the written test for the passenger endorsement can be similar or the same as on the general knowledge written test.

1. Which is not a good practice for driving a bus safely?
   (A) Have an opening beside you in the case of an emergency.
   (B) Turn around to check on your passengers.
   (C) Slowing down in high winds.
   (D) Turning on the strobe light when fog is heavy.

2. Which is the best course of action when an animal runs in front of your bus?
   (A) Step on the fuel pedal.
   (B) Take evasive action to steer around it.
   (C) Brake.
   (D) Any of these choices are good.

3. Which is the best course of action when you run off the road?
   (A) Cut the steering wheel hard to make it roll back onto the pavement.
   (B) Stop and back onto the road.
   (C) Keep driving on the shoulder until you get to an intersection.
   (D) Slow down gently and then return to the road.

4. Which of the following is a good practice for preparing for emergencies?
   (A) Giving older students some responsibility.
   (B) Training students at the beginning of the school year.
   (C) Showing the students how to work the emergency exits.
   (D) These are all good practices for emergency preparedness.

5. If your school bus gets stuck on a railroad track, which of the following should you do?
   (A) Remain on the bus.
   (B) Evacuate the bus and move far away in the same direction as an oncoming train.
   (C) Evacuate the bus and move far away in the opposite direction as an oncoming train.
   (D) Have the students push the bus off the tracks.

6. Which of the following is not a bus exit?
   (A) The hood
   (B) The roof vent/exit
   (C) Back door
   (D) The service door

7. Which of the following should be done first in a bus evacuation?
   (A) Call in to the company or school.
   (B) Put warning triangles out.
   (C) Move passengers to a safe location.
   (D) Call 911.

8. Which of the following is not a good reason to evacuate?

    (A) The bus might change its position.

    (B) The bus is hot, and the engine is not running.

    (C) Another vehicle might crash into the bus.

    (D) The bus is on fire.

9. Which of the following is not a unique item to inspect in a bus?

    (A) Seats

    (B) First aid kit

    (C) Emergency exits

    (D) Warning triangles

10. Which of the following is not a concern when picking up students at a stop?

    (A) If a student has a musical instrument.

    (B) How many students are at the stop.

    (C) If the students are a safe distance away from where the bus will stop.

    (D) If there are any students missing.

11. Which of the following is a concern when dropping students at a scheduled stop?

    (A) Traffic in the vicinity.

    (B) How many students depart the bus.

    (C) That students move at least 10 feet away from the bus.

    (D) These are all concerns when dropping students off at a scheduled stop.

12. How should you handle an unruly student on the bus?

    (A) Drop them off at the next intersection.

    (B) Slam on the brakes to make them sit down.

    (C) Restrain them in a seat.

    (D) Isolate them in a seat and call officials to meet you.

13. What is not a precaution when backing a school bus?

    (A) Let the students off the bus first.

    (B) Use a spotter.

    (C) Walk to the back of the bus, taking the keys with you.

    (D) Constantly check all mirrors.

14. High winds . . .

    (A) Can blow a high-profile vehicle like a bus over.

    (B) Should prompt a driver to slow down.

    (C) Can move a bus off the road.

    (D) These are all true statements concerning high winds and buses.

15. Which is an acceptable procedure for railroad crossings?

   (A) Slow down before crossing tracks.

   (B) Stop and look for trains at tracks.

   (C) Stop only at active crossings.

   (D) Use the left lane when on multiple-lane roads.

16. When should you require your passengers to disembark?

   (A) After you come to a full stop.

   (B) After you set the parking brake.

   (C) After you put the transmission in "Park" or neutral.

   (D) You should require your passenger to disembark after all these tasks are completed.

17. Hazardous materials . . .

   (A) Can never be hauled with passengers.

   (B) Can be hauled in any quantities in the luggage compartment.

   (C) Should be looked for by the driver.

   (D) Cannot be restricted by a bus company.

18. ABS will:

   (A) Help you control the bus during hard braking.

   (B) Give the bus more braking power.

   (C) Stop the bus faster.

   (D) Reduce maintenance.

19. When driving, a driver should avoid:

   (A) Making eye contact with passengers.

   (B) Chatting with passengers.

   (C) The right lane.

   (D) Stopping at passive railroad crossings.

20. A driver should have a DOT physical:

   (A) Only if they are receiving compensation for driving.

   (B) Only if they are operating school buses.

   (C) If they operate a bus with 15 or more passengers.

   (D) Only if they are pulling a trailer behind the bus.

21. Where should you stop a bus when approaching a railroad crossing?

   (A) 15 to 50 feet prior to the tracks.

   (B) Before a stop line.

   (C) Where you have visibility of the tracks.

   (D) These are all practices of where to stop a bus when approaching a railroad crossing.

22. The rear door of a city bus:

     (A) Might activate brakes when open.

     (B) Is for evacuations.

     (C) Is only for passengers with wheelchairs.

     (D) Is to be used to automatically set parking brakes.

23. Of the following choices, which should you do if the railroad crossing stop arms drop on your bus when you are already crossing the railroad track?

     (A) Stop and call 911.

     (B) Stop and evacuate the bus.

     (C) Back up and off the tracks.

     (D) Continue to cross the tracks.

24. What is the danger zone?

     (A) The front seats in a bus.

     (B) The areas surrounding the bus where students can be struck by other vehicles.

     (C) Dropoff locations.

     (D) Within 15 feet of a railroad crossing.

25. Why would you walk through the bus after unloading students?

     (A) To see if there is any damage.

     (B) To see if there are any students left on the bus.

     (C) To see if there are any personal items left on the bus.

     (D) These are all reasons to walk through the bus after unloading students.

Answers and Explanations

1. **B.** You don't turn around to look at your passengers. You have a mirror for that which keeps your body oriented in a position to keep a vigilant watch while driving.

2. **C.** Never swerve to miss an animal as you can lose control with such an evasive maneuver, and you are responsible for the people on your bus. You don't speed up to try to hit it either.

3. **D.** Whipping your vehicle back on a road will potentially make you lose control, possibly turning the bus over. It is not necessary to drive off the road until you get to an intersection. When you get your bus slowed down, you can safely return to the road. Never back up on the road.

4. **D.** Choices A, B, and C are all good practices for preparing for an emergency.

5. **C.** This is an example of a tricky question. You want your passengers to get away from any potential harm. To go in the opposite direction of the train is to go towards it, generally speaking. Be sure to move away from the track at the same time.

6. **A.** The hood gives you access to the engine, but it isn't a bus exit.

7. **C.** All these items are tasks to perform, but your number one task is to get your passengers to safety.

8. **B.** Another slightly tricky one. A hot bus is not enjoyable but maybe dangerous if you leave all the windows up. However, the other choices speak of eminent danger.

9. **D.** Emergency triangles or other warning devices should be common on CMVs. First aid kits are not required on most other CMVs.

10. **A.** You want to know the number of students at a stop and compare it to a roster. The students need to be a safe distance from where the bus will stop. Unless the musical instrument is a tuba, and has pyrotechnics in it, it is probably still not a main concern.

11. **D.** All these are concerns when dropping students at a scheduled stop.

12. **D.** You are not allowed to restrain students or try to get them to sit in their seats by slamming on the brakes. You are not allowed to drop them off just anywhere either. While not the only way to deal with a student, getting them away from other students and into the hands of someone official is the best choice for dealing with an unruly student.

13. **A.** Always perform the backing maneuver when all the students are on the bus. That way you don't have the extra task of keeping track of students outside the bus as you are backing.

14. **D.** All these are true statements concerning driving in high winds.

15. **B.** Don't just slow down at railroad tracks. Get in the right lane for both active and passive crossings and stop, look, and listen.

16. **D.** Choice D is the best choice because all the tasks mentioned in Choices A, B, and C need to take place prior to students departing the bus.

17. **C.** Choices A, B, and D are not true statements, but a driver should always watch what passengers are bringing on the bus.

18. **A.** ABS will not stop a vehicle faster, it does not have more braking power, nor will it reduce maintenance. ABS helps drivers to control their vehicle by helping to keep wheels rolling.

19. **B.** Bus drivers often need to make eye contact with energetic students while staying primarily in the right lane. Bus drivers must stop at both passive and active railroad crossings. Chatting with passengers while driving can be a distraction.

20. **C.** Choice C is the only completely correct statement as the others are made incorrect by the word "only."

21. **D.** You should stop a bus 15 to 50 feet from the tracks and before any stop line. You must see the tracks.

22. **A.** A city or urban transit bus might have a brake interlock with a rear door. The door is not just for evacuations and is not to be used as a parking brake by keeping it open. They generally can take passengers who are walking along with wheelchair riders.

23. **D.** Your primary responsibility is your passengers. Drive across the tracks and don't worry about equipment. It is replaceable; your passengers are not. You can call 911 after you cross.

24. **B.** While the other areas are potentially dangerous, they don't have the title of danger zone. The danger zone is around the bus where students have been struck by other vehicles.

25. **D.** Damage needs to be repaired. Students obviously should be somewhere else besides the bus, and someone should appreciate having their belongings back, especially if someone's homework assignment is in the bag.

Chapter **15**
Adding on Doubles and Triples

oubles and triples is an endorsement that can be added to your Commercial Driver's License (CDL), designated by a "T" on licenses, by just taking a written test — no driving. Scary, isn't it? Seriously, after you practice at your school driving around with a 48- or 53-foot trailer, pulling doubles won't seem that difficult. However, the truth is that it can be easier or it can be harder and more hazardous. It depends on whether you plan or if you fail to plan, ignoring safe driving practices.

Obviously, you must pass the combination written test prior to getting the doubles endorsement added to your license. While you can add the doubles and triples endorsement at any time after obtaining your CDL, I would suggest to try to do the written test on the day of the behind-the-wheel tests. But I am a nerd about taking tests, especially multiple-choice questions, just don't give me an essay test.

The main reason why it is easier to pull doubles is that making a turn is more difficult with a 53-foot trailer than with two 28-foot *pup trailers* (a short trailer commonly used in doubles). The pup trailers track behind the semi-tractor better than a 53-foot trailer. Another reason is that it's easier is that you typically drive from terminal to terminal, which are set up to accommodate doubles, versus customer locations that may be more difficult to maneuver.

In this chapter, I address the physics of driving with multiple trailers. I also cover how to hook together the trailers and semi-tractor, and how to ensure that you performed all the steps. A few practice questions are provided for you at the end of the chapter.

TIP

I encourage you to obtain a doubles and triples endorsement as it gives you more opportunities as a professional driver by making yourself more credible or desirable to employers.

Driving Double

I used to aggravate my children when they were young. They would say, "I didn't mean to do it!" I would respond saying, "Did you mean *not* to do it?" My response was meant to instruct them that they needed to plan to avoid doing certain things. When you pull doubles and triples, you must plan before you leave on a trip and all the time you are driving. Events and potential hazards are constantly unfolding that require you to be thinking about what you might need to do next.

I think it might get very annoying to say both "doubles and triples" throughout this chapter. So going forward, I will refer to as "doubles" only. Besides, triples might be popular where you live, but I am not sure that I've ever seen triples on the highway in all my years of traveling around the country.

Preventing rollovers

As you pull doubles, you will practice the same habits as when you are pulling a single long trailer, just double down on your awareness of those habits (no pun was intended here). In the chapter introduction, I mentioned that doubles track where your semi-tractor rolled better than a 53-foot trailer, which is nice for the tighter turns. However, this also means the trailers make a sharper turn, which increases rollover opportunities. The rollover can be prevented by taking the turns slower than you would when pulling a 53-foot trailer.

When you drive a straight truck around a curve or ramp, you drive it slower than a personal passenger vehicle. When you add a trailer, you decrease your speed even more. Add a second trailer and you should slow down even more. Doubles don't have the stability that most other commercial vehicles have. A safe speed on a curve or ramp for other vehicles is not a safe speed for doubles. Ignore the traffic that may be building up behind you. They will get to their destination if they take their time and stay behind you. If you turn a trailer over in front of them, they will forget that they were criticizing you for going slow (and begin criticizing you for turning the trailer over).

Cracking the whip

TIP

Crack-the-whip is a term that you might see on your written test and is another reason why doubles can turn over easier. *Rearward amplification*, where a small movement at the front of a combination vehicle, is amplified as it moves through the vehicles' connections until it culminates in a seemingly exaggerated movement in the rear trailer. This causes the crack-the-whip effect, which is discussed in Chapter 10. The last trailer in a combination is the most likely piece of equipment to turn over, and it can bring the rest of the combination with it.

REMEMBER

The traditional-sized double trailers combination has a rearward amplification of 2.0 meaning that when you are pulling doubles, it is twice as likely to turn the rear trailer over. Triples have a rearward amplification of 3.5, making them three and a half times easier to roll the last trailer over.

Planning your trip

In addition to driving at safe speeds and watching for hazards to avoid whipping the trailers, you should plan your trip because you might not be able to do certain driving maneuvers like backing up. For example, you might find yourself unable to proceed forward but you cannot back up a set of doubles like you can a single trailer, nor should you try to do so around traffic. You will need to call law enforcement (or traffic safety personnel) to help with the traffic while you disassemble your little convoy and reposition it, piece by piece, where you can be in control again.

As part of your trip planning, always check the weather forecast. Adverse driving conditions are more adverse for doubles. You can have more axles on the ground (tires actually) with less axles that are powered (drive axles). Due to the way differentials (drive axle again) work, only one wheel might be attempting to move the whole vehicle. When that wheel is on a slick surface and you are already moving, a skid is likely. Also the length of your vehicle is longer and has more surface area for the wind to catch. The bottom line is you have a greater chance of skidding, losing traction and blowing over. Remember that if it is not safe to drive, you have the authority (and responsibility) to say when it is not safe to drive. Talk to experienced drivers (who have safe driving records) about these weather-related issues.

Managing your space

REMEMBER

Increase the space between you and the vehicle in front of you — more than a semi-tractor with a trailer or similar type of combination vehicle requires. These vehicles have one pivot point (where the tow vehicle is coupled with a trailer). With doubles, there are three pivot points. Imagine coming to a fast stop with pulling two or three trailers. Have you seen a picture of a train wreck or derailment? It resembles an accordion. So, when someone cuts in front of you and reduces the space you created, it is up to you to create the space again. It is imperative that you do so!

Don't forget about the space you need to pull out of a parking spot. You must be able to drive forward when you are ready to leave. Remember that backing up is not an option. You can back a 53-foot trailer, but doubles would be more than a challenge.

Assembling Your Convoy of Equipment

Assembling your convoy of equipment is the fun part of pulling doubles (and triples) for some people. Maybe it's the exercise that they enjoy, I don't know what everyone else sees in it, but it is a change from the routine of driving and you get to perform a process. Did I hear someone say "Nerd!"?

A unique piece of equipment that is used for doubles is the converter dolly. A *converter dolly* is designed to connect two trailers together. It is equipped with air and electrical lines that connect to the front trailer and lines that connect to the rear trailer. The dolly also utilizes the air and electricity for its own brakes and lights. At the front of the dolly is an eye that hooks onto a *pintle hook*. The dolly is likely to have a pintle hook at its rear to transport another dolly as well. It has a fifth wheel mounted on it for the rear trailer to couple to. It will have one or more axles. I will be referring to the one-axle version in this chapter.

One more point, there are other types of trailer coupling, but this is by far the most common and your written test won't likely cover anything else. You should verify that this is true for where you live.

1. **Choose which trailer goes where.**

   It is a simple choice, the heaviest trailer is up front, coupled directly to the semi-tractor. The lightest trailer goes in the back. Check the paperwork to find the weights.

2. **Position the converter dolly closely in front of the last trailer (see Figure 15-1).**

   The easiest way to move the dollies is to push/roll the tires. Pushing and pulling on the tongue (the circular ring at the front of the dolly) increases the chances of injury.

You might need to pull the dolly with either the front trailer or with your semi-tractor (it might be on the other side of the lot).

Be sure to release the brakes on the dolly. You will probably figure this out fairly quickly when the dolly won't roll.

There should be enough air in the tank of the dolly to release the spring brakes (parking brake). If there isn't, you will have to drive by and hook the air lines of the truck or front trailer (when it is coupled to the semi-tractor), to the air lines of the dolly, open the valves for the lines and fill the tank with air. You can release the brakes on the dolly. Once you know how to assemble your little convoy of equipment, this will be an easy process for you to perform.

FIGURE 15-1:
A dolly in line and in front of a trailer.

3. **Hook your semi-tractor to the front trailer.**

   Again, this will be the heaviest trailer. Hook to this trailer just as you hook to any trailer.

4. **Position the semi-tractor and trailer in front of the rear trailer and the converter dolly.**

   Make a straight line with all your equipment (see Figure 15-2a).

5. **Back the semi-tractor and trailer to the dolly and rear trailer (see Figure 15-2b).**

   There will be a jack with a wheel at the bottom and a crank at the top to let you adjust the height of the tongue ring so that it will clear the bottom portion of the pintle hook.

6. **Hooking the dolly to the front trailer.**

   - Open the pintle hook by using the two-part latching system of the pintle hook as shown in Figure 15-3.

   - Lower the front of the dolly so that the tongue will set in the pintle hook.

   - Close the pintle hook.

   - Raise the jack or dolly support to its fullest height.

FIGURE 15-2:
All the
equipment
in a line,
including a
view from
the driver's
side-view
mirror.

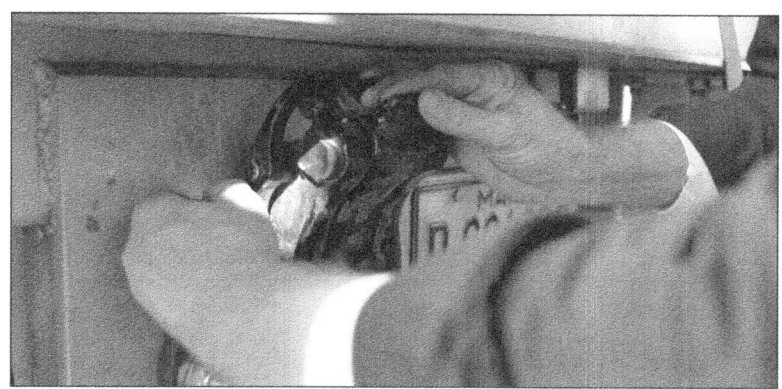

FIGURE 15-3:
Opening the
pintle hook.

7. **Prepare the rear trailer for coupling.**

- Check the height of the trailer at the kingpin and apron (refer to Chapter 12 for a coupling refresher). It should be such that when the dolly is backed under the trailer it would rise just a little, like an inch.

- Ensure that the parking brakes are set. While I include this more for the written test (because many tests will assume that some trailers don't have spring brakes), you will want the trailer to hold still as you move the dolly under it. Brakes that have been properly maintained will hold. Inspect the brakes. If you have a several-decades-old trailer, *chock* (block) the wheels.

8. **Back the assembly under the rear trailer.**

9. **Inspect your connection (fifth wheel locking bar around the kingpin).**

- Fifth wheel release handle should be all the way in.

- The jaw and locking bar should be wrapped completely around the kingpin.

- There should be no daylight between the fifth wheel and apron.

- A tug test will make the final confirmation for a secure connection.

10. **Connect all safety chains, air lines, and electrical cords.**

- Front trailer to dolly.

- Dolly to rear trailer (no chains here).

11. **Open the shutoff valves (for the air) at the rear of the front trailer.**

12. **Open the shutoff valves on the dolly.**

13. **Raise the landing gear all the way.**

14. **Push in the air supply knob in the semi-tractor to charge the air system.**

15. **Open the red emergency air line valve to ensure air comes out.**

    If no air comes out, something is connected incorrectly and your brakes are not going to work properly.

TIP

If you have triples, set everything up closely together. Assemble the trailers by starting at the front and working your way back.

Or hook the second and third trailers together as though they are the first and second trailer. Disconnect the semi-tractor and get the real first trailer and hook it up just as described above.

Disassembling Your Flotilla

In short, reverse the process of assembling the equipment. Your employer will likely have a special location for you to do this task.

1. **Park in a straight line.**

2. **Set your brakes. (For the sake of the written test, remember that they forget that trailers have spring brakes so, chock the wheels.)**

3. **Lower the landing gear of the second trailer.**

4. **Close the shutoff valves on the first trailer and the dolly.**

5. **Disconnect the air lines and the electrical cord from the last trailer and to the first trailer.**

    Store the lines and cords in the storage area of the dolly.

6. **Ensure the dolly brakes are released.**

7. **Pull the kingpin release handle to the locked release position.**

8. **Pull the rest of the assembly forward.**

9. **Lower the support or jack of the converter dolly.**

10. **Disconnect the safety chains.**

11. **Set the brakes on the dolly.**

12. **Open the pintle hook.**

13. **Safely pull forward, clearing the dolly.**

14. **Disconnect/park your front trailer as appropriate.**

WARNING

Never unlock/open the pintle lock with a trailer on the fifth wheel of the dolly. A serious injury is likely. If you don't get injured, you will have an embarrassing time fixing your mistake.

Inspecting the Equipment

You won't have to learn many new skills to inspect doubles, but you will be inspecting more lights, tires, brakes, and so on than other commercial vehicles.

Let's recap the inspection items that are special to doubles.

>> Ensure the pintle hook is locked closed.

>> Check that the chains are hooked onto the trailer in front of it.

>> Check the air lines for proper operation.

- Open the emergency valve at the rear of the rear trailer. Air should come out when the trailer air supply valve is in the released position. Close it back.

- With the trailer service brake on or the brake pedal applied, open the service line shutoff valve. Air should come out. Close it back.

- If you did not hear air escaping from both lines, check on the shutoff valves and check for correct connections.

TIP

Your written test might include a question about anti-lock brake systems (ABS) on trailers and dollies. Remember that all trailers and converter dollies manufactured on or after March 1, 1998, are to have ABS.

Practice Questions

1. What is a converter dolly?

   (A) The device that raises and lowers, holding the trailer when it is not coupled to a semi-tractor.

   (B) A one or two-axle component that joins two trailers together.

   (C) The device that lifts pallets to move in and out of trailers.

   (D) A device that lifts cargo to the floor of a trailer.

2. What is the order of coupling/assembling trailers?

   (A) Front to back.

   (B) Back to front.

   (C) There is no order.

   (D) Drivers are not allowed to assemble trailers.

3. What is the rearward amplification of triples?

   (A) 2.0

   (B) 2.5

   (C) 3.0

   (D) 3.5

4. What is the order of uncoupling trailers?

   (A) Disconnect dolly from the front trailer, then both trailers can be disconnected.

   (B) Unhook the front trailer, then the dolly, then the rear trailer.

   (C) Disconnect the rear trailer, then the dolly, then the front trailer.

   (D) There is no order as long as air lines are disconnected first.

5. Which is a concern for pulling doubles and triples?

   (A) Surges.

   (B) Crack-the-whip.

   (C) Stop arm activation.

   (D) These are all concerns for pulling doubles and triples.

6. Do converter dollies have brakes?

   (A) Yes, but just service brakes, no parking brakes.

   (B) No, the brakes of the trailers suffice.

   (C) Yes.

   (D) Yes, but not ABS.

7. Crack-the-whip phenomenon is caused by:

   (A) Rearward amplification.

   (B) Failing to connect the air lines correctly.

   (C) Surge.

   (D) High winds.

8. Which of these is not part of a safety check for doubles and triples?

   (A) Checking the safety arm for proper activation

   (B) Opening the rear shutoff valves for checking proper line connections

   (C) Checking the safety chains for proper connection

   (D) Checking that the pintle hook is closed

9. Which is the best method for checking the air connections on doubles?

   (A) Close the front trailer shutoff valves and open the valves on the rear trailer.

   (B) Release (push in) the air valve knob in the cab and open both rear trailer valves.

   (C) Apply the brakes and open the rear trailer's valves.

   (D) Push in red knob, utilize the trailer service brake handle, open both rear trailer valves.

10. Which is not an unsafe process or act?

    (A) Leaving the landing gear down on the rear trailer during operation.

    (B) Leaving the chains stowed on the dolly during operation.

    (C) Disconnecting the converter dolly from the front trailer prior to uncoupling from the rear trailer.

    (D) These are all unsafe processes or acts.

11. Which shutoff valves should be open when driving down the road?

    (A) All valves should be open.

    (B) All valves should be closed.

    (C) All valves should be open except the front trailer.

    (D) All valves should be open except the rear trailer.

12. The rearward amplification for doubles is:

    (A) 1.0.

    (B) 2.0.

    (C) 3.0.

    (D) 3.5.

Answers and Explanations

1. **B.** A sounds like landing gear. C is a pallet jack, and D is a lift gate.

2. **A.** Back to front results in catastrophe as the tongue of the dolly raises up and hits you in the head. Of course, drivers must assemble and disassemble the trailers.

3. **D.** Triples is 3.5.

4. **C.** There is definitely a safe order and part of that is for the dolly to be disconnected at its fifth wheel prior to unhooking at the pintle hook.

5. **B.** Surges are a concern for tankers and stop arms are on school buses.

6. **C.** Converter dollies have had ABS and spring brakes (parking brakes) for many years, so many that you might never see one without ABS or without spring brakes.

7. **A.** Surge is a tank driving concern and failing to connect air lines correctly doesn't lead to the crack-the-whip problem. High winds might exasperate the problem, but rear amplification is the main cause of crack-the-whip.

8. **A.** The safety arm helps to steer kids away from a bus to help the driver see them.

9. **D.** By filling the system with air and applying the brakes, it allows you to check to see that air is flowing through both lines, the supply and the service.

10. **D.** The landing gear should always get raised all the way for operation. You should always use the safety chains so that if the coupling fails, the chains can help prevent a catastrophe. Disconnecting the dolly from the pintle hook prior to uncoupling the trailer from the dolly's fifth wheel can result in the tongue end of the dolly flying up.

11. **D.** All the valves should be open so that air will flow where it needs to and so that brakes can be operated, except for the rear trailer. At the rear of that trailer, you want the air to stop flowing so that it can be utilized safely and appropriately.

12. **B.** The rearward amplification for doubles is 2.0.

IN THIS CHAPTER

» **Defining the requirements for a driver**

» **Acquiring the hazardous materials endorsement**

» **Reviewing the shipping papers**

» **Dealing with hazmat as cargo**

» **Recognizing your responsibilities**

Chapter **16**

Qualifying for Hazardous Materials

H azardous materials, often referred to hazmat or even HM, are products, materials, or ingredients that pose risk to health and safety. Hazardous materials are in different shapes, sizes, and types and can be explosives, flammable gases, liquids, or even solids. Hazmat can pose threats to the environment and/or to humans.

Shippers have a greater responsibility in shipping hazardous materials than they do for non-hazardous cargo. First, they must determine if their products are hazardous. When the cargo is hazardous, they must communicate and package the materials in compliance with regulations. Drivers, and the carriers they drive for, must acquire the credentials necessary to transport hazardous materials.

In this chapter, I provide the information on how you can obtain a hazardous materials endorsement, which is required to haul a substantial amount of hazmat. And I explain the hazmat drivers' responsibilities from picking up the cargo at the shipper to delivering the material to the *consignee* (the receiver). What to do in case of an emergency is also discussed. There is a lot of information in this chapter, so read it in small bites at a time and then read the chapter again.

What you will not find in this chapter is training on working with specific hazardous materials. For that matter, I do not go into how to work with hazardous materials any deeper than the regulations for the endorsement. So you will find what might seem to be a serious omission of some materials like toxic substances. The endorsement training teaches that often you must be more thoroughly trained on the specific hazardous materials, especially when the handling is more than your casual loading and unloading by your employer.

You will be able to pass your hazardous materials endorsement test with the information in this chapter, but don't stop learning about hazardous materials after that accomplishment. There is so much information to know, especially about any specific material that you would transport, to safely and legally do your job. If you want a job where your attention to detail and safety is paramount, haul hazardous materials for a reputable transportation company whose sole purpose is to transport hazardous materials safely and legally.

Meeting the Initial Requirements

To add a hazardous materials endorsement (for the first time) to your Commercial Driver's License (CDL), you will have a set of tasks. First, you will need proof of who you are and that you are at least 21 years old. You must be a citizen of the United States or a legal permanent resident. To obtain a hazardous material endorsement (designated by "H"), a third party will have a part in proving you are worthy to have a hazardous material endorsement.

Completing a background check

REMEMBER

It is important to check with your state's licensing department to know how they enforce the federal requirements to obtain the hazmat endorsement. There will be an application to fill out, and you will have a background check, which is called a *Security Threat Assessment* (STA). Some states will initiate the process by taking your fingerprints, but the application and the prints will ultimately go to the federal government. The Transportation Security Administration (TSA) oversees the process of these assessments. This assessment will look for criminal records, mental health records, and immigration status.

Passing ELDT on hazardous materials

You will need to pass an Entry-Level Driver Training (ELDT) for hazmat course, but that won't be difficult for you. You are reading this chapter, so you have what it takes to take an ELDT course. There are online providers for the ELDT, but there are some driving schools that offer ELDT for hazmat.

This training will be helpful as the training provider should be able to answer questions for you as you start to wrap your mind around hauling hazardous materials. Then you can start working on studying for the hazmat endorsement exam — at your testing facility (a Department of Motor Vehicles or similar state department).

When you are successful completing the ELDT on hazardous materials, you will receive a certificate or letter showing your successful completion. You won't need to take that certificate/letter to the testing facility because the EDLT provider must register your completion of the ELDT in just a couple of days after completion. Without it, the licensing facility can't give you the endorsement. Access `https://tpr.fmcsa.dot.gov` for a list of ELDT hazmat providers.

Regulating the Endorsement

The hazardous materials endorsement has been around for a while, but with increased awareness of terrorist threat — from both foreign and domestic — there is more scrutiny on who can obtain the endorsement. Hazmat drivers must also have thorough understanding of their responsibilities.

Having the hazmat endorsement guides you on what you must know and do to provide safe transportation of hazardous materials. Two things you have to do as a driver are to know where to find the critical emergency information and how to load your material. Depending on what you are hauling, it might be too difficult to always remember all the aspects of your responsibilities, so have the information handy to reference in order to confirm that you are doing your job correctly.

Understanding the regulations

Hauling hazardous materials is a huge responsibility to undertake. Think about the ramifications of materials getting into the wrong hands. Or the driver who loads two different chemicals into a truck that shouldn't be in the same vehicle together. If someone runs a red light and slams into the vehicle, it can cause the chemicals to mix.

After you obtain your hazmat endorsement, refresh your memory often of the requirements. One of the most important points to remember is you *must* reference the hazmat tables and guides to ensure safe transportation of those materials. More of the tables and guides in sections to follow.

REMEMBER

The regulations can be summarized in three categories:

>> **Containing the material.** You and shippers have the responsibility to contain hazardous materials. The regulations are there to protect you, those around you, and the environment.

>> **Communicating the risk.** Shippers start the communication process. You should be informed that you have hazardous material to haul. As shippers package their material, they have specific labels to apply to the packaging. They are to provide you with properly completed shipping papers, emergency response information, and placards (which identifies hazardous materials) when required. With these items, you have what you need to communicate information for first responders and other motorists.

>> **Assuring safety.** The regulations help assure safety by requiring drivers to pass a test on transporting hazardous materials. The regulations require drivers to identify when cargo is hazardous and then to load it safely. There are rules that are unique to hauling hazardous materials in the regulations.

AUTHOR SAYS

Breaking regulations when hauling hazardous materials can result in more than a citation. Along with fines you can face jail time. I say this for two reasons and one of them is not to scare you. One is the possibility that this can be on a written test. The other is for you to conduct yourself as a true professional and verify that you are following regulations.

Shipper responsibilities

As the driver, you are not alone when hauling hazardous materials, at least at times. When you are hauling regular cargo, shippers can get a little sloppy with loading but may be able to get by with it. However, with hazardous materials, there are regulations for which a shipper can receive citations when they fail to perform their responsibilities properly.

The *shipper* is the entity that is sending cargo to another location. They contract with a carrier, or they might haul it themselves. Shippers are obligated to:

>> Investigate the hazardous materials regulations to determine their products:
   - Proper shipping name
   - Hazard class

- Identification number
- Packing group
- Correct packaging
- Necessary placards (if required)

>> Prepares the shipment with:

- Proper packaging
- Proper labels
- Emergency response information
- Shipping papers
- Placards (if required)

>> Certifies that the shipment has been properly prepared, according to the regulations, on the shipping papers. However, the shipper does not have to *certify* that the shipment is properly prepared if you or your company supplied the cargo tank(s).

Carrier and driver responsibilities

The carrier and driver have much of the same duties, especially when the driver is the representative for the carrier. By definition, the carrier is the one transporting the material from the shipper to its destination even though the driver is doing the work. So ultimately, the driver, as the carrier representative, has the following responsibilities.

>> Checks the paperwork and packages for correct markings and refuses shipments that are improperly marked or damaged.

>> Reports accidents and incidents to the proper government agencies. (The driver can have some help with this one.)

>> Places the placards on the vehicle when required, and safely and expeditiously transports the material to its destination.

>> Keeps the shipping papers and emergency response information in the driver's door pocket.

See the section "Understanding the Driver's Responsibilities" for more information about hazmat driver's duties.

Unpacking the Shipping Papers

You have plenty of information to remember about hauling hazardous materials, but you don't have to memorize everything. There are tables of information for you to reference that help you comply with the regulations.

Placards and placard tables

REMEMBER

Placards are square signs, turned to "sit" on their point like a diamond, that communicate what type of hazard drivers are hauling. You must *place the placards on all four sides* of the truck or trailer before you start driving (when they are required). If you have a semi-tractor trailer combination, you can choose to put the front sign on the front of the towing unit or on the front of the trailer — it's your choice. Personally, I would put a placard on the trailer. That way if the semi-tractor breaks down and you receive a replacement, you will still be in compliance with the regulations. The following are additional requirements:

>> The words must be level and read from left to right.

>> The placards should be seen easily from any direction.

>> The placards should be at least 3 inches away from other markings.

>> The background should be a contrasting color to the placards.

>> The placards should be clean and undamaged, and the message must be clear.

>> Keep the placards clear of attachments.

The placard tables in Figures 16-1 and 16-2 (and in the Federal Motor Carriers Safety Regulations 49 CFR Section 172.504) identify when placards are needed and which placards are to be used. Shippers should know this information, but you need to use the tables to ensure they are correct.

Placard Any Amount	
IF YOUR VEHICLE CONTAINS ANY AMOUNT OF...	PLACARD AS...
1.1 Mass Explosives	Explosives 1.1
1.2 Project Hazards	Explosives 1.2
1.3 Mass Fire Hazards	Explosives 1.3
2.3 Poisonous/Toxic Gases	Poison Gas
4.3 Dangerous When Wet	Dangerous When Wet
5.2 (Organic Peroxide, Type B, liquid or solid, Temperature controlled)	Organic Peroxide
6.1 (Inhalation hazard zone A & B only)	Poison/toxic inhalation
7 (Radioactive Yellow III label only)	Radioactive

FIGURE 16-1: Placard Table 1.

If you are hauling hazardous materials that are in Table 1, placards are required. If you are hauling hazardous materials that are in Table 2, you are required to attach placards when the combined weight of the hazardous materials is 1,001 pounds or more. If it is under 1,001 pounds, it is optional, providing you have a hazardous material endorsement.

Hazardous materials table

The hazardous materials table is a resource that lists hazardous materials, their proper identity, and information for safe transportation (see Figure 16-3). It lists requirements for hauling the material and includes some packaging and handling requirements. It can be found at 49 CFR §172.101 (Code of Federal Regulations), which is available in print and online.

Placard 1,001 Pounds Or More	
Category of Material (Hazard class or division number and additional description, as appropriate)	Placard Name
1.4 Minor Explosion	Explosives 1.4
1.5 Very Insensitive	Explosives 1.5
1.6 Extremely Insensitive	Explosives 1.6
2.1 Flammable Gases	Flammable Gas
2.2 Non- Flammable Gases	Non-Flammable Gas
3 Flammable Liquids	Flammable
Combustible Liquid	Combustible*
4.1 Flammable Solids	Flammable Solid
4.2 Spontaneously Combustible	Spontaneously Combustible
5.1 Oxidizers	Oxidizer
5.2 (other than organic peroxide, Type B, liquid or solid, Temperature Controlled)	Organic Peroxide
6.1 (other than inhalation hazard zone A or B)	Poison
6.2 Infectious Substances	(None)
8 Corrosives	Corrosive
9 Miscellaneous Hazardous Materials	Class 9**
ORM-D	(None)
* FLAMMABLE may be used in place of a COMBUSTIBLE on a cargo tank or portable tank.	
** Class 9 Placard is not required for domestic transportation.	

FIGURE 16-2: Placard Table 2.

§ 172.101 Hazardous Materials Table

1	2	3	4	5	6	7	8			9, 10
Symbols	Hazardous materials descriptions and proper shipping names	Hazard class or division	Identification numbers	PG	Label codes	Special provisions	Packaging			Air and water transportation information
							Exceptions	Non-bulk	Bulk	
	Acetone	3	UN1090	II	3	IB2, T4, TP1	150	202	242	

FIGURE 16-3: A portion of a hazardous materials table.

Here's how to read the hazardous materials table:

>> **Column 1** indicates the shipping conditions on the material for various types of transportation.

>> **Column 2** lists the proper shipping names of the regulated materials. Anything showing in italics is not the proper shipping name. The shipping papers must show the proper shipping names.

>> **Column 3** has the material's hazard class or division. If the word "Forbidden" is entered, do not haul it! Use the placard table to help ensure when placards are required and if the shipper is supplying the correct placards. You will need to know the material's hazard class, the quantity of it, and the amount of all the hazardous materials on your vehicle.

>> **Column 4** lists the identification number of the materials. "UN" or "NA" will precede the number. "NA" is for use in the United States and for to and from Canada. This number is to be on the packaging and the shipping papers. The number is to be on bulk tanks and other bulk packaging. First responders use these numbers to quickly identify what they are dealing with.

>> **Column 5** shows the packing group. A *packing group* indicates what level of hazard the material is. Packing group I has the highest risk, the most dangerous with III having the least for a hazardous material. This guides first responders as much as it does a shipper.

>> **Column 6** shows the codes that indicate which labels shippers are to attach to hazardous material packaging.

>> **Column 7** lists any additional provisions that apply to the hazardous material. If there is an entry in this column, refer to the federal regulations for specific information. Numbers 1 to 6 indicate a poison inhalation hazard (PIH). PIH materials have special requirements for shipping papers, markings, and placards.

>> **Column 8** is a three-part column indicating the section number for the packaging requirements of each hazardous material.

>> **Columns 9 and 10** are for water, rail, and air transportation, so you don't need to be concerned about these columns for highway transportation.

Appendix A

REMEMBER

Appendix A to the list of hazardous materials table is called, "List of Hazardous Substances and Reportable Quantities." Both the US Department of Environmental Protections (EPA) and the US Department of Transportation (DOT) need to know about any spills that are equal to or greater than the quantity in the right column of Figure 16-4. You can see "RQ" reportable quantities on shipping papers.

If "INHALATION HAZARD" appears on the shipping paper or the package, you must display the appropriate placards of either POISON INHALATION HAZARD or POISON GAS. These placards will be used in addition to other required placards. Display the hazard class placard *and* the POISON INHALATION HAZARD PLACARD, even for small amounts.

List of Hazardous Substances and Reportable Quantities	
Table 1. Hazardous Substances Other than Radionuclides	
Hazardous Substance	**Reportable Quantity (RQ) Pounds (Kilograms)**
Acenaphthene	100 (45.4)
Acenaphthylene	5,000 (2270)
Acetaldehyde	1,000 (454)
Acetaldehyde, chloro-	1,000 (454)
Acetaldehyde, trichloro-	5,000 (2270)
Acetamide	100 (45.4)
Acetamide, N-(aminothioxomethyl)-	1,000 (454)
Acetamide, N-(4-ethoxyphenyl)-	100 (45.4)
Acetamide, N-fluoren-2-yl-	1 (0.454)

FIGURE 16-4: A partial list of hazardous substances and reportable quantities.

Appendix B

Appendix B is a list of chemicals that are marine pollutants. This list is only needed when the chemical's container is 119 gallons or more (bulk container). Bulk packages/containers of any marine pollutant must display the Marine Pollutant marking. A *marking* is the descriptive name, identification number, instructions, cautions, weight, specification, or "UN" marks, or combinations thereof required by the regulations on outer packaging of hazardous materials. More commonly, at least from a driver's perspective, a marking is a label with the identification number and is not a placard and is more often in the shape of a rectangle. The placement of markings can be on the vehicle, not just the package.

Figure 16-5 shows a current marking on the left. The marking on the right is obsolete but is still referenced in CDL study guides and thus, might be referenced as on some written tests. The shape and size of this current marking may make you think it is a placard, but it is officially a marking.

FIGURE 16-5: Two examples of Marine Pollutant markings.

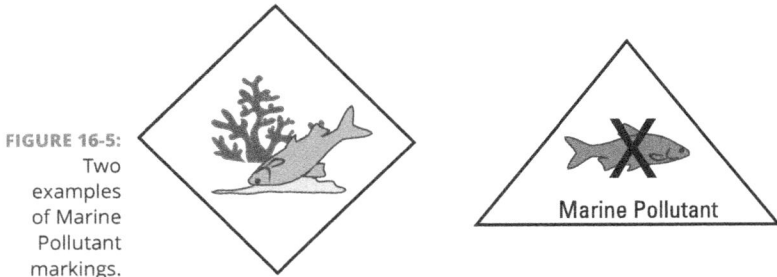

Hazardous waste manifest

A Uniform Hazardous Waste Manifest is required when transporting hazardous waste. It acts like a chain of custody. Everyone signs the manifest by hand. As the material is handed off to the next *registered carrier or disposal/treatment center,* another signature is added. When you deliver the shipment, keep your copy, which should have the signature of the shipper, your signature and any other carrier, and the signature of the person to whom you delivered the waste.

The manifest must have the name of the shipper and their EPA registration number, and the carrier(s), and the destination. The shipper must prepare and date the manifest along with signing by hand.

Identifying Hazardous Materials

When you are the driver picking up a hazardous material shipment, you are the representative of the carrier, thus, the carrier. You have a responsibility to keep your eyes open, to be vigilant concerning your cargo, and discern if it is hazardous material. This section provides a few things for you to watch for as the carrier.

TIP

The shipper that you are picking up from might be a strong indicator as to whether you are picking up hazardous materials. Paint, agricultural chemicals, pesticide or weed control companies, and scientific supply warehouses are all prime candidates for shipping hazardous materials. Expect hazardous materials at these locations and inspect the paperwork and cargo for any hazardous materials. All your observations as the carrier should come to the conclusion that there are (or are not) any hazardous materials.

Package labels

TIP

Shippers are required to print markings on packages or attach a label or tag with the name of the hazardous material. The same name should be on the shipping papers. If you see products, packages, and so on that have hazardous material warnings on them, ensure that the shipping papers do as well.

Hazardous material will likely have the name and address of the shipper on it along with the hazardous material shipping name and identification number, although this will depend on what the requirements are for that particular material.

Pay attention to arrows directing which way to set the container. Also on the containers will be the caution labels when required, such as Marine Pollutant, Biohazard, the Reportable Quantity (RQ), Hot, or Inhalation Hazard. Labels should be close together when there is more than one.

Shipping papers

Shipping papers have a variety of requirements and functions. The carrier (or you on behalf of your employer) will require the shipper's signature on paperwork stating that the shipment was prepared according to the regulations. All appropriate labels should be applied, and packages should contain the product. Emergency response information and placards should be given to you as the driver. Shipping papers that are longer than one page, are to be numbered; each page needs a page number *and* the total number of pages listed on the first page.

However, a shipper acting as a private carrier or is carrying their own product in a container, like a cargo tank for the transportation of the material, does not need signed shipping papers.

REMEMBER

Each hazardous material is to be listed with its proper shipping description in this order:

1. The identification number.
2. The proper shipping name.
3. The hazard class or the division and possibly the packaging group.

Hazardous materials must be distinguished on the shipping papers in one of the following ways:

>> Identified by an "X" in a column designated "XM."

>> Identified by an "RQ" in the column.

>> Highlighted in a contrasting color.

>> Described first.

The emergency response information, printed in English, is required for the purpose of mitigating the effects of an incident involving hazardous materials. This information should include:

>> The basic description and technical name

>> Immediate hazards to health

>> First aid measures

>> The risks of fire or explosion

>> Precautions to be taken if there is an accident or an incident

>> How to handle spills and leaks when there is no fire

The following are additional requirements for a shipper's paperwork:

>> The shipping papers should include the quantity and type of containers with the description.

>> If the hazardous material is waste, then the word "WASTE" is to appear before the proper name of the material.

>> This information is to be accessible by first responders by placing it in the pocket of the driver's door.

>> Shippers are to keep copies of shipping papers for two years, and carriers who are not also the shippers are to keep shipping papers for one year.

Loading Hazardous Materials

You can summarize your responsibilities by the philosophy that you are to protect the materials from damage or interacting with anything other than its prescribed environment. (See the sidebar, "Special loading precautions," for information about the hazardous waste classes mentioned in this section.)

Preparing the loading

It always seems as though there is an inspection to do. Hauling hazardous material adds a different aspect to that process. First, ensure your vehicle is safely parked with the parking brake set.

Ensure there are no leaks. A leak can be big trouble, and you are not allowed to move a vehicle when there is a leak of hazardous materials. Check your shipping papers for information or in this case where loading is taking place, notify the shipper.

Keep heat sources away from hazardous materials. Do not load hazardous materials in units with cargo heaters/air conditioner units unless you have read all the rules relating to your cargo.

Specifically, do not load the following materials with cargo heaters:

>> Class 1: Explosives

>> Class 2.1: Flammable Gas

>> Class 3: Flammable Liquids

Your hazardous materials containers must be restrained. Blocking, bracing, and strapping can be used and in combination with each other to keep containers from moving. When you restrain hazardous materials containers, be sure not to damage any valves or gauges or any fittings or pipes. *All* hazardous materials containers and packages must be secured when you are transporting them.

Don't open any package or transfer any material to another one. The only exception is you can empty a cargo tank when it is still on the vehicle.

Note: There are products that you are not allowed to load together in the same cargo space. In the regulations, there is a table called the Segregation Table for Hazardous Materials. Refer to this table, located in the Federal Motor Carriers Safety Regulations, to know what materials you are to keep separated.

Smoking

WARNING

Generally speaking, keep fire and any smoking cigarettes away from hazardous materials. Specifically, never smoke around:

>> Class 1: Explosives

>> Class 2: Flammable Gas

>> Class 3: Flammable Liquids

>> Class 4: Flammable Solids

>> Class 5: Oxidizers

WARNING

Never smoke or allow anyone within 25 feet of an empty container previously placarded for Class 2.1 flammable gases and Class 3 flammable liquids.

Use closed spaces for the following hazardous materials (no hanging over the bed or on a tailgate):

>> Class 1: Explosives

>> Class 4: Flammable Solids

>> Class 5: Oxidizers

SPECIAL LOADING PRECAUTIONS

Most classes of hazardous materials have some special loading precautions that must be adhered to. Some precautions seem like sound advice for any cargo, but in these special instances, a more devastating effect can occur than just upsetting a customer with poor handling of their cargo.

Class 1: Explosives

Before you load or unload any explosives, turn your engine off, and safely park the vehicle. Check your cargo space for any sharp points, bolts, screws, nails, broken panels, and broken floorboards that might damage cargo.

Disable any cargo heaters by disconnecting their power sources and drain heater fuel tanks.

I probably don't have to tell you this, however, handle explosives with care. Don't throw, drop, roll, handle with hooks, or use other metal tools on them.

If a package is damaged, don't transport it. If any explosive package shows moisture or oil, refuse to take it.

(continued)

(continued)

For Division 1.1, 1.2, or 1.3:

- Use a floor liner that is either a non metallic material or a nonferrous material.

- Don't transfer a Division 1.1, 1.2, or 1.3, to another vehicle on a public road unless it is an emergency. In the case of such emergency, set out red reflective triangles, electric lanterns, and/or flags. Others must be warned!

- Is not to be transported in vehicle combinations if:

  - A cargo tank is marked or placarded.

  - A vehicle contains Division 1.1 A: Initiating explosives.

  - A vehicle contains packages of Class 7: Radioactive materials labeled "Yellow III."

  - A vehicle contains Division 2.3: Poisonous gas or Division 6.1: Poisonous materials.

  - A vehicle contains hazardous materials in a portable tank on a DOT Spec 106A or a 110A tank.

  (This is strangely worded for vehicles like doubles, but it might be similarly worded on the test.)

Class 2: Compressed Gases, Cryogenic Liquids

Cylinders must be held *standing upright* and in racks that keep them from turning over. Cylinders may be loaded in a horizontal position if the relief valve is in the vapor space (space in the tank that is vapor not liquid).

Division 2.3: Poisonous gas or Division 6.1: Poisonous materials

These materials are never to be transported in containers that have interconnections, compartmentalized containers that have connections between the compartments.

A package labeled POISON or POISON INHALATION HAZARD is never to be loaded in the vehicle's cab or with any food material. There are special rules for loading and unloading Class 2 materials for which you need special training.

Class 4: Flammable Solids and Class 5: Oxidizers

Class 4 materials are solids that react to water, heat, air, or even spontaneously. The reactions can be fire and explosion.

Class 4 and Class 5 materials must be completely enclosed or securely covered. These materials are *unstable, dangerous when wet,* so they must be kept dry. Any materials subject to spontaneous combustion or heating must be transported with sufficient ventilation.

Class 7: Radioactive Materials

Some Class 7 materials will have a "Transport Index" number. These materials, labeled Radioactive I or II, will have a Transport Index number printed on the label. All such packages have the Transport Index numbers added together. Radiation surrounds these packages and passes through surrounding packages. The amount of time; number of packages; distance to people, animals, and undeveloped film are controlled, meaning that the number of packages of these materials that can be loaded together in a vehicle is limited. Figure 16-6 shows the distance, combined with time, based on the total Transport Index number, that film and people can be near to the packages.

Class 8: Corrosive Materials

When you load corrosive materials by hand, handle breakable containers one by one, keeping them right side up. Don't drop or roll them. Place them on an even floor surface. *Carboys* (containers much like the 5-gallon containers that are used with water coolers) can be stacked only if the upper-layer will be safe and stable.

Don't load nitric acid above any other product.

Storage batteries should always be stored upright and ensure that other cargo will not fall against them or short circuit them if they are charged.

Never load corrosive liquids next to or above	Never load corrosive liquids with
Division 1.4: Explosives C	Division 1.1, 1.2, or 1.3
Division 4.1: Flammable Solids	Division 1.5: Blasting Agents
Division 4.3: Dangerous When Wet	Division 2.3, Zone A: Poisonous Gases
Class 5: Oxidizers	Division 4.2: Spontaneously Combustible Materials
Division 2.3, Zone B: Poisonous Gases	Division 6.1, PGI, Zone A: Poison Liquids

FIGURE 16-6:
Transport
Index or
Radioactive
Separation
Table.

Radioactive Separation Table A						
TRANSPORT	MINIMUM DISTANCE IN FEET TO NEAREST UNDEVELOPED FILM					TO PEOPLE OR CARGO COMPARTMENT PARTITIONS
TOTAL INDEX	0–2 Hrs.	2–4 Hrs.	4–8 Hrs.	8–12 Hrs.	Over 12 Hrs.	
None	0	0	0	0	0	0
0.1 to 1.0	1	2	3	4	5	1
1.1 to 5.0	3	4	6	8	11	2
5.1 to 10.0	4	6	9	11	15	3
10.1 to 20.0	5	8	12	16	22	4
20.1 to 30.0	7	10	15	20	29	5
30.1 to 40.0	8	11	17	22	33	6
40.1 to 50.0	9	12	19	24	36	

Loading bulk

Hazardous materials take on a few additional rules when they are loaded in bulk packaging. It is important to know that both cargo tanks and portable tanks are bulk packaging. Cargo tanks are tanks permanently attached to the vehicle, while portable containers might be loaded and unloaded either on or off the vehicle.

Bulk packaging is defined as:

>> **Liquid** — capacity greater than 119 gallons (450 liters).

>> **Solid** — maximum net mass greater than 882 pounds (400 kilograms) or a capacity greater than 119 gallons (450 liters).

>> **Gas** — a water capacity greater than 1,000 pounds (454 kilograms).

Regulatory speaking, markings communicate information on the bulk containers (which can include dump trucks). Bulk packaging must display the identification number, and this number is found in Column 4 of the Hazardous Materials Table, which is discussed earlier in the chapter. Figure 16-7 lists the markings on bulk packaging.

FIGURE 16-7: Bulk packaging markings information.

Identification number must be on bulk packaging	
The mark description	Location
Black writing (100 mm, 3.9 inch) on orange panels	1,000 gallon or more tank; all four sides
When no placard is required, diamond shape white background	Less than a 1,000 gallon tank; opposing sides

Specification tanks (tanks built to specific DOT regulations that undergo regular testing and inspections) must show retest date markings.

When *portable tanks* are loaded on a vehicle, identification numbers must remain visible, but if not (in a box truck or box trailer instead of an open type of truck or trailer — stakes and rails for sides), then they must be on the four sides of a vehicle. Portable tanks must display the owner's or lessee's name.

Intermediate bulk containers (IBC) are bulk containers, but the owner's name and the shipping name aren't required (see Figure 16-8).

FIGURE 16-8: An IBC container.

Loading tanks

REMEMBER

Someone has to be a person in charge of the loading and unloading of a cargo tank — either you as the driver or an employee of the shipper or consignee. That person is to ensure that a qualified person is always watching the unloading. (Ensure that you receive the proper training for either of these two responsibilities.)

The "watcher" must:

>> Be within 25 feet of the tank.

>> Have a clear view of the tank.

>> Stay alert.

>> Be authorized and able to move the cargo tank.

>> Know the hazards of the materials being loaded or unloaded.

>> Know the procedures in the event of an emergency.

There are special attendance rules for cargo tanks transporting propane and anhydrous ammonia, but those rules will not be on the written test.

Before you move your vehicle, make another check to ensure all valves and manhole covers are closed. This will, of course, help to prevent leaks and keep you from getting in trouble with the law as it is illegal to move a cargo tank with either of these open (no matter the quantity nor the distance) unless the cargo tank is empty.

The following are special handling instructions:

REMEMBER

>> **Flammable liquids.** Turn your engine off prior to loading and unloading flammable liquids. The engine may run only if a pump must be operated by it. Cargo tanks are to be grounded (literally connected to the ground with a cable and a rod). Ground the tank prior to opening the "lid" and don't disconnect it until the opening is closed. By the way, setting a gas can on the ground before filling it with gasoline is also a safety instruction at gas stations.

>> **Compressed gases.** Having gas in a liquid form makes transportation and storage more efficient. Knowing this will help you understand that there can be liquid transfer valves for compressed gases. Keep these valves closed except when you are loading or unloading. Also, keep the engine off except when you have to use the engine to run a pump but even then have the engine off when you are connecting and disconnecting hoses.

Unhook all connections before coupling, uncoupling, or moving the cargo tank. When a trailer is unhooked from the tow vehicle, the regulations require wheels to be chocked (blocked).

Understanding the Driver's Responsibilities

I encourage you to get some driving time under your belt prior to hauling hazardous materials, at least on a large scale, and especially with the materials that have more regulations. You should be competent with being a safe driver when you start hauling hazardous materials.

After safely loading your cargo, you will implement other regulations for your trip. Hauling hazardous materials requires more responsibilities when driving.

Preventing fires and explosions

No one ever wants a fire and that is even more important when hauling hazardous materials. Remember the following rules, and you might have to encourage someone near your vehicle to follow them as well. (See the section, "Preparing for emergencies" later in this chapter for handling fire-related events.)

WARNING

>> **No flares.** Anyone coming into the area must be warned but flares and fuses must not be used. (*Fuses* are pyrotechnic items that were commonly used years before the reflective triangle but are still around today. They might be mentioned on the written test but should not be confused with the fuses required for your vehicle's electric system.) My advice is to carry just the reflective triangles, electric lights, and flags. But by all means, do not use flares or fuses around a vehicle loaded with Division 1.1, 1.2, or 1.3 explosives, or around a tank used for Class 3: Flammable Liquids or Division 2.1: Flammable Gas. It doesn't matter if the tank is loaded or empty.

>> **No smoking.** Keep in mind the no-smoking rules listed in this chapter under Loading Hazardous Materials.

>> **Fueling.** You might have guessed that your engine is to be turned off when fueling. Not only should you turn the engine off, you or someone else must hold the fuel nozzle, controlling the flow.

Parking

When I was a kid, my sister and I would have to suffer going to town to shop with our mom and we would suffer the agony of driving around and around the block, looking for a parking spot to free up. You won't get to drive around looking for a parking spot while hauling hazmat, but you might be able to plan ahead as where you can park.

Hauling Class 1.1, 1.2, or 1.3 Explosives

If you must park when doing your job, do so briefly. You are allowed to park and leave your vehicle unattended in a safe haven — a place that is approved for parking unattended vehicles loaded with explosives. These authorized safe havens are usually designated by authorities.

REMEMBER

Never park within 5 feet of the traveled part of a public road. In addition to that, don't park (unless needed for operational necessities like fueling) within 300 feet of:

>> A tunnel, bridge, or building

>> A gathering place for people

>> An open fire

Don't park on private property without the owner being aware of the danger. Someone else may watch your vehicle only if it is on the:

>> Shipper's property

>> Carrier's property

>> Consignee's property

Finding a parking spot

When your vehicle is placarded but *it is not* Class 1.1, 1.2, or 1.3: Explosives, you are permitted to park within 5 feet of the traveled part of the road if your work requires it, but make it brief. Someone must always be watching the vehicle when it is parked on a public road or on a shoulder. You are not allowed to uncouple from a trailer with hazardous materials on a public road. Don't park within 300 feet of an open fire.

Using a parking attendant

You can use someone to watch your vehicle, but they must:

>> Be awake and in the vehicle but not in the sleeper berth or is at least within 100 feet of the vehicle and have a clear view of it.

>> Know what to do if there is an emergency.

>> Be aware of the hazards of your cargo.

>> Be able to move your vehicle if it becomes necessary.

Planning your route

REMEMBER

If you are transporting Division 1.1, 1.2, or 1.3 explosives, you must have a *written route plan* from the shipper to the receiver (yes, an actual paper in hand). This is a great practice for anytime that you are planning your routes but, in this case, it is the regulation to do so. In fact, the carrier you are driving for has the responsibility to provide the route. You must write it down and keep it in your vehicle as you do other papers. It is possible for you to plan and write the route down instead of the people back at the office, especially when the shipper is located remotely from your employer.

Deliver the explosives only to authorized personnel. You may also deliver them to a locked room designed for explosives.

In planning your route, whether it is for the explosives or not, you must investigate local laws. Your employer, the carrier, should have helpful information. Also, consult the National Hazardous Materials Route Registry to know which roads are restricted; the registry is found at online at www.fmcsa.dot.gov/regulations/hazardous-materials/national-hazardous-materials-route-registry. Besides planning to drive around these roads, plan to stay away from more heavily populated areas, tunnels, gathering places, narrow streets, and alleys. Some tunnels and bridges have restrictions making your choices of routing limited. Having a placarded load or not usually makes a difference in the restrictions. Route away from open fires unless you can safely drive by them without stopping.

Some municipalities and states require permits to haul hazardous materials and wastes. These materials might restrict your choice of route. Ensure you have all the permits that any municipality or state requires before you leave with the hazmat. And you should know where the permits are when an officer asks to see them.

Transporting placarded *Radioactive Materials* requires the carrier to plan the safest route. Then you as the driver must be informed of the route to take, considering that the cargo is a radioactive shipment as well as any ramifications of hauling that load.

Checking your tires

Hazmat regulations state that you must ensure that your tires are properly inflated with a tire pressure gauge. (An emphasis is placed on dual tires.) Remember that it is normal and expected that the tire pressures will rise as you drive down the road. *Don't let air out of your tires* when you see that they gained 20 PSI (on a tire with a cold tire pressure is 100 to 110 PSI) after driving. However, if you have a tire leaking air or flat, drive immediately to the nearest safe place to have it repaired. Also, remove any overheated tire and find what caused it to overheat before driving again.

Keeping your shipping papers and ERG

REMEMBER

You must have a properly prepared shipping paper which, in addition to other items, is easily recognized as being for hazardous materials. The papers must be easily and quickly found in case of a crash. Here are some guidelines to follow:

>> Make it easy for others to distinguish the hazardous materials papers from others by keeping them on top of other paperwork.

>> When you are driving, you must keep the papers within your reach with the seatbelt on. Keeping them in the driver's door pouch will keep you in compliance.

>> When you aren't behind the wheel, it is acceptable to place the papers on your seat.

>> The Emergency Response Guidebook (ERG) is to be kept with the shipping papers. (See the section, "Preparing for emergencies," for more information.)

When your cargo is Division 1.1, 1.2, or 1.3: Explosives, the carrier must supply you as the driver with the Federal Motor Carrier Safety Regulations (FMCSR), Part 397 (`www.ecfr.gov/current/title-49/subtitle-B/chapter-III/subchapter-B/part-397`). The carrier must also supply you with *written* instructions on what you should do if you are delayed or in an accident. These instructions must include:

>> Contact names and numbers including carrier agents and shippers.

>> The characteristics or nature of the explosives you are hauling.

>> Precautions to take in the case of fire, accidents, and leaks.

REMEMBER

To summarize, you must sign a receipt for these documents and be familiar with them. Keep the documents in your possession while driving. Keep all of the following, in readiness, when driving:

>> The shipping papers

>> The written emergency instructions

>> The written route plan

>> FMCSR, Part 397

Crossing railroad tracks

REMEMBER

The rules for stopping at railroad tracks are simple and you should remember them fairly easily. You must stop prior to crossing railroad tracks if your vehicle is *placarded*, if you have any amount of *chlorine*, or if you have *cargo tanks* that are used for hazardous materials — whether they are loaded or empty.

Stop 15 to 50 feet from the nearest track and proceed only when you are sure there is no train coming and you can clear the tracks without stopping. Additionally, ensure there is nothing on the other side that will impede your progress over the tracks, and do not shift gears if you are driving a manual transmission vehicle.

Preparing for emergencies

AUTHOR SAYS

I am thinking of an emergency situation I was in and everyone around me froze and did nothing. Was it because of shock? Good chance the answer is "yes." On the other hand, the people around me had not prepared for an emergency to happen, so they can not react properly. Fortunately, someone came along to assist me in handling the situation. Prepare your mind and in some cases, practice physically for emergency situations. You want to be able to do the right thing when an emergency occurs.

Having the guidebook

I hope you don't run into an emergency while hauling hazardous materials, but if you do, I hope you have already examined your Emergency Response Guidebook (EGR) before you hauled the hazardous materials. As I previously stated, the book should be near the shipping papers, marking the page in the book related to the load you're carrying to help in properly responding to an emergency.

This EGR directs first responders on how to protect themselves and others when they react to an emergency. For this reason, it is vital for the shipping papers, placards, and markings to have all the correct information. The EGR can also be accessed online *for reference only* at www.phmsa.dot. gov/training/hazmat/erg/emergency-response-guidebook-erg.

Putting out a fire

You are required to have a fire extinguisher rated at 10 B:C or more. Remember that the first task you have when you detect a fire is to *make a call for help.* The CDL rules are a little confusing at this point as they will tell you not to fight a hazardous material fire unless you have had training to handle a fire but will then tell you that you can use your extinguisher to keep small fires from spreading until help arrives. The difference is whether it is *the hazardous material* that is on fire or not.

Just like in a burning building, you feel a door (like the rear door of the vehicle) before you open it. Opening a door adds the oxygen needed for fires. If you discover a fire and the fire has spread to your hazardous materials, it is not safe to fight it. *Keep the shipping papers with you and keep everyone away from the danger.*

Discovering leaks

REMEMBER

If you discover a leak but no fire (yet), you must identify the type of hazardous material that is leaking. Then there are several points that you must remember (for your sake and for your written test), starting with some "don'ts":

>> Don't touch the leaking material. Serious injury can occur.

>> Don't smell for the chemical. Serious injuries or death can occur.

>> Don't continue driving with a hazmat leak:

- Don't move the vehicle any more than what safety would mandate, considering if the movement might endanger you and others.

- Don't move it to get to a phone. (This is an old school, "before cell phones" recommendation, but there are areas without cell service. This might be on your test as well.)

- *Note:* The carrier pays for the cleanup of spilled materials. Spreading that material farther on roads, into ditches, and onto parking lots increases the cleanup costs (which are enormous).

>> Don't try to repackage the hazardous material nor try to repair the leak unless you have been trained to do so and can still do it safely.

>> Don't forget or put off any longer than is necessary for safety, notifying your dispatcher or other person designated to receive such calls from you.

So if hazardous materials are leaking from your vehicle:

>> Park.

>> Secure the area.

>> Don't leave the area (but not in harm's way).

>> Call 911 (or send someone for help if necessary) with the following information. It might help to write down the information or take photos if it can be done safely.

- Description of the emergency.

- Your location and the direction you were traveling.

- Your name and the carrier's name and address.

- The name of the product, its identification number, and hazard class.

Responding to specific hazards

There are specific responses for certain hazards. This section gives some essential information by class. In the event of a breakdown, accident, or other hazardous situations like a container leaking, do the following.

CLASS 1: EXPLOSIVES

Warn others of the danger, keeping people (especially anyone smoking) and open flames away. If there is a fire, warn everyone of the danger. If you have to separate vehicles after a collision, unload the explosives first, placing them at least 200 feet away from vehicles and buildings.

CLASS 2: COMPRESSED GASES

In the event that gas is leaking, warn everyone of the danger, keeping everyone away except those removing wreckage. Notify the shipper if compressed gas is involved in an accident.

Never transfer compressed gases to another tank on public roads unless you are filling road construction equipment.

If you haul chlorine, you must have an approved gas mask within your vehicle. You must also have a kit for controlling leaks in the dome cover plate fitting on the cargo tank.

CLASS 3: FLAMMABLE LIQUIDS

Warn people of the dangers and keep them away and keep them from smoking. Don't transfer the flammable liquid on a public road unless it is an emergency.

CLASS 4: FLAMMABLE SOLIDS

Warn others of the dangers when one of these materials leaks. However, if a package is smoldering, you can remove it from the vehicle if you can do so safely. Remove undamaged, intact packages to help prevent the chance of fire.

CLASS 5: OXIDIZERS

While the Class 5 oxidizers work differently from the Class 4 flammable solids, your reaction in a critical situation is the same. You should warn others of the dangers when there is a leak, and, if a package is smoldering, you can still remove it from the vehicle if you can do so safely. Like Class 4, you can remove undamaged, intact packages to help prevent the chance of fire. (The aforementioned information is how your written tests will be constructed. However, an oxidizer, if leaking and gets on you, and permeates your clothing, makes you susceptible for combustion.)

CLASS 6: POISONOUS MATERIALS AND INFECTIOUS SUBSTANCES

Keep other people from harm and protect yourself. The difference with these materials is when there has been a leak, the vehicle must be checked for stray poison. If an infectious substance package is damaged in transport, you must report it to your supervisor and don't accept any shipments that show signs of damage or leaks.

CLASS 7: RADIOACTIVE MATERIALS

WARNING

Report to your supervisor as soon as possible about any leak or damage of a radioactive material package. Do not touch or inhale where a spill occurred or where there is damage. Before you drive it again, ensure that it has been cleaned and checked with a *survey meter* (radiation detector).

CLASS 8: CORROSIVE MATERIALS

If a leak occurs of a corrosive material, don't cause extra damage when handling the leaking container. Any parts of the vehicle coming in contact with the corrosive material must be thoroughly washed and washed again after unloading all the product. This should be done as soon as possible to mitigate the damage of the corrosive material and to be ready for the next load.

Experiencing a traffic accident

REMEMBER

I hope you are never involved in any kind of accident and definitely not when hazardous materials are involved. However, if you are involved in a crash while hauling hazmat, you have work to do if you are able. Your first priority is to protect yourself and others, so effective communication must take place. Here's a task list:

>> Call 911.

>> Warn others of the danger.

>> Keep people away from the area, upwind and far away.

>> Check to see that any occupants in any vehicle are okay.

>> Keep the shipping papers with you.

>> Limit the spread of the material if it is safe for you to do.

>> Communicate the danger of the hazardous materials with first responders.

>> Provide first responders with your shipping papers and your ERG.

CALLING THE NATIONAL RESPONSE CENTER

If you are involved in an accident and hazardous materials cause an injury or damage, you must call the *National Response Center* (NRC) to notify authorities within 12 hours.

Call the NRC's 24-hour number at 800-454-8802 when:

>> There is a fatality.

>> Hospitalization is required for an injured person.

>> The estimated property damage exceeds $50,000. (This is not in the regulations but is in CDL study guides.)

>> The public has to be evacuated for at least an hour.

>> The accident prompts closure of a major transportation artery or facility for an hour or more.

>> Flight plans or routines of aircraft are altered.

>> Fire, breakage, spillage, or suspected radioactive contamination occurs involving radioactive material.

>> Fire, breakage, spillage, or suspected contamination occurs involving an infectious substance but not for a regulated medical waste.

>> A release of a marine pollutant with a quantity greater than 119 gallons (450 liters) for liquid or 882 pounds (400 kilograms) for a solid.

>> A continuing danger to life exists even though none of the above events occurred.

When you (or your employer) call the center, be prepared to give the following information:

>> Your name.

>> The name and address of the carrier.

>> Your phone number or a phone number where you can be reached.

>> Date, time, and location of the accident.

>> The list of any injuries.

>> The class, name, and the quantity of the hazardous materials involved (add the shipper's name if it was a reportable quantity).

>> The type of incident, the nature of the hazmat, and whether there is still a threat endangering life or not.

A written detailed report will be required of the carrier within 30 days.

NOTIFYING CHEMTREC

The Chemical Transportation Emergency Center (CHEMTREC) has a 24-hour line as well, which helps emergency personnel with technical information about the hazardous materials. CHEMTREC and the National Response Center are in communication with each other — when one is called, the other is notified.

Practice Questions

1. Which of the following is a shipper's responsibility?

    (A) To contain the material.

    (B) To provide flares for emergencies.

    (C) To provide the receiver with a delivery time.

    (D) These are all responsibilities of the shipper.

2. Why do drivers place placards on the vehicle?

    (A) To contain the product

    (B) To communicate the hazard

    (C) To provide a phone number for first responders to call

    (D) To show they have bulk packaging on board

3. How many sides of the vehicle should placards be displayed?

    (A) 1

    (B) 2

    (C) 3

    (D) 4

4. Where should you keep shipping papers?

    (A) In a lock box in the cab

    (B) In a sealed packet on the product

    (C) In the pocket of the driver's door

    (D) In the document holder in the front of the trailer or the front of the truck's bed (cargo area) of a straight truck

5. Which is a definition of bulk packaging?

    (A) Tanks over 1,000 gallons

    (B) Packages over 1,000 pounds

    (C) Packages over 250 gallons or the equivalent weight

    (D) Tanks over 119 gallons

6. Which of the following can utilize the 1,000-pound exception to placarding?

    (A) Oxygen.

    (B) Alcohol.

    (C) Batteries.

    (D) All these hazards can utilize the 1,000-pound exception to placarding.

7. When determining if placards are required, remember:

    (A) You can add the total weight of the materials and if they weigh more than 2,205 pounds, you must placard the vehicle.

    (B) As long as any chemical is under 1,000 pounds, placards are not required.

    (C) You can always substitute the DANGEROUS placard for any placards.

    (D) Placards can be displayed even when they are not required as long as they identify the hazard of the material being transported.

8. Which of the following hazard classes use a Transport Index?

(A) Explosives

(B) Radioactive

(C) Poisonous

(D) Organic peroxide

9. Which of the following may be loaded in a space with a heater?

(A) Oxidizers

(B) Flammable liquids

(C) Flammable gas

(D) Explosives

10. What type of floor liner is prohibited for Division 1.1 or 1.2?

(A) Steel

(B) Aluminum

(C) Nonmetallic

(D) Zinc

11. What can be on a marking?

(A) The descriptive name and cautions.

(B) The identification number and weight.

(C) Instructions and UN marks.

(D) All these items can be a marking or a part of a marking.

12. If your engine runs a pump for unloading a compressed gas, when should the engine be turned off?

(A) When loading.

(B) When unloading.

(C) When unhooking the hose.

(D) None of these are times to turn the engine off.

13. What is a portable tank?

(A) A tank designed to be loaded and unloaded from a transport vehicle.

(B) A tank that is temporarily attached to a transport vehicle.

(C) A tank that has mountings and accessories to allow machinery to handle it.

(D) These are all descriptions of portable tanks.

14. What should you do if you have a corrosive leak from a container?

(A) Avoid further damage or injury when handling the container.

(B) Wash parts of the vehicle that came in contact with the corrosive.

(C) Wash out all of the interior where the corrosive leaked once all the cargo is unloaded.

(D) All these are tasks or something to do with a corrosive leak.

15. Which of the following devices is the best to carry for emergencies when hauling hazardous materials?

   (A) Flares.

   (B) Reflective triangles.

   (C) Fuses (the pyrotechnic type).

   (D) These are all fine for hauling hazardous materials.

16. Which of the following is not a reason to notify the National Response Center?

   (A) A situation exists that the carrier believes should be reported due to danger to life.

   (B) A person is killed as a result of walking in front of a vehicle hauling HM.

   (C) The general public had to be evacuated for three hours due to an HM vehicle having an accident.

   (D) The interstate highway was shut down for two hours due to a fuel tanker spill.

17. What is a safe haven?

   (A) A rest area

   (B) Any location for a 10-hour break

   (C) A location where the property owners give you permission to park

   (D) An approved place for parking unattended vehicles loaded with explosives

18. Which of the following hazardous materials divisions require a written route plan?

   (A) Division 1.1, 1.2, 1.3: Explosives

   (B) Division 4.1: Flammable solids

   (C) Class 5.1: Oxidizers

   (D) Class 9

19. Which type of fire extinguisher is required for hauling hazmat?

   (A) 10 B:C extinguisher

   (B) Specialist dry powder extinguisher

   (C) Water extinguisher

   (D) Wet chemical extinguisher

20. Which of the following is not a rule for watching tank loading?

   (A) The ability to drive the vehicle away.

   (B) To know what to do in case of an emergency.

   (C) To be within 25 feet and have a clear view of the tank.

   (D) These are all rules for someone watching tank loading and unloading.

21. Which of the following is a good location for parking a vehicle with explosives?

   (A) Near a bridge

   (B) At the consignee property

   (C) At a park

   (D) At a rest area

22. What does the Radioactive Separation chart provide?

   (A) States how close different radioactive materials can be to each other

   (B) Limits quantity of radioactive materials based on an index number

   (C) Sets a minimum distance of radioactive materials to people

   (D) Both B and C

23. Which of the following conditions do not require stopping at railroad tracks?

   (A) The vehicle is placarded.

   (B) The vehicle has chlorine.

   (C) The vehicle has empty cargo tanks used for hazardous materials.

   (D) The vehicle is hauling coils of steel.

24. Which of the following chemicals during transportation, require a gas mask?

   (A) Radioactive

   (B) Corrosives

   (C) Flammable liquids

   (D) Chlorine

25. Which of the following conditions requires the engine to be turned off?

   (A) Refueling.

   (B) Loading a cargo tank.

   (C) Unloading a cargo tank.

   (D) These are all conditions that require the engine to be turned off.

26. What is not a consideration for proper hazmat routing?

   (A) If a tunnel is on the route

   (B) If the route goes by a truck washing facility

   (C) If local or state agencies have placed restrictions on a bridge

   (D) If the street is narrow

27. How far away is the minimum distance for smoking around explosives and most flammables?

   (A) 25 feet

   (B) 50 feet

   (C) 75 feet

   (D) 100 feet

28. What does RQ stand for?

   (A) Requested Qualifications

   (B) Required Quantity

   (C) Real Quotient

   (D) Resident Qualifier

29. Who must develop a route for hauling radioactive materials?

   (A) Shipper

   (B) Carrier

   (C) Driver

   (D) Both B and C

Answers and Explanations

1. **A.** The shipper is responsible for containing their hazardous materials in a container, but they are not responsible for flares, routing, or the carrier's delivery time.

2. **B.** The driver must communicate with the public what is being hauled by displaying placards. A bulk container is irrelevant, and the shipper provides phone numbers and generally contains the product.

3. **D.** All four sides of the vehicle are to have placards displayed.

4. **C.** The papers are to be in the reach of the driver and of the first responders who need to have a quick place to access the emergency response information.

5. **D.** As far as liquids are concerned, a tank over 119 gallons is bulk packaging. What confuses some people is when they start thinking about a tanker endorsement. A tanker endorsement is required when the packaging is over 119 gallons and has a combined volume of over 1,000 gallons.

6. **D.** All these materials are listed in Placard Table 2, materials under 1,001 pounds, don't require placards.

7. **D.** This is the only true statement. Some materials require placards no matter the quantity. The combined quantity of 2,205 pounds refers to the possibility of using the DANGEROUS placard, and the DANGEROUS placard can't be used just anytime you want. That would be too easy. (Just remember that you can only use placards when you have a hazmat endorsement and vice versa.)

8. **B.** Radioactivity leaks through packaging. The radioactive separation table prescribes the minimum separation distances that must be maintained between materials labeled RADIOACTIVE YELLOW-II or RADIOACTIVE YELLOW-III and people.

9. **A.** While oxidizers are not one of the materials that are not allowed to be loaded in spaces with heaters, when you combine heat, fuel, and oxygen (transportation defines oxidizers differently than the scientific world), a fire is the general result. But that result is not as spectacular as explosives would be. The other choices are on the list and not allowed in a space with a heater.

10. **A.** Steel is not allowed to be the floor or floor liner for explosives. The floor must be a nonferrous metal or nonmetal.

11. **D.** All these answers can be a component on a marking.

12. **C.** This question might be tricky. (Your written tests will be trickier as those people have more fun tricking you than finding out if you know the material.) A vehicle that has the engine running a pump to load and unload the material obviously must be running to do it. The engine is to be off when disconnecting the hose.

13. **D.** These are all defining characteristics of a portable tank.

14. **D.** All these are tasks that you must remember and do when one of your packages leaks a corrosive.

15. **B.** Reflective triangles are safe around any hazardous materials as they do not have a flame like flares and pyrotechnic fuses.

16. **B.** While B is a tragedy, the death was not due to a hazardous material, so the National Response Center is not the authorities to give a report to.

17. **D.** A safe haven is an official designation and has typically been approved by local or state jurisdiction officials.

18. **A.** Explosives are the materials out of this list that require a written route plan. My opinion is that drivers need to make such a plan for any trip they take as this would reduce the occurrences of an 18-wheeler going down a bike path or across a historic wooden bridge.

19. **A.** A 10 B:C fire extinguisher is the required fire extinguisher.

20. **D.** These are all requirements for the watcher of a tank being loaded.

21. **B.** Of these choices, only at the consignee's parking lot is a good choice to park.

22. **D.** The chart guides a driver in the material being separated from people and film, both in time, distance, and quantity. It is not a chart to show how far to distance one radioactive package from the next.

23. **D.** Coils of steel do not require stopping at a railroad crossing but the other items do. However, be careful when crossing tracks with any commodity.

24. **D.** Chlorine is nasty stuff and will do terrible things to your body. (I need a gas mask when my wife is cleaning somewhere in the house.)

25. **D.** I bet you didn't believe that it would be D again. The engine should be turned off at all these times. However, there is an exception when there is a pump that is run by the engine.

26. **B.** You are allowed to drive by truck washing businesses — no worries — but the other choices you should route away from.

27. **A.** A person only has to be 25 feet away from the vehicle when they smoke.

28. **B.** RQ is the minimum quantity of spilled material that must be reported to various government agencies.

29. **D.** Both the driver and the carrier have responsibilities in developing a written route. The situation can determine who must do it. However, the driver must always review and verify a route someone else devised. People will make mistakes, trust me, and GPS devices may be incorrect as well.

6

Passing the Tests

Know more about inspecting a commercial motor vehicle than many experienced professionals.

Add to your inspection knowledge the ability to inspect combination vehicles and buses.

Keep your cool and know what to expect on the skills and road tests.

Chapter **17**

Conducting the Pre-Trip Inspection for Any Vehicle

You have surely read somewhere in this book where I say something about inspecting your vehicle (unless you chose to read this chapter first), and you might feel overwhelmed by the responsibility that I have stressed. Don't be fearful of the enormity of conducting an inspection because there is one important aspect that I want you to remember — *don't try to memorize the inspection!*

When you had to write a paper in school, did you have to create an outline first? If so, picture your vehicle as the outline, except you don't have to write it! Right in front of you is what you need to remember — the vehicle itself. Look at the component, inspect it, and move in an orderly fashion to the next component. Don't skip around the truck. When you look at a component, ask yourself, "What does it do?" "What can happen if I fail to inspect it?" Also remember, if it contains fluid or compressed air, it should not leak. Electric wiring should not be frayed or show signs of arcing. Pretty much everything should be properly mounted and secure and not cracked, bent, or broken.

There are two main testing methods used by the State Departments of Transportation (DOTs) to examine future drivers' inspection competence. One is more of the traditional seven-step inspection, and the other is called *the modernized test*. I don't know of any state that will have you inspect everything that their method incorporates. They don't have that much time. It takes a driver, and even an experienced instructor, several times longer to state what they are inspecting, what they are looking for, and how to inspect it than to just inspect the vehicle. An experienced driver can inspect a vehicle in 15 minutes if they don't have to talk about it. I intend to be thorough so you can be confident that the officer inspecting your vehicle someday will give you a pass.

In this chapter, I explain inspecting a basic commercial motor vehicle (CMV). You can use the information I cover in this chapter for most commercial vehicles.

REMEMBER

Don't stop inspecting your vehicle when you obtain your Commercial Driver's License (CDL). Make it your daily habit.

Walking Up to Your Vehicle

When you approach your vehicle at the beginning of your driving day, scan it for an overall survey that can quickly reveal potential problems. This scan is performed at a very high level and is not necessarily meant to catch little defects. Many items will receive closer scrutiny later in the inspection. Some of these items are not in the modernized test, but an officer inspecting your vehicle does not use the modernized test to evaluate your vehicle.

Overall view

This is a high level, quick scan as you are 20 to 30 feet from the vehicle.

>> **Why inspect:** A major problem can be detected when you are standing away from the vehicle.

>> **How to inspect:** Take an overall view of the vehicle. Is it level? If it is not level, there can be a problem with a tire or the suspension, or it might have a tire sitting in a hole. You need to know why this is an issue.

>> Examine the roof, the hood, and the grill. Do you see any damage? While you are looking up, will there be anything such as buildings, trees, or outcroppings that your vehicle can strike when moving?

>> As you move closer, check the license plate. Is it mounted correctly, and is it current?

>> Does the windshield and wipers appear to be in proper condition? You are looking for visible cracks, and a proper seal around the windshield and the wiper blades to be present.

>> Look at the bumper, grill, roof, and hood to see that they are properly mounted and are in safe working condition.

>> Go to the driver vehicle inspection report if there is one. See if there is anything reported on the vehicle that still needs addressed.

Lenses

These are headlight covers or the covers on any of the lamps on the front of the CMV. There are lamps for the ID (identification) lights and marker lights, which you can find at the top, front, and rear of the vehicle. There are turn signals and headlights similar to what are on personal vehicles.

>> **Why inspect:** Light lenses or covers must be clean and free of damage for lights to work effectively. Lights are required to be visible from a distance and have specific colors.

>> **How to inspect:** Inspect that lenses are the proper color, are not broken or missing. You will inspect the operation of the lights later.

Mirrors

These are the mirrors that enable you to see areas of the vehicle that would otherwise be a blind spot while driving. If your vehicle has cameras instead of mirrors, inspect them.

>> **Why inspect:** You must be able to see pedestrians, traffic, and other potential hazards around your vehicle.

>> **How to inspect:** During the overall inspection, you are quickly identifying that the mirrors are intact and are properly mounted and secure. You will inspect the mirrors and cameras more closely when in the cab.

Looking Under the Hood

REMEMBER

When you are being tested by the license examiner, the examiner might have you conduct the in-cab inspection first. In the real world, this is a mistake. You must check under the hood first in order to know that it is safe to start the engine. However, examiners often choose the in-cab inspection first as it fails more people than any other part of the inspection test. So, why not get it over with sooner, rather than later?

Fluid and air leaks

This inspection is to check all the fluids, power steering fluid, engine oil, engine coolant, brake fluid (for hydraulic brake vehicles), and windshield washer fluid that can leak from the engine or specific components. Also, compressed air that can leak from air lines and connections.

>> **Why inspect:** Fluid loss can indicate a component failure, which is ultimately a safety issue. Air leaks can contribute to failure of components that use air, and leaks can lead to emergency situations.

>> **How to inspect:** Look for puddles on the ground and for fluids dripping, leaking from the engine or surrounding components. Be sure to identify the difference between water that the air conditioner produces and other fluids. If it doesn't look or feel like water, it is probably another type of fluid. Keep your engine area clean to help make your inspections easier.

>> Inspect air lines for condition and leaks. This is what you tell the license examiner that you are doing. However, if there is a leak in the air system, there will be no indication of it when you are checking under the hood because the air has leaked out and air pressure must be built up in order for a leak to show itself. So, in reality, you would check for air leaks after you start the engine and build up pressure. The air system test that you will perform later will help you determine if you need to find an air leak. In short, listen for air leaks when the vehicle's air system is charged.

Critical fluid levels

Engine oil, coolant, steering fluid, brake fluid (for hydraulic brake vehicles), and windshield washer fluid are critical fluids.

>> **Why inspect:** Proper levels of fluids help to ensure continued safe operation of the vehicle.

>> **How to inspect:** The engine should be turned off and cool for accurate assessments of some fluid levels. Ensure that levels are at the manufacturers' operating levels. Check the *engine oil*

on the dip stick by pulling the dipstick, wiping the dip stick, reinserting it in its tube, and pulling and checking the level of oil on the stick again. Add oil if you find that the oil is at or below the add line and report it to the person in charge of maintenance.

>> Both the *engine coolant* and *power steering fluid* are likely to have reservoirs with marks on them for easy identification of sufficient fluid. For the *windshield washer fluid,* it is sometimes easier to fill the tank than to see how much fluid is in the reservoir as it can be partially hidden.

Steering system

Mechanisms that transform steering column action to wheel-turning action

>> **Why inspect:** Worn, cracked, loose, or broken steering parts can result in a loss of steering control.

>> **How to inspect:** Inspect that the power steering box is securely mounted and not leaking.

>> Inspect that all steering hoses and connections are not cracked, worn, or leaking.

>> Inspect that the steering system has no missing nuts, bolts, or cotter pins.

>> Inspect that visible connecting links, arms, and rods from the steering box to the wheel are not worn or cracked and that joints and sockets are not worn or loose.

Figure 17-1 shows some major components of a steering system as found in many big trucks. The steering wheel (not pictured) is connected to the steering shaft (1). The steering shaft connects to the steering box (2). At the steering box is the Pitman arm (3), which is attached to the drag link (4). The drag link connects to a steering arm (5), which is part of the steering knuckle. Attached to the steering knuckle is the tie rod (6), which connects the two sides of the steering system together. *Castle nuts* (7), nuts that look like castles with cannon turrets, combined with cotter pins that hold much of the steering system components together.

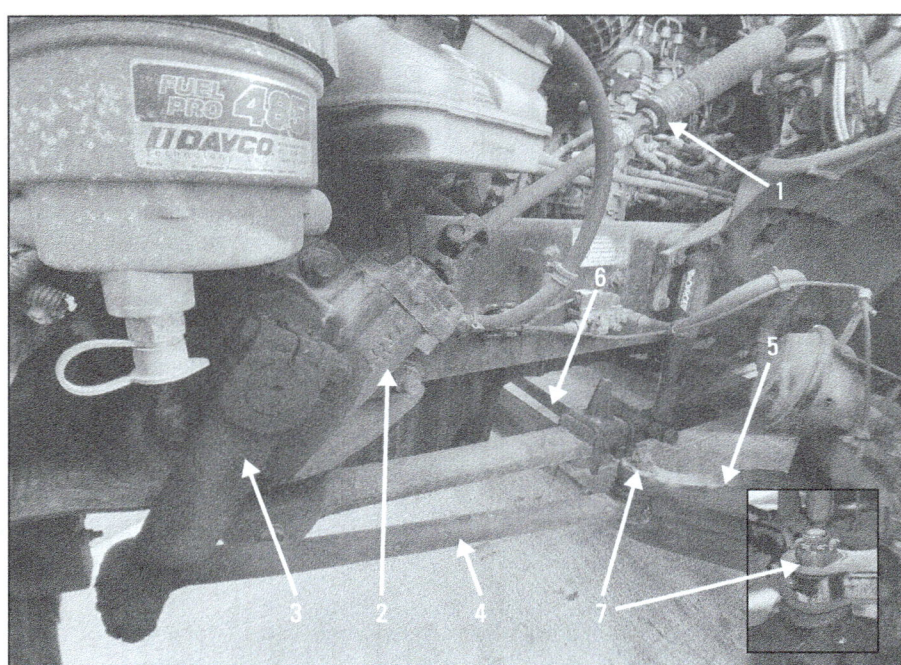

FIGURE 17-1: Components of a steering system.

NOT INCLUDED IN THE MODERNIZED TEST

The modernized test does not include all components under the hood, but I will include more components not on that test. So when you inspect under the hood, start from your upper-left when you are on the driver's side of the vehicle. Examine what you can see. Some vehicles don't make all the components you want to inspect very accessible. Here's a list of several components for you to inspect (if you have access to them) along with some brief information on the component.

Remember: Don't put your hands on hot components!

- **Air intake.** It should not be cracked or broken. Air flowing in *and* out of a diesel engine efficiently and without leaks is imperative.

- **Fuel rail.** A conduit for pressurized diesel to injectors. It should not be leaking. Leaks will affect the performance of the engine.

- **Coolant reservoir.** You have already checked the reservoir for the coolant to be at an acceptable level, so now you are looking for leaks and that it is properly mounted and secure.

- **Radiator.** The radiator should be properly mounted, not leaking, and fins allowing air flow.

- **Radiator hoses.** The hoses should be squeezable, secure, and not leaking. Any leaks associated with the coolant can lead to engine failure if you ignore them. There is a lower and upper hose.

- **Fan.** The fan helps cool the radiator and thus the coolant. *Any of the components associated with the coolant or radiator have a function in keeping the engine cool,* at least at proper operating temperatures. It should be properly mounted, and the blades should not be broken and none missing.

- **Fan clutch.** The fan clutch engages and disengages the fan. It should not be leaking air (not usually able to be verified at this point) or any fluid, depending on the type of clutch.

- **Water pump.** The water pump is another coolant-associated component as it circulates the coolant. It should be properly mounted and not leaking. Identify if it is operated by a belt or is gear driven.

- **Belts.** Belts transfer power from the engine to components near the engine like the alternator and air conditioner compressor. Belts should not be frayed or stretched. They should not be worn or loose. Modern belts aren't usually worn and simply need to be replaced on a maintenance schedule. However, you need to check the longest span of belt between pulleys for each belt. Push and pull on it to see how much deflection there is. While I have read several different amounts of how much deflection is okay, it really depends on the length of the distance between the two pulleys. Shorter distance means shorter deflection and longer distance means longer deflection. Generally speaking, around ¾ inch would be the most. If you hear squealing from the engine at times, you might have an adjustment pulley or component that needs adjusting so that the belt is tighter. If you ever hear a solid prolonged squeal, find a safe place to park soon and find the problem causing the squeal.

- **Oil fill.** There should be a tube or at least a cap marked for engine oil. The cap should be secure. The dip stick is mentioned under checking critical fluids levels.

- **Oil pump and filter.** There is an oil pump with a filter nearby. They should be properly mounted with no leaks.

- **Fuel pump and filter.** There is a fuel pump with a filter(s) that should have no leaks and securely mounted. Fuel lines attached to the pump should not be leaking.

- **Air compressor.** There is an air compressor on vehicles with air brakes. It should be properly and securely mounted with no leaks.

- **Air lines.** All air lines should not be rubbing, chafing, bulging, or leaking.

(continued)

(continued)

- **Electrical lines.** All electrical lines should be free of corrosion and arcing. Wires should not be bare.

- **Air conditioner compressor.** The air conditioner compressor is just one of a few parts of the air conditioning system that you can see under the hood. Other parts are the condenser and the receiver/dryer. Make sure that these parts are secure and not leaking.

- **Alternator.** This component works at keeping the voltage up in the batteries, so you can start the engine and operate electrical devices. Ensure that it is properly mounted, and there is no arcing where wires are connected.

- **Turbo.** This component increases the power of the engine. Look for leaks that will be indicated by black soot. These leaks will rob you of engine power.

- **Exhaust.** Look for leaks in the exhaust as far as you can see. You don't want to be breathing these fumes. You also don't want the exhaust falling apart.

- **Air to air.** This is a tube-looking component that is part of getting air into the engine. Components that are part of getting air into the engine to be used for combustion; they should not leak and should be properly mounted.

Checking in the Cab

I already mentioned that some license examiners will have you do an in-cab inspection first instead of going under the hood due to the failure rate for the in-cab inspection. Everything in the cab is important, but the air system is a new component in the student's experience. After all, don't most personal vehicles have visors, steering wheels, and so on? The air brake inspection will carry the most weight and that is likely where the candidate might fail.

Preparing to start the engine

REMEMBER

Prior to starting the engine, you must ensure that it is safe to start. Part of that safe start was ensured when you checked under the hood. Now you will ensure the engine can be started and the vehicle operates safely.

Pedals

The pedals are operated by your feet and are the fuel pedal, the brake pedal, and clutch pedal.

>> **Why inspect:** Unsafe pedals can result in accidents.

>> **How to inspect:** Check for grooves in all pedals and that they are clean.

- The clutch pedal should have 1½- to 2-inch free play.

- The brake pedal should be firm to the touch.

- The fuel (or accelerator) pedal moves freely.

Miscellaneous items in the cab

These are any loose items that are not part of the truck but in the cab, such as water bottles, bottles of cleaner, spray lubricants; or if the last driver was really messy, old fountain drink cups.

>> **Why inspect:** Items can fall, roll, obstruct your view, or affect safe driving.

>> **How to inspect:** Visually check for objects that can fall, roll under your pedals, block your view, or distract you while driving.

Permit book

This is a binder or device that holds important papers.

>> **Why inspect:** The papers are required to operate a CMV on roads. Permit books are possibly the most common item inspected by an officer.

>> **How to inspect:** Examine each document, International Fuel Tax Agreement (IFTA), registration, operating authority, proof of insurance, and so on for being present and current.

Dash area

These are the gauges and controls located in the dash area.

>> **Why inspect:** The controls are to be operational, and the gauges enable you to monitor the vehicles systems for safe travel.

>> **How to inspect:** Inspect gauges for location and expected readings (once the engine is started).

>> Inspect the controls for proper condition and their apparent functionality.

Gauges readings

REMEMBER

At this point, you should have determined whether your vehicle is safe to start the engine or not. If it is safe to start, ensure that the parking brakes are set, the transmission is in neutral or in park, and start the engine.

Immediately observe the anti-lock brake system (ABS) light. Remember that it is a malfunction light, so it should come on for a few seconds and then turn off. If it does not turn off, there is a malfunction, and you need to have your maintenance technician repair the system. If this happens on your test, the license examiner will possibly end the test, or at the least, not allow the driving portion of the test.

There are gauges informing you of critical systems operating condition. They can be analog or digital.

>> **Why inspect:** Improper operating levels can lead to breakdowns and emergency events.

>> **How to inspect:** Check the gauges for proper operating levels:

- **Voltage gauge.** A reading of 12 to 14 volts is normal.
- **Fuel.** Should match a visual inspection inside the fuel tanks.
- **DEF.** Should show expected quantity.
- **Air pressure.** Normal operating pressure is 100 to 125 PSI.

- **Coolant.** Should start to rise in 5 minutes, 180 to 200 degrees Fahrenheit is normal operating range.

- **Tachometer.** Diesel engines typically show idle RPM around 600. Know the RPMs at which your engine should idle.

- **Speedometer.** Should show zero miles per hour (mph).

Steering wheel

The steering wheel controls the steering system and should not have any looseness (steering wheel play).

>> **Why inspect:** Excessive wear or loose operation in the steering components results in catastrophic accidents.

>> With the engine still running and the steer tires pointing straight ahead, turn the wheel in one direction until you see the steer tire start to turn. Line a point on the steering wheel with something else like the turn signal stalk. Now turn the steering wheel the other direction until the steer tire starts to move again. The wheel should move no more than 2 inches on a 16-inch wheel and no more than 2¾ inches on a 22-inch wheel.

Visor

The visor is a device that shields bright sunlight from your eyes.

>> **Why inspect:** You must be able to see traffic, surroundings, and possible hazards, having the sunshine blocked is regularly necessary.

>> **How to inspect:** Grasp the visor to see if it stays in any position you place it in.

Heater and defroster

The heater heats the cab, and the defroster clears or prevents frost and condensation on the windshield.

>> **Why inspect:** The defroster improves visibility, helping to eliminate a hazardous situation. The heater keeps driver from freezing.

>> **How to inspect:** Operate both the heater and defroster, verifying air blows onto windshield and out the heater duct(s) at your feet.

Horn

Horns sound a loud alarming noise when activated.

>> **Why inspect:** Horns are used to warn other motorists of their eminent danger when they cross into your path.

>> **How to inspect:** Check that all the horns work by activating them.

Windshield wipers and washers

Windshield wipers clear the windshield, and washers aid them in cleaning the glass.

>> **Why inspect:** Wipers improve visibility during rain and snow. Worn blades can leave streaks on the windshield and fail to clear rain and snow properly — all reducing visibility. Washer fluid assists the wipers in cleaning the windshield, improving visibility.

>> **How to inspect:** Operate the wipers and washer. Wipers should sit flat on the windshield and effectively remove the washer fluid from the windshield, leaving a clear windshield.

Windshield and traffic monitoring devices

Obviously, the windshield is the glass in front of you in the cab. Any mirrors and cameras are traffic-monitoring devices.

>> **Why inspect:** Cracks, stickers, devices, and unclean glass in the viewing area can keep you from seeing any potential hazards, changes in road conditions, other vehicles, or pedestrians.

>> **How to inspect:** The windshield is to be clean with no illegal stickers, no cracks over an inch or chips that cannot be covered by a quarter. The seal is to be soft and pliable and not leaking.

>> Any cameras should be properly mounted and working properly as far as you can ascertain.

>> Mirrors must be clean, secure, and properly adjusted for you.

Emergency equipment

Fire extinguisher, devices to warn motorists of your vehicle disabled on the side of the road, and spare fuses are required emergency equipment.

>> **Why inspect:** Emergency equipment is required to be available, secure, and usable.

>> **How to inspect:** Inspect that you have three reflective triangles or six fuses, or three liquid burning flares. The triangles are the current popular item in this list.

>> Inspect that the fire extinguisher is rated for what you haul, fully charged with the safety pin in place and is securely mounted. The inspection should be up to date. Remember that there are five items.

>> Inspect that there is a spare fuse for every size and type of circuit for your vehicle. Inform the license examiner if your vehicle operates on circuit breakers.

Seatbelt

The seatbelt is the device that restrains your movement in the event of a collision.

>> **Why inspect:** A seatbelt must keep you in the most protected position in your vehicle in the case of a collision.

>> **How to inspect:** The seat belt should have no cuts or frays and be securely mounted. Latch and unlatch the belt to ensure that it is operational.

Lighting indicators

Indicators are on the dash for four-way flashing lights, high beam lights, ABS malfunction and turn signals. These indicate when the lights are presumably on. (The outside lights will be inspected during a different part of the inspection.)

>> **Why inspect:** Indicators must communicate to the driver when lights are being utilized.

>> **How to inspect:** Operate the four-way lights, left and right turn signal lever, and the high beam switch to verify that the indicators are operational.

Gear selectors

Whether you have a manual transmission or an automatic or automated transmission, there is a lever, stick, button — something that you control to select a different gear. In a manual transmission vehicle, in addition to a stick-type selector, there should be a rubber boot at the bottom of manual gear shift selectors.

>> **Why inspect:** Device must function as designed so that you can control the transmission. Rubber boots must keep out dust, exhaust fumes, and any other outside elements.

>> **How to inspect:** Physically operate the selector, verify it moves in all directions as designed. On a manual transmission that has a splitter (you will understand the splitter by the time you take the test), verify that it is operable and that you hear it operate. The boot should keep the outside environment out, so it doesn't have holes.

Conducting the brake tests

REMEMBER

You will only be tested on the vehicle you bring to the test. However, if you want the air brake endorsement, you must bring a vehicle with air brakes.

Air brake system check

The following is the procedure to inspect air brake systems. If you can't describe for the tests what is outlined below, review Chapter 9.

REMEMBER

>> **Why inspect:** This procedure is to help identify a problem in the air brake system, which can cause an abrupt and uncontrolled stop by the emergency spring brakes.

>> **How to inspect:** Here are the seven basic steps.

1. **Governor cut-off (out).** Chock wheels, start the engine, observe the air gauge build to 120 to 140 PSI (depending on the individual vehicle specifications) before the governor cuts out. This also checks the *air supply gauge* operation.

2. **Governor cut-in.** Bleed down the air pressure by repeatedly pressing and releasing the brake pedal. Slow down when the pressure drops below 100 PSI. Observe when the pressure starts building again: 90 PSI is the minimum pressure that air should start building again. Some vehicles might have different specifications. Be sure to know what your vehicle's minimum pressure should be.

3. **Air leakage Rate Test — Static.** Shut off the engine once the governor has cut out again but return the key to the "on" position (100 PSI + needed for these tests). Release the parking brake(s). No more than 3 PSI should be lost in a minute for a combination vehicle; 2 PSI maximum loss for a single vehicle.

4. **Air leakage Rate Test — Applied.** Apply the brakes (put your foot on the brake pedal) and hold. No more than 4 PSI is to be lost in a minute for a combination vehicle; 3 PSI maximum loss for a single vehicle.

5. **Air pressure warning test.** Fan the brakes (push and release the brake pedal repeatedly). Audible and visual alarms are to come on by 60 PSI. (Some official CDL publications say 55 PSI.)

6. **Emergency brake test.** Continue to fan the brakes; the parking brake and trailer air supply (if equipped to pull trailers and coupled to a trailer) valve knobs should pop out between 20 and 45 PSI.

7. **Build-up rate.** The air pressure should build up from 85 to 100 PSI within 45 seconds at normal operating RPMs.

WARNING

Be sure to learn this process. Failure to do so will likely cause the license examiner to fail you.

There is a memory technique for the air brake system inspection, which is *GGLLEEB* as in:

>> **GG:** Governor cut-in and governor cut-out.

>> **LL:** Leak tests — static leak test and the applied brake leak test.

>> **EE:** Emergency tests — low air pressure warning and emergency brake test.

>> **B:** Build the pressure back up!

Parking, trailer, service brakes check

This is a check of all the brake operations, for both single vehicles and combination vehicles. See Chapter 9 for a detailed process for checking air brakes.

Parking brakes keep vehicles from moving when parked, and emergency brakes stop the vehicle when in motion in emergency situations. Service brakes are the brakes that are applied when you use the brake pedal.

>> **Why inspect:** The brakes must function when a vehicle is parked and when it is in operation. An uncontrolled rolling vehicle can cause damage and injury.

>> **How to inspect:** Use the following list for brake inspections.

- **Parking brake.** With the parking brake engaged, trailer brakes released, remove your foot from the brake pedal and gently attempt to move the vehicle forward. The parking brake should prevent the movement of the truck.

- **Trailer parking brake.** With the trailer brake engaged, parking brake released, on the tow vehicle, remove your foot from the brake pedal, place it on the fuel pedal, and gently attempt to move the vehicle forward. This test can also be called the *trailer spring brake test* for air brake-equipped vehicles.

- **Trailer service brake.** With the trailer *and* parking brake released, remove your foot from the brake pedal and gently attempt to move the vehicle forward while holding down on the trailer brake handle or using the manual operation of the trailer brake (if your tow vehicle has one).

- **Service brakes.** With the trailer *and* parking brakes released, remove your foot from the brake pedal and gently move the vehicle forward at 5 mph, keeping your hands off the steering wheel. Apply the service brakes with the brake pedal. The steering wheel should not turn in either direction as your vehicle stops. Doing so indicates a mechanical problem.

Verifying the hydraulic brakes

This is a process in testing brakes that use a fluid as the conduit of power. Note that hydraulic brakes systems vary, and it is most important to follow the manufacturer's instructions for testing their brakes.

>> **Why inspect:** Leaks of the fluid will result in brake failure, which can result in a crash.

>> **How to inspect:** Explain and demonstrate the hydraulic brake check for the license examiner, based on your manufacturer's instructions. Inspect the warning systems and any indicators your vehicle might have.

>> Identify the position/height of the brake pedal. Inspect the pressure by pumping the brake pedal three times and then holding the pedal down for five seconds. The brake pedal should not depress any more after the initial application. The pedal should be firm.

>> Be sure to follow the manufacturer's process for testing any power assist system that your vehicle might have.

Inspecting the Brakes

You inspected the brake performance from inside the cab, now you can inspect the actual brakes.

Brake lines and hoses

Brake lines and hoses carry pressurized air or hydraulic fluid to the wheel brake assembly or such device that activates the brakes.

>> **Why inspect:** Loss of hydraulic fluid may lead to loss of brake power and loss of response in time and power. Loss of air pressure may cause wheel/brake lockup.

>> **How to inspect:** Inspect that hoses or lines can supply air or hydraulic fluid to the brakes and are not leaking.

>> Inspect for cracked, worn, or frayed hoses or lines.

Brake contaminates

This is brake contamination, such as grease, or oil that can be on brake pads, rotors, and drums.

>> **Why inspect:** Contaminants on the brakes can cause a reduction in braking friction, which may lead to a crash. Contaminants can also create a fire hazard.

>> **How to inspect:** When accessible, inspect for contaminants such as grease, oil, or other substances on the brake lining or pads and the brake drum or disc/rotor that can affect braking capabilities.

REMEMBER

If your state requires you to describe the brake components, review Chapter 8.

Examining the Suspension

Leaf or coil *springs* dampen wheel vibration and shocks created by rolling along the roads and terrain. *Air bags* can accompany springs or serve as the primary suspension system. Gas or hydraulic devices (*shocks*) cushion vehicle suspension and stabilize the vehicle.

» **Why inspect:** Damaged or missing leaf springs or broken coils may lead to loss of control or rollover if the vehicle falls on the frame or on a tire. Shifted springs may strike a tire causing a blowout or interfere with steering. Damaged air bags or shocks can affect vehicle handling and stopping distances.

» **How to inspect:** The following items must be inspected, where visible and accessible, on each axle every driving day after you obtain your license. Your vehicle will not have every one of these components. For the test, you will only inspect one axle.

» Inspect for missing, shifted, cracked, or broken *leaf springs* and inspect that spring mounts, shackles, and hangers are not cracked, broken, or missing any parts.

» Inspect that any *u-bolts* are present and properly secured.

» Inspect for broken or distorted *coil springs* and inspect that mounts are not cracked, broken, or have any missing parts.

» Inspect that the *air bags* for an air ride suspension are secure, not damaged, and not leaking.

» Inspect that *shock absorbers* are secure, not damaged, and not leaking (if equipped).

» Inspect that the vehicle is sitting level (front to rear and side to side).

Note: Inform the license examiner if the suspension components are not visible or accessible on vehicles such as transit or motor coach buses and inspect that the vehicle is sitting level (front to rear and side to side). And note that a leaning vehicle may indicate a suspension problem unless your vehicle is sitting in a pothole.

Thumping Your Tires

I can get in a good argument with myself on which component of a CMV is the most critical. Maybe it is like your children, each getting your attention at different times. Take the time to ensure that the tires — that are in contact with the ground while you are barreling down the road at 65 mph — are in good and proper condition.

Tires

The tire/wheel assemblies are in contact with the pavement and need to be checked.

» **Why inspect:** Underinflation increases the chance of blowout from excessive heat buildup due to increased flexing of the tire. Low tread depth increases the effect of hydroplaning, reduces traction, and increases stopping distance.

Overinflation increases the chances of damage to the tire from curbs and potholes as well as loss of traction due to less tread in contact with the road. Cuts and bulges may cause tire failure, blowouts, and sudden loss of control.

MORE ON TIRES

Tires should be the same size and type on each end of an axle.

When you have dual wheels (two wheels together at the end of an axle) check for debris or objects that can be lodged between tires. Besides possibly ruining the tires, the object can fly out and strike another vehicle.

Buses cannot have regrooved, recapped, or retreaded tires on the front wheels.

» **How to inspect:** The following items must be inspected on each tire:

- **Tire inflation:** Inspect for proper inflation using a tire gauge. Make sure all valve stems are accessible. Tire can have no audible leaks.

- **Tire condition:** Inspect for cuts and damage that expose body plies of the tire in the tread and sidewall. Make sure that valve caps are not missing, and valve stems are not damaged or broken. Look for bumps and bulges in the sidewall and mismatched diameters in dual tires.

» **Tread depth:** Inspect for minimum tread depth with a tread depth gauge on all major tread grooves containing wear bars (4/32 on steering axle tires, 2/32 on all other tires).

TIP

You do not use a tire gauge on a hot tire, only on cold tires. If you have been driving, you have a warm tire. Check the pressure at the beginning of your driving day, during your pre-trip inspection. During other inspections, you check to ensure that your tire isn't losing pressure by thumping them.

AUTHOR SAYS

For your CDL test, you will not get credit if you simply kick the tires or use a mallet to inspect for proper inflation (thumping your tires). You are being tested on how you do a pre-trip inspection, so you mention that a tire pressure gauge is what you use. *Have a truck tire pressure gauge with you and show it.*

A truck tire pressure gauge, shown in Figure 17-2, has two *chucks* (ends) to connect to valve stems facing either direction. Dual tires have valve stems in both directions.

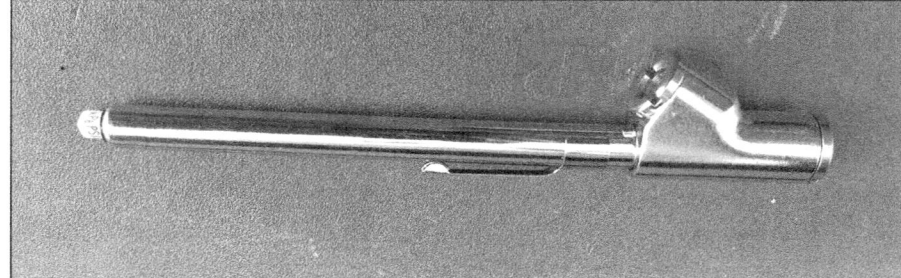

FIGURE 17-2:
A truck tire pressure gauge.

Note: If the tires are equipped with an automatic tire inflation system (ATIS) or tire pressure monitoring system (TPMS) that has hoses connected to the tire valve stems, you need only mention that tire pressure is monitored and adjusted by an automatic system and inspect that it is working properly.

Lug nuts

Lug nuts hold the wheels on to the axles.

>> **Why inspect:** Loose or missing lug nuts can result in the loss of a wheel and lead to a crash.

>> **How to inspect:** Inspect that all lug nuts are present.

Inspect that lug nuts are not loose. Check that there are no signs of rust trails on steel wheels, powdery trail on aluminum wheels, or shiny threads that would indicate loose lug nuts.

>> Inspect that there are no broken studs.

Wheels/rims

Tires are mounted on wheels. The outer portion of the wheel at the extreme edge is called the rim, which keeps the tire on the wheel.

>> **Why inspect:** Damaged rims can cause the loss of a tire, the wheel can come off an axle, air pressure can be lost, or a tire can roll off a rim due to damage to a flange or split rim. A damaged wheel can result in loss of vehicle control.

>> **How to inspect:** Inspect for damaged, cracked, or bent rims. Rims/wheels cannot be repaired by welding. Inspect for rust trails or powder trails.

>> Inspect studs and bolt holes to make sure they are not elongated (out of round) and there are no missing or loose nuts or bolts.

Checking Your Lights

Nothing gets the attention of an officer like having a light out on your vehicle, and you never know when a light is going to quit operating. So check your lights — often.

Lights

Your vehicle has headlights, hi-beam lights, four-way flashers, clearance lights, marker lights, taillights, license plate light, and brake lights. There are lights on all sides of the vehicle.

>> **Why inspect:** Lights allow the driver to see and be seen. Lights are communication devices.

>> **How to inspect:** Inspect that all lights operate and illuminate.

Lights on testing day

Your behind-the-wheel test can go one of two basic ways. The first way is the license examiner will have you operate the various light switches and verify that all the lights are operational.

REMEMBER

The second way is when using the modernized test, which states that you can ask the examiner to help with the light inspection. If they help, you are to call out which lights you are asking the examiner to observe. So, speak loudly, with your window down, not forgetting any of the lights. Most examiners have a set amount of time to conduct a test, so an examiner might just want to verify that your lights work themselves so that they can move on to the next test.

Seeing the Side of Vehicle

You know where the side of your vehicle is as you are driving down the road, but you need to see just a bit of it in relation to the road and other vehicles and obstacles near you. The sides of the vehicle need attention just like the rest of the components because it is usually what you don't see that gets you into trouble.

Mirrors and other traffic monitoring devices

As you walked up to your CMV to start your inspection, you saw the big picture that included the mirrors (which other drivers can damage with their vehicles). Now you look at details.

Mirrors are glass reflectors for the purpose of helping you comfortably see what you can not otherwise easily see. Cameras with display screens have the same function.

>> **Why inspect:** It is imperative that you know where traffic and hazards are around you.

>> **How to inspect:** These devices were inspected during the in-cab inspection for adjustment, cracks, and cleanliness. You are now inspecting them for secure mounting.

Lenses of lights and reflectors

During your walk-up inspection, you inspected some of your light and lenses. As you inspect the rest of your vehicle, you will inspect all the lights, their lenses, and reflectors as you move around the vehicle. Included in this inspection are the required reflectors.

Lights generally have lenses covering them and reflectors reflect the lights of oncoming traffic back to the driver, communicating which part of a vehicle they are seeing.

>> **Why inspect:** Other drivers must be able to see you and correctly interpret what they are seeing. Lights are protected by lenses.

>> **How to inspect:** Observe that lenses are unbroken and are covering lights. Look for evidence of damaged or removed reflectors.

Batteries

Batteries are the devices that store electrical power for the vehicle.

>> **Why inspect:** Unsecure batteries don't only have the potential to disable a vehicle, they can cause a hazard for other motorists. Batteries with loose connections can cause vehicular failure.

>> **How to inspect:** Inspect that any door or cover for the batteries is secure. Battery terminal connections should be secure and be free of excessive corrosion. Cables should not be worn.

Fuel tanks

These are the containers that hold fuel. These can also be Diesel Exhaust Fluid (DEF), which is used in reducing the exhaust soot released into the air.

>> **Why inspect:** Defective holding brackets, leaks, and unsecured caps can cause fuel to be lost, creating potential hazards.

>> **How to inspect:** All tanks must be secure. Any steel straps holding aluminum tanks *must* have rubber between the strap and the tank. Caps to the tanks must be tight. There should be no leaks.

Frame

The frame is the structure to which everything is attached. The frame supports beds and bodies of vehicles.

>> **Why inspect:** A damaged or loose frame member can cause a hazardous situation. There can be handling problems or loss of cargo.

>> **How to inspect:** Look for cracks, broken welds, welds made after the manufacturer made the vehicle to the frame and its members. (No one should weld on the frame or drill holes in it because those types of modifications would compromise the integrity of the frame, thereby violating the regulations unless done so per manufacturer's specifications.) Look for holes in the cargo holding area of the vehicle.

Other side inspections

There are other items not listed in the modernized test that you should inspect in real life. If you are driving the same vehicle each day, some of these items can be inspected quickly.

The door area

>> **Why inspect:** Doors must be secure at the hinges and the latches and need to keep the weather environment outside.

>> **How to inspect:** Check the seals around the doors. They should be present, soft, and pliable, and able to seal out the elements.

>> The door hinges, latch, striker, and handles (inside and outside) should all operate and are mounted properly.

>> The wiring harness should be protected with no bare wires or any corrosion.

>> You inspected the glass while in the truck, so move on to the steps. The steps should be secure and well grooved. The steps should be free of dirt, mud, snow, and ice so that you are not forced to test your three points of contact.

REMEMBER

Have I mentioned the proper way to enter and exit the vehicle? It is very important that you always have three points of contact when entering and exiting the vehicle — both for your exam and for the rest of your career. This means that you should always have at least two feet and one hand or one foot and two hands in a secure position on the truck when climbing in and out.

Stickers

IFTA sticker. Many companies are required to have an International Fuel Tax Agreement (IFTA) sticker. This fuel tax agreement greatly simplified the administrative fuel tax costs that companies incur.

>> **Why inspect:** Generally speaking, trucks traveling across state lines that require Class A or B licenses are required to have the sticker (which also means your company needs an IFTA license with the paperwork in your permit book).

>> **How to inspect:** Check that this sticker is in place and current.

Inspection sticker. A sticker indicating a DOT inspection was conducted on your vehicle.

>> **Why inspect:** The sticker for a federal DOT inspection has no specific location on the vehicle nor is it required, but it will usually suffice at a roadside inspection as an indication that the federal requirement for an annual inspection has been performed. The actual copy should then be in the company's office records.

>> **How to inspect:** Check for a current inspection sticker. The date on the sticker is the date of the inspection. You have a year to perform the next inspection. If there is no sticker, you must have a copy with the vehicle or in your possession — on paper or digitally.

Knowing the Rear of Vehicle

Often, what an officer sees first of your vehicle will be the rear. For that matter, it will be what most everyone will see first who is coming up from behind you. Therefore, containing your cargo is critical and must be inspected.

Lenses of lights and reflectors

These are the transparent covers of lights and the tape or devices that reflect the lights of other vehicles. Now that you are at the rear of the vehicle, repeat the process for inspecting the lenses and reflectors.

>> **Why inspect:** Lights and reflectors must convey your vehicle's presence and intentions. Missing or broken lenses and missing or damaged reflectors can compromise this communication.

>> **How to inspect:** Look for broken or missing lenses of lights and missing or damaged reflectors and tape. There is a whole section of regulations on what vehicles require which types of lights and reflectors. Your vehicle was likely assembled in accordance with the regulations so ensure all lights are intact (and working when you are inspecting) and that no reflectors are missing.

Doors

Doors usually confine cargo, like the doors on a dump truck, or keep the weather and pilferers out of the cargo area of a box trailer. Doors also cover controls of tankers, any and all components that are part of the back of a trailer are to be inspected, unique or not.

THE UNDERRIDE BUMPER

The modernized test does not mention the underride bumper — the bumper at the back of any CMV that doesn't have its rear wheels all the way to the back of the vehicle. This bumper is designed to help keep another vehicle from traveling under the CMV when it fails to stop prior to hitting the CMV. It should be secure with no cracked welds.

>> **Why inspect:** Cargo can spill from the vehicle, or swinging doors can be a hazard for other motorists. Doors should protect the cargo and controls from potential damage from the outside.

>> **How to inspect:** Check that doors close and seal appropriately. Hinges should be present and operable. Verify that the seals and locks are in place when applicable.

Verifying Your Competence with Questions

There are no practice questions in this chapter, but I am giving you questions (without multiple-choice answers) to help you check your competence. Any questions that you might receive on a written test have practice questions in another chapter. When you are successful, these questions will ensure your competence and improve your confidence.

If you find yourself stumped on the answers, go back and reread the appropriate section(s) and refresh your memory.

1. Why do you inspect *tires*?
2. Why do you inspect the *air system*?
3. What defects can a *wheel/rim* have?
4. How do you conduct the *air system tests*?
5. What do you inspect the *fuel tank* for?
6. Why do you inspect the *frame*?
7. What defects can *tires* have?
8. What are the *critical fluids* under the hood?
9. What can go wrong if you don't inspect the *lug nuts*?
10. What are the *seven tests* for the *air system*?
11. What do you look for when you inspect your *batteries*?
12. How do you check your *lights* on the day of the driving test?
13. Can you name the basic components of a *steering system*? (Start with the steering wheel and mention the next component until you reach the steer tires.)
14. What device do you have with you when checking *tires*?
15. What can be wrong with a *coil or leaf spring*?
16. What can be found *leaking* under the hood?

17. What do you expect to see when inspecting the following items?

- Voltmeter
- Oil pressure gauge
- Coolant temperature gauge
- Fuel gauge
- Speedometer
- Tachometer

18. What are the three *emergency items* that should be found in the cab?

19. How do you inspect *hydraulic brakes*?

20. How can a *windshield* be defective?

21. How do you inspect the following components?

- Horns
- Defroster and heater
- Windshield wipers and washer fluid
- Visors

22. How do you inspect *pedals*?

23. What are some *miscellaneous items* to check?

24. How do you inspect a *permit book*?

Chapter **18**

Handling the Pre-Trip Inspection on Special Vehicles

At this point in the book, I have shared with you a lot about inspections, and I am not done yet. If this is all new to you, I don't want you to be overwhelmed. You can do a competent job inspecting a vehicle, just do it a step at a time. Do your inspection in the same logical order. When you see a component that you can't remember how to inspect, don't immediately rush to this book or your flash cards for the answer. Think about it, rule out some options, and make your mind do the problem-solving. When you have the answer, pause, and think about how you can have remembered that information more readily. This will help you remember next time.

In this chapter, I discuss the pre-trip inspections for a combination vehicle and for a passenger vehicle, primarily a school bus. Both of these inspections are critical when you are driving one of these vehicles. When you have conducted the inspection, you will have the satisfaction and comfort in knowing that you have done everything you can to make the vehicle safe. Then you can focus on safe driving.

On your pre-trip inspection test day, you will only perform your pre-inspection on the vehicle you are using, so you will not have to talk about a school bus when you have a semi-tractor and trailer with you. If you test at a facility that uses the *modernized test,* you are allowed to have an "official" cheat sheet with the areas they want inspected.

One final note, you will inspect your vehicle much faster, say in 15 minutes, when you don't have to verbalize everything you are doing. Just remember that the experts say to always inspect everything, and to always inspect everything in the same order.

Inspecting Specifics for a Combination Vehicle

When you inspect a combination vehicle, you will incorporate what you would inspect for any commercial vehicle plus some particulars specific to combination vehicles. With the two vehicles joined together (a power unit and a trailer), special conditions now exist. You should use the information from the previous chapter and add the specifics for inspecting the combination vehicle.

Rear of semi-tractor

Behind the semi-tractor cab of a combination vehicle, especially your semi-tractor/trailer, you will have a few items that are somewhat unique to inspect. In addition, there will be some common items that are more accessible at this location than elsewhere around the vehicle. If you drive a straight truck coupled with a trailer after you get your Commercial Driver's License (CDL), be sure to study any user manuals or get training on the specific vehicles you will be operating to ensure you perform a quality inspection.

Air and electrical lines/connectors

Air lines are the conduit for air to the trailer from the truck or semi-tractor and an electrical cord for electricity to the trailer.

REMEMBER

>> **Why inspect:** For air lines, loss of air to the trailer will result in a partial or total loss of brake control to the towed unit. A low air condition in modern trailers will cause sudden application of the trailer's spring brakes, which might result in loss of control.

>> For electric lines, damaged lines may result in loss of communication to other drivers (no turn signal lights or brake lights). You can fail to be seen by other vehicles at night.

>> **How to inspect:** Inspect that air lines are properly and securely connected and are not leaking. Inspect that electric connectors on the power unit *and* the trailer are fully connected, secure, and free of damage on both ends of the lines (see Figure 18-1).

>> Inspect that both air lines and electrical lines are not cut, cracked, chafed, nor taped and are not in contact with the frame or other such components. Listen for air leaks.

Reflectors

There are reflectors (tape or plastic) shaped as inverted "Ls" (see Figure 18-2 on the back of the cab near the top).

>> **Why inspect:** It is a violation to not have these reflectors. If the reflectors are made of plastic rather than tape, they are often missing.

>> **How to inspect:** Verify the reflectors are present.

Fifth wheel area

The fifth wheel area of a combination vehicle is a unique and critical area where the trailer couples to the semi-tractor. Some of the components are best inspected when the semi-tractor and trailer are unhooked while some of the inspection must be performed when the semi-tractor and trailer are coupled together.

FIGURE 18-1:
Air and
electric lines.

FIGURE 18-2:
Reflectors
at the top of
the cab.

OTHER ITEMS BEHIND THE CAB

When you are behind the cab of the towing unit, especially a semi tractor, inspect everything you can see, not just what is in the test. Remember that officers don't receive the same type of training that you will receive when you go through Entry-Level Driver Training (ELDT). They will look for anything unsafe and cite you for anything they find, and rightly so. Neither you nor I want unsafe vehicles on the road with us or with our families.

As you inspect your combination vehicle, when you see the frame, which will be often, check it for illegal welds or drilled holes. Also, check the drive shaft to see that it is straight; a drive shaft that has any twist to it has been over torqued and has become more prone to break. Don't forget to inspect under the fifth wheel area, where it is hard to see. So inspect the suspension, brakes, tires, and wheels again.

Kingpin apron and gap

The kingpin is a part of the semitrailer, which is permanently mounted to the metal plate (apron) of the trailer and couples with the fifth wheel. The apron rests on the fifth wheel and rotates on the fifth wheel when the combination vehicle is turning.

>> **Why inspect:** Wear or damage to the kingpin can result in handling problems, a rollover, or the uncoupling of the semi-tractor and trailer.

>> **How to inspect:** Inspect the kingpin for damage or wear (see Figure 18-3).

>> Inspect the apron for bends or cracks.

>> Inspect that there is no daylight or no gap between the trailer and the fifth wheel skid plate when the two units are connected.

>> Inspect for proper lubrication where possible and especially when the semi-tractor is uncoupled from a trailer.

FIGURE 18-3: A straight, nonworn kingpin.

TIP

Fifth wheels are made with extremely strong components and precise mechanisms. So while they are heavy duty, you still must inspect the parts of the fifth wheel to ensure the connection will stay secure. Inspect what you can see when there is a trailer already coupled to the semi-tractor. But when you don't have a trailer connected to your semi-tractor, stop for a minute and inspect the upper and lower parts of the fifth wheel area and the chassis below it before hooking to another trailer.

Fifth wheel

The fifth wheel, the flat roundish steel component that is secured to a semi-tractor, is where the trailer rests and where the trailer kingpin is secured. The fifth wheel also pivots from the front to the back, keeping a secure connection when the two units are on uneven surfaces.

>> **Why inspect:** A faulty or damaged fifth wheel or an improper connection between the semi-tractor and the trailer can result in handling problems, a rollover, or separation of the semi-tractor and trailer.

>> **How to inspect:** Inspect that the fifth wheel is securely mounted, referring to Figure 18-4. The horizontal and vertical bolts (1) that hold the fifth wheel to the fifth wheel bracket and the bracket to the vehicle must be present and secure. Fifth wheels that slide must have the locking pins in the out position (2). Pivot pins (3) must each be secured with a plate (4) that is also secured to the fifth wheel. This plate keeps the pivot pins in place when the fifth wheel pivots.

FIGURE 18-4:
Sliding fifth
wheel pins
in locked
position.

Fifth wheel connection

Locking connection and safety device keep the trailer locked into place.

>> **Why inspect:** The trailer can uncouple during travel if the locking mechanism is not secured.

>> **How to inspect:** Look into the fifth wheel gap (go underneath the trailer and look from the back side of the fifth wheel) and inspect that the locking jaws are fully secured around the kingpin. Inspect for play between the kingpin and locking jaws (see Figure 18-5).

>> Inspect that the release arm is in the engaged position and the safety latch or lock (if equipped) is in place.

>> Ensure there is no space between the fifth wheel and the trailer apron.

>> Inspect for cracks, breaks, or excessive wear. Inspect for proper lubrication or undamaged Teflon plate as applicable. Again, inspect for secure connection or open jaws ready for coupling (when unhooked from a trailer).

Pintle hook combination

Most truck driving schools won't have a truck with a pintle hook, so be sure someone gives you proper training when you have to use that combination. *Pintle hooks* are the typical connection of a *converter dolly* (used in pulling doubles) and for many construction trucks pulling construction–type trailers.

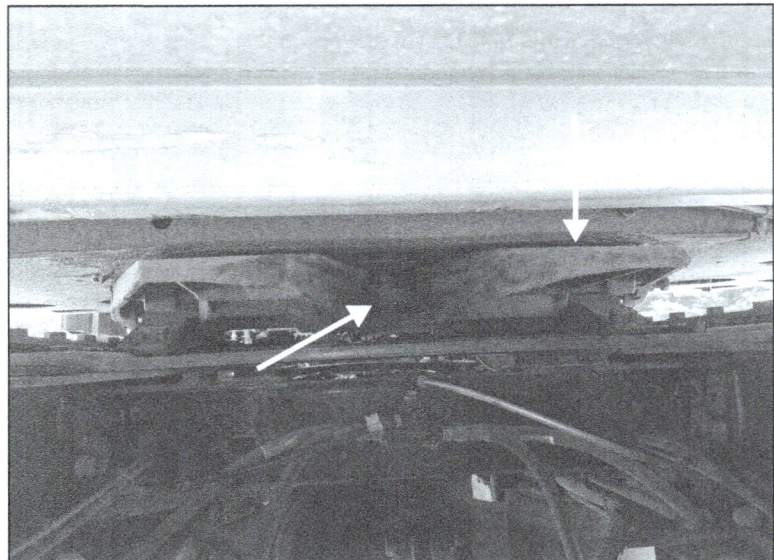

FIGURE 18-5:
A jaw
(hidden
behind the
locking
bar) locked
around the
kingpin.

Pintle hook

This is the specially designed hitch that a drawbar ring is locked into. It can be found on a trailer, semi-tractor, or converter dolly.

>> **Why inspect:** A faulty hook or connection can result in a trailer leaving the towing vehicle, causing a crash.

>> **How to inspect:** The pintle hook is to be securely mounted to the frame. No parts should be missing, and the hook should function properly (see Figure 18-6).

Drawbar ring and tongue

This is the specially designed ring found on converter dollies and some trailers and is secured into a pintle hook.

>> **Why inspect:** A faulty ring can result in a trailer becoming detached from the towing vehicle, causing a crash.

>> **How to inspect:** Inspect that the ring has not been bent or broken. No welds are broken. All bolts are present and all components that connect the trailer or dolly to the unit in front of it are secure and no fasteners are missing (see Figure 18-7).

Tow hitch and coupler combination

This coupler is more common among lighter vehicles and trailers, but a few of these are heavy duty enough to require a Class A license. Even when this combination is used for a boat trailer, which often wouldn't require anything more than a passenger vehicle license, inspecting the coupling is paramount. After all, who would want to see their boat pass them on the highway?

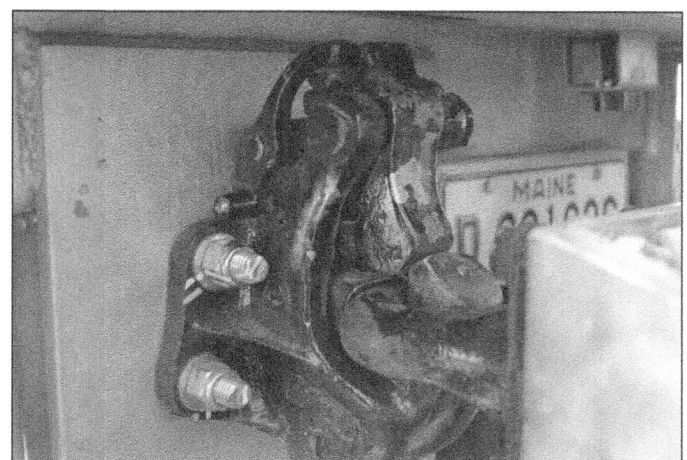

FIGURE 18-6:
A pintle
hook.

FIGURE 18-7:
A drawbar
ring and
tongue.

Tow hitch

This is a hitch receiver to which a trailer ball is attached, and a trailer coupler attaches and pivots on (see Figure 18-8).

» **Why inspect:** An improperly mounted receiver can cause handling problems and a trailer to disconnect, resulting in a crash.

» **How to inspect:** Check for cracks and broken welds. Look for loose fasteners. The hitch should be secure to the frame. Ensure that the size of the ball matches the coupler of the trailer and that the hitch and vehicle are sufficiently rated for the trailer that would be attached to it.

Trailer coupler

This is the device connected to the front of a trailer that locks onto a trailer ball (see Figure 18-9).

» **Why inspect:** A defective coupler or tongue can cause a trailer to disconnect from the towing unit, resulting in a crash.

FIGURE 18-8:
A hitch
receiver and
trailer ball.

FIGURE 18-9:
A trailer
coupler with
chains.

>> **How to inspect:** Inspect that the coupler is properly mounted and has no broken welds, and all fasteners are present and secure. Inspect that the coupler is not worn and is able to work as designed.

>> Inspect that the safety chains, cables, and other safety mechanisms are properly implemented and secure. For the best practice (and to possibly comply with laws where you live), safety chains should form a cradle where possible. Chains should not drag the ground and should be long enough to make turns.

Side and rear of trailer

Drivers can walk by the side of a trailer, missing critical components. Be sure to look at the top and all the way down taller trailers to look for damage and holes. The rear of a combination vehicle should receive the same inspection as the rear of the vehicle as described in Chapter 17.

Reflective tape

Reflective tape, also known as DOT or conspicuity tape, is on the side and rear of the trailer.

>> **Why inspect:** Reflective tape on a trailer helps a commercial vehicle to be seen and communicate presence among other vehicles.

>> **Inspection:** Inspect that the tape covers 50 percent of the length of the sides (spaced fairly even) and 100 percent across the back (see Figure 18-10). There should be reflectors at the top outside corners at the rear of the trailer, in the shape of an "L" when possible. Ensure that none of the tape has been removed.

FIGURE 18-10:
Reflective
tape.

Landing gear and clearance

Landing gear supports the front end of a trailer when it is not coupled to a truck or semi-tractor.

>> **Why inspect:** Landing gear must be raised all the way up so that it will not strike the ground or any raised surface during travel. It must clear the back of the power unit while turning. Its handle must be secured in its holder, so it will not move and strike other vehicles. Damage to landing gear supports can result in the trailer tipping or falling over when uncoupled. If debris is on the landing gear, it can fall off and be a hazard to other motorists.

>> **How to inspect:** Inspect that the landing gear is fully raised, has no missing parts, and is operational. The crank handle should be stowed correctly, and the support frame and landing pads are not damaged (see Figure 18-11).

>> Inspect that the fifth wheel is positioned far enough back so that the semi-tractor frame, tires, and mudflaps will clear the landing gear during turns.

>> Inspect that powered landing gears are not leaking.

>> Landing gear is to be clear of debris, such as rocks, snow, and ice.

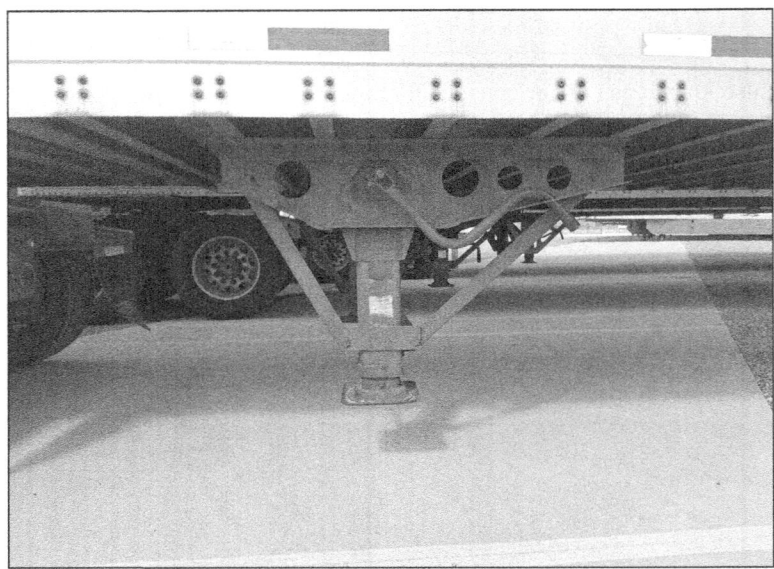

FIGURE 18-11:
Fully raised
landing
gear.

Air lines

There are air and electrical lines hanging below many trailers. Trailers with axles that have the ability to slide back and forth will have the air and electrical lines connected to a spring(s) to keep them off the ground in whatever position the axles are in.

>> **Why inspect:** Springs can deteriorate and break causing the lines to come in contact with the ground, creating a possible emergency stop. Lines can rub on each other or on other components creating a hazardous (or at least potentially hazardous) situation.

>> **How to inspect:** Springs should hold the lines sufficiently above the ground, so that they will not get damaged or hooked on any obstacles. There is no federal height clearance for these lines (most likely because there are many different types of trailers), but there might be some state requirements. Ensure that the springs are in good working condition, holding the air lines off the ground as the manufacturer recommends. Replace sprung springs or corroded springs (see Figure 18-12).

>> Ensure that lines are in good condition, that they are not rubbing on each other and on other components causing chafing. Separators as seen in Figure 18-12, keep lines from rubbing on each other.

Tandem (sliding) area of the trailer

Many box trailers and some flatbed trailers have tandems (the tires, wheels, and axles of the trailer) with the ability to slide forward or backward. This feature helps you adjust the weight on the axles to be within legal limits. This section is on inspecting the sliding tandem. A trailer without a sliding tandem will be inspected the same as any other axle, suspension, brakes, tires, and so on.

Locking pins

There are four pins that should be in the "out" position, holding the tandems in a particular position.

FIGURE 18-12:
Springs
holding
lines off the
ground.

>> **Why inspect:** If pins are not out, the whole tandem set can come out from under the trailer when you have to stop.

>> **How to inspect:** Look on both sides of the tandems to see that all four pins are in the out position (see "A" in Figure 18-13).

Slide rail and slider clips

Sliding tandems have a rail to slide on and clips that keep components in position.

>> **Why inspect:** Tandems should slide with reasonable effort and clips help tandems to stay in place when sliding.

>> **How to inspect:** Inspect both tandem slide rails as they should not be cracked, bent, or broken. They should be clear of anything adding undue friction between the sliding components. Clips should be present, properly mounted, and not bent (see "B" in Figure 18-13).

Stop bars

There are bars that limit how far the tandems can slide forward or backward. Sometimes these stops are not bars but smaller metal pieces in the place of bars.

>> **Why inspect:** Without the bars, a tandem set can come completely out from under the trailer when it is being slid.

>> **How to inspect:** Look at the front and rear area of the slider rails for stop bars (or their equivalent) to be securely in place (see "C" in Figure 18-13).

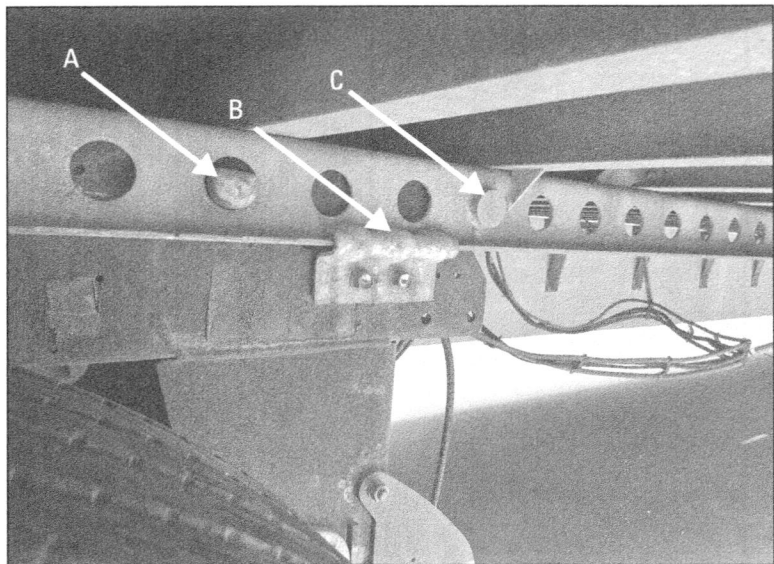

FIGURE 18-13:
Tandem
slide rails.

Inspecting a School Bus or Other Passenger Bus

It is interesting to note that seats are in the inspection list for buses, but the seat in a commercial vehicles is rarely mentioned in an inspection list. In this section, you will inspect the special components that passenger buses and school buses have, including the seats!

Seats

All passenger seats, frames, and attachment points should be inspected.

>> **Why inspect:** Seats must be safe for passengers. Seats on buses are designed to keep passengers safe in the event of an accident.

>> **How to inspect:** Inspect by grasping and attempting to move or wiggle the seats with your hand and by visually observing the condition. Seats should be mounted securely, and the cushions should be secure.

Exits

Entry and emergency doors, push-out windows, and roof hatches need to be operational for use during emergencies.

>> **Why inspect:** Emergency exits must be accessible and usable in the event of a crash or other emergency.

>> **How to inspect:** Inspect that all possible exits are labeled; and they should open, close, and fasten properly. Inspect that exterior release handles operate. Inspect that all emergency exit warning devices are working. The ignition key needs to be on or in an operating mode to make this inspection (see Figure 18-14).

FIGURE 18-14:
A roof
emergency
exit and
a window
emergency.

Extra lights (school bus only)

Alternating lights are used for approaches and pickups. Strobe lights are for low visibility situations, and interior lights provide lighting inside the bus.

» **Why inspect:** Alternating lights must communicate intentions and actions. Strobe lights alert other motorists to your presence. Interior lights are needed to ensure safe nighttime operation.

» **How to inspect:** Inspect that the alternating amber and red lights are operating on both the rear and front of the bus and at the controls if the bus is so equipped (see Figure 18-15).

» Inspect that the strobe light is secure and operational, and the dashboard indicator is working.

FIGURE 18-15:
(A) Flashing
lights, (B)
stop arm,
and (C) rear
emergency
exit.

First aid kit

Required item for emergencies, first aid and body fluid cleanup kit on passenger vehicles (see Figure 18-16).

>> **Why inspect:** First aid kit and body fluid cleanup kits must be available and usable.

>> **How to inspect:** First aid kit and body fluids cleanup kit must be present and the seals intact. Broken seals mean the possibility of missing items. Requirements of both items on passenger buses can vary between states.

Stop arm(s) and safety arm (school bus only)

These are the devices with the stop signs on the left side and the arm on the front of the bus that force children away from the bus when they cross in front of the bus. The devices are activated when loading and unloading children.

>> **Why inspect:** The stop arms must deploy and communicate to other drivers that the bus is stopping, and children will be present. The safety arm must deploy so the bus driver can see and account for all the children when they are crossing in front of the bus.

>> **How to inspect:** Operate the devices, verify that they are secure, and deploy to their proper position. Ensure all the controls on the operating panel are secure and in proper working order (see Figure 18-17).

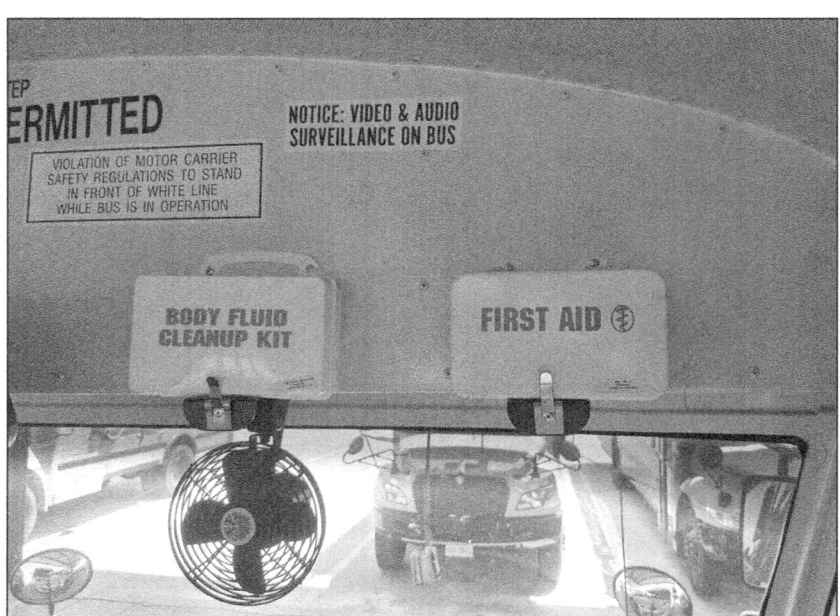

FIGURE 18-16:
First aid kit and a body fluid cleanup kit.

FIGURE 18-17:
The
operating
panel for a
school bus.

Verifying Your Competence with Questions

There are no practice questions in this chapter, but I am giving you questions (without multiple-choice answers) to help you check your competence. Any questions that you might receive on a written test have practice questions in another chapter. When you are successful, these questions will ensure your competence and improve your confidence.

If you find yourself stumped on the answers, go back and reread the appropriate section(s) and refresh your memory.

1. Where are all the possible emergency exits?

2. What do you inspect a fifth wheel for?

3. What do you inspect a locking pin for?

4. How do you inspect emergency exits?

5. What do you inspect air lines for underneath a trailer?

6. What extra emergency equipment do you find on a school bus?

7. What do you inspect between a semi-tractor and a semitrailer?

8. How do you inspect the connection between the semi-tractor's fifth wheel and the trailer?

9. How much reflective tape should there be on the side of a trailer? On the rear?

10. How do you inspect the seats on a bus?

Chapter **19**

Passing the Behind-the-Wheel Tests

You passed your written tests long ago, at least it seems like it. You were successful in your pre-trip inspection test. You have practiced the skills course many times. So, clear your mind of all other matters. Listen to the voice of your license examiner and perform the skills. After passing the skills, you are going to get behind the wheel and drive. Yes, I know your nerves are likely on edge. . . Take a deep breath, and don't forget to breath.

In this chapter, I describe the various skills that testing facilities use on a special course and give you tips for passing those tests. I also share the components of a road test for you to begin thinking about and preparing for, even before you start your driving class.

Passing the Skills Course

There are four basic skills that many State Departments of Transportation (DOT) have adopted. But if some states have not gone to the modernized course (with the four basic tests), it is okay. Most of the principles I discuss in this chapter are adaptable.

The total amount of points allowed for passing the test is different state to state. State DOTs will put their own spin on the tests by determining how many points for an *encroachment* (part of your vehicle passing over a boundary line), or how many points for an extra look, or how many points to assess for an extra pull-up. Therefore, I can't be specific about the assessing the various ways to lose (or gain) points on a test. If I give guidance that contradicts your state's testing process, I ask for your forgiveness.

Seeing yourself succeed

TIP

Adjust your mirrors and do so when the trailer is straight with the semi-tractor if you are driving a combination vehicle. Adjust your seat as well, positioning it as you always do.

As you practice in the weeks prior to test day, sit still in your seat to use your mirrors. Keeping your back to the seat and using your properly adjusted mirrors will help give you consistency, especially if you are testing in a combination vehicle.

Practice your allotted "look." A look is the same as the *Get Out and Look* (GOAL) that is mentioned often in this book. The proper look is to turn off the engine, take the key, use three points of contact as you get down to the ground and shut the door (see Chapter 17). Failure to perform your look in this manner might result in an automatic fail.

TIP

How do college athletes accomplish something like making a free throw when there are 500 wild students screaming behind a clear backboard, waving big foam fingers? How does your kid sit there, playing a video game and not hearing you say, "go brush your teeth"? Concentration in these examples requires focusing the mind on the task at hand, especially removing the thought of failing. Rather, think of how you succeed. Good free-throw shooters can make a free throw with their eyes closed because they are picturing what they do to make the ball go into the hoop, and then they do it. Picture in your mind what has to happen for your maneuvers, and then do it (except don't close your eyes).

Preparing for the forward drive and stop

AUTHOR SAYS

An interesting story: there was a lady interviewing people to be her new limo driver. There were three candidates for the job. She asked each of the drivers the following question, "If we were on a mountain road and there was a cliff that dropped off the side of the road, how close can you drive to that edge?" The first driver said, "I can drive that car within a foot, and you would be safe." The second driver said, "I can drive that car within six inches of that cliff and keep you safe." The third driver responded, "Ma'am, I would keep that car as far away from that cliff as possible to keep you safe." The third driver got the job.

Good or bad, the *drive forward and stop test* requires you to stop your front bumper within inches of a couple of lines, without getting out and looking, which is similar to the first two drivers in my story. After you receive your Commercial Driver's License (CDL), you can be more like the third driver and stop much farther back when behind another vehicle at a traffic light. Alternatively, you can get out and look when you must maneuver in tight areas. After all, that lady who wants a driver might be the owner of a company where you want to apply.

The driving forward part of this test is easy. The real test is for you to come to a stop with the front edge of your bumper within a three-foot box (see Figure 19-1). If you have something like a *cherry picker* (the bucket for a person to be lifted in) on top of your vehicle that is sticking out over the cab of the truck, it does not count. The measurement needs to be from your bumper.

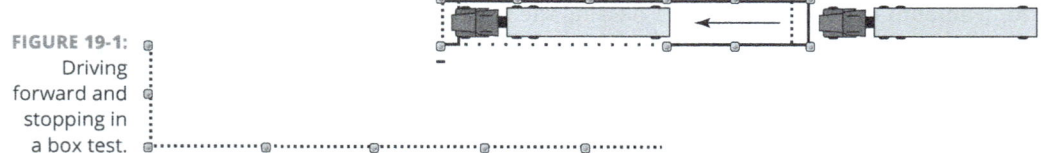

FIGURE 19-1: Driving forward and stopping in a box test.

This test is easier to complete successfully if you simply *creep* up to the box. You will only be allowed to stop once. In the weeks prior to test day, practice by lining up a cone with something on your truck and associate the two together. Be sure to figure this out during your practice sessions.

Follow what your license examiner says, but if you are not given any other instructions, sound your horn when you have completed this test. I know that sounds unnecessary since stopping ends the test anyway. Your examiner might have you sound your horn on subsequent tests. Any test that requires the horn to be sounded and you fail to sound it, the examiner might score an unnecessary move (if you move to start the next test) and penalize you. So it's a good habit to honk your horn when you complete a test. Failing to stop with the front edge of your bumper inside the box is a substantial penalty.

Backing in a straight line

A driver must be able to *back the vehicle in a straight line*. This test has you backing within a 12-foot-wide lane for 200 feet (see Figure 19-2).

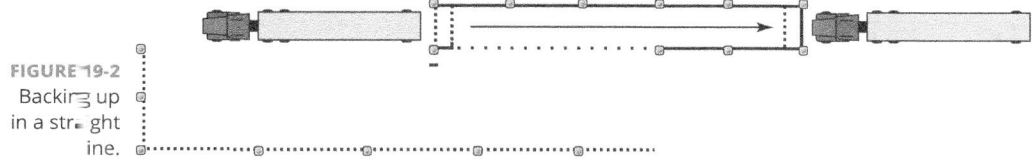

FIGURE 19-2
Backing up
in a straight
line.

The license examiner will have you drive forward to the end of the course. There shouldn't be a line there, but you should stop at the end or when the examiner says stop. Then you will back in a straight line for a couple hundred feet or so until you drive out of the course (passing two three-foot boxes with the front of your vehicle).

Remember to drive slowly and keep your head on a swivel, checking your mirrors constantly. Correct trailer drift immediately but with small quick movements, moving the steering wheel back to center quickly. There will be a line at the end of the course, but it is not a line where you have to stop. The examiner should tell you when to stop, but if not, continue until your entire vehicle is clear of the course lines. You are typically allowed one free pull-up and one free look for this test to help correct your trailer's direction of travel. Any part of your vehicle passing over one of the lines beside your vehicle is an encroachment and thus negative points are assessed. How many points are assessed for minor and major errors are not published by most states, but your Entry-Level Driver Training (ELDT) instructor will probably have some information on the points system for your state.

Managing the forward offset

The *forward offset test* is testing your ability to maneuver your vehicle while driving forward.

If you are driving a semi-tractor with a 53-foot trailer, don't turn too soon on the first turn you are to execute. Otherwise, you might roll over *cone A*. Next, don't swing out too far when you make your maneuver around cone B, as your *right rear tire* is to pass in between the cone and a line four feet out from *cone B*.

Keeping your right rear wheel between that line and the cone, bring your *vehicle back to the right,* and then *straighten to make your vehicle line up parallel* with the lines to the sides of your vehicle. *Stop when your vehicle is parallel* (see Figure 19-3).

Perform this exercise *without stopping* until your vehicle is parallel with the side lines. Points are assessed for encroachments, stopping prior to finishing, and for failing to have the right rear tire go between the line and cone B.

CHAPTER 19 **Passing the Behind-the-Wheel Tests** 347

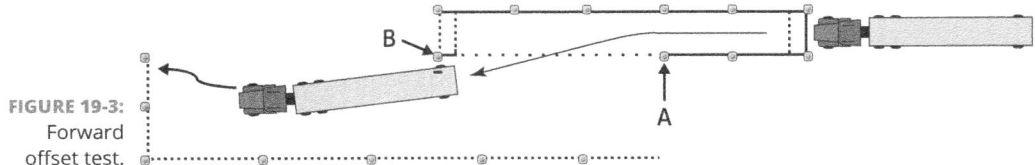

FIGURE 19-3:
Forward
offset test.

Handling the reverse offset

You will literally reverse the path you took in the forward offset (see Figure 19-4). Don't perform this maneuver at too much of an angle when you are driving your vehicle back into the space because that will make the final turn into the lane more difficult.

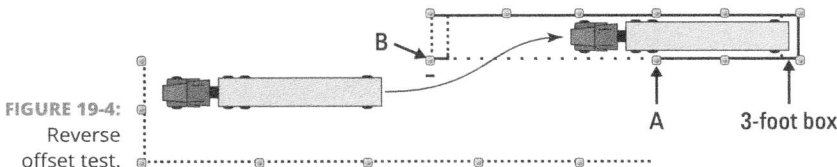

FIGURE 19-4:
Reverse
offset test.

For a combination vehicle:

1. **After completing the forward offset, position your rear axle beside cone B located at the front end of the stop box.**

2. **Turn your steering wheel to the left so your trailer can go right then back up.**

3. **Once you have the rear of your trailer pointing a little to the right, turn your steering wheel back to the left.** The trailer will continue to turn until the semi-tractor is straight with the trailer.

4. **When the semi-tractor and trailer form a straight line, straighten the steering wheel.**

5. **Find the cones that are in your mirrors.** Your goal is to have cone A in your left mirror where the likely path of your left rear wheels will miss it by a foot or less. Cone B should be in your right mirror, possibly your convex mirror.

6. **Continue with your backing.** Steer to the right when it is time to start curving your trailer around cone A. Do not wait any later than when your rear wheel is on the same line as cone A. Trailers with more overhang will need to start curving around the cone sooner than trailers with no overhang.

7. **Watch your right mirror for timing on turning your steering wheel back to the left.** You don't want to encroach (pass over boundary lines) with your tires or mudflaps by going over lines on the right side.

   - If your truck is going to encroach on the line to the right, this is a good time to stop and perform a pull-up. Do so by turning your wheel to the right and pulling forward. Don't overdo this step. Your goal is to keep the trailer pointing in the correct general direction and to be able to go in reverse again without encroaching the lines.

   - After you stop (to avoid a different encroachment), turn the steering wheel back to the left and back the vehicle. This will put the front of the truck to the right.

   - If your truck isn't going to encroach on the line to the right in this step, make that left turn with your steering wheel and back-up until the towing unit is in line with the trailer.

8. **Back the trailer, tweaking your position as needed and the instant your trailer needs it!**

9. **Stop the trailer prior to placing the rear bumper in the box.** This will help you avoid encroaching over the end line.

10. **Get out and look to see how much farther you should back the vehicle.**

11. **Back up the distance that puts you in the center of the box and stop.**

12. **Honk your horn when you are done.**

For a non-combination vehicle:

1. **After completing the forward offset, position your rear axle beside the cone located at the front end of the stop box.**

2. **Start backing up, steering to the right to go right.**

3. **Look for cone A to appear in your driver's side mirror and straighten the steering wheel.**

4. **Continue backing, aiming for your left rear tire to miss cone A by a foot or less.**

5. **Steer to the left enough to keep the left rear wheel parallel with cone A until your vehicle is straight between the lines.**

6. **Back the vehicle until you are just shy of the box.**

7. **Perform a "look." See how much farther you must go to place the rearmost portion of the vehicle in the box.**

8. **Back the appropriate distance.**

9. **Sound your horn when you are done and successful.**

TIP

You can stop (and should stop) without getting dinged any points. So, stop when you need to check your position in the mirrors or to alter your steering. An allotted pull-up (depending on your state, you might be allowed two) gets used only when you pull forward. You will be dinged for extra pull-ups.

The tests I took a few decades ago examined how close you can get without touching the cone or going over a line with your bumper. The worst score was stopping 24 inches away. Every 6 inches the score got better. Within 6 inches and you got the best score, until you touched the cone or line, then it was a fail. (There might be some locations that still use this scoring system, but I don't know for sure.)

Taking other tests

State DOTs have done their own thing for years when it comes to CDL tests. There are guidelines that are to be followed since the CDL is a federal program, but states are allowed to have variations for maneuvers and for the scoring criteria. Here are some skill tests that might still used and a description of each.

>> **Parallel parking.** If there are locations that are not using the modernized testing, one of the tests they can give can be parallel parking. Parallel parking is almost the same as the reverse offset. One difference is that the examiner can choose which side you park — on your left or your right (see Figure 19-5).

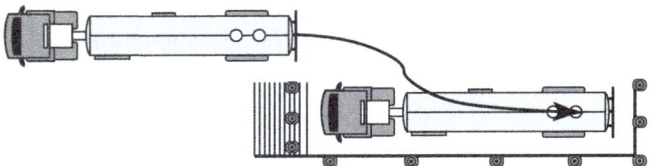

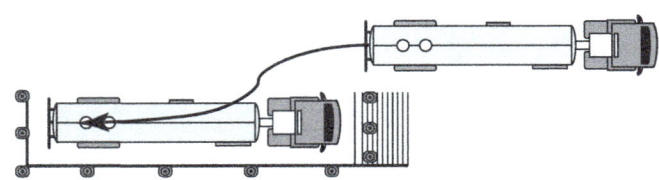

>> **Alley dock backing.** This task tests whether a driver can back into a dock from the street (see Figure 19-6). This is called an alley dock back or a 90-degree backing test. It is not as difficult as it sounds as long as you have practiced it. The odds are not likely that you would have to perform this maneuver. But if you do, your driving school would prepare you by having a nice easy formula to use. Combine this formula with the chapter on backing for a good understanding of performing this skill and correcting mistakes.

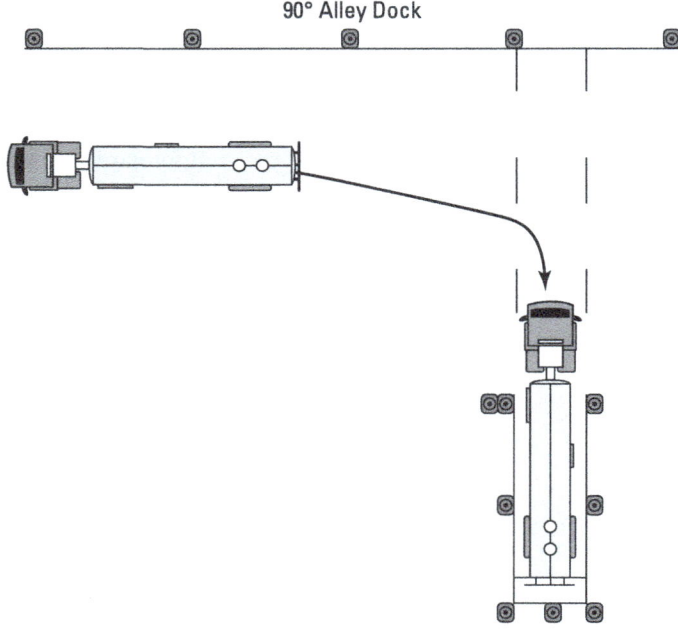

90° Alley Dock

>> **Backing into a dock.** This test resembles what most over-the-road box trailer drivers do day in and day out — back into a dock. The testing facility will probably just have some lines and maybe a prop to simulate a dock. As you should do with other tests that allow it, use your GOAL technique. Chapter 11 on backing a combination vehicle can possibly be helpful for you.

>> **Other offsets.** Testing facilities can have other offset backings, and they can be performed to the left or to the right (see Figure 19-7). The process is the same as the "reverse offset," as described earlier in the chapter, but is mirrored for the left offset.

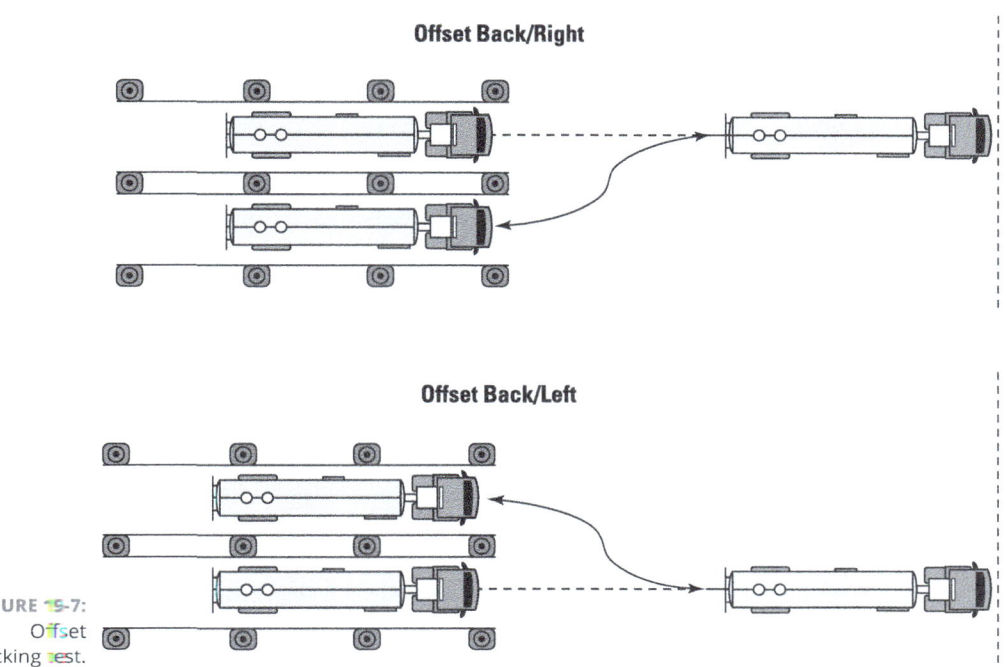

FIGURE 19-7: Offset backing test.

Tipping the Test in Your Favor

REMEMBER

Often when drivers fail a test, it is because they do something that is simply careless like: jumping out of the vehicle to check on their position and failing to turn off the engine or to take the key or failing to use three points of contact while exiting. I want to help you turn the tables and instead of making careless mistakes, perform each task successfully.

TIP

>> **Being smart.** When you back up your vehicle, you use your last opportunity to get out and look. You are checking to see how close you are to placing the rear of your semi-tractor in the box. You have several inches to go yet. Measure in your mind the distance left to go to the center of the box. Walk back to the front of the vehicle and line up a spot on the ground (like a crack in the concrete or a rock — anything) with a spot on your vehicle and move the distance needed. Just don't stick your head out the window!

TIP

>> **Correcting a mistake.** When you are performing the reverse offset or any other backing maneuver and see that you steered incorrectly, use one of your pull-ups to drive right back to where you started the mistake. When you drive forward, don't move your steering wheel until you have returned to the spot where you started your mistake. Now, do the opposite or a modification of the technique.

>> **Taking advantage of the looks and pull-ups.** The ability to do your GOALs and pull-ups is to be appreciated. Use them sparingly, but don't try to be a showoff by not using any at all. Use them if they will assure your success. If not using them means risking failure, it seems prudent to take advantage of a look or pull-up.

Passing the Road Test

Your license examiner will test you on a variety of common driver skills and situations. The road test should cover familiar maneuvers because your ELDT instructor should have prepared you for the same skills and to react appropriately.

If driving responsibly is still a new practice for you, you should review the chapter on driving safely (see Chapter 4). It wouldn't hurt to review the guidelines on driving safely in all types of conditions (see Chapter 5).

REMEMBER

Don't touch your cell phone during your road test! You will receive an automatic fail. Turn your cell phone off and, if possible, keep it out of reach. Use three points of contact when getting in and out of the cab. When in a bus, use the handholds and don't jump out the door.

AUTHOR SAYS

If the weather is too treacherous for driving, your test will probably be postponed.

Here are driving scenarios that your license examiner will likely test your competence on:

>> **Turns.** Safety and proper execution, especially for combination vehicles, is important as you make your turns.

- Slow down for your turns, signal, safely change lanes when needed for the turn, remember which lane you are to turn into.

- Manual transmissions. Slow down early enough to downshift, be in proper gear for the turn, and don't coast more than the length of the vehicle.

- If you must stop, do so smoothly and behind the stop line, stop sign, or crosswalk.

>> **Intersections.** Besides checking your own driving, you must be checking the driving of other motorists.

- Slow down even when you don't anticipate stopping.

- Ensure that the intersection is clear before proceeding after a stop.

- Look for vehicles failing to stop that should be (cross traffic and oncoming traffic turning left).

- Yield to pedestrians.

- Don't change lanes in an intersection.

- When using a manual transmission, don't shift while in the intersection.

>> **Curves.** The license examiner will be looking for behavior that results in rollovers.

- Slow down prior to the curve.

- Stay in your lane, remember off-tracking.

>> **Safe distances.** Always a must with commercial motor vehicles (CMVs).

- At intersections, be far enough behind the vehicle in front of you so that you can maneuver around them if their vehicle breaks down.

- Maintain proper distance from vehicles in front of you when driving on the road.

>> **Mirror checks and scanning.** People who are very nervous might forget to do this.

- Check the mirrors often.

- Check both mirrors on turns.

>> **Limited access roads.** Interstates, freeways, expressways, and so on (some locations will not be using such roads).

- Communicate by using your turn signals properly.

- Use appropriate speed on ramps for a CMV.

- Choose the correct lane.

- Lane choice, signaling, braking, all are examined when exiting.

>> **Emergency stop.** A simulated stop.

- Safely pull off the road, downshifting appropriately if using a manual transmission.

- Use parking brakes, place the transmission in neutral or park.

- Know where and when to place warning triangles.

- Signal when stopping and when getting back on the road.

- Check for traffic using mirrors.

>> **Railroad crossings.** If there is no railroad crossing, it will be simulated when appropriate.

- If you are driving a bus, you will be expected to correctly execute the stop at the crossing.

- Stop: In the right lane, stop 15 to 50 feet from the tracks.

- Look: Open the door and window to listen and get a better view. You must be able to see if a train is coming.

- Listen: While the door and window are open, listen for any train warning.

- Regardless of the vehicle you are driving, slow down for the crossing.

>> **Underpasses.** Generally speaking, going over a bridge or under an overpass isn't much of a test. Just be prepared to tell what any signs said, especially ones listing the maximum height or the weight limit.

>> **Clutch and gear usage.** For manual transmissions only.

- Don't shift in an intersection or when crossing a railroad track.

- Always use the clutch when shifting, and for that matter, double-clutch.

- Don't rev the engine too high nor lug the engine (have too high a gear selected for the speed the vehicle is going, causing the engine to struggle at a low RPM).

- Don't grind gears.

- Don't pop the clutch (release clutch pedal fast, often resulting in killing the engine).

- Don't coast (depressing the clutch pedal and rolling the vehicle too far, like longer than the length of the vehicle).

>> **Braking.** The license examiner is looking for smooth and steady braking.

>> **Lane usage.** Your examiner might not tell you to choose the correct lane.

- Assume that you will use the right lane unless told otherwise. You can ask if it is okay to move into the right lane, you know, in case the examiner wants to turn left and hasn't mentioned it.

- Stay off shoulders and sidewalks and out of other drivers' lanes.

- Choose the correct lanes for turns.

- » **Steering.** Less is more when driving straight down the road.

  - Do not oversteer nor understeer.

  - Keep both hands on the steering wheel when feasible. I encourage using the hand-over-hand method. This helps to produce the smooth steering examiners like to see.

- » **Turn signals.** The license examiner will look for proper communication with other drivers.

  - Activate your turn signals in a timely manner. (This might seem obvious to you, however, I encourage activating the turn signal before changing lanes, not while changing lanes. And activate them prior to applying brakes when making a turn from your lane.)

  - Cancel your turn signal when your turn is complete.

  - Did you check for blinker fluid before the test? Blinker fluid is an old CB joke referring to the driver who didn't use their turn signal; thus they must have run out of blinker fluid.

AUTHOR SAYS

TIP

Don't relax until your license examiner says the test is done, and the vehicle has been shut down properly. Stay in testing mode as you take the turn back into the lot where you started. Don't start celebrating before the test is finished, and don't run over the curb with your rear axle as you turn into the lot and don't kill the engine.

FAILING THE SKILLS COURSE: BY EXAMPLE

One day I filled in for an instructor at a driving school. I jumped in the driver's seat just to illustrate how to correct a mistake. I should have left it at that as I then proceeded to continue the reverse offset and struck a cone. What did I have against that cone? Seriously, what went wrong? Well, I wasn't thinking about what I was doing because I wasn't concentrating. I didn't Get Out and Look. If I did a GOAL, I probably would have been focused on what I was doing.

7

The Part of Tens

Chapter **20**

Ten (or So) Ways to Fail a Test

You were the star pupil in truck driving school. You received a 100 on your final written test and received your Commercial Learning Permit (CLP). You passed the pre-trip inspection test without a hitch. But then on your driving test, the license examiner declares that you failed the test. What happened?

In this chapter, I give you 10 (or so) ways to fail a Commercial Driver's License (CDL) test, some of which are automatic failures while other reasons can be surprising.

Don't panic! I show you ways that people have failed so that you don't repeat their mistakes. With the information in this chapter, you will recognize that you are about to make a mistake and immediately correct it.

Directing Traffic

You would never think of directing traffic during your behind-the-wheel test. I wouldn't either. But directing traffic is what they call a driver motioning another driver to move on.

During the test, you are told to make a right turn, but there is a car sitting, waiting to make a left turn. You think that car is in your way. You see that it is clear for them to make their turn and give them a nice polite hand gesture to go ahead and make the turn. That is what the license examiner will call directing traffic.

Drivers of commercial motor vehicles (CMV) are held to a much higher standard than drivers of personal vehicles. Much is expected of you, but why not every motorist? Isn't safety paramount for every driver? You as a commercial driver are considered to be the guardians of the road because you have received professional training and have undergone testing to drive large vehicles. So when you direct someone to go ahead and move, you have declared that it is safe to do so, even though you are thinking that you simply want them to move whenever it is safe to precede.

Curbing a Tire

REMEMBER

You've driven around town and witnessed a semi-tractor trailer combination make a tight turn and one of the tires on the trailer rolls up on a curb. This just seems to be a part of driving a big vehicle. It must be the way that things have to happen.

What can go wrong in this scenario? A tire can blow, a wheel can get damaged, a street sign can be struck, a light pole can be knocked over, a traffic light can be taken out of commission, and the worst case, a pedestrian can be hit. This is the reason your license examiner will fail you if you do what we call, "curb a tire."

Getting Too Many Points on the Skills Test

On driving tests that I took a few decades ago, if I remember correctly, I was to accumulate points. If I got enough points, I passed the test. Now whether I am remembering that correctly, you do not want to receive points during your skills test. They allow you to accumulate a limited amount of points.

Points are given for crossing over lines that should not be crossed over, for getting out and looking in excess of the allowed times, and for pulling up when executing a backing maneuver in excess of the allotted times.

Disobeying Traffic Laws

REMEMBER

You approach a stop sign, and the intersection is clear, so you roll on safely through the intersection. No problem, right? A quick way to fail the driving portion of the CDL test is to disobey a traffic law, like failing to come to a complete stop behind a stop sign or a stop line. What else is the license examiner to do? They can only assume that if you don't come to a complete stop on your exam, how bad will you do out on your own?

Speeding is another way of breaking traffic laws and another way to automatically fail a road test. Many people habitually speed, thinking that 5 mph over the limit is okay. It won't be okay on your driving test. Practice keeping under the speed limit in your personal vehicle so that it will be easier for you when you are driving the CMV.

Ignoring the License Examiner

WARNING

Nobody likes being ignored. However, a license examiner is likely to fail you because you didn't follow their instructions. If you performed the wrong maneuver, you will fail the skills course. Listen to the examiner and when you don't understand or hear the examiner's instructions, ask politely to repeat the instructions.

Failing a Test Too Many Times

Obviously, this is not just simply failing but failing more than once. The good news is that you can take the test again. There are different rules on how long you have to wait before taking a test again. There are many State Departments of Transportation (DOTs) that will allow you to fail up to three times prior to having to wait a month before you are allowed to take a test again.

Driving Too Slowly

You might think that driving slowly is driving safe. However, the license examiner needs to know that you are able to drive at a speed that you are likely to drive at after getting your license. Don't bother driving right at the speed limit though. But when conditions allow, stay only about 5 mph under the posted limit.

Failing to Use Three Points of Contact

Some licensing facilities will fail you if you don't use three points of contact while entering or exiting the vehicle.

REMEMBER

Three points of contact means that of your two hands and two feet, three of those appendages are always in contact with the truck. Hands are grasping grab handles, door handles, or steering wheels. Feet are on the steps, ground, or floor of the vehicle. It makes no difference whether you are getting into the vehicle or getting out of it, always have your body facing the cab. That places your arms and shoulders in their strongest position.

Killing the Engine

If you take your driving test in a vehicle with a manual transmission, there is a chance that you can *kill* the engine, causing the engine to stop running accidentally. It is not the end of the world to have that happen after you get your license — just embarrassing. Just start the engine again and calm yourself while taking a deep breath.

TIP

However, since you will likely be failed if you kill the engine during either of the behind-the-wheel tests (skills or road), you might want some pointers.

>> From a stop, always release the clutch pedal slowly.

>> When you feel your vehicle start to move but the truck hesitates, go with your gut; it is telling you that something is wrong, so push the clutch pedal back in.

>> Ensure that your brakes are released.

>> Verify that you are in the correct gear and range.

Shifting Too Early

When you pass through an intersection, don't shift the transmission. At many testing facilities, this will be a fail. It is hard to keep from shifting when you are stopped at the traffic light and now you have a big intersection to pass through. Stay in the gear that you entered the intersection in until your truck gets through that intersection. If you have the chance to give yourself a little more space prior to going into the section, you might have enough time to grab another gear (shift into the next higher gear).

The rationale behind this is if you don't shift gears in the intersection, you won't kill the engine due to shifting and then have your vehicle blocking the intersection.

Now you might be thinking, what about shifting when passing side streets? Is that an automatic fail? It can be. Ask your driving instructor if a license examiner would fail a student for doing such a thing in your neck of the woods.

Cheating

WARNING

Cheating is not allowed on the CDL written test. I hope it is obvious to you that looking at notes on your phone or written on your arms and legs is cheating. You will be tossed out of the facility! They will let you know if and when you can come back to take the test again.

But you are a decent, honest, law-abiding citizen. I believe you! However, you must make everything appear to be honest as well as be honest. Leave your cell phone somewhere else. Don't take it into the testing area! If you so much as look at the time on your phone, they can say, "You're done!" You have been warned. Pretend this is training for driving your CMV. Don't touch your cell phone.

IN THIS CHAPTER

» Preparing to take a test

» Slowing down for a better outcome

» Confirming decisions and actions

Chapter **21**

Ten Tips for Passing a Test

t is better that you focus on how to pass your tests than to dwell on how you can fail. I have seen sports teams obtain a substantial lead in a game and then change the way they were playing (thinking they needed to play to protect the lead instead of staying the course). The result is the other team takes advantage of the change of strategy, turns the momentum in their favor, and makes a comeback. If you approach a Commercial Driver's License (CDL) test the same way, you will encourage negative results because you are not focusing on how to achieve positive results.

In this chapter, I share the mindset of someone who knows what to do to accomplish a successful test.

Listening to Instructions

REMEMBER

Listen to what the license examiner says and then follow their directions. If you do something other than what the examiner told you, you may fail. If you are unsure about what was said, ask the examiner to repeat the instructions, or you can restate what you believe to be the instructions that were given to you. Also, look at the examiner to help clarify. There might be hand gestures or nodding of their head that will help you understand what they want.

Getting Plenty of Sleep

TIP

Staying awake late to review testing material probably won't be as effective as getting a good night's sleep. Try to go to bed a little earlier than usual. If you have time before the test, glance over the chapters in this book, particularly the practice questions, or use any flash cards that you made.

Arriving Early

TIP

Any place you go, whether it is by plane, train, boat, or car, you cannot guarantee that you will be at an appointment on time. Plan on there being something to slow down your progress. Many successful drivers have a philosophy that being on time is being late and being early is being on time.

Ensuring Your Truck Passes an Inspection

Thoroughly inspect the vehicle that you are bringing to test in, and if possible, early enough to fix any minor problems or to obtain a different vehicle. Your vehicle needs to pass an inspection. If the license examiner observes lights that aren't working, you probably won't be allowed to continue the test. It might not be construed as a fail, but you won't be getting a chance to obtain your license until the problem is resolved.

Skipping Questions

You will most likely be allowed to skip a question (or more) during the written test and then be able to go back to the missed questions. Take advantage of this opportunity. By skipping a question, a later question may give you the answer for the one that you skipped. Your test might end before you have answered all the questions because 80 percent is all that is needed to pass. So don't panic and rush through the written test. Rushing can cause simple mistakes to be made, and you might miss questions that you would know the answers to.

Regrouping after a Failed Written Test

This tip appears to be focusing on a negative. However, the best thing to do after failing a test is to stop or slow down before moving forward. I have seen motorists (in various types of vehicles) make a driving mistake and then as a "sign" to other drivers around them, speed up to go faster as if to say, "I know what I am doing, look at me going faster!" Don't be like these drivers and rush into taking a test again — at least not right away. Take a little time to figure out what went wrong and what you can do to avoid those mistakes. Also, review your study material again.

Returning to Where You Made a Skills Mistake

You are not a professional driver, yet. When you realize that you made a steering mistake while backing in a skills test, you should stop, do not adjust the steering wheel, return to the spot where you made the mistake and do it over. If you attempt to fix the mistake, for example by continuing to back up, there is a good chance that you are attempting a maneuver that even a seasoned driver can not accomplish. Return to the beginning of the mistake.

Using Your GOALs

There are skills tests that allow you to get out of your vehicle to look at your vehicle and its position on the course. This action, known as Get Out and Look (GOAL), will help you ensure that your vehicle is where it needs to be, or better yet, to tell you what you need to do next. If you guess where your vehicle is positioned and you guess wrong, it might be the cause for a failed test. Don't be cocky, use your GOALs.

Remembering That You Are Not Done

If you declare that you are done performing a section of inspecting your vehicle, the license examiner will take your word for it and only give you credit for what you did say. There is no chance of adding to your accomplishment. That opportunity is gone. You have eliminated the possibility of adding any essential item. If you are allowed, leave the door open to go back and add to what you have done (not the literal door on the cab but leave the door of opportunity open).

Practicing Maneuvers

Practice your maneuvers the way you must during your test. For example, every time you get out of the vehicle (three points of contact for most vehicles) execute it like you should on your test. Practice taking the keys out of the ignition. Honk the horn when you have completed a skill. Make these little tasks a habit. Some of these habits you should continue to keep throughout your career.

In addition to that, if you live where they test the same way every time (your instructor will know), do the whole set of tests all together, in the same order, the way they will have you do it when testing.

Chapter 22

Ten Tips for Backing Successfully

B acking up (known in the trucking industry as just "backing") will bring out different emotions in people. For some drivers, the spirit of competition is awakened. For others, an impending feeling of doom washes over them.

You probably already know that there are very few driving jobs where backing is not necessary. Sooner or later, you will need to back up your vehicle, including for the behind-the-wheel tests. (See Chapters 11 and 19 for more information on backing and how backing is tested for a Commercial Driver's License.)

In this chapter, I provide some steps that you should take prior to backing so you can be successful with or without a trailer. I also explain the adjustments and tasks that you can do, making all the difference in successful backing. When you are backing your commercial motor vehicle — whether for your test or on your new job — clear your mind of other matters and focus on the task. So no matter what emotion the thought of backing brings out in you, I will steer you back towards the middle.

Adjusting and Cleaning Your Mirrors

It is amazing what clean mirrors do for backing. If you have a delivery or pickup to make where you have to back your vehicle into a building, it will likely be difficult to see in to where you are going. If it is darker inside than outside, glare is prominent in your mirrors and even more of an annoyance when the mirrors are dirty, so removing dirt also removes glare. Keep a can or bottle of your favorite cleaner with you along with clean towels. You will need to clean your mirrors at the beginning of the day as well as during the day. How often you clean the mirrors depends on the weather and the environmental conditions you operate in.

I recommend using one of two types of glass cleaner. One is in an aerosol can and doesn't leave any streaks. Detailers and people who show classic cars in competitions use this type of glass cleaner. The other glass cleaner contains a fine wax that causes water to bead up and run off the mirror. This helps you to see more easily when it is raining because there will be less raindrops on the mirrors.

After you clean your mirrors, check for proper adjustment. Your mirrors are giving you feedback as you are backing. Make sure that you just see a sliver of the side of your vehicle in each mirror. You don't need to know what the side of your vehicle looks like, but you do need to see what is beside your vehicle, while you sit firmly in your seat.

Examining Your Ultimate Goal

When you arrive at a stop and it is time to back your vehicle, examine where you are backing into. Look at the width of the space. Look at the path you intend to use to place your vehicle in the space, and don't forget about looking overhead. Are there any wires hanging down anywhere? Is there any kind of out-cropping from a building? What about tree limbs? Remember, it is what you don't see that can hurt you.

Setting Up Your Vehicle Properly

Once at a customer, I was told to put my trailer in a specific dock door. I backed my trailer up to the spot, still 53 feet away from the door, and got out of the truck to see if it was possible to put my trailer in that spot. It was impossible as my trailer was at the point of being ready to touch both trailers on either side of mine! It just wasn't going to happen. Don't try to make a backing attempt from a position that doesn't make sense to do. Set your vehicle up again, or maybe, all you have to do is keep pulling forward until you have a nice, curved path and not an "S" like path.

Using Both Mirrors

Failing to use both mirrors is setting yourself up to be blindsided. Failing to use both mirrors gives you only half a picture of what is happening. There are enough blind spots on commercial motor vehicles already, so you don't want to create more. Use both mirrors as you back to give yourself more information to be more productive.

Utilizing Your GOALS

Early in my driving career (with a combination vehicle, that is), I had a 12-foot-wide load to deliver onto a construction site. A worker was attempting to direct me, but the directions were not helpful. When I got out of the semi-tractor and saw how the path wounded around, I had a better understanding of what was going on. What you can't see can hurt you. What you can see, can shed light on that which was previously unknown! The *Get Out and Look* (GOAL) task will help to inform you about what you need to do and keep you from striking an object.

When you GOAL, you walk around your vehicle to see the best way to safely back up. Remember, it looks more professional to GOAL than to hit another vehicle or a building.

Realizing You Shouldn't Undo Everything

I have witnessed many times when a driver has their vehicle halfway into their parking spot and then pulls all the way out to start all over. Getting out of the truck and examining the situation can reveal that a slight pull-up and turn of the steering wheel will bring the truck or trailer into the desired path. Once that happens, you can often get backed into your spot with a little more tweaking. Be a student of knowing how your vehicle maneuvers. You might surprise yourself about how much you can learn about commercial vehicles that you drive.

Making Small Adjustments

"Go big or go home!" is not your motto for backing your vehicle. The bigger the turn of the steering wheel or the longer the steering wheel is held in a turn, the bigger the problem becomes. When you have a good setup, your adjustments should be small or short in duration. With a short vehicle, mistakes can happen quickly, so little movements must be made as soon as possible. When your vehicle is long, by the time you stop making a big adjustment (which is a mistake), it will take a lot of time and space to get it corrected.

Returning to the Beginning of a Mistake

In life, you can't go back in time and get a do-over. However, in backing, you can go back to where you started for a do-over. Here's how you do it. As soon as you see that you made a steering mistake, stop! Do not move the steering wheel. Put your vehicle back in a drive gear and return to where the mistake actually began. Now, try it again but steer in the correct direction. It is important though that you don't try to fix the mistake by continuing to back up. It will likely be a disaster (yes, that is hopefully an overstatement).

Anticipating

Anticipating when your semi-tractor is going to become straight with your trailer in order to back up is obviously a combination-vehicle guideline. But what about a straight truck or bus? You will still want to do some anticipating — just not for the same reason. In the straight truck, your anticipation will be in the distance it takes for the truck (or bus) to reach its proper angle. Remember to think about what is going to happen and when that is going to happen. Because you are anticipating what will happen during this maneuver, you will come closer to the correct distance needed to complete the task.

Going Slow, Even Stopping

"Just don't stand there, do something!" This statement doesn't apply to backing. Don't back until you *know* your vehicle will not hit an object. Remember, backing is not a race. If you drive too fast, you cover more ground than you have time to steer and countersteer to accomplish your maneuver or fix a mistake. If you miss making a correction or an adjustment, you are likely to hit an object or are guaranteeing that you will need to pull up and maybe start over. If you have to stop to adjust your position, get out and look, or reset your thinking or nerves, then do so. Maybe "slow and steady wins the race" from Aesop's fables is applicable to backing.

Chapter **23**

Ten Tips for Safe, Efficient Driving

D rive to obtain good fuel mileage or drive to be a safe defensive driver. Both end up with the same results — better fuel mileage and a safer driving record. The same tactics you use for one are the same for the other. Do you want to know another application of the same tactics? Use the same practices for driving on slick winter roads, just be even more deliberate executing these tips.

In this chapter, I present the best practices for obtaining good fuel mileage, driving defensively, and staying safe on hazardous winter roads.

How efficient are these tactics discussed in this chapter? Obviously, all things are relative, but drivers usually gain at least 2 mpg (miles per gallon) over their previous habits. So for a tractor trailer combination, the average driver would gain 2 mpg to achieve 9 mpg after applying these practices. If a driver logs 100,000 miles in a year (a conservative figure for an over-the-road driver; see Chapter 3), the annual savings would easily be $8,750 based on fuel at $3.50 per gallon. I can think of many things to spend that money on instead of fuel. And if you are going to own your own truck, you should put the savings back into your company to weather the normal problems that come with transportation. (It is okay to be nerdy about saving fuel. After all, isn't it the nerds who are making the big money?)

Keeping Space

Keeping plenty of space between you and the vehicle ahead of you is a fairly obvious safe driving practice. But how is it a *fuel saving* technique? If you are driving in big city rush hour traffic, you will see the flow of traffic speed up and slow down. If you drive like you are trying to rush to get ahead in stop-and-go traffic, you will use more fuel to speed up and use brakes to slow down, over and over again. Keeping space allows you to eliminate or at least reduce the repetitive fuel and brake pedal applications. When you attempt to get your commercial motor vehicle (CMV) rolling faster, especially the heavier it is, it takes a lot of fuel. To slow down a heavy vehicle, it takes plenty of braking power. So it is your choice, use fuel and brake pads or save fuel and brake pads.

TIP

How much space? You should always stay far enough away from the vehicles in front of you to brake gently if they decide to stop in the road for any reason. If you have to brake hard, you know you were too close. For the proper spacing, the Federal Motor Carrier Safety Administration recommends to allow 1 second for every 10 feet of your vehicle's length. When you are traveling over 40 miles per hour (mph), you are to add another second. This formula might not always translate to keeping enough space when including other processes of driving, like checking your gauges and mirrors.

For safety reasons, this practice saves the potential for rear-ending another vehicle. Tests have shown that if everyone drove moderately and they were content to go with the flow instead of overtaking other drivers, a smooth flow of traffic would result. Too many other drivers are not going to drive like this. So you will simply be giving yourself a cushion for anything that can happen. When you are keeping plenty of space and someone has an accident in front of you, you will be able to react, slowing down safely, turning on your hazard lights, warning others behind you.

You don't want to perform any maneuvers quickly on *slick roads.* Keeping plenty of space between you and the next vehicle will help you maintain that goal. Practicing keeping space helps other tactics be effective.

Steering with Ease

The next time you are behind the wheel, see how you can hold your steering wheel still. My experience is that the biggest vehicles drive the straightest down the road. Driving straight, with little steer tire movement, results in more fuel savings. There will be less friction from the tires rubbing or scrubbing against the road as they are no longer constantly turned back and forth. And steering smoothly as you turn corners reduces tire wear, which always correlates with reduced fuel consumption.

In the wintertime, you want to have the least amount of movement by your steering wheel. Your steer tires need to keep traction. Moving the steering wheel back and forth hinders the tires from keeping traction. Losing traction means a skid or a jackknife is possible.

Many old-time commercial drivers, who had driven an old truck with loose steering, will drive as if they are currently driving a vehicle with loose steering: moving the steering wheel back and forth, tiring themselves out, using extra fuel, and wearing out their steer tires and steering components.

REMEMBER

Don't constantly move the steering wheel back and forth. Keep the steering wheel still. You are not driving an old, neglected farm truck that is in need of a new front end.

Accelerating Smoothly

Have you ever pushed a car or pickup truck? If you pushed it with all the strength you had, how long did it take for you to get tired? Have you ever leaned against a car that was in neutral, and it just started rolling? If you have had both experiences, you spent more energy pushing hard than when you were just leaning against the car.

Transfer this principle to accelerating in a bigger vehicle. You can push it really hard and use a lot of fuel, or you can gently give it fuel to get the vehicle rolling. To measure how well you are doing with your acceleration, use your instant mpg readout (if you have one) to observe whether you are accelerating too fast. Conduct your own studies; study the gauge to see what works for your vehicle.

If you have a hill or any kind of a decline to go down, wait to accelerate because you can use gravity as a free fuel. If your hill is too short, combine fuel with gravity. It will still be a cheaper way to get up to speed.

For winter roads, remember that you always want to keep traction. Accelerating very smoothly will help with that. Heavy acceleration will be detrimental to that goal.

Braking Gradually

Your goal for stopping should always be to do so gradually and gently. Think about paying for a brake job (replacing brake pads and drums or rotors), or maybe not paying for a brake job, which will save some money. My dad never had to have brake pads replaced (his testimony) due to the way he slowed down. The effect on fuel efficiency might be harder to measure, but the *savings* on fewer brake jobs is easily measurable. Part of this tactic is to reduce the number of times you put yourself in braking situations. Whenever conditions exist for you to take your time braking, take advantage of it. Braking gradually takes planning and requires keeping plenty of space (another tactic, see how they work together).

TIP

Planning to avoid the need to use your brakes develops you into a defensive driver. You will get better at it as time goes on. Just try to avoid complaining about how everyone else is driving. It won't help your attitude.

On slick winter roads, you *must* drive in a manner that allows you to minimize the number of times you apply your brakes. You must keep traction. Braking just makes it harder to keep traction, and what do you want to do on winter roads? Keep traction!

Being Patient Up a Hill

It takes a lot of fuel to move a heavy vehicle up a hill. For this tactic, allow your vehicle to lose a little bit of momentum as you approach the crest of the hill. You don't necessarily need to let up all the way on the fuel pedal.

In fact, you might just keep the pedal pushed down the same amount from the bottom to the top of the hill, allowing your speed to drop the whole time. When you reach the crest, you will likely get to go back down the hill, gaining your momentum and speed back. Don't lose too much momentum when you go up the hill. Losing a 5-mph spread over the length of the hill will suffice. Vigilantly watching your instant fuel mileage — maybe performing a few experiments going up the same hill under similar conditions — will help demonstrate the fuel savings. For safe defensive driving, this gives you a little extra time to react to a hazard over the top of the hill that you couldn't previously see.

You need all the advantages you can gain when you are driving on a *snow packed road.* Traction comes into play again. If you start down a hill already going too fast, how are you going to get slowed down safely to stop at an intersection, navigate a curve, or avoid someone who's lost control?

Avoiding Red Lights

REMEMBER

Stopping at a red light means using your brakes to get stopped. When you stop at a traffic light, you must use fuel to get moving again, much more fuel than a truck or bus that is already moving. When you are sitting still, you are achieving 0 mpg. However, when you are moving in an 30,000-pound big rig, and a Prius is sitting still at a traffic light, you are getting the *better fuel mileage* because the Prius is getting 0 mpg.

In order to achieve this feat with any regularity, you must look for clues that will help you reach traffic lights when they are green. When you see the clues, you might need to decrease your speed or coast down to a speed where you can move faster when you go through the intersection (instead of speeding towards the lights and have to come to a stop). Let's look at clues:

>> Look for crosswalk signals. Some signals have countdowns that show the seconds when the light will change to yellow. Other signals will start blinking, "Don't Walk," for a few seconds prior to your light changing to yellow.

>> Watch the oncoming traffic. Is it starting up or is the amount of traffic dwindling down, meaning the lights might be changing?

>> Is traffic approaching from the side street? Often the presence of traffic triggers sensors that will change lights. On the other hand, the absence of traffic on the side roads might mean the lights will stay green for you.

>> The flashing lights informing you that you will be required to stop at the upcoming traffic lights are the greatest invention for traffic control since the creation of the traffic light. Seriously, if a municipality desires safer intersections, they would install these instead of red light cameras. I haven't seen one fail, and you can rely on needing to stop when it says you should. You can stop safely (with no surprises) or save fuel.

>> Study your frequent routes and watch for patterns — when do the turn lanes get their chance to move? Which direction of traffic gets to move first? Is it different in the morning than in the afternoon? If you are driving in the same area all the time, you will begin to have the answer to these questions. Even if you return to stops on an irregular basis, you will pick up on the timing patterns.

REMEMBER

Safety is enhanced by the increased scrutiny of traffic. Observing traffic coming on side roads helps to avoid having a collision with anyone running a red light.

When you can keep rolling in the wintertime though an intersection, you don't have to worry about coming to a complete stop, which can be difficult when the road is slick. And, you won't have to worry about getting your vehicle moving again (after stopping), which again, can be difficult in the winter.

Coasting When Legal

Here's a motto for you to adopt: Why keep using fuel just to have the opportunity to wear down your brake pads? When you continue to press on the fuel pedal, knowing that you're approaching a lower speed limit, does it make sense to keep doing that? In order to avoid speeding tickets, you must start applying your brakes, which means that you wasted fuel during the mile before the new lower speed limit. Attempt to be driving the speed of the speed limit that you are approaching without having to apply any brakes, including the engine brake.

Some transmissions have a coasting feature to save fuel. In certain conditions, like letting off the fuel to let your vehicle slow down, the transmission will disengage from the engine (saving fuel due to loss of friction). That automatically causes the engine to drop down to 600 RPMs (rotations per minute), but then the engine is programed to run on only half the cylinders. During this short time, your vehicle is achieving a 200+ mpg fuel rate. While this is only for a short time, imagine the increase of your fuel mileage when added with your regular 7 to 10 mpg.

You would rather avoid using your brakes any more than you have to on *slick roads.* This practice helps you maintain much-needed traction. Obviously coasting helps with this goal.

Using Your Brakes Less Frequently

TIP

Speaking in philosophical terms, any time you use your brakes, you have wasted fuel prior to using the brakes. If your foot is always on the fuel pedal or on the brake pedal (one or the other), you know that there is room for improvement. You can introduce more time by having your foot ready to apply the brake, letting your vehicle slow down in a more efficient way.

Using your brakes less frequently works directly by *keeping plenty of space* between you and traffic in front of you as well as *coasting.* Deciding to use less brakes helps with your mindset. It also helps to keep your fuel saving, defensive driving, safe winter road driving frame of mind going. The difference here is that you change your thinking. You no longer think that you have to charge ahead to the next traffic light or keep up with the traffic ahead of you.

Use this tip for driving on slick winter roads. Always look for ways to safely avoid having to use your brakes. Remember, using your brakes introduces another variable in your quest to keep traction and stay on the road.

Note: Just because I provide some tips for driving safely on winter roads doesn't mean that you should always be out on the road in any road condition. You will have to assess the slickness of the road. There is one way to ensure that you don't get into a skid — be parked!

Knowing When to Use Your Cruise Control

Since the 1970s, cruise control has been touted as a fuel-saving device, and it probably was for some people. People who sped up and slowed down at the wrong times benefited. However, the cruise control would use every bit of fuel it needed in order to go the speed you told it to go, ignoring the tactics in this list. Today, many vehicles (including CMVs) have an adaptive or predictive cruise control system. This type of system works with a GPS or radars and sensors and intends to incorporate a few of the tactics in this list as well to achieve good fuel economy.

WARNING

To maintain safe driving, at least in inclement weather, you must turn off the cruise control. *Never use the cruise control on wet roads, in the rain or snow, nor on slick winter roads.* Using cruise control in these conditions will make you lose control.

Keeping Your Speed Down

Keeping your speed down might be the hardest of these tips to adopt. It goes against most people's thought process; drivers might think they won't get the cargo delivered on time. Dispatch will think that drivers must max out the speed limit 100 percent of the time, if not worse. The following three ways may help you to keep your speed down:

>> **Staying in the sweet spot.** There is a sweet spot where your vehicle can achieve the best fuel economy. Generally speaking, it is when the transmission is in the highest gear and the engine is running comfortably. Aerodynamics plays a big role in the sweet spot as overcoming the wind, whether natural or man-made takes energy.

>> **Scheduling accomplishment.** In reality, drivers don't lose that much time, if any. A driver can't legally average a full 70 mph every legal driving hour of the day. Not all driving takes place on the interstate at top speed. Metropolitan area speed limits and construction help to limit the time spent at 70 mph. Other roads, with lower speed limits, are utilized in making our deliveries too.

When an over-the-road driver has the opportunity to drive the majority of the day at 70 mph, the likelihood of getting to take advantage of the time saved and distance accomplished in the next couple of days is slim. I know that when it does happen, it does seem to be an accomplishment, which in itself indicates that such an event is not a regular event. The reason a driver often doesn't get to take advantage of the time savings is that customer schedules don't necessarily change because a driver is early. Many businesses do not operate around the clock so if the delivery was made early, the next pickup might have to wait until the business opens.

Also, what if the person who plans your stops assumes you will have success all the time and therefore plans your driving schedule accordingly? Would that lead to any stress for you? Maybe you would start contemplating fudging on your hours-of-service limits — that isn't a good idea!

TIP

Whenever steps of a process are in your power, you can plan accordingly. Regarding your driving schedule,

- Have your vehicle fueled the day before.

- Start early enough to conduct your pre-trip inspection and find any defects in your vehicle.

- Load your vehicle early.

- Take care of personal preliminary tasks early.

- Study your route and any special instructions.

- Leave early.

  Not everything you plan works. But because you made plans, more things will work out.

Taking advantage of the company rewards program. "Show me the money!" This was the legitimate response I received when I first started working with drivers in adopting a different driving philosophy. If an employer wants something accomplished, they have to reward or somehow give an incentive for it. Not too many people will keep giving out of the goodness of their heart, while the person who is the receiver keeps all the benefits.

Fortunately, there are more companies paying for safe and fuel-efficient driving. If you drive for one of these companies, take advantage of it — you both win.

Index

exempt crossings, 252, 258. *See also* crossings
expedited freight, 25
explosives, 298
extra lights, in school bus, 341

F

factoring, in distances, 51
federal
  bridge formula, 129
  law, 10
  regulations, 9–10
Federal Motor Carrier Safety Administration (FMCSA), 9, 10, 18–19, 59, 127, 131, 132, 198, 370
  Drug and Alcohol Clearinghouse, 31
  and HOS, 106, 108
  mandate ELD, 110
  regulations, 136
  yard moves, definition, 109
Federal Motor Carrier Safety Regulations (FMCSR), 9, 289, 296
fifth wheel
  area of combination vehicle, 330–333
  in coupling of trailers, 223, 224, 227
final mile delivery, 25
first aid kit, 342
flammable liquids and solids, 293, 298
flares, 294
flashing lights, 372. *See also* lights
flatbed truck, 134, 138, 141. *See also* trucks
flotilla, 174
FMCSA. *See* Federal Motor Carrier Safety Administration (FMCSA)
FMCSR. *See* Federal Motor Carrier Safety Regulations (FMCSR)
forklift, 132
forward momentum, cargo, 132, 133
forward offset test, 347–348
foundation brakes. *See also* brakes
  disc brakes, 150
  s-cam brakes, 150
  wedge brakes, 150
14-hour rule, 108
frame, 125
free play movement, 46
front brake limiting valve, 162
front wheel skid, 79

fuel, 294
  pedals, 47, 314, 372
  state taxes on, 11
  tanks, 325
  tax agreement, 326
fuel-saving
  device, 373
  technique, 369
fuses, 294

G

garbage trucks, 26. *See also* trucks
gases
  compressed gases, 293, 298
  hydraulic devices, 321
  Poison Gas, 285, 290
gauges
  air pressure system, 158, 159, 171, 172
  driving controls and, 40–41
  readings in cab, 315–316
  trucks tire pressure, 322
GCW. *See* Gross Combination Weight (GCW)
GCWR. *See* gross combination weight rating (GCWR)
gear
  landing, 199, 225, 226, 228, 337, 338
  pattern, 47–49
  selectors in cab, 318
  shifting (*see* shifting gears)
  shift lever, 46, 170
general knowledge, 20
Get Out and Look (GOAL), 13, 45, 206, 346, 350, 351, 354, 363, 366–367
g-force (weight), 132–133
GGLLEEB, 319
gladhand, 218, 219, 220
  in coupling of trailers, 229, 230
glass cleaner, 366
GOAL. *See Get Out and Look* (GOAL)
good fuel economy, 52–53
governor (compressor), 156
  air pressure system and, 171–173
  cuts in pressure, 172
  cuts out pressure, 171
GPS, 113
granny low, 47
gross, 129
Gross Combination Weight (GCW), 16

gross combination weight rating (GCWR), 16, 129
gross vehicle weight (GVW), 16, 129
gross vehicle weight rating (GVWR), 16, 129

H

hand-over-hand method, 193
hauling
  cargo
    dynamic, stacked (tiered), 140–141
    specializing, 142
  class, 294
  hazardous materials, 282–283, 288
  hot-shot, 25
  liquid, 239
  liquid tanker (*see* tank vehicle)
  waste, 26
hazardous conditions, driving safely
  crossing railroad tracks, 88–90
  in fog, 74–75
  handling emergencies
    crash by steering, avoiding, 92–93
    failing brakes, 95
    tire failure, dealing, 94–95
    using ABS system, 93–94
  in hot weather
    examining vehicle for summertime, 86–87
    inspecting the tires, 87–88
  in the mountains
    driving down, 91–92
    lay of the land, examining, 91
    understanding brakes, 91
  at night
    adjusting body clock, 72–73
    cleaning lights, 73
    dodging wildlife, 74
    glare minimizing, 72
    poor lighting, 73
    switching beams, 73
    watching, impaired, 74
  taking curves, 90–91
  in the winter
    chaining tires, 79–85
    controlling and recovering from skids, 78–79
    parade watching, 79
    taking care of yourself, 75–76
    truck preparing, 76–77

About the Author

The son of a truck driver and a life-long enthusiast of driving "the right way" (literally creating rows and fields in the living room and yard of his childhood home), Cory Adams imparts his simple, yet strategic observations and years of experience for driving safe and efficiently. As a young teen, Cory worked on farms, owned his own mowing business (for which he pulled a trailer behind his riding mower into town and would back the trailer into a parking spot, even when he didn't have to). Speeding (not literally) through the next few decades, Cory built on his driving and transportation experience, operating forklifts and managing part logistics at the local auto plant. And before beginning an official career in the trucking industry, he regularly drove buses for school and church events.

As a driver for Nussbaum Transportation, his safety and fuel performance stood out, prompting the company to create a new position to bring him off the road and into the office, teaching hundreds of drivers "the right way" to drive and become the best on the road. Cory develops curriculum for Nussbaum Trucking Academy at Heartland Community College and for driver trainees at Nussbaum Transportation. Taking it several steps further, he provides valuable training courses and hands-on experiences for seasoned professionals as well at Nussbaum. His personal demonstration videos are a driver-favorite as he walks through a variety of skills and tasks.

Much credit to Cory's knowledge and savvy training, Nussbaum has earned numerous safety awards (including top honors from the Truckload Carriers Association) and continual recognition as an industry leader in fuel efficiency and driver performance.

More than just the skills and knowledge, Cory strives to influence drivers' way of thinking and approaching their role as professionals. Perhaps most importantly, Cory has shared and passed along this mindset, observations, experience, and skills to other already skilled drivers and trainers who continue to pass the same information and instruction along to new and seasoned drivers alike.

Additionally, Cory trains volunteer drivers through his church and its affiliated school while continuing his position as Instruction Administrator at Nussbaum Transportation.

Dedication

To my wife, Diana, and the rest of my family for their encouragement and patience through the creation of Passing the *Commercial Driver's License Exam For Dummies.*

Author's Acknowledgments

Alan Brokken, for saying that I should write the book, I might help a lot of people. My son, Phillip, for his PR work, and for helping make sure my words made sense and didn't sound like Yoda. For all the drivers including Bob P. who said, "I just don't believe it!" when he achieved 2 mpg higher than what he believed possible. Jeff King, instructor extraordinaire, for ensuring that the book was correct in all that was stated. Jeremy Strickling, for convincing people that everyone must win for ideas to work. Shelby Warner, for sharing her insight as a DOT medical examiner.

My dad, who taught me how to drive right. And my mom, who despite losing a daughter in an auto accident, took me out of school on my sixteenth birthday to get my license. Robert Pearce, for putting me behind the wheel of an 18-wheeler. Donna Wright, who might deserve a raise after editing this book. Jennifer Yee, whose efforts put this project together. Ertl, for making toys that children can steer.

Publisher's Acknowledgments

Senior Editor: Jennifer Yee

Project Editor: Donna Wright

Technical Editors: Jeff King

Senior Managing Editor: Kristie Pyles

Production Editor: Bharaneedharan Murthy

Cover Image: © grandriver/Getty Images